D0537929

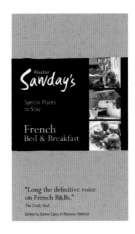

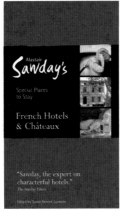

Alastair
Sawday's

Special Places to Stay

Eighth edition
Copyright © 2009 Alastair Sawday
Publishing Co. Ltd
Published in 2009
ISBN-13: 978-1-906136-09-3

Alastair Sawday Publishing Co. Ltd,
The Old Farmyard, Yanley Lane,
Long Ashton, Bristol BS41 9LR, UK
Tel: +44 (0)1275 395430
Email: info@sawdays.co.uk
Web: www.sawdays.co.uk

The Globe Pequot Press,
P. O. Box 480, Guilford,
Connecticut 06437, USA
Tel: +1 203 458 4500
Email: info@globepequot.com
Web: www.globepequot.com

Series Editor Alastair Sawday
Editor Kathie Burton
Assistant to Editor Roxy Dumble
Editorial Director Annie Shillito
Writing Jo Boissevain, Ann Cooke-
Yarborough, Viv Cripps, Nicola Crosse,
Monica Guy, Matthew Hilton-Dennis,
Helen Pickles
Inspections Kathie Burton, Monica Guy,
Virginia Hayman, Guy Hunter-Watts,
Billy Kite, José Navarro, Ken Reid,
Tristram Templer, Rosie Van Allan
Accounts Bridget Bishop,
Amy Lancastle
Editorial Sue Bourner,
Jo Boissevain, Polly Procter,
Cristina Sanchez Gonzalez, Lianka Varga
Production Julia Richardson,
Rachel Coe, Tom Germain,
Anny Mortada
Sales & Marketing & PR
Rob Richardson,
Sarah Bolton, Bethan Riach
Web & IT Joe Green,
Chris Banks, Phil Clarke, Mike Peake,
Russell Wilkinson

*We have made every effort to ensure the accuracy
of the information in this book at the time of
going to press. However, we cannot accept any
responsibility for any loss, injury or
inconvenience resulting from the use of
information contained therein.*

Maps: Maidenhead Cartographic Services
Printing: Butler, Tanner & Dennis, Frome
UK distribution: Penguin UK, London

Alastair Sawday's

Special Places to Stay

Spain

4   Contents

The buildings

Beautiful as they were, our old offices leaked heat, used electricity to heat water and rooms, flooded spaces with light to illuminate one person, and were not ours to alter.

So in 2005 we created our own eco-offices by converting some old barns to create a low-emissions building. Heating and lighting the building, which houses over 30 employees, now produces only 0.28 tonnes of carbon dioxide per year. Not bad when you compare this with the 6 tonnes emitted by the average UK household. We achieved this through a variety of innovative and energy-saving building techniques, described below.

Insulation We went to great lengths to ensure that very little heat will escape, by:
- laying insulating board 90mm thick immediately under the roof tiles and on the floor
- lining the whole of the inside of the building with plastic sheeting to ensure air-tightness
- fixing further insulation underneath the roof and between the rafters
- fixing insulated plaster-board to add another layer of insulation.

All this means we are insulated for the Arctic, and almost totally air-tight.

Heating We installed a wood-pellet boiler from Austria, in order to be largely fossil-fuel free. The pellets are made from compressed sawdust, a waste product from timber mills that work only with sustainably managed forests. The heat is conveyed by water to all corners of the building via an under-floor system.

Water We installed a 6000-litre tank to collect rainwater from the roofs. This is pumped back, via an ultra-violet filter, to the lavatories, showers and basins. There are two solar thermal panels on the roof providing heat to the one (massively insulated) hot-water cylinder.

Lighting We have a carefully planned mix of low-energy lighting: task lighting and up-lighting. We also installed three sun-pipes – polished aluminium tubes that reflect the outside light down to chosen areas of the building.

Electricity All our electricity has long come from the Good Energy Company and is 100% renewable.

Materials Virtually all materials are non-toxic or natural. Our carpets, for example, are made from (80%) Herdwick sheep-wool from National Trust farms in the Lake District.

Doors and windows Outside doors and new windows are wooden, double-glazed, beautifully constructed in Norway. Old windows have been double-glazed.

We have a building we are proud of, and architects and designers are fascinated by. But best of all, we are now in a better position to encourage our owners and readers to take sustainability more seriously.

Photo: Tom Germain

What we do

Besides moving the business to a low-carbon building, the company works in a number of ways to reduce its overall environmental footprint:

- all office travel is logged as part of a carbon sequestration programme, and money for compensatory tree-planting is dispatched to SCAD in India for a tree-planting and development project
- we avoid flying and take the train for business trips wherever possible; when we have to fly, we 'double offset'
- car-sharing and the use of a company pool car are part of company policy; recycled cooking oil is used in one car and LPG in the other

- organic and Fair Trade basic provisions are used in the staff kitchen and organic food is provided by the company at all in-house events
- green cleaning products are used throughout the office
- all kitchen waste is composted and used on the office organic allotment.

Our total 'operational' carbon footprint (including travel to and from work, plus all our trips to visit our Special Places to Stay) is just over 17 tonnes per year. We have come a long way, but we would like to get this figure as close to zero as possible.

For many years Alastair Sawday Publishing has been 'greening' the business in different ways. Our aim is to reduce our environmental footprint as far as possible – with almost everything we do we have the environmental implications in mind. (We once claimed to be the world's first carbon-neutral publishing company, but are now wary of such claims.) In recognition of our efforts we won a Business Commitment to the Environment Award in 2005, and in 2006 a Queen's Award for Enterprise in the Sustainable Development category. In that year Alastair was voted ITN's 'Eco Hero'.

But becoming 'green' is a journey and, although we began long before most companies, we still have a long way to go.

In 2008 we won the Independent Publishers Guild Environmental Award. The judging panel were effusive in their praise, stating: "With green issues currently at the forefront of publishers' minds, Alastair Sawday Publishing was singled out in this category as a model for all independents to follow. Its efforts to reduce waste in its office and supply chain have reduced the company's environmental impact, and it works closely with staff to identify more areas of improvement. Here is a publisher who lives and breathes green. Alastair Sawday has all the right principles and is clearly committed to improving its practice further."

Our Fragile Earth series is a growing collection of campaigning books about the environment. Highlighting the perilous state of the world yet offering imaginative and radical solutions and some intriguing facts, these books will make you weep and smile. They will keep you up to date and well armed for the battle with apathy.

We have created our own eco-offices by converting former barns to create a low-emissions building. Through a variety of innovative and energy-saving techniques this has reduced our carbon emissions by 35%.

Photo: Tom Germain

THE QUEEN'S AWARDS
FOR ENTERPRISE:
SUSTAINABLE DEVELOPMENT
2006

One of the saddest sights in Spain right now is the devastation wrought upon the Costas by the housing boom-and-bust. There are thousands of unwanted apartments and houses, and thousands of people whose dreams of living peacefully in the sun have come to nought. But it is good to remember that the Costas are one thing and the glory that is Spain is another.

Most of Spain looks much as it has for many years. We have always encouraged our readers to penetrate the vastnesses of this great country and get under her skin. The Special Places in this book are there to enable you to do that, with marvellous and generous people ready to help. If you have not yet walked in the Alpujarras, or the Grazalema Natural Park, or the Pyrenees or the Picos de Europa, then you have not experienced Spain fully. If you have not sauntered through the streets of any of the *pueblos blancos*, stood beneath the great cathedral of León and gasped in astonishment at her stained-glass windows, bird-watched and surf-ridden by the mighty sands in the south-west, winced at the noble cruelty of a bullfight, tucked into pea-and-ham soup after a cold climb, tasted *pata negra* ham north of Seville and washed it down with *fino* – then you need to get cracking. To have been to Spain and not tried the tapas of the Rioja region, or of Barcelona, or of – well, so many places; to have missed the Dalí museum in Figueres, the Prado in Madrid, Segovia, or Salamanca with its two cathedrals – such sadness! Spain's

vast culture and variety are among the great treats of Europe.

But the potential for sadness gets worse! To have taken this beautiful book in your hand and travelled Spain without staying in an old monastery or ex-convent; to have neglected the Picos de Europa, or the Pigüeña valley where the last of Europe's bears can be seen; to have skipped the 17th-century manor house in Galicia and the forest-skirted mountain retreat in Catalonia – all these lost opportunities are hard to bear! So take your time with this book in your hand and get to know a Spain that many have forgotten about in their desperate search for the sun.

Alastair Sawday

Photo: Tom Germain

As someone who grew up and was educated in Spain towards the end of the Franco era, editing this book has been a fascinating journey of discovery and re-discovery for me, and an opportunity to reflect on the changes in Spain.

Lots of things haven't changed of course – the passion that underpins every aspect of Spanish life, the 'can-do' attitude, the pride in history and culture, a fierce sense of regional identity. Spain has an immensely varied and rich cultural heritage; art, architecture, food, fashion, music, and literature have flourished and taken their rightful place as part of a wider European culture. Spain is producing hugely exciting work in a number of these fields, most notably architecture and food. Spain has three out of ten of the world's top restaurants and internationally famous buildings such as the Guggenheim Museum in Bilbao and the Alamillo Bridge in Seville.

Politics, too, has always been important in Spanish life, and many years have passed since it was brave to talk freely and openly. For example, when I was at school we weren't allowed to speak Catalan; now it is the language in which children are taught throughout the Catalan-speaking regions of Spain. People take their democratic rights with the utmost seriousness and have exercised these to gain a previously unthought-of degree of independence through the creation of 17 autonomous self-governing communities, each with its own parliament, government and supreme court. Where Franco once ruled by diktat, King Juan Carlos is now a staunch defender of democracy.

Above all, I have been struck by how much Spain has retained of its deep culture and values, while embracing democracy and its important role in a modern Europe with genuine enthusiasm.

One of the major delights for me has been the combination of re-visiting places I know well with the exploration of those I didn't. The huge variety of scenery to be found in Spain is astounding – from arid volcanic landscapes in the Canaries to lush green pastures, mountains and sea in northern Spain; and from the enchanting coves and beaches of the Costa Brava and the Balearics to the majestic coastline of Galicia. And, of course, the drama of the vast expanse of plains in central Spain and Andalusia in the south, with some of the

Photo left: Cortijo Las Rosas, entry 305
Photo right: El Privilegio de Tena, entry 72

the most beautiful cities in the world. Although they are steeped in history they are positively humming with new life.

This variety is reflected, too, in the places chosen for this book – from simple farmhouses to small and intimate casitas; from smart little boutique hotels to gracious and grand palacios, and everything in between. You'll find them in the remotest places and the busiest, but each has its own special charm. We continue to base our choices on the qualities we value most highly: character, place, beauty and warmth of welcome; some places are traditional, some are quirky, some luxurious and some frankly funky. We aim to avoid the pompous, the indifferent and the smug, as well as the anonymity of a chain hotel; by their very nature most of our special places are small. We most emphatically do not operate a star-rating system; our judgement is proudly subjective. Finally, one can't write about Spain without mentioning the rich array of regional food and drink: fabulous fish and seafood from the northern Atlantic coast; hearty stews; succulent beef and pork; tasty seasonal vegetable dishes; wonderful cured meats and cheeses, from the renowned Ibérico ham and Manchego cheese to local handmade specialities; delicious pastries and cakes... and mouth-watering tapas everywhere you go. Do try these, and the local wines too: delicately flavoured Albariño from Galicia (perfect with seafood), robust Rioja from northeastern Spain, sparkling cava from Catalonia, sherry and brandy from Andalusia, to name but a few.

I hope you enjoy using this book as much as I have enjoyed its creation!

Kathie Burton

Photo: Hotel La Fuente del Sol, entry 273

It's simple. There are no rules, no boxes to tick. We choose places that we like and are fiercely subjective in our choices. We also recognise that one person's idea of special is not necessarily someone else's so there is a huge variety of places, and prices, in the book. Those who are familiar with our Special Places series know that we look for comfort, originality, authenticity, and reject the insincere, the anonymous and the banal. The way guests are treated comes as high on our list as the setting, the architecture, the atmosphere and the food.

Inspections

We visit every place in the guide to get a feel for how both house and owner tick. We don't take a clipboard and we don't have a list of what is acceptable and what is not. Instead, we chat for an hour or so with the owner and look round. It's all very informal, but it gives us an excellent idea of who would enjoy staying there. If the visit happens to be the last of the day, we sometimes stay the night. Once in the book, properties are re-inspected every three to four years so that we can keep things fresh and accurate.

Feedback

In between inspections we rely on feedback from our army of readers, as well as from staff members who are encouraged to visit properties across the series. This feedback is invaluable to us and we always follow up on comments.

So do tell us whether your stay has been a joy or not, if the atmosphere was great

or stuffy, the owners cheery or bored. The accuracy of the book depends on what you, and our inspectors, tell us. A lot of the new entries in each edition are recommended by our readers, so keep telling us about new places you've discovered too. Please use the forms on our website at www.sawdays.co.uk, or later in this book (page 418).

However, please do not tell us if the bedside light was broken, or the shower head was scummy. Tell the owner, immediately, and get them to do something about it. Most owners are more than happy to correct problems and

Photo: La Torre del Visco, entry 83

will bend over backwards to help. Far better than bottling it up and then writing to us a week later!

Subscriptions

Owners pay to appear in this guide. Their fee goes towards the high costs of inspecting, of producing an all-colour book and of maintaining our website. We only include places that we like and find special for one reason or another, so it is not possible for anyone to buy their way onto these pages. Nor is it possible for the owner to write their own description. We will say if the bedrooms are small, or if a main road is near. We do our best to avoid misleading people.

Disclaimer

We make no claims to pure objectivity in choosing these places. They are here simply because we like them. Our opinions and tastes are ours alone and this book is a statement of them; we hope you will share them. We have done our utmost to get our facts right but apologise unreservedly for any mistakes that may have crept in.

You should know that we don't check such things as fire regulations, swimming pool security or any other laws with which owners of properties receiving paying guests should comply. This is the responsibility of the owners.

Photo above: Hotel Duquesa de Cardona, entry 92
Photo right: Casa Rural el Olivar, entry 304

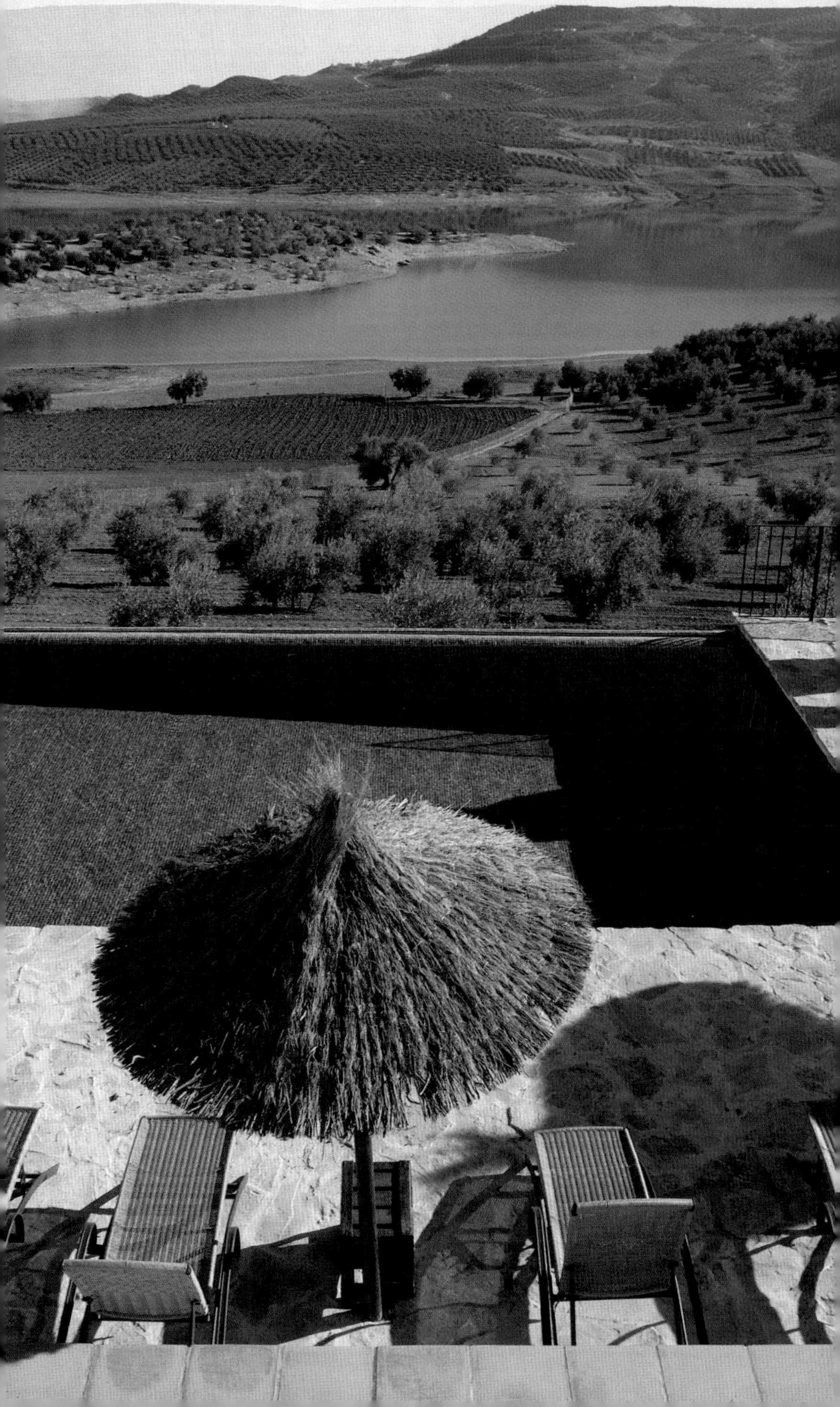

Finding the right place for you

All these places are special in one way or another. All have been visited and then written about honestly so that you can decide for yourselves which will suit you. Those of you who swear by Sawday's books trust our write-ups precisely because we don't have a blanket standard; we include places simply because we like them. But we all have different priorities, so do read the descriptions carefully and pick out the places where you will be comfortable. If something is particularly important to you then check when you book: a simple question or two can avoid misunderstandings.

We try to say when a place is a popular wedding or conference venue, or offers courses such as cookery or painting. If in

doubt, pick up the phone to check or you may find your peaceful haven does not turn out to be as peaceful as you'd expected.

Maps

Each property is flagged with its entry number on the maps at the front. These maps are a great starting point for planning your trip, but please don't use them as anything other than a general guide – use a decent road map for real navigation. Most places will send you detailed instructions once you have booked your stay.

Ethical Collection

We're always keen to draw attention to owners who are striving to have a positive impact on the world, so you'll notice that some entries are flagged as being part of our 'Ethical Collection'. These places are working hard to reduce their environmental footprint, making significant contributions to their local community, or are passionate about serving local or organic food. Owners have had to fill in a very detailed questionnaire before becoming part of this Collection – read more on page 412. This doesn't mean that other places in the guide are not taking similar initiatives – many are – but we may not yet know about them.

Symbols

Below each entry you will see some symbols, which are explained at the very back of the book. They are based on the information given to us by the owners. However, things do change: bikes may be under repair or the owners have a new pet. Please use the symbols as a guide rather than an absolute statement of fact and double-check anything that is important to you — owners occasionally bend their own rules, so it's worth asking if you may take your child or dog even if they don't have the symbol.

Children — The 🧒 symbol shows places that are happy to accept children of all ages. This does not mean that they will necessarily have cots, high chairs, etc. If an owner welcomes children but only those above a certain age, we have put these details at the end of their write-up. These houses do not have the child symbol, but even these folk may accept your younger child if you are the only guests. Many who say no to children do so not because they don't like them but because they may have a steep stair, an unfenced pond or they find balancing the needs of mixed age groups too challenging.

Pets — Our 🐕 symbol shows places which are happy to accept pets. It means they can sleep in the bedroom with you, but not on the bed. Be realistic about your pet — if it is nervous or excitable or doesn't like the company of other dogs, people, chickens, or children, then say so. Do let the owners know when booking that you intend to bring your pet — particularly if it is not the usual dog!

Owners' pets — The 🐈 symbol is given when the owners have their own pet on the premises. It may not be a cat! But it is there to warn you that you may be greeted by a dog, serenaded by a parrot, or indeed sat upon by a cat.

Quick reference indices

At the back of the book you'll find a number of quick-reference indices showing those places that offer a particular service, perhaps a room for under €100 a night, or horse-riding nearby. They are worth flicking through if you are looking for something specific.

Photo: San Bartomeo de Torres, entry 121

may not be served; Hosteria: a simple inn which often serves food; Hosteleria: an inn which may or may not serve food; Mas (or Masia): a farmhouse in the north-east of Spain; Posada: originally a coaching inn, with beds and food available; Palacio: a grand mansion; Palacete: a slightly less grand version of the above; Pazo: a grand country or village manor in Galicia; Venta: a simple restaurant, usually in the countryside, which may or may not have rooms.

Rooms

Bedrooms – We tell you the range of accommodation in single, twin/double, family rooms and suites (with a sitting area, which may be separate – we do not distinguish between suites and junior suites). Extra beds can often be added for children; check when booking. In self-catering entries we mention the number of people who can sleep comfortably in the apartment, cottage or house. Where an entry reads eg '3 + 1' this means 3 B&B rooms plus 1 self-catering apartment/cottage.

Bathrooms – Most bedrooms in this book have an en suite bath or shower room; we only mention bathroom details when they do not. If these things are important to you, please check when booking. Spaniards generally prefer an invigorating shower to a long soak in a bath; if you're keen on a bath you might want to pack one of those handy universal bath plugs just in case you find the plug missing from your bathroom in smaller places.

Types of places

This book covers all types of places to stay in Spain, as long as they are special. Each entry is simply labelled (B&B, hotel, self-catering) to guide you, but the write-ups and place names reveal several descriptive terms. This list serves as a rough guide to what you might expect to find.

Can: a farmhouse in Catalonia or the Balearic Islands, often isolated; Casita: cottage or small house; Casona: a grand house in Asturias or Cantabria, many built by returning emigrants; Cortijo: a free-standing farmhouse, generally in the south; Finca: a farm (many of those in this book are working farms); Fonda: a simple inn which may or may not serve food; Hacienda: a large estate (originally a South American term); Hostal: another type of simple inn where food may or

Photo: La Madrugada, entry 178

Meals

Breakfast can be as simple as coffee and toast, but might also include homemade jams, cheese, eggs and cold meats. In a B&B, breakfast is likely to be served at one table

A daily set meal – *el menú del día* – is often available at lunchtime and occasionally at dinner, although waiters may simply present you with the à la carte menu. But do ask for it; it tends to be great value and will often have fresher ingredients. Many restaurants serve only à la carte at weekends.

The Spanish tend to eat quite late: breakfast often doesn't get going until 9am, lunch is generally eaten from 2pm and dinner is rarely served before 8.30pm.

Prices and minimum stays

The prices we quote are per night per room unless otherwise stated. For self-catering we specify whether the price is per night or per week; for half-board it may be per room or per person (p.p.); if in any doubt, do check. Meal prices are always given per person, per meal. The room prices are inclusive of VAT at 7%; when VAT is not included we say so.

Price ranges cover seasonal differences and different types of rooms. In most of Spain high season includes Easter, Christmas, public holidays and the summer; some hotels may classify weekends as high season and weekdays as low. Some owners charge more at certain times (during festivals, for example) and some charge less for stays of more than one night. Some ask for a two-night minimum stay at weekends or in high season, and we mention this where possible. Prices quoted are those given to us for 2009–2011 but are not guaranteed, so do double-check when booking.

Booking and cancellation

Requests for deposits vary; some are non-refundable, and some owners may charge you for the whole of the booked stay in advance.

Some cancellation policies are more stringent than others. It is also worth noting that some owners will take this deposit directly from your credit/debit card without contacting you to discuss it.

Photo: Mas Fontanelles, entry 173

So ask them to explain their cancellation policy clearly before booking so you understand exactly where you stand; it may well avoid a nasty surprise.

Payment

The majority of places take credit or debit cards, but do check in advance that your particular card is acceptable. Those places that do not take cards are marked with a cash/cheque symbol. Do check before you arrive, in case you are a long way from a cash dispenser!

Tipping

Tipping is not unusual, but do not feel obliged; you will rarely be made to feel embarrassed if you don't tip. In bars you are given your change on a small saucer, and it is usual to leave a couple of small coins there. For lunch or dinner leave 5%-10%. Taxi drivers don't expect a tip but welcome the gesture of leaving the change with them. A small tip in family-run establishments is welcome, so do leave one if you wish.

Arrivals and departures

In hotels, rooms are usually available by mid-afternoon; in B&Bs and self-catering places it may be a bit later, but do try and agree an arrival time with the owners in advance or you may find nobody there. Many city hotels will only hold a reservation until early evening, even if you have booked months in advance, so do ring ahead if you are going to arrive late. It remains law that you should register on arrival, but hotels have no right to keep your passport, however much they insist.

Closed

When given in months this means the whole of the month(s) stated. So, 'Closed: November–March' means closed from 1 November to 31 March.

Photo: Hotel Chamarel, entry 185

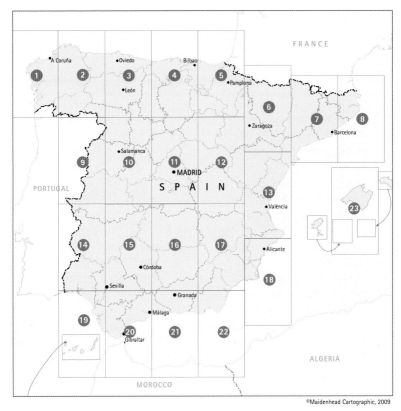

©Maidenhead Cartographic, 2009

Please remember: our maps are designed to be used as a guide, not as road maps for navigation.

On the following map pages:

self-catering properties are marked in blue   **30**

catered properties are marked in red   **12**

properties with a mixture are marked with both   **79**

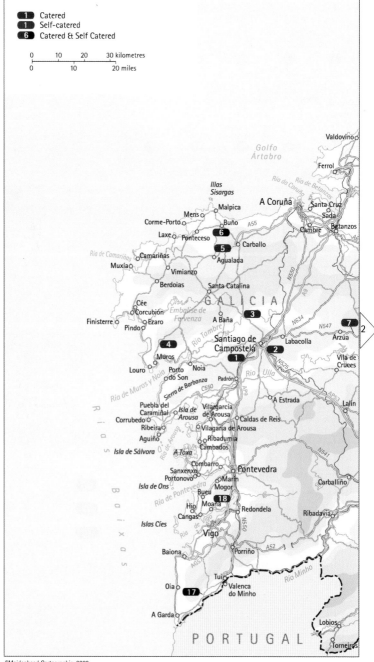

Catered
Self-catered
Catered & Self Catered

0   10   20   30 kilometres
0   10   20 miles

Map 2   23

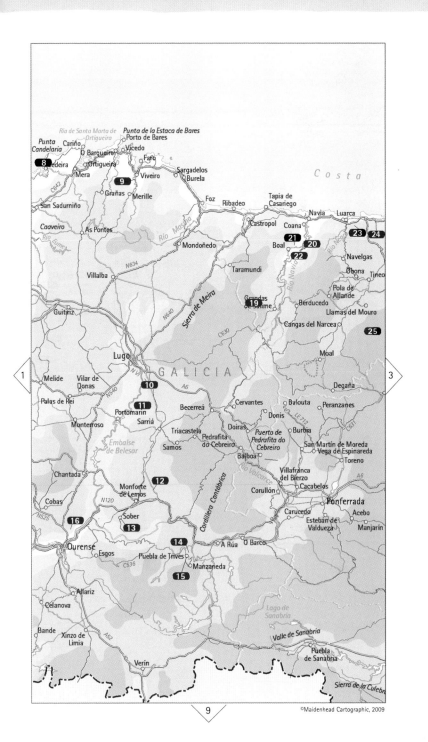

©Maidenhead Cartographic, 2009

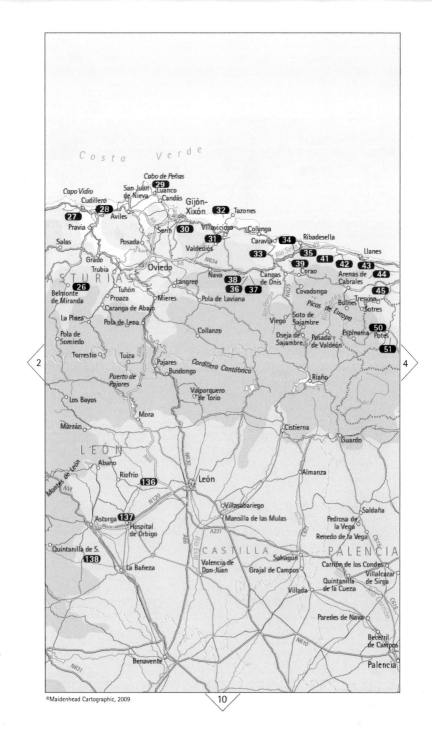

Map 4   25

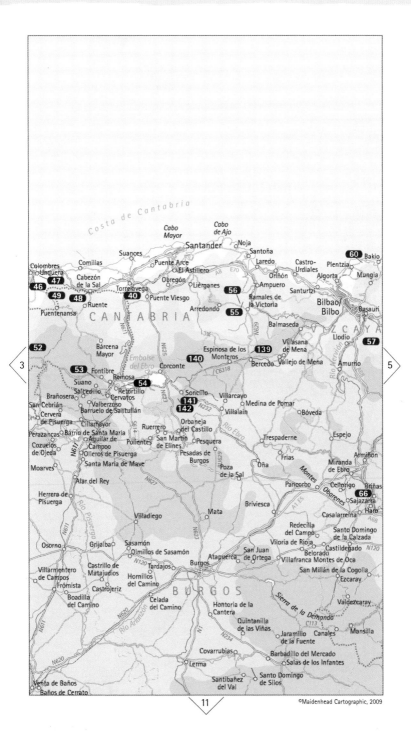

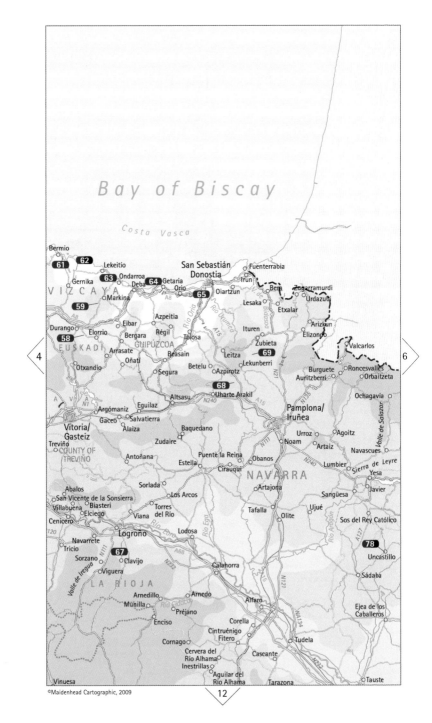

Map 6

27

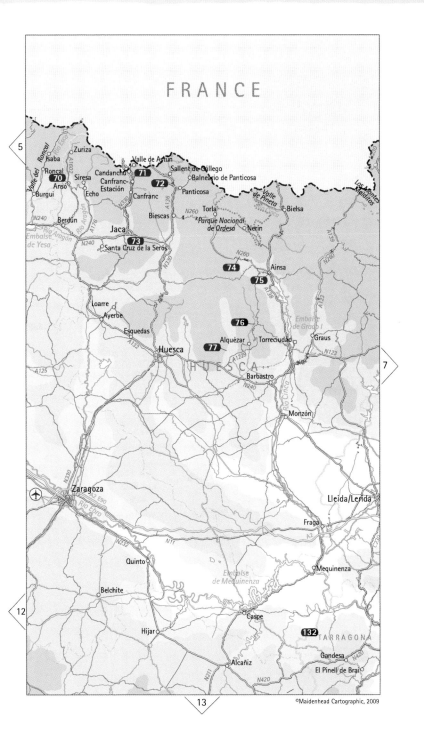

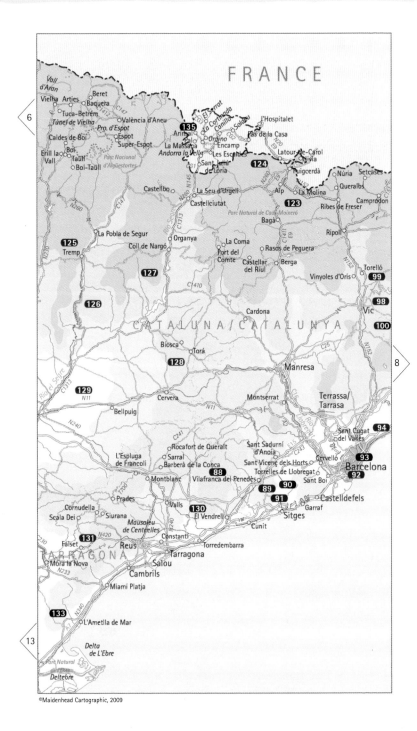

©Maidenhead Cartographic, 2009

Map 8

29

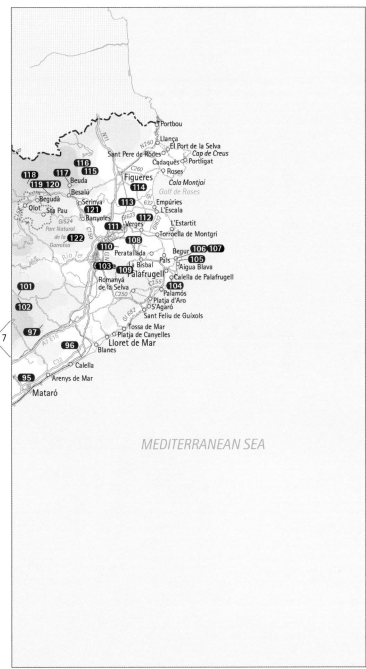

MEDITERRANEAN SEA

Map 10 31

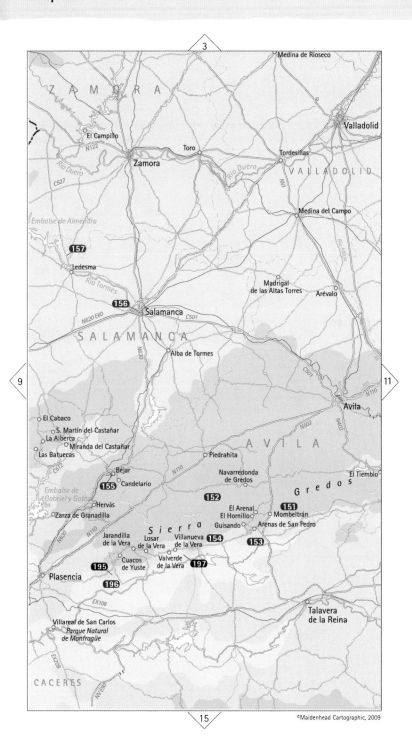

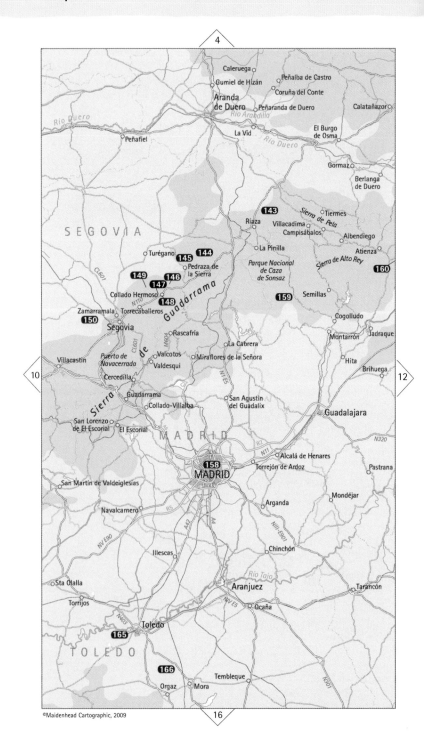

Map 12

33

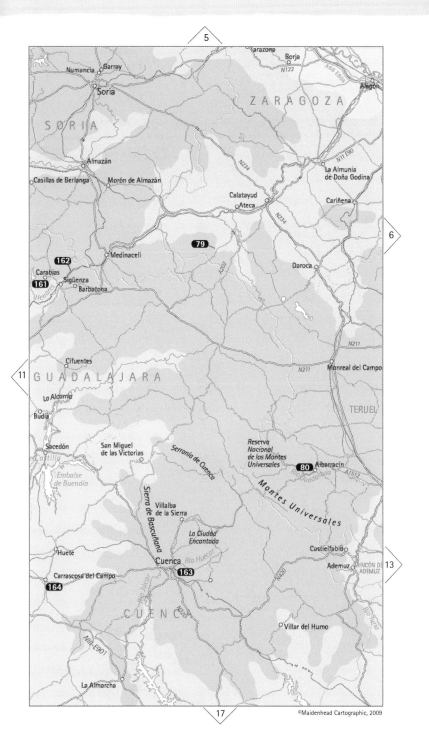

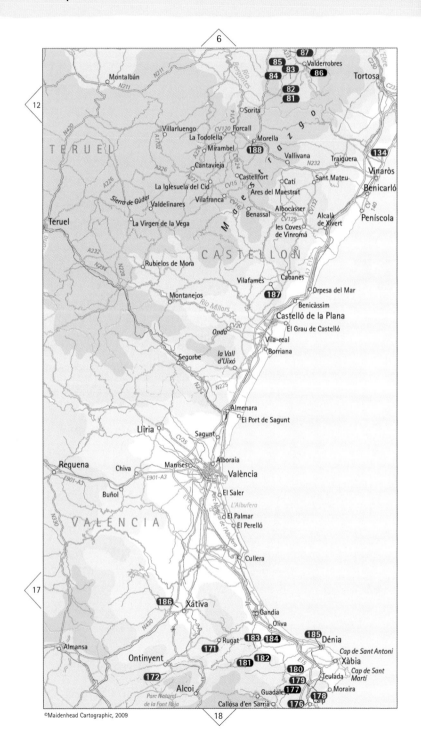

Map 14

35

©Maidenhead Cartographic, 2009

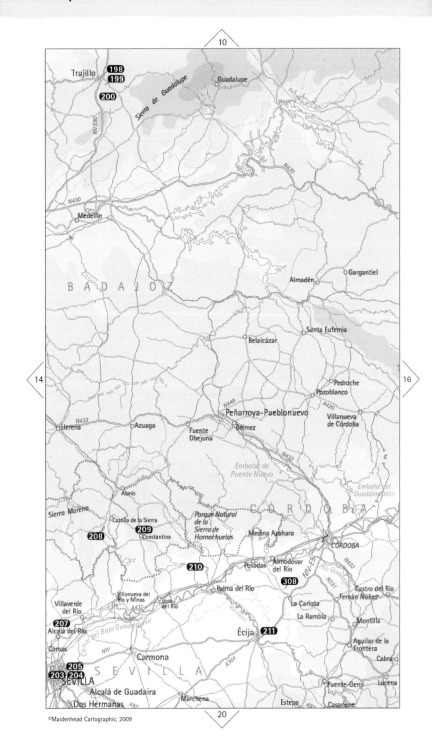

©Maidenhead Cartographic, 2009

Map 16   37

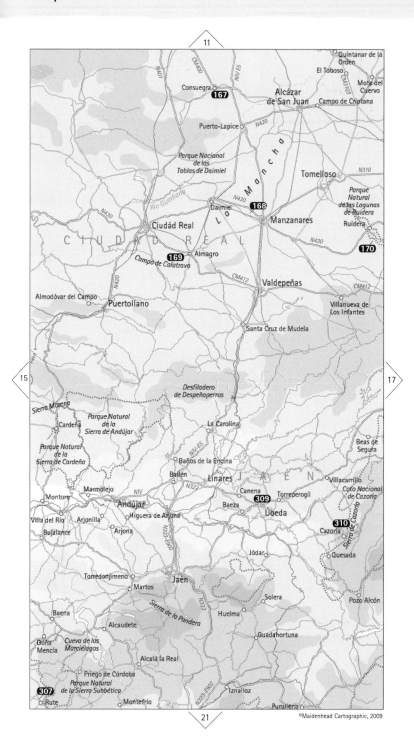

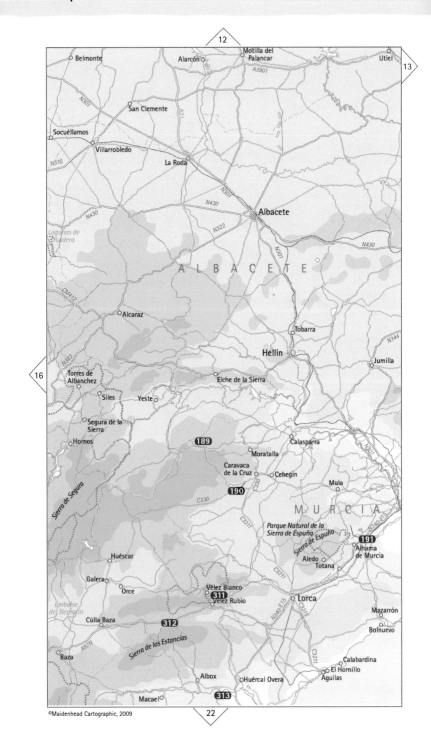

Map 18   39

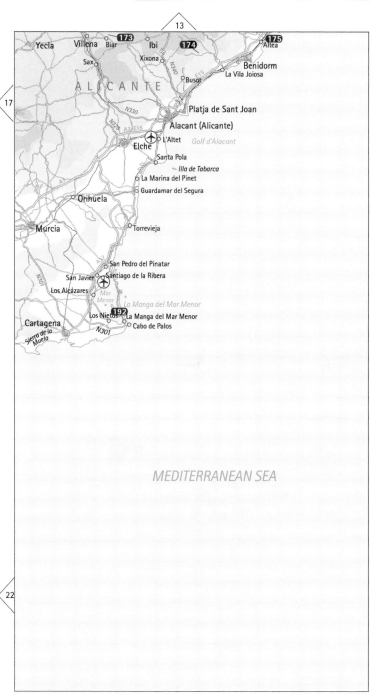

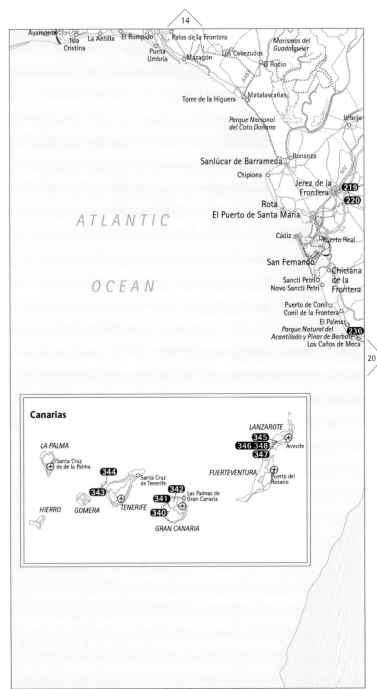

Map 20

41

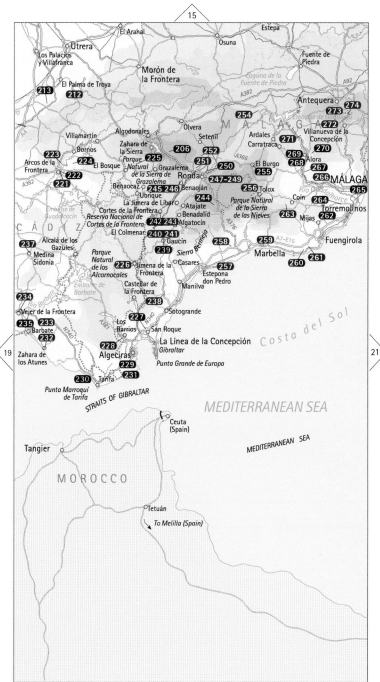

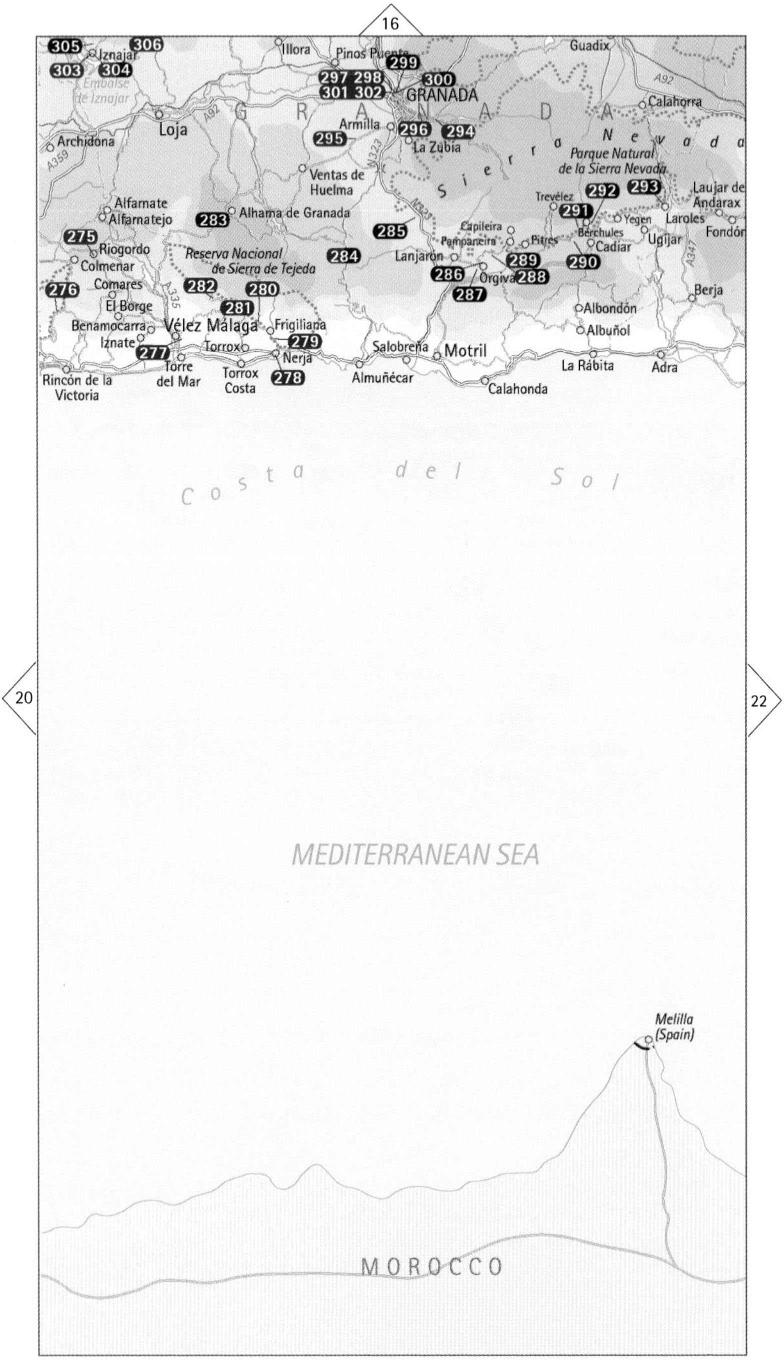
16
20
22
Iznajar
Embalse de Iznajar
Illora
Pinos Puente
GRANADA
Guadix
Calahorra
Archidona
Loja
Armilla
La Zubia
Sierra Nevada
Parque Natural de la Sierra Nevada
Ventas de Huelma
Laujar de Andarax
Alfarnate
Alfarnatejo
Alhama de Granada
Trevélez
Yegen
Laroles
Fondón
Capileira
Pampaneira
Pitres
Bérchules
Cadiar
Ugíjar
Riogordo
Colmenar
Reserva Nacional de Sierra de Tejeda
Lanjarón
Orgiva
Comares
El Borge
Berja
Albondón
Albuñol
Benamocarra
Iznate
Vélez Málaga
Frigiliana
Torrox
Nerja
Salobreña
Motril
Rincón de la Victoria
Torre del Mar
Torrox Costa
Almuñécar
Calahonda
La Rábita
Adra
305 306 303 304 299 297 298 300 301 302 296 294 295 292 293 291 283 285 275 284 289 290 286 288 287 276 282 280 281 279 277 278
Costa del Sol
MEDITERRANEAN SEA
Melilla (Spain)
MOROCCO

Map 22

43

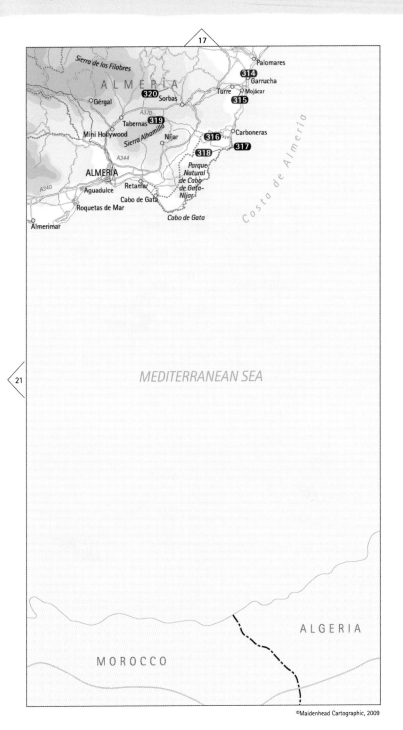

Galicia

Casa Grande de Cornide

Just 15 minutes from Santiago centre and surrounded by Galician green, Casa Grande may be likened to a good claret: refined, select, worth paying a bit more for. It houses a large collection of modern Galician paintings, hundreds of ceramic pots, a huge library and decoration that is a spicy cocktail of old and new: exposed granite, designer lamps, wooden ceilings, and, everywhere, art. Do ask to see the dovecote – converted into a charming and original winestore. A place to come to read, to paint in the beautiful mature garden full of ancient trees – and a surprising number of palms so far north – and to explore the countryside on bikes provided free for guests. The studied décor of the lounges and library is mirrored in the bedrooms and suites – they have all mod cons and the same mix of modern and old; there are books, ornaments, paintings and exquisite little details such as handmade tiles in the bathrooms to create a special feel. Some are housed in an annexe – these duplex apartments have spiral staircases and are modern in style . "A glorious place," enthused one reader. *A Pazos de Galicia hotel.*

Price	€50–€100. Singles €40–€68.
Rooms	8: 6 twins/doubles, 2 singles.
Meals	Breakfast €7. Lunch & dinner €15.
Closed	January–March.
Directions	From Santiago, N-550 dir. Pontevedra; 10km. At Casalonga, turn left, dir. Luou. After 2km, follow signs for hotel.

Javier Goyanes
Teo, 15886 Santiago de Compostela,
La Coruña

Tel	+34 981 805599
Fax	+34 981 805751
Email	cornide@casasgrandesdegalicia.com
Web	www.casasgrandesdegalicia.com

Casa Hotel As Artes

Handy when visiting big beautiful Santiago to stay close to the cathedral. Look no further than this delightful small hotel, in its bustling heart. It is the creation of friendly, dynamic Esther and Carlos – and entirely inspired by his six-month stay in a small Parisian hotel. Guest bedrooms – indisputably small but very well done – look to music and the arts for their theme: choose between Rodin, Dante, Vivaldi, Gaudí, Picasso, Duncan and Chaplin. All are stylishly furnished with new wrought-iron bedsteads on polished parquet, fashionable fabrics, paintings and prints on exposed stone walls; beds have embroidered sheets; bathrooms sport dressing gowns and thick towels. There's a little sauna, too, and physiotherapy on request. What makes it even nicer is the professionalism of the staff. Breakfast – fresh orange juice, fruit salad, charcuterie, cakes, several breads – is served at pretty red-clothed tables or in your room. The setting is unbeatable: the cathedral two steps away, bustling restaurants outside the door. *Parking is at some distance.*

Price	€52–€110.
Rooms	7 twins/doubles.
Meals	Breakfast €10.
Closed	Rarely.
Directions	In Santiago head for Praza do Obradoiro; Rua de San Francisco to left of cathedral. Hotel 50m past cathedral on right. Car park 100m from hotel. Detailed directions on hotel website.

Esther Mateos & Carlos Elizechea
Travesia de Dos Puertas 2,
15707 Santiago de Compostela, La Coruña

Tel	+34 981 572590
Fax	+34 981 577823
Email	recepcion@asartes.com
Web	www.asartes.com

Casa Grande do Bachao

Approach through a veritable forest of eucalyptus trees – and in a hillside clearing looking down the valley … not a gingerbread cottage nor the home of Red Riding Hood's grandmother, but two beautifully solid four-square houses. Inside, both houses have been carefully restored and furnished without eclipsing the original bones of the place; delightful personal touches abound and polished wood and floors gleam. Bedrooms are comfortable and uncluttered – rather grand and soberly furnished in the main house, smaller and cosier in the little one. The elegant dining room – which serves a delicious fixed menu – is light and airy; french doors open out onto the terrace. If you like splendid isolation you'll love it here – and you can actually walk to Santiago de Compostela (it's 15 kilometres). There are sauna, gym, a library stacked with books on flora and fauna, and bikes to borrow. A spot of trout fishing can also be arranged. On wet days families will appreciate the children's playroom and games and TV room; on fine ones, the swimming pool. And the freedom to explore. Good value. *A Pazos de Galicia hotel.*

Price	€50-€85. Singles €40-€68. Suite €65-€100.
Rooms	12: 9 twins/doubles, 2 singles, 1 suite.
Meals	Breakfast €7. Lunch & dinner €15. Wine from €7.
Closed	24/25 December; 1 January-12 March.
Directions	From Santiago, CP-0701/AC-404, Santa Comba road. Pazo signed on right at 8km marker. Follow forest road for 5km; signed.

Javier Goyanes
Monte Bachao s/n, sta. Cristina de Fecha,
15898 Santiago de Compostela, La Coruña

Tel	+34 981 194118
Fax	+34 981 192028
Email	bachao@casasgrandesdegalicia.com
Web	www.casasgrandesdegalicia.com

Hotel Rústico Santa Eulalia

If you're sporty and you don't demand luxury, this modest hotel between Santiago and the Atlantic could be for you. The young owners are keen to promote 'adventure tourism' on their patch so you can fish for trout, hike, mountain-bike or ride the St James's Way, sail or, perhaps most tempting of all, swim in the Atlantic off the lovely sands at Carnota. Bedrooms are in the original stone farmhouse and are surprisingly smart considering the price, the best with their own covered galleries. All are cheerfully decorated with attractive wooden furniture and floors, and central heating in bedrooms and bathrooms, a comfort when the days turn chilly. The restaurant is just across the way, new and strictly functional, its culinary philosophy to keep things "simple and local". Try the local specialities stuffed peppers and *empanada*, the Galician equivalent of Cornish pasty. The wine list is surprisingly good. Although this is a no-frills hotel, the young owners' kindness and hospitality has convinced us that Santa Eulalia deserves a place in this guide.

Price	€60–€70. Singles €45–€55.
Rooms	10 twins/doubles.
Meals	Lunch €10. Dinner €15. Wine €12–€50.
Closed	Rarely.
Directions	From A-9 exit Santiago Sur/Noia. Signs for Noia, then right to Serra de Outes. Here, 1st road towards Mazaricos. Hotel on right after 8km.

John Pritchard & María Angeles Cuadrós
Santa Baia s/n, 15256 Chacín-Mazaricos,
La Coruña

Tel	+34 981 877262
Fax	+34 981 852062
Email	reservas@andanzasrural.com
Web	www.hotelsantaeulalia.com

Pazo de Souto

The atmosphere of religiosity is tangible: the fine old manor, lost among fields of maize and wooded glades, was built by a member of the Inquisition in 1672. Later it became the school that José attended as a boy; now he and his son-in-law Tito have one of the friendliest and most authentic family-run hotels in this corner of Galicia. The house is dimly lit and labyrinthine, full of stuffed animals and antiques; the vast sitting room has a 'lareira' (inglenook) and chunky chestnut beams, the dining room is lovely, with a gallery; lighting is subdued and the bar is deliciously cosy. Some bedrooms are on the ground floor; a granite staircase leads to more above. Those on the first floor have classic Spanish beds and a certain decadent flair, some with hydromassage baths, but the simplest and sweetest, reached by a winding wooden stair, are in the attic. Tito's daughter is chef; eggs come from the hens, fresh fish from Malpica, and the locals like to dine here. Fine views from the daisy-filled lawn, a new squash court and pool, bikes to borrow and all the rugged beauty of the north coast. *A Pazos de Galicia hotel.*

Price	€50–€90. Singles €36–€70.
Rooms	11: 8 twins/doubles, 3 family rooms.
Meals	Lunch & dinner €15.
	À la carte from €22. Wine from €8.
Closed	Rarely.
Directions	From A Coruña AG-55, exit Carballo Norte. Follow signs Carballo & enter town; right for Sisamo just before BP petrol station (signed). Follow road 2.5km; on right after church.

Maria del Carmen & Taibo Pombo
Lugar de la Torre 1,
15106 Sisamo-Carballo, La Coruña

Tel	+34 981 756065
Fax	+34 981 756191
Email	reservas@pazodosouto.com
Web	www.pazodosouto.com

Casa Entremuros

Here are long stretches of fine, sandy beaches, hidden coves and a number of old fishing villages where the seafood is among the best in Spain. Rest awhile at Santiago and Rosa's solid old granite house and B&B, and let them unlock the secrets of this wonderfully unspoilt region. You approach through the pretty stable yard, with an annexe to one side, lawns, flowers and a fold-away swimming pool in one corner. There are six bedrooms, not huge but handsome; expect shining parquet-clad floors, fitted wardrobes, white bedspreads and matching rag rugs, carefully restored antique beds, a modern upholstered chair or two, and good (though somewhat small) bathrooms. There is a large, light-filled lounge with a dresser and a wood-burner in the huge stone *lareira*. Rosa makes fresh fruit juices and gives you local cheeses and honey and cake. No meals apart from breakfast but the popular Casa Elias is only two miles away — you can have a great meal there at any time of year. A quiet, unassuming and good value place to stay on the wild, indented coastline of the Rías Altas, little known beyond Galicia.

Price	€44-€55. Singles €37.40-€46.70. Whole house (sleeps 12-16) €160-€260. Prices per night. Plus VAT at 7%.
Rooms	6 twins/doubles. House available for self-catering.
Meals	Breakfast €5. Restaurants nearby.
Closed	15 December-15 January.
Directions	From Santiago de Compostela, by Alameda, road for 'Hospital General'. On to Carballo, then towards Malpica to Cances; signed by petrol station.

       Santiago Luaces de La-Herrán
       & Rosa Alvarez
       Cances Grandes 77, 15107 Carballo,
       La Coruña

Tel	+34 981 757099
Email	info@casaentremuros.com
Web	www.casaentremuros.com

Entry 6   Map 1

Pazo de Sedor

One of a number of grand Galician *pazos* open to guests, and a delectable place to stay if you're on the road to Santiago. It is an imposing, 18th-century country house in a fairly remote position, surrounded by wooded hillsides and fields of maize and cattle. Inside you get a proper sense of its aristocratic past: great big rooms and a beautiful wide stone staircase between the two floors. Equally memorable is the open fireplace that spans an entire wall of the dining room, with bread ovens at each side; an airier second dining room has been created in an outbuilding with sweeping views. The bedrooms are a treat; high-ceilinged and parquet-floored, they have family antiques (some Art Deco, some older) and embroidered bedcovers. Some come with a balcony; all have space for an extra bed. Meals are as authentic as the house, and promise the flavours of Galicia – most of the vegetables are home-grown and the meats free range. Your hosts are charming, and fill the house with garden flowers. Superb value. *A Pazos de Galicia hotel.*

Price	€58.40–€73. Singles €44–€55.
Rooms	7 twins/doubles. Extra beds available.
Meals	Breakfast €6. Dinner €15. Wine €5–€35.
Closed	January & February.
Directions	From Lugo N-540, then N-547 for Santiago. 400m past km57 marker, right to Pazo.

Joaquín Saavedra
Castañeda, 15819 Arzua, La Coruña

Tel	+34 981 501600
Fax	+34 981 501600
Email	info@pazodesedor.com
Web	www.pazodesedor.com

Golmar 13

Clinging to a forested ridge, gazing at a vast expanse of sea, this fine old 'casa grande' invites you to share its spectacular position on the northernmost tip of Spain. Inviting and charming, with traditional furniture and original features, the ground floor is warmed by an open fire and glows with prints and paintings. Upstairs, breathtaking views take in 90 kms of coastline; gaze through the telescope in the family room – next stop Newfoundland! Simple bedrooms sport pretty pastel shades and chestnut furniture, while the master bedroom is more luxurious, with its claw-foot bath (and loo) on the open-plan mezzanine above. Village elder Manolo has the keys, neighbours are welcoming and there's masses of information about walks, activities and adventures for rainy days. Kids will love climbing trees in the lawned garden while you swing in the hammock. Another world… yet you are mere minutes from Cedeira with its fishing boats and famous tapas bars. The beaches are Spain's best-kept secret: a vision of blues and greens, white sands and tree-fringed coves along Galicia's breathtaking coast.

Price	€1,100-€1,850 per week. Ask about low season stays.
Rooms	House for 10 (2 doubles, 1 twin, 1 quadruple; 3 bathrooms).
Meals	Restaurant 4km.
Closed	Never.
Directions	Exit 34F at Ferrol; AC566 to Cedeira. Cross river immediately after r'bout, right at T-junc. Follow forest road 4km; at top of hill, left to Trasmontes, right after 100m. Thro' hamlet; on left.

Andrew Platt
15350 Cedeira, La Coruña

Mobile	+34 619 096140
Email	plattperez@gmail.com
Web	www.dosxtremos.com

Pazo da Trave

Plants scramble over old stone, vines hang heavy under the trellis, big trees give shade. The lovely gardens, with fruit trees everywhere and sculptures dotted amongst the greenery, are an integral part of this place. Outside, there is also a children's play garden, a dovecote, an old 'hórreo' – a traditional wooden food store – and a chapel exhibiting more art. Striking decorative art abounds inside too, much of it created by the previous artist and potter owner. Food is taken seriously at Pazo da Trave and dinners are a delight, served by attentive staff in a romantically lit dining area, accompanied by excellent wines. Beautiful bedrooms have big oak beds and beamed ceilings; children are thoughtfully taken care of, with small beds and cots. There is a lovely whitewashed beamy sitting room with an open fire – perfect for cosy winter nights – and a comfortable smokers' gallery on the first floor. A wide range of outdoor activities are further reasons to stay in this friendly and unstuffy hotel. The enthusiastic new owner and manager are full of great plans for the future. *A Pazos de Galicia hotel.*

Price	€60-€100. Singles €45-€60. Suites €90-€145.
Rooms	18: 15 twins/doubles, 3 suites.
Meals	Breakfast €8. Lunch & dinner €22. Wine €9-€30. Restaurant closed 1-30 November.
Closed	Rarely.
Directions	From A Coruna, AG-64 past As Pontes to Chao, left on LU-540 dir. Viveiro. 2km before Viveiro, left to Galdo. Through village, on right (signed).

Antonio Palacios
Galdo, 27850 Viveiro, Lugo

Tel	+34 982 598163
Fax	+34 982 598040
Email	pazo@pazodatrave.com
Web	www.pazodatrave.com

Casa Grande de Camposo

Inside and out – a rare, intriguing place. A high stone wall encloses the four-square farmhouse and its grounds, fortifying Casa Grande against the outside world. There's a new pool just outside the garden wall, the unfussy garden is perfect for kids (grandchildren regularly visit) and guests love the dovecote turned wine cellar. Flowers romp. As for the house, built in the 1730s by a wealthy farmer, it's a fascinating labyrinth of passages, landings and rooms. Gentle Arturo and warm, spirited María Luisa – who inherited it all – preside. An old-fashioned family atmosphere and traditional meals at neat tables set the tone; breakfasts are a treat. Be welcomed into a softly lit, stone-floored hall, with oak and chestnut beams and a massive open fireplace. Big airy bedrooms have pretty rugs on shining wooden floors and bright immaculate bathrooms. The village is tiny – 14 inhabitants; it grew organically around the house. The area is not yet on the tourist trail – this is deeply, undeniably rural – but you're within easy reach of the Sierra de los Ancares and the Neira teems with trout.

Price	€57–€78. Singles €42–€52.
Rooms	8: 6 twins/doubles, 2 suites.
Meals	Breakfast €5.60.
	Lunch & dinner with wine, €18.
Closed	1 November–1 March.
Directions	From Lugo, A-6 dir. Madrid, exit
	479 dir. Corgo. At r'bout, DP-1611 for
	Puebla de San Julián. After 10km, left
	to Camposo (signed).

	María Luisa Sánchez
	Lugar de Camposo 7,
	27364 O Corgo, Lugo
Tel	+34 982 543800
Fax	+34 982 543800
Email	info@camposo.com
Web	www.camposo.com

Casa Grande da Fervenza

The river Miño is a stone's throw from this house and ancient working mill. The 18 hectares of magnificent ancient woodland that girdle it won the 2007 'Forest of the Year' prize and have been declared a Unesco Biosphere Reserve. The Casa, named after the amazing rocky waterfall outside, is both hotel-restaurant and working museum; delightful staff will happily give you a guided tour. There's a cosy bar; the restaurant, with its own spring, glorious open fireplace and wood-fired oven, is in the oldest part, dating from the 17th century. Locally sourced menus are based on traditional regional specialities … try suckling pig and wild boar stew. Wines are outstanding, the region's best. After a day out walking or on the river (with canoe or traditional *batuxo*) return to quiet and simple bedrooms. The restoration has been meticulous in its respect for local tradition. Country furniture has been restored, rugs woven on their own looms, there are linen curtains, chestnut beams and hand-painted sinks. No stinting on creature comforts but here the setting is the thing. *A Rusticae hotel.*

Price	€62–€76. Singles €49–€60. Suite €80–€100.
Rooms	9: 8 doubles, 1 suite.
Meals	Breakfast €8. Lunch & dinner, with wine, €15. À la carte €15–€30.
Closed	Never.
Directions	From Madrid/La Coruña A-6 exit km488 marker. N-VI for Lugo. 2km to Conturiz & left at r'bout by Hotel Torre de Núñez for Páramo; 11km; right at A Fervenza sign; 1km.

Ethical Collection: Environment; Community. See page 412.

Norman Pérez Sánchez-Orozco
Ctra. Lugo-Páramo km11,
27163 O Corgo, Lugo

Tel	+34 982 150610
Fax	+34 982 150610
Email	info@fervenza.com
Web	www.fervenza.com

Casa de Labranza Arza

Glorious views, a farmhouse-family welcome, the smell of newly baked bread… this place is special. The views really *are* something, the 6,000-foot-high peaks strung together like a dowager's diamonds; in the foreground is a rural patchwork of green fields and hedgerows. On a clear day you can see as far as Portugal. Casa Arza is on the slopes of Monte Oribio and is a working dairy farm – hence the delicious butter and soft cheeses served at breakfast. Rosy-cheeked Ramona, who seems to belong to another age, makes jams, butter, bread, cooks meat in a wood-fired oven and vegetables straight from the farm. (The bread is kneaded in an old bread chest and baked daily in a 1700s stone oven.) This is back to basics in the best possible sense, and the warmth of the hospitality is the cherry on the cake. The slate walls and roof of the Casa are typical of the area; spotless bedrooms have rafters and exposed stone walls and beds are wooden and antique, widened to take modern mattresses. Be sure to visit the Monasterio de Samos nearby – it's the biggest monastic cloister in Spain. Stunning value.

Price	€35. Singles €28. VAT included.
Rooms	9 twins/doubles.
Meals	Breakfast €4. Dinner with wine, €11.
Closed	Rarely.
Directions	From Lugo, N-VI for Ponferrada; C-546 to Sarria-Monforte. Left at Sarria on LU-633 to Samos. Through San Cristobo; signed to right at end of village; 4km uphill on left, on entering Reigosa.

Cristina Arza Río
Reigosa-San Cristobo do Real,
27633 Samos, Lugo

Tel	+34 982 216027
Fax	+34 982 216027
Email	asesoria@ingenieriaarza.com

Casa Grande de Rosende

This monument to medieval life is full of fascination – from its suits of armour to its vast stone-walled rooms. The tower dates from 1511, the rest is noble 18th century. Having suffered a devastating fire in 2006, the public areas have been lovingly and carefully restored using a mix of family heirlooms, antiques and some reproduction pieces; the sweet family chapel is being restored too. Bedrooms in the side wing were unaffected and are stupendously raftered, with furnishings to match; refurbished rooms are comfortable and more sober, with a mix of antique and reproduction furniture. The charming personalities of Pauloba, Manuel and son Alejandro, a tourism graduate, add to the fun of being here – and Manuel's knowledge of history is a delight. Enjoy hearty and delicious regional dishes, many made with veg from the garden, in the vaulted dining room – do try Pauloba's fresh almond pudding. You are in the heart of the Ribeira Sacra – wine and hermit country – and one of the most beautiful corners of Galicia; from here you can visit any number of bodegas. *A Pazos de Galicia hotel.*

Price	€65. Suite €84.
Rooms	13: 10 twins/doubles, 3 singles.
Meals	Breakfast €6. Lunch €21. Dinner €17. Wine €3-€20.
Closed	15 December-15 January.
Directions	From Orense, N-120 for Monforte. At km530 marker, exit for Canaval. Right at 1st T-junc., following signs for house. Casa Grande 3km down road.

Manuel Vieítez
Rosende, 27466 Sober, Lugo

Tel	+34 982 460627
Fax	+34 982 460089
Email	rosende@infonegocio.com
Web	www.casagrandederosende.com

Pazo Paradela

A treat for all seasons: a 17th-century manor house with views to the Galician hills. Delightful Manuel, who speaks perfect English, goes out of his way to make your stay a happy one. He grew up in America, dreamed of returning to his native soil, and ended up restoring the imposing old granite house that his father bought. Manuel's natural generosity is reflected in the renovation; "be proud of your work," is his philosophy. Bedrooms and bathrooms have been treated to the simple best: chestnut floors and furniture, Portuguese marble, antique mirrors, rustic stone walls. There's central heating for winter, air con for summer, views are long and green and the peace supreme. The treats continue at table: in the vast granite-hearthed dining room you get homemade honey and jams for breakfast. For dinner, the best of Galician country cooking: perhaps roast leg of lamb from the wood-fired oven and vegetables from the kitchen garden. And the ultimate in hospitality: a *queimada* shared with your hosts, the local hot brandied brew that keeps evil spirits at bay. Close to Trives, a bucolic delight.

Price	€60. Singles €45. Suite €70.
Rooms	8: 7 twins/doubles, 1 suite.
Meals	Breakfast €8. Dinner with wine, €24.
Closed	22 December–2 January.
Directions	From León, N-VI to Ponferrada; N-120 into A Rua Petin; C-636 to Trives. Through centre of town, cross bridge, 1st right; follow signs.

Manuel Rodríguez Rodríguez
Carretera Barrio km2,
32780 Pobra de Trives, Orense

Tel	+34 988 330714
Fax	+34 988 330714
Email	1pa712e1@infonegocio.com

Entry 14 Map 2

Casa Grande de Trives

This noble village house with its own chapel was left abandoned when Alfredo's great-grandmother died; Alfredo and his mother have spent 15 painstaking years on the restoration. Now rooms are filled with very fine antique pieces, many exquisitely upholstered or carved; there's even a restored piano rescued from the ruin. Bedrooms in a separate wing are a quiet delight, with polished floors and (in some cases) French windows to the gardens. And the garden is huge, like something out of a fairytale, full of shady hidden corners and heaven for kids. There are three lovely sitting rooms where you can have a quiet drink (or excellent tea, poured from fine china) and an elegant dining room where breakfast is served. Here rich furnishings, cut flowers and classical music vie with homemade cakes, fresh fruits, big pots of coffee and croissants that make their way up from the kitchen via a dumb waiter. A marvellous place in a charming little town, with plenty to do and see in the area, and a most gracious and charming welcome from mother and son.

Price	€53–€73. Singles €42–€58.
Rooms	9 twins/doubles.
Meals	Breakfast €5.60.
Closed	Rarely.
Directions	Madrid A-6 for La Coruña. Exit 400 for N-120 Monforte de Lemos. At km468 marker, branch off for Pobra de Trives, signed Terra de Trives; right at lights onto OU-636 Trives. On left in village.

Alfredo Araujo & Adelaida Alvarez
c/Marqués de Trives 17,
32780 Pobra de Trives, Orense

Tel	+34 988 332066
Fax	+34 988 332066
Email	info@casagrandetrives.com
Web	www.casagrandetrives.com

Casa Grande de Soutullo

Come for charming owners and stylish country living. This was Benito's great-grandfather's house, a pile of stones in 1973; Gill, Benito and two expert stonemasons nurtured it back to life. From the breezy and beautiful internal courtyard radiate a series of elegantly raftered galleries and rooms decorated with beautiful artworks, some Gill's, and many antiques. Breakfasts are a treat – delicious and homemade. Wooden-floored bedrooms are inviting, naturally cool and enhanced with period pieces and lively colours; lovers should ask for the bridal suite. Bathrooms have delightful hand-painted washbasins. Outside are vast and delightful grounds through which a 100-year-old tortoise roams; and fruit trees galore, woodland, a babbling brook, sun loggia, a serene pool and tennis court. And a terraced organic vegetable and herb garden – a feast for the senses. Hard to tear yourself away… but make time for Ourense's fine seven-arched bridge and amazing Bishop's Baths. Your hosts' friendliness, and their attention to detail and quality, make this very special. *A Pazos de Galicia hotel.*

Price	€66–€86. Singles €52–€68.
Rooms	8 twins/doubles.
Meals	Breakfast €8. Restaurants nearby.
Closed	Rarely.
Directions	From Ourense, N-525 for Santiago to Gustei; CP-6 to A Peroxa; 1st turning on right to Soutullo de Abaixo.

Benito Vázquez
Soutullo de Abaixo,
32152 Coles, Orense

Tel	+34 988 205611
Fax	+34 988 205694
Email	turismorural@pazodesoutullo.com
Web	www.pazodesoutullo.com

Os Bravos I

Take your pick of freshly plucked fruit from the lush garden – kiwis, peaches, cherries, apples, oranges, pears, plums, pomegranates, nectarines. The beautiful and fragrant garden is the star of the show here – stroll around feeling proprietorial. Slipped into this unspoilt pocket of Spain, the sprawling five-bedroom colonial-style house marries modernity with Galician charm. Local chestnut furniture, sloping ceilings and touches of English chintz are married with modern sofas; the owners' paintings and sculptures add interest. There is also a carefully renovated 500-year old cottage where rooms are simple, there are sofabeds for children and the generous porch is perfect for breakfast. Judith and Carlos are welcoming and always on hand – they know all the best beaches, walks and romantic ruins. On a good day it's just too tempting to do nothing – apart from drift around gardens and lovely pool, or sketch or paint. Wine-expert Judith can advise on the region's finest. At night, you'll be hard pushed to hear anything more than the soft plop of an over-ripe peach. *Wine appreciation & art classes available. B&B sometimes available in villa.*

Price	Villa from £1,000 per week. Cottage from £400 per week.
Rooms	Villa for 10 (3 twins, 2 family). Cottage for 2-4.
Meals	Dinner with wine, €25. Restaurant 20-minute walk. Optional maid service.
Closed	Rarely.
Directions	From Vigo N-550 for Tui, then PO-552 dir. A Guarda. After 12km, right for Estas (signed). Through village, bear left to Os Bravos.

Judith Mary Goater & Carlos Abreu
Estas, 36730 Tomiño, Pontevedra
Tel   +34 986 623337
Email   osbravos1@telefonica.net

Rectoral de Cobres 1729

Mussel platforms, fishing boats and the majestic sweep of the Ría de Vigo – a special site for a special place. The house was built for a priest in 1729 and has been beautifully renovated by vivacious Randi, a Norwegian architect, and her husband, the equally hospitable Juan Carlos. Relax in the long living room divided by an old stone arch and graced with a delicate Persian carpet and red sofas; dip into a tome from the library (3,000 books and almost as many maps), take a drink to the terrace with the estuary views. Bedrooms are sensitively designed and reveal a designer's love of clean lines and uncluttered spaces. One lovely double has a sweep of polished parquet, French windows to a balcony (more views) and an entire wall of ancient stone. Gravitate to the bar, where strong Galician beer is served; Juan Carlos may pick up the guitar or the Gallic pipes and serenade you. The stunning outdoor *hórreo* (granary) has been converted into a further sitting area: a magical place to watch the sun go down. And there are some wonderful fish restaurants close by. *A Pazos de Galicia hotel.*

Price	€80–€170.
Rooms	8 twins/doubles.
Meals	Breakfast €8. Restaurants 500m.
Closed	Rarely.
Directions	From Pontevedra, A-9 for Vigo; exit 146 Cangas. After toll, left following signs for Vilaboa & Cobres. 2km from junction, at km8 marker, take track on left; 100m from road.

Juan Carlos Madriñán & Randi Hanssen
San Adrian de Cobres,
36142 Vilaboa, Pontevedra

Tel	+34 986 673810
Fax	+34 986 673803
Email	info@rectoral.com
Web	www.rectoral.com

Asturias & Cantabria

Casona Cantiga del Agüeira

In the fold of lush, green mountains by the Agüeira river, a house of song and laughter owned by two passionate musicians. The striking red casona exudes centuries-old solidity but music is now its raison d'être – fitting for the 'House of Song'. Inside is rustic yet refined, with high chestnut beams, slate floors and atmospheric lighting by Patricia's artistic father. Windows are small but the views are tantalising. Bedrooms are generously simple, with soft beds, polished wood floors and neat floral tables. Join in evening recitals round a grand piano in the big stone-walled sitting room, or sink into the pink velvet seats that once graced Madrid's Teatro Alfil. Reinhold, a professional guitarist, holds master classes too. It's a steep walk up to the restaurants of sweet Santa Eulalia, but an easy walk down; return to a nightcap from the confession box (now an honesty bar). Breakfasts are a treat, with fresh cheese and local honey. On the remote Asturian–Galician border, there are walks galore and life in the villages; charming Patricia tells you all. When the music stops, listen to the sound of silence.

Price	€82–€116.
Rooms	9 twins/doubles.
Meals	Breakfast €7.
	Restaurants 10-minute walk.
Closed	10 January-10 February.
Directions	From Oviedo, west on N-634. At Castropol, N-640 for Vegadeo; AS-11 for Puerto de la Garganta. Here, follow signs Santa Eulalia de Oscos. At x-roads for village, right down hill (signed Pumares/Ventoso) for 1km.

Patricia Cid
Pumares s/n,
33776 Santa Eulalia de Oscos, Asturias
Tel   +34 985 626224
Fax   +34 985 626225
Email info@cantigadelagueira.com
Web   www.cantigadelagueira.com

Entry 19   Map 2

Chao de Pendia

The road twists and slices through rocky, wooded valleys up to this solid old casona, now a charming and smart little hotel. Exposed stone and soft colourwashed walls, old beams and polished dark wood floors combine with modern furniture, bright prints and pools of light. Some bedrooms nestle under eaves with light pouring in through skylights; others have stunning views of the surrounding nature. All have ergonomic mattresses and generous bathrooms. Less is more in the stylish dining room, opening out to a huge lawned garden, great for games for all ages. Take a drink from the bar and sit on old railway sleeper steps: imaginative seating for the grassy terrace. Young and welcoming, Blanca and Amalio calmly take care of every need, while their baby daughter adds to the family feel. Watch the moon rise over wide, wooded mountains to illuminate the river below – disturbed only by the hooting of owls or tinkle of cowbells. Such peace. You can still hit the coast in minutes for beaches and seafood… or explore inland the riverside paths, pre-Roman forts, wooded walks and mountains beyond.

Price	€69–€94.
Rooms	9 doubles.
Meals	Dinner by arrangement. Restaurants 5-minute drive.
Closed	Never.
Directions	From Gijón, A-8 to Navia. Thro' town centre,1st left after bridge over estuary (signed AS12 to Boal). Left at km18 marker, signed Castro de Pendia. Follow asphalt track down hill for 1km; on left.

Blanca Glez. Iparrraguirre
c/Pendia s/n, Pendia,
33798 Concejo de Boal, Asturias

Tel	+34 985 620754
Fax	+34 985 620359
Email	contacto@chaodependia.es
Web	www.chaodependia.es

El Bosque de las Viñas

It takes love and dedication to create something as special as these apartments, set in an old Asturian farmhouse near the charming village of Boal. Revelling in distinct characters (Earth, Air, Fire, Water, Wood), these quirky holiday spaces proudly bare their chunky beams, rustic stonework and fabulous colours. A stunning slate mirror, a stained-glass screen, chequerboard tiles, a claw foot bath – each open-plan space delivers its own delights. All are squeaky clean and smartly comfortable. Some beds are on a mezzanine, others behind screens on a high-ceilinged ground floor, and bathrooms promise hydromassage showers or baths. Cook in sweet kitchens, dine al fresco or pop to Boal for a *menú del día*. Navia is 20 minutes away, for fish restaurants and the sea; wooded valleys surround you. Smiling Nuria is always to hand, and you can order breakfast – and even buy local produce – at reception. There's almost too much to do: beaches, markets, forts, goldmines, biking, climbing, water sports… this lovely place between the mountains and the wide blue sea really does have something for everyone.

Price	€78 per night. Plus VAT at 7%.
Rooms	5 apartments for 2.
Meals	Breakfast €6. Plus VAT at 7%. Restaurants 2km.
Closed	Never.
Directions	N-632, E-70 to Navia; then AS-12 towards Grandas de Salime and Boal. As Viñas 2km before Boal.

Nuria Santana Menéndez
As Viñas s/n, 33720 Boal, Asturias

Tel	+34 985 620284
Fax	+34 985 620284
Email	boal@elbosquedelasvinas.com
Web	www.elbosquedelasvinas.com

Palacio de Prelo

Rediscover the meaning of silence. It is broken only by the echo of footsteps on ancient floors. Alicia will guide you through reading rooms and vaulted doors to your room, relating on the way the story of the Oxford doctor of economics who has so beautifully restored this 16th-century palace to its former glory. Your room will be large, plush and outrageously comfortable. Noble old wardrobes and delicately embroidered bedspreads reflect the owner's delight in fine antiques and rich fabrics, but our favourite room is the one in the tower, its contemporary furnishings enhanced by a feast of ancient rafters. Or choose a room at the front of the house, for pastoral views and the sound of cowbells. If you are in the tower bedroom, no excuse not to write that novel: the mezzanine gallery has writing desks strategically positioned in front of tiny windows. In-palace entertainment includes an atmospheric billiard room and a home cinema with a fine selection of classic and foreign films. You may be a 30-minute drive from fine Asturian beaches but this feels a million miles away.

Price	€139-€155. Suites €180-€225.
Rooms	5: 3 twins/doubles, 2 suites.
Meals	Dinner, with wine, €25.60. Lunch by arrangement only.
Closed	10 January-10 February.
Directions	From Navia on AS-12 through Boal to San Luís. Here, follow signs to Villayón/Castrillón. After sign for Prelo, Palacio on hillside on left.

Alicia Alvarez
Prelo s/n, 33728 Prelo-Boal, Asturias

Tel	+34 985 620718
Fax	+34 985 620038
Email	info@palaciodeprelo.com
Web	www.palaciodeprelo.com

Hotel Villa La Argentina

This aristocratic villa was constructed in 1899 by an emigrant who'd made his fortune in South America – hence the name. It was later abandoned, then rediscovered by the González Fernández family who saw in the crumbling stucco a brighter future. Once again it breathes an air of old-fashioned charm. Painted ceilings have been painstakingly restored by Antonio's mother, as has much of the original furniture; huge land and seascapes are also by her. The best bedrooms breathe in harmony with the house and have glorious garden views; most are large with stuccoed and corniced ceilings and king-sized beds and there are also four new colourful self-catering apartments. There's a cosy and popular sailor-style bar, serving regional home cooking in the evenings. The working fishing port of Luarca is down the hill – or slip off for a swim or a dip in the jacuzzi here and wander the superb botanical gardens with their rare and tropical plants. There's also a charming little chapel cum library. The pilgrim route, Camino de Santiago, passes by the front door. Antonio and his family are warm and generous and adore children.

Price	€69–€95. Suites €81–€102. Apartments €150. All prices per night.
Rooms	12 + 4: 9 twins/doubles, 3 suites. 4 apartments for 4.
Meals	Breakfast €5.50–€9.50. Tapas available. Restaurant 100m.
Closed	7 Jan to end Feb (open 14 Feb).
Directions	From Oviedo & Gijón on A-8/N-632 for Avilés. Exit onto N-634 for Luarca. At AGIP petrol station just before Luarca, right on LU-1; yellow signs to hotel.

Antonio González
Parque de la Barrera, Villar de Luarca,
33700 Luarca, Asturias

Tel	+34 985 640102
Fax	+34 985 640973
Email	villalaargentina@villalaargentina.com
Web	www.villalaargentina.com

La Torre de Villademoros

In meadow land high above the coast stands this elegant retreat – hike down to undiscovered shingle beaches. The original medieval tower is the stuff of local legends; the interiors have been beautified by young welcoming Manolo and his delightful family. La Torre's 18th-century Asturian exterior gives little hint as to the delights within – the interior spaces are intimate, cosy, hugely appealing. Gleaming wooden or slate floors are the background to sleek sofas and sculpted lighting; warm colours, modern art and an open hearth add depth. Serene bedrooms and private sitting rooms are finished with polished chestnut and pine, bathrooms are sleek and large. And there is a stupendously romantic and luxurious new suite, occupying all four floors of the medieval tower. Views are grand – over the sea or the lush eucalyptus forests – while the semi-wild grounds encourage wildlife. Enjoy tapas and a glass of wine in the bar; scrumptious breakfasts are taken on the covered terrrace and will set you up for the coastal path to Cudillero – superb. Not easy but well worth the effort to find! *A Rusticae hotel.*

Price	€84–€120. Singles €63–€92.
Rooms	11: 10 twins/doubles, 1 suite.
Meals	Breakfast €8. Dinner €16.
Closed	7 January–2 March.
Directions	From Oviedo, N-632/E-70 for La Coruña; exit for Cadavedo. Through village & into Villademoros. 30m after Villademoros road sign, right; signed.

Manolo Santullano Méndez
Villademoros s/n (Cadavedo),
33788 Valdés, Asturias

Tel	+34 985 645264
Fax	+34 985 645265
Email	correo@torrevillademoros.com
Web	www.torrevillademoros.com

La Corte

Here you are *cerca del cielo* – close to heaven. Up the scenic road to a delightful working village deep in the Parque Natural de Somiedo. The inn is a 19th-century wood and stone farmhouse, converted by its charismatic owner into a small restaurant with rooms. You enter via a small courtyard, then up old stone steps to a wooden-floored sitting room. Here are books and photographs (some of your host as a young boy), a brass-studded chest of drawers, old crockery, a handsome hearth and a gallery with amazing mountain views. A metal spiral staircase leads to the bedrooms, some big, some small. All have good bathrooms, new pine furniture and comfy beds; two have dormer windows so you can study the stars from your bed. The self-catering studio in the 150-year-old granary has a Heidi feel, the apartment comes with an open-plan living room. Locals pop in for a drink or a fine meaty meal in the restaurant – cosy, low-ceilinged, beamed and with basket lamps. No simpler or sweeter place from which to go walking in the Pigüeña Valley, where some of Europe's last bears roam free.

Price	€60. Studio €65. Apartment €100. All prices per night.
Rooms	5 + 2: 5 doubles. Studio for 2, apartment for 4.
Meals	Breakfast €4. Lunch & dinner €15.
Closed	Rarely.
Directions	From Oviedo N-634 west. Just before Cornellana, left on AS-15 to Puente de San Martín. Here, AS-227 south to Aguasmestas. Here, right to Pigüeña; up via Cores; 11km to Villar.

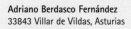

Adriano Berdasco Fernández
33843 Villar de Vildas, Asturias

Tel	+34 985 763131
Fax	+34 985 763117
Email	lacorte_somiedorural@hotmail.com
Web	www.lacortesomiedo.com

Entry 25   Map 2

Pisón de Fondón

High in an unspoilt hamlet where wooded hills give way to steep mountains is a sweet house owned by a charming family. Originally a mill for the 'escanda' grain grown in the mountains, the old stone building has been transformed by Carmen into a delightful home from home. Step in through a cheery courtyard to feel peace envelop you: inside is simple and pretty with polished chestnut floors, exposed stone and pastel colours. The cosy kitchen, dining room and sitting room blend into one, with a warm wood stove, restored chairs and a comfy sofa. Welcoming and homely bedrooms upstairs – with organic linen and towels – share a snug bathroom. Gentle and genuine, Carmen and Jason are passionate about green living: they use eco paints and products, local suppliers and have an organic vegetable patch and an orchard; they can provide delicious organic breakfasts, too. There's nature on your doorstep, so pop across the patio for maps, advice or to borrow a bike; Carmen's children may take yours exploring. No cars or shops distract from the soothing caress of this rural peace – breathe in deeply and unwind.

Price	€525–€700 per week.
Rooms	Cottage for 2-4.
Meals	Breakfast €7.50. Restaurants 4km.
Closed	Rarely.
Directions	From Grado AS-311 for Tameza. After 8km, right in San Pedro (GR-4) for Restiello. Continue for 9km; sharp left after narrow bridge to Villandás (1km).

Carmen Fernandez Mayo
Villandás, 33827 Grado, Asturias

Mobile	+34 649 058437
Email	capison@gmail.com
Web	www.fade.es/pisondefondon

La Casona de Pío

Hard to believe Pío ever had a fish-salting factory here, in this elegant little hotel one street back from the main square. Cudillero is one of the prettiest fishing villages of the Asturian coast, a huddle of houses around a sheltered cove where you can still watch the catch being landed first thing. La Casona de Pío is one of the area's best known fish restaurants – beautifully presented tables and food, an extraordinarily crafted wooden ceiling, and a chef who knows his stuff. We were ushered through to the kitchen to see all kinds of good things on the go in boiling pots and sizzling pans. Out of season Pío's charming owners will give you a choice of rooms – we might choose no. 104 for its private terrace, or a top-floor room for its light. All the rooms are compact but smart, with chestnut furniture, matching bedcovers and drapes, rugs on gleaming tiled floors and swish bathrooms with hydromassage baths. Picnics can be prepared for walks and other sorties. You should know that steep steps climb from the street to the reception hall and parking is some distance away. Excellent value, lovely people.

Price	€58-€92. Singles €45-€73. Suite €87-€111.
Rooms	11: 10 doubles, 1 suite.
Meals	Breakfast €7. Lunch & dinner €20-€30. Wine €8-€36.
Closed	10 January-15 February.
Directions	From Oviedo, N-634 for La Coruña; on for Luarca. Turn right off road for Cudillero. Hotel in town centre, just off main square. Park in front of bollards to unload. Car park 250m, by harbour.

Rosario Fernández Martínez
c/Riofrío 3, 33150 Cudillero, Asturias

Tel	+34 985 591512
Fax	+34 985 591519
Email	casonadepio@arrakis.es
Web	www.arrakis.es/~casonadepio/

Casona de la Paca

Worth coming here for the breakfasts alone... Asturian cheeses, smoked meats, *torrijas*, *maranuelas*, *frixuelos*, doughnuts and crêpes – all superb. The Casona's strawberry-coloured façade and exotic gardens packed with New World species grab the attention on arrival – as was intended. This is one of Asturias's many flamboyant edifices built by emigrants who made their fortune in the Americas, then returned home. Revived from ruin only 15 years ago, the house contains an elegant mix of classic and colonial styles in sympathy with the spirit of the place. There's mahogany and teak in abundance, contemporary fabrics and handmade, Deco-style floor tiles. The conservatory is exquisite, the well-upholstered lounge is a lovely place to read and there are plenty of books in the library. Bedrooms are divided between the main house and the annexe; splash out on the Tower Suite with its wraparound terrace. There are also ten immaculate self-catering apartments. Casona de la Paca runs on well-oiled wheels, and the fishing town of Cudillero lies delightfully nearby. *A Rusticae hotel.*

Price	€70-€95. Singles €57-€81. Suites €100-€123. Studios for 2, €64-€87; for 4, €86-€110. All prices per night.
Rooms	20 + 10: 11 twins/doubles, 1 single, 8 suites. 10 studios for 2-4.
Meals	Breakfast €7.80. Restaurants 600m.
Closed	11 December-end January.
Directions	From Oviedo/Gijón on A-8/N-632 for La Coruña. After Soto de Barco, right at signs for Cudillero. House on right after 1km.

	Montserrat Abad
	El Pito, 33150 Cudillero, Asturias
Tel	+34 985 591303
Fax	+34 985 591316
Email	hotel@casonadelapaca.com
Web	www.casonadelapaca.com

La Quintana de la Ería

Members for years of the guest-exchange organisation SERVAS, good-natured Clara and Guti make delightful hosts. Be prepared for a traditional welcome: a glass of local cider poured from an impossible height! Their Asturian farmhouse is surrounded by dairy farms and big skies, while cool sea breezes help build up appetites for hearty breakfasts of fried eggs, chorizo and... cider. All this is cheerfully served on old wooden tables in a cosy sitting room with roughly plastered mauve and terracotta walls, robust beams and a roaring stove. Simple but spacious bedrooms are colour coordinated and named after herbs found in Clara's garden; we like the Rosemary Room best, with its own balcony. A rustic and earthy feel runs throughout, complemented by delicate embroidered covers and old wrought-iron bedsteads; all around you are views of rolling hills to the serrated skyline of the Picos de Europa. Plan trips to fishing villages or to the awesome Cabo de Peñas, as you rest awhile under the courtyard's weeping willow, your sole companions a clutch of contented free-ranging hens.

Price	€45–€68.
Rooms	4 twins/doubles.
Meals	Breakfast €5.50. Dinner €14, by arrangement. Wine €7.
Closed	Rarely.
Directions	A-8/E-70 from Gijon; exit 404 for Luanco onto AS-238/AS-239a. At km7.5 marker, right to La Ería, opposite Bar Peláez. Follow track for 400m; house has tarmac driveway.

Clara Sierra & Guti Lagares
La Eria, 33449 Luanco, Asturias

Tel	+34 985 882023
Fax	+34 985 882023
Email	clara@quintanadelaeria.com
Web	www.quintanadelaeria.com

Hotel Quinta Duro

The family estate is a haven of greenery and mature trees, girdled by a high stone wall. It lies just to the east of Gijón and you overlook the city; 800m from the main road yet you hear nothing but birds. Carlos, a delightfully warm presence, has turned the stately house and large veranda into a rather grand and very comfortable small hotel. Panelled walls, family heirlooms and period Portuguese and English furniture show the family's love of quality and detail, and bedrooms are distinguished, one with its own terrace. The bronze statue in the lovely gardens is of Carlos's grandfather who casts a wistful eye on all those who visit – he would surely approve of his grandson giving the house this new lease of life. Breakfasts are excellent and there are two restaurants close by – or head for the nearby lively seaside city of Gijon. The beach gets busy, but on the harbour front you'll find two Asturian specialities in abundance: fish and cider. Carlos's devoted red setter, Jarra, is as charming as his owner. A warm and memorable experience for those in search of quiet comfort. *Pottery courses available.*

Price	€82.64–€144.24. Singles €58.25–€73.06.
Rooms	11 twins/doubles.
Meals	Breakfast €6.42. Restaurants 400m.
Closed	Rarely.
Directions	A-8 exit 385 Gijón, then to Jardín Botánico at 1st & 2nd r'bouts. At r'bout by Jardín Botánico 1st right for Santurio y Cefontes; after 200m left for Santurio; 200m, right for Deva; 350m on right.

	Carlos Velázquez-Duro
	Camino de las Quintas 384,
	33394 Cabueñes-Gijón, Asturias
Tel	+34 985 330443
Fax	+34 985 335815
Email	info@hotelquintaduro.com
Web	www.hotelquintaduro.com

La Corte de Lugás

Secluded, surrounded by eucalyptus and walnut forests – and in cider country's delicious heart – this family venture is a showcase for the decorative talents of welcoming owners. The whole place has a fabulously, tongue-in-cheek 'royalty' theme; bedrooms, named after the kings of Asturias, are divided between the 17th-century house and the old bakery. They vary in size and theme: some feel darkly medieval, others bohemian, all are bold, stylish, eye-catching and decked in royal colours. Some of the wrought-iron furniture was commissioned by local artists, a few beds are country antiques; fabrics are subtle and of fine quality, real art adds a special touch. And now four luscious garden suites have been added – sloping ceilings, waterfall showers, huge jacuzzis: over the top maybe but quite irresistible. There's a popular restaurant, a café and a bar; outside are lawns and field and forest views. Explore the conveniently close town of Villaviciosa and the seafront city of Gijon; return to deep leather armchairs before a fire, and dinner that's worth waiting for. Grand – with a family touch. *A Rusticae hotel.*

Price	€100-€130. Singles €70-€90. Suites €130-€160. Garden suites €200-€250.
Rooms	14: 5 twins/doubles, 5 suites, 4 garden suites.
Meals	Lunch & dinner, with wine, €30.
Closed	7 January-7 February.
Directions	From Villaviciosa towards Infiesto; at km3 marker, left for Lugás. Hotel 2km.

Daniel González Alvarez
c/Lugás s/n, 33311 Villaviciosa, Asturias

Tel	+34 985 890203
Fax	+34 985 890203
Email	info@lacortedelugas.com
Web	www.lacortedelugas.com

La Quintana de la Foncalada

Severino greets you with unaffected simplicity at this honeysuckle-clad farmhouse in the flat, coastal *mariña* area of Asturias. The garden, full of flowers, shady corners and fruit trees, is bliss for children, with both treehouse and slide. The inside of the house is what you'd expect for the price; bedrooms have basic furniture, dim lighting, artistic splashes of colour; bathrooms are small. Make yourself a hot drink in the rustic kitchen whenever you like; find out about the area and its traditions in the lounge replete with leaflets and guides. There is an organic apple orchard and much is home-produced: juices, cider, jam, delicious breakfast cakes. Make the most of the wonderful beaches and the excursions from La Quintana – by pony or bike. Your hosts run pottery courses too, for adults and kids: every plate, lamp and tile in the house is homemade. But Severino's great passion (to which he has dedicated a museum) is the Asturian pony, the *asturcón*, which he also breeds. Children can help with them and he also runs very popular 'à la carte' riding courses. Perfect for pony-lovers, and kids.

Price	€45-€55. Singles €40. Apartment €90-€120. All prices per night.
Rooms	5 + 1: 5 twins/doubles. 1 apartment for 4-5.
Meals	Breakfast €5. Lunch & dinner, with wine, €17.
Closed	Rarely.
Directions	A-8 Santander-Oviedo, at exit to Villaviciosa AS-256 for Gijón. Arguero 8km further; follow signs.

Severino García
Argüero, 33314 Villaviciosa, Asturias
Tel   +34 985 999001
Email   foncalada@asturcon-museo.com
Web   www.asturcon-museo.com

Hotel Posada del Valle

After two years spent searching the hills and valleys of Asturias, your hosts found the home of their dreams – a century-old farmhouse just inland from the rugged north coast, with sensational views to mountain, hill and meadow. Find a seat in the green hillside garden and gaze! Now they are nurturing new life from the soil – theirs is a fully registered organic farm – while running this small and beguiling Asturian hotel with an English feel. The apple orchard has matured, the sheep munch the hillside, the menu celebrates the best of things local and organic. Bedrooms, sensitively converted, are seductive affairs with shutters and old beams, polished wooden floors, exposed stone, colourful modern fabrics and washed walls to match. There's a stylishly uncluttered living room with an open brick fire, and a dining room with more views. You are close to the soaring Picos, the little-known sandy beaches of the Cantabrian coast and some of the most exceptional wildlife in Europe. Your hosts have compiled well-researched notes on self-guided walks.

Price	€62–€86. Singles €49.60–€60. Triples €82–€95.
Rooms	12: 10 twins/doubles, 2 triples.
Meals	Breakfast €8. Dinner €23. Wine from €10.60.
Closed	Early November to late March.
Directions	N-634 Arriondas; AS-260 for Mirador del Fito. After 1km, right for Collia. Through village (don't turn to Ribadesella). 300m on left after village.

Nigel & Joann Burch
Collia, 33549 Arriondas, Asturias
Tel   +34 985 841157
Fax   +34 985 841559
Email   hotel@posadadelvalle.com
Web   www.posadadelvalle.com

Ethical Collection: Environment; Community; Food.
See page 412.

El Correntiu

It must be the swishest grain silo in Spain. In nine acres, it stands to one side of the farmhouse on a quiet road outside Ribadesella. It's a stunning renovation, not huge but sylish, original and inventive: ochre tones impart warmth, discreet lighting gives character. There are two apartments here, each with a circular bedroom upstairs and its own fragrant kitchen garden – pick to your heart's content. There is also an abundance of kiwi, avocado and citrus trees: in this micro-climate everything thrives. Inside, a feast for the eye – chunky rafters, chestnut floors, country furniture, hand-painted ceramics – and all you need: books, games, linen, towels. If you're a traditionalist you may prefer the little cottage, not swish but just as well equipped. It's a steep, 90-minute walk down to the lovely fishing village of Ribadesella at the mouth of the Sella; the beaches are magnificent, and there's canoeing, bike hire and horse riding too. You can walk to the cave paintings at Tito Bustillo, and drive to the national park. Your hosts are a delight and thoughtful personal touches abound.

Price	Apartments €55–€75. Cottage €85–€110. All prices per night.
Rooms	2 apartments for 2, 1 cottage for 4.
Meals	Restaurant 2km.
Closed	Rarely.
Directions	From Santander A-8/N-632. At Ribadesella N-632 for Gijón. Immed. after bridge, left for Cuevas & Sardalla. From here, 2km to El Correntiu.

María Luisa Bravo & Jose Luis Valdés
Ctra. Piconera 42, 33560 Ribadesella, Asturias
Tel   +34 985 861436
Email elcorrentiu@fade.es
Web   www.correntiu.com

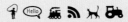

Bajo los Tilos

The hamlet materialises, as if by magic, out of nowhere. As do steep green mountainsides and lush chestnut forests; a wild and wonderful eco-system thrives outside Elena and Juan Luis's front door. These two ex-bankers left Madrid mayhem for memories of childhood summers spent here. Now, bold colour schemes enliven interior spaces; uncluttered bedrooms with sweeping wooden floors reveal deep hues and dazzling white crochet covers. Indian and south-east Asian pieces of furniture add intriguing ethnic touches; paintings and canvasses by Juan Luis's brother strike a bold note. You are only two miles from the nearest FEVE train station, so drop the car and take a trip into the mountains or along the coast. Elena can also tell you about walks in search of hidden springs. Return to a pretty, shady garden and woodpeckers at work; get out the binoculars and spot a few deer. Come evening, there's a huge selection of DVDs, including many classics, to choose from. Charming hosts are the cherry on this very special cake.

Price	€56–€70.
Rooms	6 twins/doubles.
Meals	Breakfast €6. Dinner €17.
Closed	Rarely.
Directions	From Santander/Oviedo on E-70; exit fpr Ribadesella/Picos de Europa onto N-634. At r'bout, signs for Arriondas. After 1km, Santianes del Agua; left into village opposite church. Bear left; 300m to hotel.

Elena de Haro & Juan Luis Toribio
Santianes del Agua 6, 33569 Ribadesella,
Asturias

Tel	+34 985 857527
Email	info@bajolostilos.com
Web	www.bajolostilos.com

Entry 35   Map 3

Palacio de Rubianes, Hotel & Golf

Like a castle on a cloud, this 16th-century palacio sits high on the skyline, above the rolling hills and hamlets of its large estate. Magnificent but not over-precious, sumptuous but serene, its blend of style and comfort is delicious. Behind the restored walls and modernity lie layers of history: the mansion became a farmhouse, then a barracks, then home to the ancestors of its present owners, who have transformed it into this enchanting hotel. A staircase still spirals up a defence tower and the old chapel hosts events. Modern extras attach themselves to stylish, understated bedrooms (some romantically under the eaves), while marble bathrooms breathe indulgence. Sip aperitifs in the sitting room or on the terrace as the sun sinks into the mountains, then dine on light-touch gourmet meals in the quietly stylish restaurant. As serene as the hotel itself, general manager Montse prides herself on her service; just ask her staff about horse riding, golf (the estate has a nine-hole course) and the loveliest places to visit in Asturias. A place of welcome, peacefulness and delicious food.

Price	€110. Half-board extra €18-€25 p.p. Plus VAT at 7%.
Rooms	23: 20 twins/doubles, 1 single, 2 suites.
Meals	Lunch & dinner €18-€25. À la carte €35.
Closed	Never.
Directions	From Oviedo, A64 to Villaviciosa, exit 14; continue on N634, pass Villamayor, then 1st left; follow signs for Pl-11; straight on through La Goleta & La Trapa to La Cereceda. Signs to hotel.

Montse Ortega
Palacio de Rubianes s/n,
33583 Cereceda, Asturias

Tel	+34 985 707612
Fax	+34 985 707139
Email	reservas@palacioderubianes.com
Web	www.palacioderubianes.com

Caserías Sorribas

The hills and mountains around this large family estate are home to mountain goats and Asturcón ponies; its green rolling expanse is dotted with sweet old houses. Lovingly restored by Isabel in Asturian style, they're brilliant for walkers and families looking for cosy comfort and undisturbed peace. Some snuggle into a hamlet, with small gardens and balconies; others stand alone hugged by woodland, and fields where kids can roll around. Décor is repro-rustic with patterned prints and polished pine around wood-burning stoves and fires. Everywhere is spick, span, light and airy, but the refurbished places are the smartest. Bedrooms are generous and pretty, some en suite; others share ample bathrooms. If the weather's not right for barbecues or you fancy a treat, fill up on rich game in nearby restaurants, washed down with scrumpy. You're sandwiched between the Picos de Europa and the Sierra del Sueve; it's a walker's paradise but a mere leap over the hills for unspoilt beaches. You can hire horses on site or fish in the river. Activities abound and nature surrounds you. *Wireless access in reception.*

Price	Houses €441–€987.
	Apartments €462–497. Plus VAT at 7%.
Rooms	10 houses for 2-8; 4 apartments for 2.
Meals	Restaurants 4km.
Closed	Rarely.
Directions	From Oviedo, A64 to Villaviciosa, exit J14; continue on N634 to Sevares next to the restaurant La Pergola, where owner will meet & pick up.

	Isabel Campozano
	33584 Sevares, Asturias
Tel	+34 985 706232
Fax	+34 985 706264
Email	caseriassorribas@fade.es
Web	www.caseriassorribas.com

L'Ayalga Posada Ecológica

Abandon the car and take a train on the narrow-gauge railway to Infiesto. Or come by bus. Either way, if you let them know beforehand, Luis or Concepción will be there to meet you. They are a friendly, caring couple who've taken infinite pains in restoring their farmhouse and use only healthy, non-contaminating materials. Sand is used as sound insulation between floorboards and ceiling and the cleaning products are homemade from borax and essential oils. Herbs scent the garden, a pair of Asturcon ponies graze quietly and green slopes lead the eye inexorably to dramatic mountain profiles. The rooms are attractive and unadorned, with simple white walls, plain wood and warm-coloured fabrics. Thanks to solar panels, the showers have constant hot water and the wooden beds, treated with natural oils, wear decent mattresses. Your hosts, who manage without staff, give 1% of their income from guests to charity. If you crave a massage in peace, your children will be looked after – you may even find them harvesting watermelons for lunch... Peacefulness and tranquillity.

Price	€49. Singles €43. Plus VAT at 7%.
Rooms	5 twins/doubles.
Meals	Vegetarian dinner €13. Plus VAT at 7%. Wine €6-€12.20.
Closed	21 December-8 January.
Directions	From Santander/Bilbao on A-8; exit 326 for Ribadesella/Arriondas. At r'bout, exit N-634 for Arriondas. At km361 marker, towards Infiesto; then AS-254 for Campo de Caso. After 3km, left for La Pandiella. Or bus/train to Infiesto for pick-up.

Ethical Collection: Environment.
See page 412.

Luis A. Díaz & Conchi de la Iglesia
La Pandiella s/n,
33537 Piloña, Asturias

Mobile	+34 616 897638
Fax	+34 985 710431
Email	layalga@terrae.net
Web	www.terrae.net/layalga

Hotel Aultre Naray

You'll be captivated by the views. The green-sloped, grey-peaked Cuera mountains have the quality of a life-size pop-up book: every tree, every rock, every gully appears with such clarity that you feel you could reach out and touch them. This grand *casona* dates from the time when 19th-century Spanish emigrants invested the gains of their adventures overseas in deliberately ostentatious houses. The transition from grand home to fine hotel has been a seamless one here. Vintage flags greet you on arrival, and an exquisite chestnut staircase leads from reception to cosy, comfortable rooms upstairs. The name comes from a medieval motto meaning, 'I'll have no other' and the hotel flourishes under new ownership, the mood remaining warm and relaxed. Designer prints, fabric and furniture marry well with the core elements of beams and stone walls. And it is a treat to breakfast on the terrace in the English-style garden faced with a choice of crêpes, homemade cakes — and eggs and bacon! — to accompany those out-of-this-world views. *A Rusticae hotel.*

Price	€70–€115. Singles €60–€85. Family €113–€163.
Rooms	11: 10 twins/doubles, 1 family.
Meals	Breakfast €4.50–€9. Lunch & dinner €20–€25 à la carte. Wine €11–€25.
Closed	Never.
Directions	From Oviedo for Santander on m'way, then N-634. After passing Arriondas at km335 marker, right for Peruyes. Climb for 1km to village; hotel on left after 150m.

Iñaki Sabando & Susana Marcos
Peruyes, 33457 Cangas de Onis, Asturias

Tel   +34 985 840808
Fax   +34 985 840848
Email   aultre@aultrenaray.com
Web   www.aultrenaray.com

Hotel Rural Arredondo

Feisty bulls once romped around this sunny 18th-century farmhouse; now it's a charming small hotel amid a sea of green. Décor reveals simplicity and comfort with a splash of Ana's quirky retro style: split-colour walls, a 60s cigarette machine, decorative bottles and old ships' lamps. There's a playroom glasshouse, a lover's bench in a two-wheeled cart, and morning papers for a lazy breakfast on the shady terrace (if the weather breaks, a conservatory too). Dine in on home-reared organic meat and fresh farm eggs – cows graze around you – or head to nearby Llanes for seafood and nightlife. Organic cider is made each autumn in the on-site press – watch, if you're there, or simply taste and buy. Bedrooms are generous, with local artist-designed wrought iron beds; suites have an open fireplace, terrace and hydromassage baths. Wake to birdsong and sunlight. Between the high Picos de Europa and the lush Cantabrian coast, cushioned by tranquillity yet so close to beaches, hikes, main roads, the city of Santander... Arredondo really is all things to all people, and Ana's easy generosity shines through.

Price	€80–€104.
Rooms	16: 4 twins/doubles, 5 suites, 7 triples.
Meals	Half-board extra €25. Wine €8.
Closed	2-15 January.
Directions	From Santander, N-634/A-8 dir. Gijón; exit 307 dir. Celorio/Porrúa. After 200m, right to Porrúa; after 300m, right to Arredondo. Follow to end.

Ana Bueno Sánchez
c/Arredondo s/n, 33595 Celorio, Asturias

Tel	+34 985 925627
Fax	+34 985 925930
Email	info@hotelrural-arredondo.com
Web	www.hotelrural-arredondo.com

La Montaña Mágica

Wedged between beaches and the mighty Picos, the hill-perched village hotel has a privileged position and the approach up a mountain-road is amazing... but scary at night! Warm and welcoming Carlos has sensitively rebuilt and added to old farm ruins: the finish is rustic, generous and cheerful. Warm colours and furniture in walnut and oak mingle beautifully with stonework and rafters. There's a log-fired sitting room and library and a map room for walkers and riders: Asturian ponies are available for lessons or hire. There are six lovely suites in the main house, with hydromassage baths and an Alpine feel; other bedrooms are practical, bright and have bathrooms stocked with MM towels and toiletries. Words cannot do justice to the views; ask for a room facing south. The restaurant stands beside the old granary (now a children's playroom) and the food is delicious and great value, the lamb straight from the mountain. Carlos is gradually replacing eucalyptus with indigenous species, and the garden and grounds are full of fragrant delights. The views – clouds permitting – are fabulous. Lots to explore, too.

Price	€50–€85. Suites €70–€105.
Rooms	16: 10 twins/doubles, 6 suites.
Meals	Breakfast €5.40. Dinner à la carte €30. Set menu €14.70. Restaurant 4km.
Closed	Rarely.
Directions	From Santander W on E-70/N-634. Past Llanes; at km307 marker right for Celorio; AS-263 to Posada. Here left on AS-115 for Cabrales to La Herreria. At Allende right over bridge; right, following signs; 3km.

Carlos Bueno & Pilar Pando
El Allende, 33508 Llanes, Asturias

Tel	+34 985 925176
Fax	+34 985 925780
Email	magica@llanes.as
Web	www.lamontanamagica.com

Entry 41   Map 3

La Posada de Babel

Space and light — a treat for the eye! The cool lines, bold colours and extravagant glazing of this trio of buildings add up to a modernist's dream. Designed with an architect's attention to detail, floor to ceiling windows make the most of the wide expanse of undulating lawns and meadows, as the foothills of the Cuera rise behind. White walls, polished tiles, sleek lighting, bursts of colour — the lofty cobalt blue ceiling of the entrance hall will make you gasp. The open-plan spaces of the dining and drawing rooms are languorous, large and washed with light. Bedrooms in the Cube (just that: a cube of glass and oiled teak) and the Garden Suite are ultra-modern and swish, those in the main house are more traditional; young Lucas and Blanca, both from Madrid, attract a mature and sophisticated crowd. Breakfasts are bountiful and delicious; in the evening, the dining room takes on a cool elegance. Cooking is inventive, giving modern twists to the local Asturian cuisine. Your gentle hosts will also steer you towards the best walking, riding and fishing. Or just stay put and unwind.

Price	€91–€115. Suite €140–€160.
Rooms	12: 10 twins/doubles, 2 suites.
Meals	Breakfast €10. Dinner €27.
Closed	November–February.
Directions	From Oviedo, A-8/E-70 dir. Santander. Exit at Llanes; but take turn opposite Llanes for La Pereda. Over railway tracks & left at village. Posada 2km down road, signed.

	Lucas Cajiao & Blanca Fernández
	La Pereda s/n, 33509 Llanes, Asturias
Tel	+34 985 402525
Fax	+34 985 402622
Email	info@laposadadebabel.com
Web	www.laposadadebabel.com

Hotel

El Habana Country Hotel

Lush meadows, grazing cows, dry-stone walls – such is the rural beauty of Asturia, where gently rolling farmland gives way to the foothills of the Cuera Mountains. The hotel is a contemporary version of the traditional Asturian house, and is charming within. Plants, rugs on warm terracotta floors, modern art, subtle lighting. Much of the furniture comes from Mariá Eugenia's home in New Delhi and an air of colonial elegance – touched with modern Deco – prevails. The friendly atmosphere goes up a notch in the dining room, the elegant hub of the hotel. Here, regulars and visitors congregate to sample excellent Asturian dishes, served from 9pm. Bedrooms are big and light, the two with patios leading to the garden (Sirio & María's creation, with 300 species of trees, shrubs, ferns and stunning pergola) being our favourites. Spin off on one of the bikes, take a put on the golf course by the sea, set out on a coastal pony trek, dip into the pool. Your multi-lingual hosts will advise – and if sporting pursuits do not appeal, head for nearby Llanes with its handsome galleried buildings. *A Rusticae hotel.*

Price	€85-€131. Suite €135-€161.
Rooms	12: 9 twins/doubles, 3 suites.
Meals	Breakfast €8.50. Dinner, with wine, from €24 à la carte.
Closed	November to mid-March.
Directions	Santander-Oviedo on N-634; at km301 marker, Llanes exit, do a U-turn & cross over N-634 for La Pereda, following signs on right for Prau Riu Hotel. 1.5km; signed.

	María Eugenia Caumel & Sirio Sáinz
	La Pereda s/n, 33509 Llanes, Asturias
Tel	+34 985 402526
Fax	+34 985 402075
Email	hotel@elhabana.net
Web	www.elhabana.net

Entry 43   Map 3

Casa de Aldea La Valleja

Drive up to La Valleja through some of the Picos de Europa's most spectacular scenery – turn up the Vivaldi! – with sheer craggy rock faces on one side and fast-flowing rivers on the other. Eagles, hawks and vultures circle overhead; goats, sheep, foxes and wolves roam the forest. The house was built in 1927 and the original bricks, tiles, stones and chestnut exude rustic charm. Each bedroom, gaily coloured, has been named after wild berries; if yours feels sombre, throw open the shutters and drink in the views. There's relaxed simple comfort too; clean yet not over-polished, and good heating for winter. After a rugged walk in the Peñamellera Alta – don't miss the spectacular Cares gorge – you'll be well fortified: meals are delicious, hearty, organic and lovingly prepared. Whether you want to take advantage of La Valleja's setting, sandwiched between the Picos and the coast, or stay here for the views and the birds (bring the binoculars), this is the place. Paula and family are welcoming, kind and friendly – buy some of their homemade preserves and jams as a memory of your stay. Bliss.

Price	€52.
Rooms	5 twins/doubles.
Meals	Packed lunch €7. Dinner, with wine, €15.
Closed	Christmas & January.
Directions	N-634; at Unquera, left for Panes. Here, right onto AS-114 for Cangas de Onís. 10km beyond, at Niserias, right to Ruenes. Through Alles; 800m after Pastorias, right up a steep track to Rieña. Park at top.

Ethical Collection: Environment; Food.
See page 412.

Paula Valero Sáez
Rieña, 33576 Ruenes, Asturias

Tel	+34 985 415895
Fax	+34 985 415895
Email	valleycas@yahoo.es

Casona D'Alevia

An improbable setting for a village: a pocket of greenery, an old church and a cluster of lovely old buildings – until this year, at the end of a recently widened vertiginous mountain road! The eagle-eye views are breathtaking. Step into the 15th-century farmhouse and you step back in time; the house could be a museum of ethnography. If you ask, softly-spoken Gregorio will tell you all about his family, who have been basket-makers for generations. The hall is decorated with tools that belonged to his father-in-law, the bedrooms sport damask-covered tables and kilims on chestnut boards, and in the sitting room are fascinating curios and an old piano. Such rustic interiors are timeless and enchanting and the homely feel is epitomised by displays of family items on each landing, including some of Gregorio's daughter's beautiful, symbolic sculptures. New mattresses on old wrought-iron beds guarantee a good night's sleep, and you wake to a breakfast as good as any in Spain. It is a privilege to stay in such a place.

Price	€70–€85. €85–€100.
Rooms	9: 6 doubles, 3 suites.
Meals	Breakfast €8. Restaurants in Panes, 3km.
Closed	7 January–7 February.
Directions	N-634 to Oviedo-Santander; exit for Unquera onto N-621. At Panes, right to Cabrales on the AS-114, right again at sign to Alevia; follow new road for 3km to Alevía. On left of main square.

Gregorio Sánchez Benito
LG. Alevia s/n, 33579 Peñamellera Baja, Asturias

Tel	+34 985 414176
Email	alevia@casonadalevia.com
Web	www.casonadalevia.com

Quinta Villanueva

Locals remember when this eye-catching 'casa de indiano' housed a young Mexican widow who dedicated her life to good works. A century on, its bold blue exterior is still visible for miles. Impressive to see how Montse mingles modern touches (contemporary art, cut-velvet fabrics, dramatic touches of red) with the elegance of a period house. Montse and her staff shower love and attention on the place, and everything gleams in polished perfection. From the welcoming entrance sporting original tiles, wind up a grand staircase to smart, soothing and peaceful rooms. Several have galleries or balconies; all gaze onto nature. All around are breathtaking views; watch the sun sink into the Picos while you recline on cream sofas in the drawing room, complete with classical music and candelabra. Breakfast is a treat – homemade pastries and local ham and cheeses in the light, bright breakfast room – and you can sample the best of local in the villages. It's a beautiful drive through the Picos to Potes, the heart of the National Park, and a short hop to white sand beaches. A place to unwind.

Price	€60–€94. Plus VAT at 7%.
Rooms	19: 6 doubles, 13 twins.
Meals	Breakfast €7.30. Plus VAT at 7%. Restaurants 2km.
Closed	Mid-October to Easter.
Directions	From Santander, A-8/E-70 dir. Llanes & Gijón then N-634. Take exit for Bustio, then AS-344 through Colombres, continue to Villanueva de Colombres. Hotel in centre of village.

Montserrat Abad
Villanueva de Colombres s/n,
33590 Ribadedeva, Asturias

Tel	+34 985 412804
Fax	+34 985 412283
Email	hotel@quintadevillanueva.com
Web	www.quintadevillanueva.com

Hotel

Casa de Aldea las Helgueras

Carmen and Miguel opened this elegant B&B on their wedding day. Enter Miguel's grandmother's estate house and you'll feel immediately at home; tradition blends with comfort in a cosy, fire-warmed sitting room. They've an eye for antiques and every heirloom tells a story: a shiny 1890s piano, a centuries-old trousseau, rare clocks and treasures. Bedrooms are intimate, bath and shower rooms gleam and beds are heaven, with ornate headboards and classic bedspreads; pick the south-facing room with the full-length balcony. Tuck into tasty home-cooked meals and local cider in the dining room that catches the sun – a different menu every night, a hearty breakfast too. A brick wall protects you from the village road, so you can relax among geraniums in the shade of the terrace while children make daisy chains on the lawn. Unwind completely in sleepy Noriega, hugged by Asturias' delights: hiking in the Picos de Europa, shopping in lively Llanes, visiting prehistoric caves... Miguel can arrange kayaking, horse riding, golf and more. This is a lovely home and you'll feel part of the family.

Price	€60-€95. Suite €100-€107.
Rooms	8: 7 twins/doubles, 1 suite.
Meals	Dinner €25, by arrangement. Wine €12-€25. Restaurant 3km.
Closed	January & February.
Directions	From Santander, A-67 for Oviedo. Past Unquera, at El Peral, left to Noriega. Right at stop sign in village; 200m on right.

Carmen Fernández Villar
Noriega s/n, 33590 Ribadedeva, Asturias
Tel   +34 985 412394
Email   reservas@lashelgueras.com
Web   www.lashelgueras.com

Asturias

El Jardín de Carrejo

Swings and sequoias in the grounds, the odd swaying palm and weeping willow, vast lawns and ancient trees. Everyone loves this small hotel, with its clean lines and modern design. The huge 1901 stable and hayloft have been stylishly re-crafted into a comfortable haven between the Cabuérniga Valley and the golden beaches of Comillas. Expect a cool symphony of creams, taupes and warm hues, stone floors and polished parquet. Over 100 photographs by contemporary Spanish photographers enliven the interor spaces; there is masses of light, not a curlicue in sight, and suave leather sofas and chestnut and walnut pieces represent the best of modern design. Bedrooms, two with balconies, all with garden views, are serene. Bathrooms are chic and lack nothing. The new garden suites are the swishest of all: high ceilings, black slate and an open-plan layouts with sliding doors to private gardens. Hire a tandem from the hotel, practice your golf in the grounds, head off for a Parque Natural (there are two nearby), laze under a posh parasol. And the staff are great. *A Rusticae hotel.*

No

Price	€88–€120. Singles €77–€97. Suites €131–€225.
Rooms	12: 8 twins/doubles, 4 suites.
Meals	Breakfast €9.25. Dinner €25.
Closed	5 January–5 February.
Directions	A-8 exit 249 for Cabezón de la Sal; right at entrance of town following signs for Reinosa. Drive through town & into Carrejo. Pass narrow section & traffic lights, turn immediately left. Hotel signed.

Isabel Alvarez García
Carrejo, 39500 Cabezón de la Sal, Cantabria

Tel	+34 942 701516
Fax	+34 942 701871
Email	hotel@eljardindecarrejo.com
Web	www.eljardindecarrejo.com

Fuente de las Anjanas

It's hard to miss: a medieval tower stands by the road 50 metres from this *casa de colonos*. Inside, charming, caring Nieves has put together modern country furniture with sumptuous fabrics to dramatic effect. The first impression is that of a hunter's lodge: roaring fire, checked armchairs, mounted wild boar's head. Animated dinners take place around a large wooden table. On the stairs is a bizarre collection of masks from West Africa and Venice, agricultural yokes, and photos of Nieves in regional dress. Comfortable, cool bedrooms are eye-catching, with their dark wooden beams, pristine bed linen and vibrant walls; bedsteads from Seville and embroidered fabrics coexist with rather more twee furnishings. Choose a colour to match your mood, or a Cantabrian fairy after which each room is named; Nieves will tell you — in Spanish — about their quirks and qualities. Most rooms overlook rolling meadows and indigenous forest; we like best those with balconies over the young front garden. Charming San Vicente de la Barquera is nearby, and the famous Camino de Santiago slips just by the house.

Price	€55–€90.
Rooms	12 twins/doubles.
Meals	Breakfast €6. Dinner with wine €18.
Closed	7–31 January.
Directions	From Santander on E-70; exit 264 for San Vicente de la Barquera. At 2nd r'bout, CA-843 for Abanillos. After 4.5km, right at tower. House 100m beyond.

Miguel & Nieves Cuevas–Villar
Canal de los Bueyes s/n,
Val de San Vicente, 39549 Estrada,
Cantabria

Tel	+34 942 718539
Email	fdelasanjanas@hotmail.com
Web	www.fuentedelasanjanas.com

Entry 49   Map 4

Casa la Yosa

Walkers won't find a better value launch pad for the Picos de Europa than this lovely old four-square farmhouse. Decked out in pale stone with wonderful chestnut beams, the generous open-plan living spaces hold practical kitchens equipped with all you need; pretty walls need no artwork and bathrooms are white and spotless. Calming pastel colours wash over soothingly plain and simple bedrooms, dominated by the views. One apartment has a balcony, two spill outside through French windows; all share the front terrace for al fresco dining in the sparkling air. Enjoy the birdsong in the sweet lawned garden, edged at the rear by woods and gurgling stream. The tiny hamlet is a short hop from lively Potes, where you can stock up for your kitchen – and tuck into hearty local dishes. The mountains are so close you can almost touch them; this is three minutes from the start of the National Park trail. Hospitable owner Manuel, an ex-park ranger, can show you the best routes – as can Jesús and Eva who look after the house (he's a ranger too). Outdoor adventure or sedentary peace – it's all here.

Price	Apartment for 2, €50–€70. Apartments for 4, €70–€105. All prices per night.
Rooms	4 apartments: 1 for 2; 3 for 4. Extra beds available.
Meals	Restaurants 3km.
Closed	Rarely.
Directions	From Santander, A-8/E-70 dir. Llanes, exit 272 for N-621, dir. Unquer/Panes. Onto N-621 to Potes. Thro' town, dir. Fuente De 1.5km; right signed Arguebanes; on 3km, through village. House signed at end, on right.

Manuel Bahillo & María Eugenia Herrero
39571 Arguebanes, Cantabria

Tel	+34 942 735085
Fax	+34 942 735085
Email	manelbahillo@hotmail.com
Web	www.casalayosa.com

La Casa de las Chimeneas

The road meanders comfortably up up through the Picos de Europa to tiny Tudes – and a 14-chimneyed cluster of apartments with stunning views. British host Tony greets you warmly and shows you around his meticulously reconstructed farmstead, where old hen coops, barns and pigsty have been transformed into super apartments in new pine and rustic stone, comfortably equipped with wooden furniture and smart kitchens. Splendid murals cover the walls – 'Natura' depicts local plants and animals, 'Cielo' the stars and the zodiac. The rest of the décor has been fashioned by Tony's bubbly Spanish wife Lucía; Tiffany lights, bright fabrics, rustic ornaments, a red sofa. Tony and Lucía have thought of everything: put on a DVD, play billiards or table football over drinks in the courtyard or their village bar, dream in the infinity pool. Tudes is tiny, just 30 souls, but you're only ten minutes from Potes, the Picos' beating heart. Try hiking, biking, horse riding and canyoning, be thrilled by the cable car at Fuente Dé or the prehistoric Altamira cave, spend the day on the coast. Remote – but a gem!

Price	Apartments €330–€910 per week. Extra beds €35.
Rooms	7 apartments: 3 for 2; 4 for 4. Extra beds available.
Meals	Restaurants 10-minute drive.
Closed	Never.
Directions	From A-8 Santander-Oviedo, take Unquera exit N-621 to Potes. Left at Potes to continue on N-621; 100m past Naroba left up mountain road to Tudes. House in main square, signed.

Tony Bastian
Plaza Mayor s/n, 39575 Tudes, Cantabria

Tel	+34 942 736300
Fax	+34 942 736300
Email	lacasadelaschimeneas@telefonica.net
Web	www.lacasadelaschimeneas.es

Posada La Trébede

The smell of wood smoke seduces you even before your eyes adjust to the light. Gnarled old beams still stand strong, eagle-eye views take in distant mountains. It's a child-friendly house that tucks itself into the steep hillsides of the Liebana Valley, a rich forested landscape of cork, chestnut and oak with a thriving eco-system. Hens, dogs and children roam freely on the cobalt and stone patio and even the dogs have personalities here (John Wayne with bow legs, muppet-like Fermín). The solid old house, named after the hearth above which the very young and the very old would sleep when winters were winters, is as authentic as can be. Comfortable rooms have a homely, rustic feel, good fabrics, woollen blankets and crisp white sheets guarantee deep sleep, bathrooms sparkle, stone and terracotta brickwork on the walls is a treat for the eye, and attic rooms have sloping roofs and dormer windows – mind your head! The Liébana Monastery is nearby, as are the Picos de Europa; Manuel was a National Park ranger so you are in excellent hands – discover the best routes to get to know its flora and fauna.

Price	€45–€58.
Rooms	6 twins/doubles.
Meals	Breakfast €5. Dinner €12.
Closed	Rarely.
Directions	From Santander E-70 to Oviedo, then N-630 Unquera to Potes. Continue for Cervera/Pto. de Piedrasluengas. 1km after Puente Asni, left for Perroza. Signed.

Manuel Bahillo & María Eugenia Herrero
Perrozo, 39573 Cabezón de Liebana,
Cantabria

Tel	+34 942 735085
Fax	+34 942 735085
Email	manelbahillo@hotmail.com
Web	www.perrozo.com

Casona de Naveda de Campóo

Step out of the front door and back in time onto the quiet village square. The *casona* is 300 years old and was converted into a home grand enough to announce the newfound riches of one of those enterprising indianos who returned from Cuba. Floors, ceilings and fire surrounds of stone, rich walnut and oak have the soft patina that only centuries of polishing can achieve. Ancient stone pillars in the sitting room, rumoured to be Roman, would not look out of place in one of Cantabria's churches. Rooms 6 and 7, with their wooden galleried sitting areas, have a very special charm, but every room is distinctive in its own way. The menu is a celebration of simple food beautifully cooked, accompanied by some of Spain's great wines. The area is studded with Romanesque churches; there are Roman ruins too, and nearby Reinosa, with its galleried houses and fine central square, is a real find. There's an 18-hole golf course and carp fishing, the source of the mighty Ebro is nearby and you are only a short drive from the ski terrain of Alto Campóo with its breathtaking views. *A Rusticae hotel.*

Price	€78-€86. Singles €63-€69. Suites €86-€105.
Rooms	9: 2 twins/doubles, 1 single, 6 suites.
Meals	Breakfast €7. Dinner, with wine, €20.
Closed	Never.
Directions	From Santander on A-67; exit 136 onto CA-183 for Alto Campóo. Drive through Nestanes, Salcos & Fontibre. In Náveda, on village square.

Paloma López Sarasa
Plaza del Medio Lugar 37,
Hermandad de Campóo de Suso,
39211 Naveda, Cantabria

Tel	+34 942 779515
Email	info@casonadenaveda.com
Web	www.casonadenaveda.com

Casa del Lago de Cantabria

Migratory geese flap across the magnificent lake created by the damming of the mighty Ebro. Gaze across its sparkling waters to rolling hills from the large lawned garden of this pretty old house, perched right on the water's edge. Lovingly and completely refurbished with comfort in mind by owner Jesús, its spacious interiors are enhanced by bright walls, polished wood and exposed stone. Fine old features mingle with modern details in your three bright sitting rooms: wood-burning stoves, antique poker table, quirky lamps, a fancy sound system (bring your iPod). Generous modern bedrooms (one a duplex, two with a mezzanine) are as comfortable as the rest, and there are super showers in classy bathrooms. Cook up a feast in the state-of-the-art white kitchen with walk-in larder; dine under the stone porch overlooking the lake. There are walks whatever the weather, and much to explore: the source of the Ebro, Roman ruins and Romanesque churches. Fish for carp or play golf; ski in winter, windsurf in summer. Perfect for large groups or families seeking a peaceful escape with plenty to do.

Price	€2,200 for 10 people; extra €140 per person. Prices per week.
Rooms	House for 4–16.
Meals	Restaurant 2km.
Closed	Rarely.
Directions	From Reinosa, CA-171 dir. La Costana & Corconte; at Orzales, 1st right & follow road to end; follow path round side of house to entrance.

Jesus Mantilla
Barrio del Bergen s/n, 39292 Orzales, Cantabria

Tel	+34 942 779515
Fax	+34 942 750174
Email	jmblanc@ya.com
Web	www.casadecampoo.com

Hotel Posada Aire de Ruesga

Amazing to think you are 20 minutes from some of the best beaches in Spain. Up here, in glorious 180-degree mountain scenery, is Josu's casona, a beautifully restored 17th-century country-house hotel that beats with a modern heart. On a clear day you can distinctly see five layers of mountain ridges; in autumn, four shades of brown on the highest slopes. It is a place that encourages meditation, and the San Esteban hermitage opposite shows that you are not the first one to feel the magic. Big, comfortable, contemporary bedrooms are loosely themed: 'Arab' has mint walls and Moroccan furniture, 'Colonial' a Balinese four-poster and wardrobe. Josu's sister, a professional chef, buys fish and seafood from Laredo's market, her special menus and the *menú del día* – superb value – served in an elegant restaurant with Añil-blue walls and nicely dressed tables. Enjoy a wild mushroom and prawn pie in full view of the mountains: all-glass walls pull in the Parque Natural de Collados del Asón. The sunsets are to die for and the staff are wonderful.

Price	€75–€120.
Rooms	10 twins/doubles.
Meals	Dinner €14.50–€35. Wine €12–€30.
Closed	6-31 January.
Directions	From Santander/Bilbao on A-8; exit 173 Colindres/Burgos onto N-629. At Ramales, right for Valle/Arreonda. After 5km, just before Valle, right for Mentera. Hotel at entrance of village, on left.

Josu Madariaga Páez
Mentera, 39813 Valle de Ruesga,
Cantabria

Tel	+34 942 641000
Email	airederuesga@telefonica.net
Web	www.airederuesga.com

La Torre de Ruesga

On the lush banks of the Asón and within easy reach of its spectacular waterfall, this 1610 stronghold matches old-fashioned elegance with theatrical extravagance, and is surrounded by beautiful gardens. The grander rooms have been embellished with impressive frescos by the Catalan painter, Leon Criach, the finest in the pink-washed banqueting hall on the first floor. Antiques, heirlooms and art books abound, rooms have been set aside for videos, games or quiet reads and there's a piano to play. Bedrooms are ornate, with hand-painted details, polished wooden floors, chunky rafters and antique beds; bathrooms are luxurious. Breakfast in the conservatory is a treat; dinner — made with locally sourced meat, veg and fish — is an accomplished mix of Cantabrian and international, accompanied by fine wines from a well-stocked bodega. Take tea on the terrace or relax on the immaculate lawns; the views of Torre de Ruesga are stunning. There's also a lovely large outdoor pool, and five casita suites in the garden. Every possible need has been anticipated, and charming Carmen is the star of the show. *A Rusticae hotel.*

Price	€95–€125. Singles €70–€80. Suites €117–€140. Casitas €135–€150.
Rooms	15: 6 twins/doubles, 4 suites, 5 casitas.
Meals	Breakfast €12. Lunch & dinner €21. À la carte €35–€40.
Closed	Last 3 weeks in January.
Directions	From Santander, S-10 for Bilbao. Exit 173 for Colindres; N-629 for Burgos to Ramales de V. Right on C-261 to Arredondo & Valle; right at sign. On right just over bridge.

Carmen Caprile & Giorgio García de Leaniz
La Barcena s/n, 39810 Valle de Ruesga,
Cantabria

Tel	+34 942 641060
Fax	+34 942 641172
Email	reservas@t-ruesga.com
Web	www.t-ruesga.com

Basque Country

Ametzola

This fine Basque farmhouse has risen like a phoenix after destruction by fire three centuries ago – the result of a family feud. Mikel, your unfailingly affable host, has undertaken a laborious and sympathic restoration. And the serenity of the setting is extraordinary; watch the early mists lift from the valley below and an idyllic pastoral scene unfolds. The ancient wooden structure of the house is revealed in beams, walls and ceilings; look closely at the wafer brickwork and you'll see evidence of a time when tools were simple but ingenuity compensated. Bedrooms here are rustic affairs but with plenty of comfort, thanks to plump duvets and hydromassage showers, while shelved, curtained alcoves make simple storage space. After one of several circular walks starting from the door, how comforting to return to Mikel's hearty dishes, accompanied by robust wines. Savour his port-flavoured chicken and raisins, or his quails' legs in chocolate sauce; you'll be glad this former economist swapped his spreadsheets for an apron. Friendly, authentic, charming and special.

Price	€65–€80.
Rooms	6 twins/doubles.
Meals	Breakfast €6. Dinner, with wine, €20.
Closed	Rarely.
Directions	AP-68 Burgos-Logroño, exit 1 for Arrigorriaga onto A-625. Cont. dir. Laudio-Llodio on BI-625. After 3km, right for Ugas/Miraballes onto BI-3524. At Ermitabarri, sharp left by church for Ametzola; 1km; left again on very steep road to house.

Mikel Azaola
Barrio Ametzola 1, 48499 Zeberio, Vizcaya

Tel	+34 944 046076
Email	house@ametzola.net
Web	www.ametzola.net

Mendi Goikoa

All you hear is the wind. Peaceful it is, and majestic. The hotel is made up of two handsome 19th-century farm buildings divided by cobblestones and flights of steps, surrounded by meadow land and spectacular mountain views. The main restaurant, once the old barn, is vast and high-ceilinged and packed with fine country antiques; the beautiful aroma of traditional cooking on the wood fire pervades the space, and we hear the food is fantastic. There is a small breakfast room and a gem of a restaurant/bar in the stables above, set aside for weddings, but the best spot for breakfast is the glazed veranda overlooking fields and village below: stunning. The bedrooms on the hayloft floor, not huge, are equally good-looking: original rafters and small windows, some lovely old pieces of furniture, carpeting and seductive views. Shower rooms are functional; thick stone walls keep you cool. There are great walks up to (or towards!) the surrounding peaks, so make sure you work up an appetite for dinner. Do book – it's a popular place – but note, this is a wedding-feast venue and can get lively at weekends.

Price	€110. Singles €75. Plus VAT at 7%.
Rooms	11 twins/doubles.
Meals	Lunch & dinner €25. À la carte from €50. Plus VAT at 7%. Restaurant closed Sunday evening & all Monday.
Closed	November-March.
Directions	From A-8, exit 17 for Durango. N-636 for Elorrio. In Atxondo, right to Axpe. After 1km, right following signs; through village. House above village, at foot of mountain. Park at rear.

Agurtzane Telleria; Iñaki & Jose Luís Ibarra
Barrio San Juan 33, 48291 Axpe-Atxondo,
Vizcaya

Tel	+34 946 820833
Fax	+34 946 821136
Email	reservas@mendigoikoa.com
Web	www.mendigoikoa.com

Ziortza-Beitia

It's beautiful here, and so peaceful. Bilbao and San Sebastian are an hour's drive but this is another world… and it's not unusual to see donkeys on the road with cartloads of hay. The old farmhouse sits in remote countryside below a Cistercian monastery on the famous pilgrim route to Santiago de Compostela and the drive here is stunning. The new owner is keen to build a reputation for the restaurant as a place where you come to enjoy the best of traditional Basque cooking; there's cabrito (kid marinated in sherry), cochinillo (suckling pig) and gatzatu (sheep's rennet with honey), and breakfast's cakes are homemade and delicious. Now a wood-fired oven dominates the restaurant, which has had a welcome facelift, and there's a good selection of affordable wines. As for the rooms, they are plain, comfortable and squeaky clean – fine for pilgrims and walkers – with a laundry on the top floor. The nights are blissfully quiet – just the hoot of the owl to lull you to sleep. Nearby Bolibar is the birthplace of Simon Bolibar, the liberator of South America – the museum is well worth a visit.

Price	€45. Bunkbed €15 p.p. Breakfast not included.
Rooms	12: 7 twins/doubles, 5 bunkbed dormitories for 6.
Meals	Breakfast €5. Lunch & dinner €10. Weekend special menu €25.
Closed	Christmas.
Directions	Directions on booking. Not easy to find.

Iñaki Eguía
Goiherria 13, 48279 Bolibar, Vizcaya
Tel +34 946 165259
Fax +34 946 165259
Email irurokziortza@telefonica.net
Web www.irurokziortza.com

Hotel Arresi

Driving off the ferry, whether you're arriving at Bilbao or Santander, this hotel is a godsend: family-friendly and perfectly situated. The approach is informal and from the outside it may not look that special but step in and you could be entering the home of a gracious friend. An imposing staircase leads to an impressive landing and on to spacious bedrooms spread over two floors. All are comfortable and hotel-smart, with excellent bathrooms, private terraces and – in most – breathtaking views. So you wake to a panorama that takes in the hotel's gardens, the harbour and the hills. The children will love the beautifully tended lawns, the cool shady pine grove behind and the swimming pool, safely fenced. Enjoy the shaded pergola by day, and the cosy reading room by night. There's no restaurant as such but the staff are so good-natured they may rustle up a meal if you ask in advance, and we hear excellent reports of the breakfasts. Note: they host weddings in late spring and in autumn, so it can get busy. *A Rusticae hotel. Self-catering apartments due to open summer 2009.*

Price	€110–€138. Singles €90–€111. Suite €170.
Rooms	10: 9 twins/doubles, 1 suite.
Meals	Restaurants 300m.
Closed	24 December-8 January.
Directions	Signs to Bilbao airport, then Mungia on BI-631. At Mungia exit for Plentzia (BI-2120). At Andraka, on BI-3153 to Armintza. At entrance of town, hotel signed on left.

Estibaliz & Borja Aranbarri Uresandi
c/Portugane 7, 48620 Armintza, Vizcaya

Tel	+34 946 879208
Fax	+34 946 879310
Email	hotelarresi@hotelarresi.com
Web	www.hotelarresi.com

Atalaya Hotel

Fernando, Jesús and Alaín are keen to make your stay a happy one, here in one of the most 'family' of Vizcaya's small hotels. You couldn't better the position, either, right by the fish market and a step from the beach of a deep inlet carved by the Cantabrian sea. The house was built in 1911 and is listed. An open galleried frontage lets in the ever-changing light, encouraging contemplation of sand, sea and the church tower of Santa María. The owners and staff are kind, straightforward people who cheerfully help you plan your visits. The best rooms have sea views but they're all worth a night: somewhat dated, quiet, clean and comfortable with modern furniture and king-size beds. A smart little bar serves sandwiches and snacks. This would be a good place to spend a night en route to the ferry, and your car and belongings should be safe in the car park. It's a great launchpad from which to explore the Urdaibai Biosphere Reserve and the magnificent coastline, while the stunning and world-famous Guggenheim Museum is just over an hour by train — and the station is five minutes away.

Price	€95-€105. Singles €76-€84.
Rooms	12: 10 twins/doubles, 2 family.
Meals	Breakfast €9. Bar meal around €30.
Closed	Rarely.
Directions	From Bilbao, A-8/E-70 exit 18 onto N-634. BI-635 via Gernika to Mundaka; left to village centre. Hotel near Santa María church; one way system, narrow roads. Park at free hotel car park.

Fernando Rodriguez & Jesús Alkorta
Itxaropen Kalea 1, 48360 Mundaka,
Vizcaya

Tel	+34 946 177000
Fax	+34 946 876899
Email	reservas@atalayahotel.es
Web	www.atalayahotel.es

Urresti

It's been a dream come true for Urresti's two charming owners, to transform the ruins of a farmhouse in green Vizcaya. From the outside it looks 17th century; inside is more modern in feel. Breakfast is excellent value, served in the large sitting/dining room: local cheeses, homemade jams, farm fruits, plenty of coffee. For other meals there's an open-plan, fully-equipped kitchen/living area you may share. Smart, impeccably clean little bedrooms have laminate floors and pine beds; the one under the eaves (hot in summer) has a balcony and rafters; another has space for an extra sofabed. The bath and shower rooms are very good, and you wake to the trilling of birds. Outside: a greenhouse and organic plot, and a small charge for produce. The house stands in beautiful rolling countryside with stunning beaches a short drive – such a great place for families. There are emus, sheep, goats, horses and hens to fuss over, bikes to borrow and ancient forests of oak and chestnut to explore. Guernica (Gernika) is close, and the whole area is a biosphere reserve; many come for the birdlife.

Price	€47–€55. Apartment for 2, €71–€77. Apartment for 4, €103. All prices per night plus VAT at 7%.	
Rooms	6 + 2: 6 twins/doubles. 2 apartments: 1 for 2, 1 for 4.	
Meals	Breakfast €6.50. Guest kitchen.	
Closed	Rarely.	
Directions	From Gernika for Lekeitio on BI-2238. After 6km, left at roundabout for Elanchobe. On right, below road level, after 1.2km at sign 'Nekazal Turismoa Agroturismo'.	

María Goitia & Jose María Ríos
Barrio Zendokiz 12,
48314 Gautegiz de Arteaga, Vizcaya

Tel	+34 946 251843
Fax	+34 946 251843
Email	urresti@wanadoo.es
Web	www.urresti.net

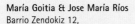

Hotel Zubieta

The inauspicious surroundings are misleading; through the arch, up the drive to the former stables, and you arrive at somewhere special. The hotel, enfolded by forests of eucalyptus, is a temple to stylish rusticity. Smart sofas, old teracotta brick floors, carved wooden columns, a small library: the atmosphere is that of an old inn touched with a contemporary elegance, a place where you would happily settle in for the day. Bedrooms match crisp patterned fabrics with some fine pieces of old family furniture – wrought-iron bedsteads, armoires, delicate four-posters – while subdued lighting adds to the immaculate but warm feel. After a deep sleep, start the day with homemade pastries on a large terrace that overlooks the family's 18th-century manor house. Venture further and you enter Lekeitio, a town where, according to owners Mikel and Zenaida, "tourism is only accidental." It's an authentic Basque fishing town with a startling energy; fishermen pull in the catch daily, women mend nets by the sea. Local 'fiestas' have special ethnographic interest and local Basque tapas – 'pintxos' – are particularly good. *A Rusticae hotel.*

Price	€78-€90. Family €90-€106. Suite €100-€112.
Rooms	24: 12 twins/doubles, 11 family, 1 suite.
Meals	Breakfast €9.50.
Closed	November to early February.
Directions	In Lekeitio, right at main x-roads for Ondarroa. After 500m, at the end of tree-lined avenue, on left.

Zenaida & Mikel Solano
c/Portal de Atea s/n, 48280 Lekeitio,
Vizcaya

Tel	+34 946 843030
Fax	+34 946 841099
Email	hotelzubieta@hotelzubieta.com
Web	www.hotelzubieta.com

Hotel Iturregi

The setting is pastoral, and timeless — shepherds watch their flock in the fields below. The hotel is sophisticated and exclusive — a modern retreat. As for the drive to get here, it's along the coastal road from surfers' Zarautz to picturesque Getaia and perched just above the sea: breathtaking. On arrival you're greeted by charming staff and taken up (by lift or stair) to immaculate bedrooms designed with flair. Classic-modern furniture of excellent quality is the order of the day, along with smooth carpets, thick drapes, soft lights and chunky rafters; bathrooms are plush, with elegant mosaics and smart curtains. The lofty suite under the eaves is particularly lavish, with velvety slate-blue fabrics, perfect framed views and a private terrace. (Three further rooms on the ground floor have front terraces, too: fabulous.) Outside are open lawned areas on which children may play, and landscaped gardens that lead to a stylish decked pool… more lush views over vineyards and sea. No restaurant, but who needs one when there are world-renowned restaurants so close by? A treat.

Price	€150–€320. Suites €270–€450.
Rooms	8: 6 doubles, 2 suites.
Meals	Restaurants 1-3km.
Closed	Never.
Directions	A-8 exit 11 for Getaria/Zarauz; follow N-634 thro' Zarauz. Right at Santa María La Real church; bear right, follow coastal road to Getaria. Right at fork by handball court; continue on N-634 signed Zuhaia. Left for San Prudenzio; left after 1 km. Hotel 800m.

Gonzalo Pardo
Barrio Azkizu, 20808 Getaria,
Guipúzcoa

Tel	+34 943 896134
Fax	+34 943 140418
Email	info@hoteliturregi.com
Web	www.hoteliturregi.com

Villa Soro

Classy, different and in San Sebastián. Built in 1898 for a prominent Basque family, the conversion from house to hotel was completed in 2003. Only two of the original 20 chimneys remain, but this is a small price to pay for an exquisite transformation. The carpeted and carved oak staircase sets the tone of elegance and grace; drawings by the contemporary artist Oteiza adorn the walls; the radiators are not merely radiators, but beautiful examples of what can be done with cast iron... Parquet floors gleam, chandeliers glisten, staff glide. Retreat with tea or cocktail to one of two sitting rooms, fire-lit in winter, or the lovely patio. Big, serene bedrooms – some in the main house, others in the carriage house with small terraces, and just as good – have pure-wool carpets, classic furniture and exemplary beds. Marble bathrooms come with fine toiletries and dressing gowns, while double glazing ensures peace from the busy avenue. New: an air-conditioned gym. Michelin stars are a hop away, but don't drive into town where the parking is tricky: spin off on one of the hotel's city-shoppers instead.

Price	€144–€285. Singles €117–€180. Extra bed €70. Plus VAT at 7%.
Rooms	25: 23 twins/doubles, 2 singles.
Meals	Breakfast €14. Room service available.
Closed	Rarely.
Directions	A-8 exit Donostia/Ondarreta. Follow main road into town, along seafront until road becomes c/San Martin. Over bridge & up c/Miracruz, which becomes Avda. de Ategorrieta. Hotel on left; on to next crossroads & turn around; very busy road.

Jaione Gastañares
Avda. de Ategorrieta 61,
20013 San Sebastián, Guipúzcoa

Tel	+34 943 297970
Fax	+34 943 297971
Email	info@villasoro.com
Web	www.villasoro.com

La Rioja & Navarre

Hospedería Señorío de Briñas

In a village of shady squares and peacefulness, Briñas's stately houses and ornate churches pay witness to its golden age, the 16th century, when the region reached its economic zenith and noble families set up house. Don't let the exterior of this *casona* (or the apartment blocks next door) put you off: behind the sober façade is a hotel of character and modernity. Charming, gregarious Angela is a designer who embarked on the project when the building was little more than a ruin; now you find chunky terracotta tiles, antique chairs, chandeliers and luxurious linen. Most intriguing are the trompe l'oeil frescos, the surreal creations of a Polish artist that will have you gazing out of an imaginary window or pulling back a drape... There are six new rooms upstairs, one a vast suite with fashionably turquoise walls; a stylish new spa, massage and aromatherapy with wine-based oils, and a cosy bar where you can try Rioja's most famous export (do visit a bodega). No air con for hot nights and limited soundproofing in some rooms, but the staff are delightful and a distinctive elegance prevails. *A Rusticae hotel.*

Price	€119. Singles €90. Suites €160–€190. Dogs €15. Plus VAT at 7%.
Rooms	20: 15 twins/doubles, 5 suites.
Meals	Evening snacks available. Restaurants in Haro.
Closed	Rarely.
Directions	From A-68, exit 8 for Zambrana; N-124 for Logroño. Through tunnel, up hill; after 8km, left for Briñas. After 300m right; 50m down dead-end road. Park in front, or in car park.

Angela Gómez
Travesía de la Calle Real 3,
26290 Briñas, La Rioja

Tel	+34 941 304224
Fax	+34 941 304345
Email	info@hotelesconencantodelarioja.com
Web	www.hotelesconencantodelarioja.com

La Casa del Cofrade

You could drive past this and not take a second look. But this roadside hotel, opened in 2004 on the outskirts of a small Riojan town, has its fair share of surprises. Yes, you have a good bed for the night, in a stylish room that is double glazed, air conditioned, internet-wired and vastly comfortable. What makes La Casa del Cofrade special is what lies below: a warren of vaulted galleries containing the hotel's own bodega. They produce their own highly regarded Riojan wines here, of which '200 Monjes' ('200 Monks') is the star. One hundred thousand bottles are arranged in eye-catching rows in the underground alcoves. A tour is a must; you'll see the process from start to finish, from burgundy fruits to nectar maturing in 900 wooden barrels. Leticia, the sparky young director, will tell you all. She can also book you on the Vinobus, a bodega-themed tour that leaves from Logroño at weekends (July-October) – a fantastic idea. Back above, bedrooms sport bold stripes and gleaming parquet, our favourite being La Tentación (Temptation). *Groups of 12 may book the old wine cellar for meals.*

Price	€72-€105.
Rooms	18: 17 twins/doubles, 1 single.
Meals	Restaurant 15-minute walk.
Closed	24 December-6 January.
Directions	From Bilbao on AP-68; exit 12 for Logroño. Continue on N-111 for Soria. After 14km, left to Albelda de Iregua; through here, following signs for Nalda/Soria. Hotel at exit of town, on left. Hotel car park 100m, on left.

	Leticia Villegas
	Ctra. Nalda km9,
	26120 Albelda de Iregua, La Rioja
Tel	+34 941 444426
Fax	+34 941 444427
Email	reservas@lacasadelcofrade.com
Web	www.lacasadelcofrade.com

Etxatoa

The forests are an enticement to walkers, the old railway track is a gift for cyclists (they rent bikes here) and the road up to the Santuario de San Miguel is spectacular. The house is a listed 17th-century building with a coat of arms and a three-sided roof, and its freshly restored façade is fronted by a veranda with stunning views. Charming, English-speaking Alicia looks after guests and her homemade breakfasts are organic and delicious. Inside, as much has been recycled as possible: the washstand of reclaimed oak is charming, a fine restoration job has been done on the antique pieces (many for sale) and the large, frill-free living/dining/kitchen area exudes comfort and style. Darkly austere bedrooms exude a sweet rusticity, with their chunky rafters and open-stone walls, new wrought-iron beds and country antiques; the suite, impeccably restored and with a small bathroom, gets its own terrace under the plum trees. Though the village is tiny and remote there are restaurants in Pamplona, 20 minutes away, where Basque, Spanish and French cuisines meet. In autumn the Aralar forests are pure joy.

Price	€65–€93. Suites €84–€186. Plus VAT.
Rooms	6: 4 twins/doubles, 2 suites.
Meals	Breakfast €9. Plus VAT.
Closed	Rarely.
Directions	From S. Sebastián A-15 for Pamplona; exit 127. Through Lekunberri; at exit of town NA-7510 for Baraibar; 500m, left at junc. for Madotz on NA-7500; 6.5km to Oderitz. House opp. as you drive into village.

Iñaki Etxebarria
31879 Oderitz, Navarra

Tel	+34 948 504449
Email	info@etxatoa.com
Web	www.etxatoa.com

Donamariako Benta

A mouthwatering address! Donamaría is hidden away off to one side of a pass through the mountains between France and Spain, within striking distance of San Sebastian and Pamplona; it was a farmers' rest until this family arrived. They and their daughters, who are gradually taking over the business, are sophisticated and delightful people. These two old village houses are packed full of old furniture, vintage toys, dried flowers and a few surprises to boot; the atmosphere is intimate, authentic, easy. This is a place to linger long over lunch or dinner; connoisseurs rave about the traditional Navarra cooking with a modern French touch. Menus change according to season; warm duck salad with hazelnut vinaigrette, stuffed hake with garlic sauce, apple cake with cinnamon ice cream... all of it memorable. Bedrooms are spotless, uncluttered, stylish and charming, bathrooms are small but pristine; two rooms have superb little terraces overlooking the river. The garden is beautiful, secluded, with weeping willows children may hide in; the oak forests make the heart soar. *Wine-tasting & salmon fishing.*

Price	€70–€80.
Rooms	5 twins/doubles.
Meals	Breakfast €6. Lunch & dinner €18. À la carte €25–€30. No meals Sunday evenings or Mondays.
Closed	Rarely.
Directions	From San Sebastián, N-121-A for Pamplona. Right into Santesteban (Doneztebe); here, just before bridge, left for Saldías. On for 2km to junc. with Donamaría road; hotel opp. junc. on right.

Elixabet Badiola & Imanol Luzuriaga
Barrio Ventas 4, 31750 Donamaría,
Navarra

Tel	+34 948 450708
Fax	+34 948 450708
Email	info@donamariako.com
Web	www.donamariako.com

Aragon

Posada Magoría

This very special 1920s house in the lee of the church has been restored by Enrique, pioneer of eco tourism. It's a well-insulated home, cool in summer, warm in winter; old radiators belt out the heat, louvred shutters let in the light, the pale interior is finely furnished, and the top-floor bedrooms are elegantly sober, with magical views. New mattresses dress 1920s beds, and shower rooms have glass-brick walls. But the heart of the place is the dining area where a huge rock juts into the room beside the long convivial table and the full-length wall tapestry lends the space weight. Here you are served organic and vegetarian soups, salads, cheeses, homemade bread and lashings of cider, while breakfast is a purifying selection of muesli, cereals and mountain honey. Enrique, a well-travelled and charming host, has an intimate knowledge of this undiscovered region; it is a joy to converse with him. Walking, mushroom-picking, advanced yoga... make a trip to this peaceful, remote, deeply serene place. The garden shares its walls with the ramparts, the fortified village is a gem. *Vegetarian cookery courses.*

Price	€45–€55.
Rooms	6 twins/doubles.
Meals	Breakfast €6. Vegetarian dinner €14. Wine €6–€20.
Closed	Rarely.
Directions	Pamplona-Jaca N-240. Left at Berdun on HU-202 to Ansó. Here, 2nd left into village past mill; left along narrow street to church; last house on right. Steep walk from car park: unload at house first.

Enrique Ipas & Teresa Garayoa
c/Milagro 32, 22728 Ansó, Huesca

Tel	+34 974 370049
Email	posadamagoria@gmail.com
Web	www.posadamagoria.com

Ethical Collection: Environment; Food.
See page 412.

Hotel Santa Cristina

The Pyrenees tower majestically before you, and from this idyllic valley you can walk straight into France. In a former headquarters of the 19th-century *carabineros* (whose joyful role it was to seize smugglers) is this stunning hotel. Friendly and attentive staff have replaced the armed police, stylish rooms have supplanted spartan soldiers' quarters and the former canteen is a celebrated restaurant. Roomy, relaxing bedrooms reveal clean lines, earthy hues and a warm minimalism. Stunning views of the Aragón Valley flood the spa (sauna, gym and heated pool – no charge for residents.) The pilgrim's way to Santiago meanders beside the hotel and if you're fit, you could walk the 20 kilometres to Jaca, a town with an active cultural agenda and a Romanesque cathedral. Return on the scenic train, to a charming welcome and a delightful dinner: red-shrimp and monkfish carpaccio perhaps, or slow-roasted lamb shoulder with thyme. This would make a superb winter sporting base: you're a snow-ball's throw from two of the best ski resorts in the Pyrenees – Candanchú and Astún.

Price	€85–€100. Singles €60–€107. Half-board option available.
Rooms	56: 54 twins/doubles, 2 singles. Extra beds available.
Meals	Lunch & dinner €21.50.
Closed	12 October to end November.
Directions	From Zaragoza A-23 to Nueno; m'way becomes N-330. Continue on N-330 to Canfranc Estación; follow direction Astún/Candanchú. Signed after 2km.

Conchita Murrieta
Ctra. Astún-Candanchu km.669,
22880 Canfranc-Estación, Huesca

Tel	+34 974 373300
Fax	+34 974 373310
Email	hotel@santacristina.es
Web	www.santacristina.es

El Privilegio de Tena

The name of this gorgeous place echoes the privileges granted long ago by the Kingdom of Aragón. Because of the valley's isolation, it suffered terrible hardship in the long winter months. Despite the village's summer-tourist train, there's a remoteness and silence still – though you'll find the privations hard to credit now. Rooms are divided between those in the abbey (five) and the rest in the main building. All are big, beautiful, instantly warm and welcoming, elegant with designer and sometimes whacky touches. Marble bathrooms flaunt Bulgari toiletries. If you really want to push the boat out, book the raftered Suite Privilegio at the very top – it has everything, from cosy new wood-burner to brass telescope for the views. Swan downstairs to the restaurant with its tasting menus and super-exclusive feel; the food is extraordinary. More perfection in the spa – marble, decking and Japanese pebbling – where you may combine your swims with a spectacular view. Themed weekend events include sloe-gin making and singing evenings with soprano and tenor. *Reserve parking at time of booking: €15.*

Price	€155–€220. Singles €116–€166. Suites €230–€730.
Rooms	25: 17 twins/doubles, 8 suites.
Meals	Lunch & dinner €30. À la carte from €45.
Closed	Rarely.
Directions	Huesca N-136 for Jaca. Follow road round to Biescas. 12km on, at junc. for Biescas, on towards France. 10km after junc. left; 1.5km to Tramacastilla. Thro' village; hotel behind 'Ayuntamiento'.

Anabel Costas & Juan Ignacio Pérez
Plaza Mayor,
22663 Tramacastilla de Tena, Huesca

Tel	+34 974 487206
Fax	+34 974 487270
Email	info@elprivilegio.com
Web	www.elprivilegio.com

Barosse

Rather than going for over-the-top design extravaganza, Jose's restrained approach has resulted in a modern house as charming as any we have seen. He and Gustavo are delightful, attentive and determined to make your stay memorable – and Gustavo's little pug dog adds to the home-from-home feel. The position, just below the iconic Peña Ordel mountain, is superb: Pyrenean views, all-day sunshine, refreshing breezes. What you get here is modern elegance combined with great value; there are reclaimed stones, high rafters and comfy furnishings. The hotel sits on the new residential outskirts of the village, its six bedrooms named after the local forge (Herreria), laundry (Lavadero), fountain (Fuente) etc. Each room is different, the most private being on the ground floor; shower rooms are decorative and colourful. The lovely breakfast room has a long convivial table, the sitting room sports twirls of wrought-iron and a collection of sofas (books and maps too), the cosy little spa has a sauna and jacuzzi (therapies are an extra). A great little find. *A Rusticae hotel.*

Price	€100–€155.
Rooms	6 twins/doubles.
Meals	Dinner €30–€40, by arrangement. Restaurants 10-minute drive.
Closed	Rarely.
Directions	From Huesca-Sabiñanigo, continue towards Jaca. Take exit 'Jaca Sur/Pamplona' onto N-330. At town entrance, 100m after 'Jaca' sign, left at x-roads to Barós. Through new residential area; hotel on right before old village. Signed.

José Pérez Poyato
c/Estiras 4, 22712 Barós, Huesca

Tel	+34 974 360582
Fax	+34 974 360582
Email	info@barosse.com
Web	www.barosse.com

Casa de San Martín

A retreat that manages to be both rustic and chic. Once you've left the main road, prepare to stay in second gear for a tortuous three-mile track: the hotel rests on a little green knoll surrounded by the foothills of the Pyrenees. A dwelling is said to have stood here since 1200 but the tall, stone, galleried front is 500 years older. Enter the hall, where pride of place is given to the portrait of a clergyman owner who gave the artist shelter during the War of Independence. In the chunky beamed sitting room – once a chapel – are voguishly clad tartan sofas and country chairs, exposed stones, soft lighting, a big fire – a rustic contemporary décor. Bedrooms, too, are decorated in glowing good taste. The scent of lavender lingers in the lawned gardens where cool breezes caress the trees, and food is a mix of regional Spanish and Brazilian, with some produce straight from the garden; it couldn't be fresher. The Somontano wines are delicious, too, and Mario is a gracious and welcoming host. A treasure. *A Rusticae hotel.*

Price	€150–€210. Singles €120.
Rooms	9 doubles.
Meals	Dinner €40. Wine from €14.
Closed	Occasionally.
Directions	Barcelona A-2/E-90 for Lleida; N-240 for Huesca. Before Barbastro, right on N-123, then A-138 Ainsa. Left for Boltaña onto N-260; 10km after Boltaña, right for San Martín. Rough track 5km; right onto tarmac; right to hotel.

Mario Reis & David Robinson
22372 San Martín de la Solana, Huesca

Tel	+34 974 503105
Fax	+34 974 341456
Email	info@casadesanmartin.com
Web	www.casadesanmartin.com

Hotel Los Arcos

At the heart of enchanting Aínsa, minutes from the carpark, is a cobbled square overlooked by a fine church tower. Tucked away down its exquisite alleys are restaurants and cafés; it's lively in summer. On one side of the square is a terrace of old houses — warm stone, shuttered windows, tiny balconies. Oscar, an engineer born in Aragón who returned to his roots, has turned one of these tall slender houses into a charming, and unexpectedly spacious, hotel. He pays great attention to detail, cleanliness and the comfort of his guests. The communal areas are of necessity small, but the spaces have been cleverly used and the walls hung with art. Exposed stone, reclaimed beams and solid flagstones on the stair coexist with steel and glass; soft, tawny colours and fabrics contrast with snow-white linens. The bedrooms are generous and pleasing, some facing the square, others the Peña Montañesa; the 'special' room has a splendid four-poster. Come for Romanesque architecture, wild boar in the Ordesa National Park, and a bird sanctuary on the edge of the village. A great little place.

Price	€70–€150.
Rooms	7 twins/doubles.
Meals	Restaurants in village.
Closed	Rarely.
Directions	From Barcelona to Lleida (Lérida) on A-2; exit 458 onto N-123 for Huesca. Before Barbastro right for Aínsa. Left at main x-roads in Aínsa. After 250m, right at sign 'casco historico'; 500m to car park; 5-minute walk to hotel.

Oscar Fantova & Marisol Cheliz
Plaza Mayor 23, 22330 Aínsa, Huesca

Tel	+34 974 500016
Fax	+34 974 500136
Email	info@hotellosarcosainsa.com
Web	www.hotellosarcosainsa.com

La Choca

The road is steep and twisting, the drive from Colungo is exhilarating and spectacular. In a privileged position on the village square, in a tiny hamlet in a wild part of Huesca, Miguel and Ana restored this centuries-old fortified farmhouse for themselves; but La Choca cried out to be shared so they opened to all. Old beams and stone stairs, woodsmoke and polish – there's an enchanting rusticity. Fall asleep to the hooting owl, wake to church bells: the tranquillity is intoxicating. The bedrooms are simple, without air con but with tiny homemade soaps and captivating views. The most light-filled are the twins at the front; the top one has its own terrace. You breakfast well on redcurrant jam and traditional doughnuts, as classical music gently plays. Ana's seasonal dishes are accompanied by local Somontano wines at dinner. There's a garden flanked by the church, and an ancient green oak for shade. Cave paintings nearby, walks from the door, mushroom picking in the forest – and the loveliest people. The self-catering apartments are as authentic as all the rest.

Price	Half-board €90. Singles €58. Apartments €45-€65 (minimum stay 2 nights). All prices per night, plus VAT at 7%.	
Rooms	9 + 2: 9 twins/doubles. 2 apartments for max. 6.	
Meals	Half-board only. Lunch (weekends only) €30-€35 à la carte. Picnic lunch by arrangement.	
Closed	December-February for B&B.	
Directions	Directions on booking.	

Ana Zamora & Miguel Angel Blasco
Plaza Mayor 1, 22148 Lecina, Huesca

Tel	+34 974 343070
Fax	+34 974 343304
Email	chocala@gmail.com
Web	www.lachoca.com

Hostería de Guara

There's inn-keeping in the family: this well-established roadside hosteria was started by Ana and Eva's parents. A spectacular drive on narrow scenic roads brings you to the unassuming village of Bierge; the Parque Natural de Guara, criss-crossed with canyons of emerald waters, is a short drive away. The front garden, packed with thyme, rosemary, lavender and roses, provides an explosion of Mediterranean colour against the perennial blue sky. Hotel-smart bedrooms have polished tiles, beds have white metal bedheads and flowing muslin drapes, and perhaps an armchair or two. Take a sundowner to the terrace for views of the hilltop church, floodlit at night. In the restaurant some dishes are cooked over an open fire; and don't miss the 'olive oil menu' – they produce their own. At the back is an almond orchard, a cloud of white and pink in February when the blossom begins. Delightful Eva can arrange guided tours of the many bodegas of the Somontano region, and then there's rafting, riding, climbing and ravine-spotting. Or book onto a birdwatching tour and see eagles and vultures feeding. *A Rusticae hotel.*

Price	€82-€138. Singles €63-€77. Half-board €120-€176 for 2.
Rooms	14 twins/doubles.
Meals	Lunch & dinner with wine, €25.
Closed	January.
Directions	From Huesca, N-240 for Lleida. 5km after Angües, left to Abiego, then left to Bierge. Hostería on left, at entrance to village.

Ana & Eva Viñuales Ferrando
c/Oriente 2, 22144 Bierge, Huesca

Tel	+34 974 318107
Fax	+34 974 318107
Email	info@hosteriadeguara.com
Web	www.hosteriadeguara.com

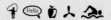

Posada La Pastora

Uncastillo, as the name implies, is an attractive castle-topped town – too often passed by – in the Sierra de Santo Domingo. Just behind the beautiful Iglésia Santa María is this grand, 18th-century house: the nicest place to stay in town. The traditional elements of old flagstones, wrought-iron grilles, terracotta tiles and wooden beams have been preserved and restored, and matched by an eye-catching décor. Massively thick outer walls mean that even at the height of the Spanish summer it remains cool; in winter, a wood-burner keeps the sitting room as warm as toast. Inma and Miguel are as charming as the guest house they have created. With those heavy stone walls, thick bedspreads and antique (or ultra-modern) washbasins they feel wonderfully comfortable. The new suites, designer gorgeous with massive beds and tubs, have perfect views – of terracotta roofs, countryside and three Romanesque churches. The apartments, in another part of town, are equally good. Another medieval town to visit is Sos del Rey Católico, whose claim to fame is that the local-boy-made-good was Fernando II. *A Rusticae hotel.*

Price	€74. Singles €52. Suites €124. Apartments €135. All prices per night.
Rooms	10 + 3: 8 doubles, 2 suites. 3 apartments for 6.
Meals	Breakfast €6.
Closed	8 January-28 February; Sundays to Thursdays 15 October-26 December.
Directions	From Pamplona N-121 south, then N-240 Huesca; NA-127 to Sangüesa. There, A-127 to Uncastillo. Here, round church of S. María; park on Plaza del Ordinario, just behind church.

Inma Navarro Labat & Miguel Pemán
c/Roncesvalles 1, 50678 Uncastillo,
Zaragoza

Tel	+34 976 679499
Fax	+34 976 679499
Email	lapastora@lapastora.net
Web	www.lapastora.net

Hotel Monasterio de Piedra

This 800-year-old monastery up in the hills is one of those gems of Spanish culture that ravish the senses and make exploration a joy. Impressively long corridors still invite contemplation but there's not a horsehair mattress in sight: big bedrooms, each converted from a quartet of monks' cells, are smart with antiques and fine fabrics and cool in scorching summer. Best of all, they overlook a monastic garden. Vaulted sitting areas echo; ancient cream stone walls and alabaster windows soothe the soul. Unwind, and take a guided tour of the cloisters, altars and tombs – and the first European kitchen where chocolate was made. In one of the former cellars, the Calatayud Wine Museum gives another glimpse of life in days gone by. But it's the dense natural ecosystem of the park that is the jewel in this particular Aragonese crown: a 174-foot waterfall, a mirror lake, a sunken grotto. Go lose yourself in the gardens and walkways, then return to a cool pool on an immaculate lawn. Wedding warning: they are often booked at weekends throughout the summer. *Bird of prey demonstrations.*

Price	€136. Singles €73–€103. Extra bed available.
Rooms	61 twins/doubles.
Meals	Lunch & dinner €27. Combined lunch & dinner €52.
Closed	Rarely.
Directions	From Barcelona & Zaragoza exit 231 for Monasterio de P. In Nuévalos, signs for Monasterio de P. Hotel 2.5km outside village in monastery grounds.

Antonio Carmona Fernández
Afueras s/n, 50210 Nuévalos, Zaragoza

Tel	+34 902 196052
Fax	+34 976 849054
Email	hotel@monasteriopiedra.com
Web	www.monasteriopiedra.com

Hostal Los Palacios

Albarracín is one of Teruel's most amazing walled towns, its medieval streets tumbling down the hillside to a beautiful square and blue-domed cathedral. Los Palacios is a tall, balconied building just outside the city walls whose earthy colours appear to fix it to the hillside on which it stands. The 1950s building was not long ago thoroughly revived and thus was born this small *hostal*. Bedrooms are furnished with workaday wooden furniture, floors are decked in modern tiles and the fabrics are a shade satiny, but forgive this little lapse – these are impeccably clean, typically Spanish rooms and, from their small balconies, have views that are second to none. (And more from the breakfast room/bar.) An unpretentious little place, amazingly cheap, and wholeheartedly recommended if you are happy in simple surroundings. Make time for the new animal farm nearby, Masía Monteagudo, with its horse riding and restaurant, and follow in the footsteps of semi-nomadic shepherds on the Ruta de la Trashumancia. Great value, and views to die for.
Meals available July/August, Easter & bank holidays only.

Price	€40-€45. Singles €25-€28.
Rooms	16: 15 twins/doubles, 1 single.
Meals	Breakfast €3.
	Lunch & dinner, with wine, €10.
Closed	Rarely.
Directions	From Teruel N-234 north for Zaragoza. After 8km, left on TE-901 to Albarracín. Here, through tunnel, right after 200m. Hostal 2nd house on right. Unload; park 50m below.

Valeriano Saez & Maite Argente
c/Palacios 21, 44100 Albarracín, Teruel

Tel	+34 978 700327
Fax	+34 978 700358
Email	hostallospalacios@montepalacios.com
Web	www.montepalacios.com

Masía del Aragonés

Its 16th-century tower rising above the pastures, at the end of a long track, is a rustic farm. The old stone walls of this onetime retreat for wealthy Aragonese are now hung with old farm implements, and floors laid with plain new tiles. Furniture is simple new pine, heating is from a wood-burning stove. This is where you enjoy Pilar's cooking with nearly all ingredients home-grown or reared: wholesome soups and stews, simple puddings and pastries, homemade liqueurs and home-brewed wine (strong stuff!). Bedrooms are a good size but as basic as the price suggests; there are iron bedsteads, homespun curtains, spotless bathrooms, exposed stone walls. The downstairs rooms could be damp, so ask for a room at the top; reached by a steep stair, they have arched windows and share an open bit of wall. Wonderful to be woken by the sun as it rises from the hills, home to ibex and eagles. There are crystalline rock pools above Beceite, and Valderrobres is worth a visit. The older members of the Andreu family speak not a word of English but will surely find time to make sure your stay is memorable.

Price	€34–€46.
Rooms	6 twins/doubles.
Meals	Lunch & dinner, with wine, €14–€18, by arrangement.
Closed	Rarely.
Directions	Barcelona A-7, exit 38 for L'Hospitalet de L'Infant. On to Valderrobres. There, left to Fuentespalda, on for Monroyo, left for Peñarroya de T. After 500m, right to Herbes; signs to Masía. After 1.5km, right for 3km track.

Pilar Andreu & Manuel Lombarte
44586 Peñarroya de Tastavins, Teruel
Tel +34 978 769048
Web www.masaragones.com

Mas de la Serra

A stylish rebuilt 1600s tower soars above the wild isolation of Teruel's landscape, and woodland stretches to the horizon over clay-red hills. The *masia* hits you after a rocky 4km road: a shock of stone-built shapes and styles, a maze of steps, stairs and high sloping ceilings – not a straight angle or rectangular room in sight. Inside, find contemporary décor with a dash of tradition and a pinch of exotica; modern bathrooms and a luxury spa gleam in Moroccan tadelakht plaster. So many places to relax: endless sitting areas and terraces, a swimming pool with the same fabulous valley views. Delightful Luis, and Jenny from Peru, take care of every whim, from tasty meals to drinks on the terrace; charming owner Alasdair regales you with tales of filming and the Territorial Army. Use the space to get away from it all: a drink in unspoilt Fuentespalda's square, gorge walks in Els Ports park. The only life around you are horned Spanish ibex, the only sound the whistling breeze. A house-party hotel with five-star comfort amid beautiful untamed surroundings – just the place for adventurous young bloods.

Price	€120–€230. Half-board extra €25 p.p. Whole house €6,000–€9,500 per week (catered).
Rooms	8: 5 twins/doubles, 3 suites for 2.
Meals	Dinner with wine, €25. Restaurants 6km.
Closed	7-21 January.
Directions	From Reus, N-420 for Alcañiz to Calaceite. Left on A-1413; at junc., right on A-231 to Valderrobres. Left on A1414 to Fuentespalda. Between km14 & 15 markers, left up steep track for 4km, bear left at white post.

	Alasdair Grant
	44587 Fuentespalda, Teruel
Mobile	+44 (0)7970 610316
Email	al@masdelaserra.com
Web	www.masdelaserra.com

La Torre del Visco

Quiet, soothing, exquisite. Inland, an hour's drive from the coast, the hotel is surrounded by farmland and ancient peace. Bajo Aragón is beautiful, wild, unspoilt, stacked with natural and man-made treasures. Inside the 500-year-old estate house each piece of furniture, antique, rustic or modern, blends beautifully with ancient tiles, brickwork and beams. No bedroom phones, no TVs, just embroidered linen, flowers from the garden and a suite in the tower fit for a king. The food is another reason to come, served in a beautiful, split-level restaurant where the emphasis is on seasonal and regional produce. Fruit, vegetables and olive oil come from their big, certified organic farm, there are black truffles, wild mushrooms, the freshest fish. Then there are the gardens, the summer breakfasts on the terrace, the library with backgammon and books in English and Spanish, the bodega (a wine-lover's dream), and the river to cool off in on a hot summer's day. Although the hotel is owned and run by an English couple, the majority of guests are Spanish. Understated luxury: an exceptional treat. *Ask about cookery courses.*

Price	€275–€355. Suites €350–€450.
Rooms	17: 11 twins/doubles, 6 suites.
Meals	Half-board only. Lunch €47.
Closed	Never.
Directions	Barcelona AP-7 for Valencia; junc. 38 for L'H.de L'Infant, then C-44 & C-12 to Tivissa; N-420 to Calaceite, onto A-1413 & A-231 to Valderrobres. There, left at x-roads on A-1414 for Fuentespalda; at km19 marker, track for 5.5km; right.

Piers Dutton & Jemma Markham
44587 Fuentespalda, Teruel

Tel	+34 978 769121
Fax	+34 978 769016
Email	casasdelvisco@casasdelvisco.com
Web	www.torredelvisco.com

Molí de l'Hereu

Spanish olive oil was once pressed and bottled in this remarkable 18th-century building, now transformed into a captivating blend of museum, spa, restaurant and hotel. Fabulously restored, the huge wooden levers and enormous cogs are the showpiece: you can browse at will or sip a drink among the machinery. Moody lighting and a flickering fire illuminate the stone-pillared restaurant next door, where Agustin serves roast suckling pig and other Spanish treats. Upstairs to neat bedrooms, finely dressed in classic colours and the best quality linen – nothing is lacking here, nor in the generous modern bathrooms. Gaze out to tranquil gardens from the indoor swimming pool and jacuzzi, or visit the spa for a steam, sauna or massage; the peace is palpable. From here it's a long and swooping drive through Teruel's craggy clay-tinged hills to find civilisation (and restaurants) beyond sleepy towns and villages, but energetic Agustin and Pilar can give you some ideas – that's if you can tear yourself away. Come for an authentic taste of rural life, with every creature comfort thrown in.

Price	€120. Suites €150–€190. Whole hotel available July/August on half-board basis (minimum 5 nights).
Rooms	12: 10 twins/doubles, 2 suites.
Meals	Dinner €30. Wine from €15. Restaurants 30-minute drive.
Closed	Never.
Directions	From Reus, N-420 for Alcañiz; past Calaceite & Valdeltormo; left on N-232 for Morella. Left on TE-V-3005; 8km, to Ráfales. Continue past entrance to village, following green/white signs to hotel.

Agustin & Pilar Cáceres Valdivieso
Rabanella s/n, 44589 Ráfales, Teruel

Tel	+34 978 856266
Fax	+34 978 856266
Email	agustinrafales@yahoo.es
Web	www.molidelhereu.com

Mas del Colomé

Pine forests above, almond groves below – Paul may entice you into helping with the harvest. A serene, wonderfully remote setting for the 'house of the dovecote': from the top of the valley you just see the tiny road below. Bilingual Yorkshireman Paul has left the City of London to become a town councillor in the hamlet of Fórnoles, and run a B&B. And he has given the old olive-curing warehouse a most sympathetic restoration: the robust beams and honey-coloured stones glow. Bedrooms are modern-rustic and inviting, with comfortable beds and subtle colours; one has a balcony, the others have sun terraces, all have views. Rolling slatted blinds help keep the heat at bay, though welcome breezes blow; bathrooms have beautifully polished limestone washstands. The house and its garden fit perfectly into the landscape, though the high stone walls and uneven terrain look unsafe for young ones. In the living room are a massive fireplace and sturdy tables for sociable dining: home-baked muffins and homemade quince jams, salmon wrapped in jamon de Teruel, peach crumble. Great base for a great region.

Price	€75–€100.
Rooms	4 twins/doubles.
Meals	Dinner €20. Wine €8.
Closed	Christmas & New Year.
Directions	From Barcelona/Reus N-420 for Alcañiz; N-232 for Castellón. After 8km, left on TE-V-3004 for La Portellada/Fornoles. After 3km of narrow mountain road, house on right before bridge.

Paul Reynolds
& Reginald Thomas Doherty
44650 Fórnoles, Teruel

Tel	+34 978 853017
Email	info@masdelcolome.com
Web	www.masdelcolome.com

Las Casas del Visco

Self-catering doesn't get swisher than this. Your quarters are in an 1800s house and a 14th-century tower, part of the ramparts of Valderrobres. They are as stylish as they are historic. Perhaps the bedrooms get a trifle hot in summer, perhaps the house is unsuitable for the very old or very young – all those labyrinthine stairs, all those door-free spaces – but it is hugely distinctive and it is a privilege to stay. The kitchen/dining area is in the lofty basement, a gorgeous mix of sleek units and rustic stone. Upstairs, divided from the landing by a sheer glass wall, is the sitting room: geometric rugs on terracotta floors, stylish sofas, a real fire, art on the walls. Bathroom one is above, with a stair up to its bedroom: both spaces delightful with white sloping beams. Bedroom two, reached via another stair, has a carved bedstead from India… then it's three flights to the top room (mind your head): a small double bed, a tiny mosaic'd bathroom, spectacular views of the castle above. Sumptuous are the breakfasts, deep are the comforts, and you are guided up cobblestone streets right to the door.

Price	€1,500 for 2. Extra person €350. Plus VAT. Prices per week.
Rooms	House for 6.
Meals	Restaurant 7km.
Closed	Never.
Directions	From Barcelona A-7 S for Valencia; exit 38 for L'Hospitalet, then C44 Tivessa; C12 Móra la Nova; N420 through Gandesa to Calaceite; left for Valderrobres; follow signs right to castle.

Piers Dutton & Jemma Markham
El Portal de Bergos 5, 44580 Valderrobes,
Teruel

Tel	+34 978 769121
Fax	+34 978 769016
Email	casasdelvisco@casasdelvisco.com
Web	www.casasdelvisco.com

El Convent 1613

Its huge front door is set in a creamy stone archway, flanked by a pair of cypresses; a quarter of the door opens to embrace, then seduce you. The site was acquired around 1900 by a forebear of today's owners; with the land came the ruins of a church built in 1613. By the time the forebear arrived on the scene, little remained other than the outer walls – the shell for an elegant and contemporary new dwelling. Now it's a delightful hotel run by an even more delightful family. Spaces are lofty and unexpected, with an arresting mix of ancient and modern: beamed vaulted ceilings and sheets of glass, exposed stone walls and high spec fittings. The bedrooms have huge period appeal and old frescos; those on the top floor are more contemporary and one has a fabulous view. Particularly striking are the central patio and restaurant in the old choir and nave; the former side chapels make intimate dining areas (and cosy reading rooms). The food is elegant, contemporary, delicious. The spreading gardens have a soothing, breezy air; birds sing, water plays, the hammock swings, there's a lovely pool. Special.

Price	€115–€150. Suites €150–€185.
Rooms	12: 9 twins/doubles, 1 family room for 3, 2 suites.
Meals	Lunch & dinner, à la carte with wine, €40–€60.
Closed	10–27 December.
Directions	5km before Valderrobres, right to La F. There, left fork to square; park. Hotel 50m below square on right, at bottom of dead-end alley; staff will show you how to get to hotel car park.

Ana & Diana Romeo Villoro
c/Convento 1, 44596 La Fresneda,
Teruel

Tel	+34 978 854850
Fax	+34 978 854851
Email	hotel@hotelelconvent.com
Web	www.hotelelconvent.com

Catalonia & Andorra

Arianella de Can Coral

Sample a slice of Catalan life with Ariane and Rayner who count local winemakers and members of Vilafranca's Castellet team – human-tower racers – among their friends. The sun ripens olives and almonds and lends a glow to this 19th-century burnt-yellow farmhouse. Great stone floors in the living room surround a huge sandstone pillar that glows in firelight during winter. Outside, mulberry trees grow and are harvested to make a delicious sweet sauce for ice cream. Fruity by name, charming by nature, rooms like 'Melocotón' have slanted ceilings that shelter sweet wrought-iron four-poster beds and little sinks in the corner. Swimming pool, mountains and vines fill the view before it plunges toward Vall de Penedés. The self-catering apartment is a smart modern renovation with a fabulous terrace overlooking vineyards. Catalan specialities like *fideua* and *butifarra* are enjoyed outside under the tree by candlelight. On one night of the year, all 150 flowers of the cactus that climbs the wall suddenly burst into bloom; come morning, they're gone.

Price	€69. Suite €97. Apartment €118–€134 (€700–€840 per week).
Rooms	6 + 1: 5 twins/doubles, 1 family suite. Apartment for 4.
Meals	Breakfast €7. Dinner €18–€22, by arrangement.
Closed	Occasionally in winter.
Directions	A-7 Barcelona-Tarragona; exit Vilafranca del Penedés & follow signs & Sant Martí BP-2121. Continue to Torrelles de Foix; right 50m after church; hotel 1.5km, signed.

Ariane Paasch
Avda. Can Coral s/n, Alt Penedés,
08737 Torelles de Foix, Barcelona

Tel	+34 938 971579
Fax	+34 938 971579
Email	arianella@cancoral.com
Web	www.arianella.com

Hotel Masía Sumidors

Perched quietly on its own, high on a hill surrounded by pine trees and vineyards, the crumbling *venta* oozes history and charm. Delightful new English owners have introduced a bohemian yet classical style with African and oriental undertones; scattered around are interesting objets d'art (Japanese umbrellas, musical intruments) and paintings old and new on low, thick walls. Bedrooms are atmospheric, showers are simple and one suite has a rustic four-poster; the other lies in a bright and cool bungalow (no kitchen). Outside on the upper terrace, a Bedouin tent hung with lamps protects intimate clusters of wrought-iron tables and chairs. Sit out by the terracotta, crescent-shaped bar for sunset drinks before candlelit dinner; there is also a barbecue, which is often used. On the lower terrace, the figure-of-eight pool is fabulous and the views awesome. Explore the surrounding countryside on foot or by mountain bike. For day trips there's classy Sitges and the medieval towns of Olivella or Montserrat, while Tarragona and Barcelona are a short drive. A simple but special place – relax and revive.

Price	€75-€115. Suites €115-€200.
Rooms	9: 7 twins/doubles, 2 suites.
Meals	Dinner €25. Wine €10-€30.
Closed	Rarely.
Directions	Barcelona C-32 to Sitges; exit 28 onto C-15B dir. Sant Pere de Ribes/Vilafranca. 2km past turning to Sant Pere de Ribes, immed. after Restaurant Carnivor, right onto 1km track; hotel signed on apex of bend.

Neil Stock & Iain Murray
Ctra. de Vilafranca km4.6,
08810 Sant Pere de Ribes-Sitges,
Barcelona

Tel	+34 938 962061
Email	info@sumidors.com
Web	www.sumidors.com

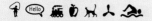

Entry 89   Map 7

Cal Mestre

Breakfast overlooking the rugged outline of Mount Montserrat, then choose whether to spend the day on the beaches or among Barcelona's riches: this village house (built 1643) is within reach of both. Marian and Martin have soberly, sensitively restored it all, in faultless Dutch style, blending restorable old with perfectly designed new. Polished wooden floors, exposed stones and rustic doors mix with modern art, paper globe lanterns, fine bed linen and big flowers. Modern furniture with clean lines is juxtaposed with atmospheric country pieces, small alcoves glow and you dine off white china. Dreamy 'Penedès' has a free-standing bath, 'Stable' has shuttered doors that open to the village street. Spend the day exploring Roman Tarragona or tasting the wines of Penedès. Back here there's massage and meditation; a terrace romantic with jasmine and views – or candles; a saltwater pool buried in the greenery below. Spanish guitar mixes with tractor hum and twice-weekly Catalan suppers are served at the long Spanish table – as perfect as all the rest. An exclusive retreat. *Two saunas (extra charge) & honesty bar. Ask about yoga breaks.*

Price	€100–€130. Apartment €550–€850 per week.
Rooms	3 + 1: 3 twins/doubles. 1 apartment for 2.
Meals	Lunch €14–€20. Dinner (occasionally) €25. Wine €12–€20.
Closed	Winter months.
Directions	From Barcelona N-340 to Vilafranca. At Avinyó Nou, signs to Olessa-Gavà-Begues. After 100m, right, signed Les Gunyoles. In village, bear right up very narrow road; yellow house near church.

Marian & Martin Badoux
c/Torre Romana 2-4,
08793 Les Gunyoles d'Avinyonet,
Barcelona

Tel	+34 938 970761
Email	info@cal-mestre.com
Web	www.cal-mestre.com

Hotel Santa María

Sitges was fashionable among rich Catalans for years. The crowd is cosmopolitan now, but it has kept its intimate feel and life still centres on the busy promenade and beach. At the heart of it all is the pretty Santa María, its white façade enhanced by apricot awnings, the largest one spanning the front terrace. There's a glistening array of fresh seafood from the modern open kitchen, the sea almost laps to the table and everything ticks over nicely in the popular restaurant, thanks to the still indefatigable Señora Ute who switches between half a dozen languages at any given time. Some bedrooms have beautiful shuttered balconies and a view across the palm trees to the bay; seafront rooms will be noisy in summer. There's a rolling programme of improvements and the newly done rooms are simple, neat and polished; older ones have gilded mirrors and big solid wardrobes. For Sitges it's well priced but do book ahead in season; if there's no room here, there may be space in sister hotels La Niña and La Pinta (not inspected). You're at the centre of this bustling resort — and it's child-friendly, too.

Price	€80–€120. Singles €68–€91. Family rooms €115–€140.
Rooms	57: 51 twins/doubles, 6 family rooms.
Meals	Lunch & dinner €12. À la carte, with wine, from €25. Wine €7.50.
Closed	20 December–10 February.
Directions	From Barcelona, A-2 to Sitges. Follow signs to Sitges centre & seafront; left past Hotel Calipolis. 50m, on left. Limited parking.

Ute Arcas Sánchez
Passeig de la Ribera 52, 08870 Sitges,
Barcelona

Tel	+34 938 940999
Fax	+34 938 947871
Email	info@lasantamaria.com
Web	www.lasantamaria.com

Hotel Duquesa de Cardona

Where would you choose to stay in Barcelona? Near Las Ramblas, by the atmospheric marina? The Duquesa de Cardona has a near-perfect site – vibrant until the small hours! – and a sophistication to match that of the city. You can safely expect the best of everything here: service, comfort, food, and a high-ceilinged, columned and vaulted restaurant that is quite something. This imposing 19th-century building, in palm-lined Paseo Colón in the city's famous gothic quarter, was once home to nobles and kings. The aristocratic mood is reflected in original chequered marble floors and stone arches and carvings, while elegant bedrooms, some small, some large, come in contemporary chocolates and taupes with carpeted floors and high ceilings... ask for a harbourside view, but rooms at the back may be quieter. Bathrooms are stunning. After a day exploring one of the world's best-loved cities, return to a sleek teak table on the top terrace, sip a cocktail beneath a vast parasol, take a dip in the splash pool and watch the sun going down. Everything is close to perfection.

Price	€140–€305. Suites, €250–€450. Plus VAT at 7%.
Rooms	40: 35 twins/doubles, 5 suites.
Meals	Buffet breakfast €14. Lunch & dinner €30. Plus VAT at 7%.
Closed	Never.
Directions	From airport, C-32 dir. Barcelona; exit 'Ronda Litoral' onto B-10; exit 21 'Ciutat Vella direction Paseo Colón/Puerto'. Hotel opp. marina. See map on hotel website.

Déborah Sarrazin
Paseo Colón 12, 08002 Barcelona

Tel	+34 932 689090
Fax	+34 932 682931
Email	comercial@hduquesadecardona.com
Web	www.hduquesadecardona.com

Casa Capella 2

The perfect place for an extended stay in Barcelona: a fully serviced apartment two steps from the Passeig de Gràcia. The building's classic façade doesn't hint at the delights on the second floor: a gleaming urban flat – cool, light and oozing contemporary chic. Smart design features pepper the place. A sleek cube-shaped kitchen doubles as a room-sized lamp for the stylish lounge, and a glazed gallery converts to an open balcony in summer. Bedrooms have huge plush beds and practical cupboards, while bathrooms are a luxury with waterfall showers and all the extras; nothing has been skimped on. Welcoming, efficient John and Josefina take care of every little service (just ask): fully equipped office facilities, cleaning... Roaring traffic outside, but inside, cool silence thanks to clever insulation and air conditioning; opera singers stay happily here. Gaudí's buildings are scattered around you, exclusive shops and restaurants abound and transport connections converge: Barcelona's best both inside and outside the door. *Welcome hamper.*

Price	€410–€492 per night.
Rooms	Apartment for 6-8 (3 doubles).
Meals	Restaurants close by.
Closed	Never.
Directions	On corner of Carrer d'Aragó & Carrer de Pau Claris. Apartment on 2nd floor; ring bell for entry Metro: Passeig de Gràcia. .

John Barnard & Josefina Bias
2nd floor, Carrer d'Aragó 288,
08008 Barcelona

Tel	+34 932 093650
Fax	+34 932 053550
Email	barcelona@casa-capella.com
Web	www.casa-capella.com

Can Casadellà

At the end of a bougainvillea-bright drive stands Josep's old family summer home, a solid proud masia that blends colonial-style trappings with a pinch of nostalgia. Gilt-framed mirrors, patterned tiles, oil-painted ancestors cover the thick stone walls; low lighting and chandeliers add to the sense of a house lost in time. Old-fashioned bedrooms nestle under thick-beamed eaves, simple with their brick floors, antique headboards and candelabra. Some bathrooms are slightly makeshift, with shower, basin and loo in the bedroom itself. If windows are small, the sense of space outside is not; take a stroll through the cacti, pines and cypress trees to discover a children's play park and a simple pool. Friendly Magda's four young children are always hoping for playmates, so in these grounds you can let yours run free. On request, Magda will serve you a Catalan meal around the summer room's table, or in the fire-warmed salon. Trains run straight to Barcelona from nearby Premià de Mar, but you'll need a car to explore the monastery and mountains at Montserrat, while the beach is a ten-minute drive.

Price	€85–€119. Extra beds €25–€39.
Rooms	5 doubles/twins. Extra beds.
Meals	Occasional dinner. Restaurants 400m.
Closed	Never.
Directions	From Barcelona, C-32 exit 92 Premià de Mar; signs to Premià de Dalt. Here, follow Carretera de Enllaç to end; right at junction onto Riera de Premià de Mar; 1st right onto Careterra de la Cisa. Round corner, house on left; ring bell at gates.

Josep Botey Galindo
Carrer de la Cisa 53,
08338 Premià de Dalt, Barcelona

Mobile	+34 636 252440
Fax	+34 933 875005
Email	magda@cancasadella.com
Web	www.cancasadella.com

Vilaclara Art Hotel

Once a luxury residence for visiting football clubs, later a home for monks, this quietly grand hotel lies within striking distance of Barcelona, yet exudes the space and calm of a rural summer retreat. Inside is gently imposing, a sea of soft arched shapes, marble floors and forest green. Curve up a grand stone staircase to generous bedrooms on the first and second floors, and three sweet attic rooms under the eaves; clean-lined and classic with high ceilings and cool tiled floors, they have every comfort you need. Bright bathrooms are equally luxurious. Dine on coastal specialities in the smart restaurant downstairs, eat al fresco on tiered terraces, or stroll up tree-lined paths to the sunny swimming pool, hugged by yet more trees, and order a stylish snack for the poolside. There's also a shiny-floored piano bar with sofas and full-length windows, and big artworks for sale. If you manage to tear yourself away, there are buses to the beach – watersports for the energetic – and trains to Barcelona. Comfortably smart, efficiently run, the Art Hotel is a very relaxing place to get away from it all.

Price	€118–€185. Suites €140–€310.
Rooms	32: 23 doubles/twins, 9 suites.
Meals	Lunch with wine, €18.50. Dinner, à la carte, from €35. Wine from €12. (September–July: lunch Tues–Sun, dinner Thurs–Sat. Restaurant open daily in Aug.)
Closed	January.
Directions	From Barcelona, C-32 exit 105 Sant Andreu de Llavaneres. Continue towards town, then follow yellow signs left to hotel.

Cristina Viader
Avda. Catalunya 63,
08392 Sant Andreu de Llavaneres, Barcelona

Tel	+34 937 927551
Fax	+34 937 928025
Email	info@vilaclaraarthotel.com
Web	www.vilaclaraarthotel.com

Can Rosich

Handy for Barcelona, close to the beach, yet buried in bucolic loveliness. This *masía* is two centuries old but has been virtually rebuilt. Tiled bedrooms, named after the birds and animals of the region, are a good size and large enough to take a third bed. Beds are antiques, mattresses are new, and you'll find a be-ribboned and neatly ironed bundle of towels on your duvet – a typical touch from a gracious hostess. To one side of the large hallway is the rustic, white-walled dining room, its tables decked in bright checks; there's a new second room for groups and an enchanting dining area outside. Cooking is wholesome, delicious and superb value. Among Montserrat's specialities are rabbit, pork from the farm and *asado de payés*, a thick stew with three different meats, plums and pine nuts (order this one in advance!). Breakfast, too, is delicious: cheese and charcuterie, fruits, fresh juice. You are a five-minute drive to the station and trains that get you to Barcelona in an hour. Mateo and Montserrat are the loveliest hosts; no surprise that this is a favourite with our readers.

Price	€55–€70.
Rooms	6 twins/doubles.
Meals	Breakfast €7. Dinner, with wine, €18.
Closed	2 weeks in October/November.
Directions	From AP-7, exit 9 Maçanet; N-II for Barcelona to Santa Susanna; here, right at 1st r'bout for 'nucleo urbano'; signs for 2km to Can Rosich.

Montserrat Boter Fors
Camí de la Riera,
08398 Santa Susanna, Barcelona

Tel	+34 937 678473
Fax	+34 937 678473
Email	canrosich@canrosich.com
Web	www.canrosich.com

Entry 96   Map 8

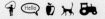

Hotel Masferrer

It takes boldness and sensitivity to turn a grand Catalan masía into a young contemporary hotel without losing its charm. In the little town of Gualba on the edge of the Parque Natural, this is a beguilingly simple blend of ancient and modern. Young manager Nils and his wife are breathing new life into the rustic old place and are brimming with plans – for dining al fresco and a play area for kids. The dining room is breezily elegant with white linen and simple vases of flowers, and the kitchen is headed by a Moroccan chef who expertly tweaks Catalan dishes. The veg comes from the gardens. Rustic oak beams and exposed stone, old wooden doors and designer lighting remain; antiques mix with books, board games and velvety sofas; soft jazz plays throughout. Bedrooms are pared down but not chilly, bathrooms are a stunning mixture of designer-sleek and rough-cast; choose the split-level suite for huge windows onto a private terrace. In several acres of woodland and garden – with a pool – it's hard to believe the coast is 15 minutes away and Barcelona half an hour. Peace without the isolation. *A Rusticae hotel.*

Price	€130. Singles €120. Suites €165–€195.
Rooms	11: 9 twins/doubles, 2 suites.
Meals	Breakfast €15. Lunch & dinner €25. Wine €10–€50.
Closed	Rarely.
Directions	From Barcelona AP-7 to Gerona; exit 11 onto C-35 to Hostalric; left at r'bout to Gualba. Hotel siged on right, after 200m.

Mr Nils Garcia
08474 Gualba, Barcelona

Tel	+34 938 487705
Fax	+34 938 487084
Email	hmasferrer@husa.es
Web	www.hotelmasferrer.com

Hotel Torre Martí

Stunning! A doctor's summer retreat, now a boutique hotel, created by artistic Pere and son Roger. You may think you'd washed up at a Tuscan villa – the solidity and the squareness, the porticoed first floor, the rich red exterior. Enter a world of terracottas and ochres, pistachios and Moroccan blues, a classy backdrop for flamboyant furnishings: gilt mirrors, twinkly chandeliers. Add Asian and modern art (including Pere originals), old theatre seats for dining on and a barber's chair on the landing – this is eclectic in the best possible way. Be soothed by soft classical music as you float down for dinner; Pere's cooking lures locals, ever a good sign (breakfasts are delectable too). Big windows allow views onto the elegant terrace and lawn with its fountain'd pond. Bedrooms, some in the main house, some with balconies, the rest in the old guards' house next door, are surprising, original and have sparkling bathrooms. There's more: the vivid blue library with its traditional leather chairs, the open fires, the magnificent grounds, the warm and charming staff… curl up and purr. *A Rusticae hotel.*

Price	€140–€170. Singles €100–€120. Suite €275.
Rooms	8: 6 twins/doubles, 1 single, 1 suite.
Meals	Lunch & dinner €35. Wine €30–€50.
Closed	Rarely.
Directions	From Gerona, south on N-II then C-25 direction Vic. Just before, right on N-141; follow signs to Sant Julia de V. Signed in village. Parking.

Roger Morral Palacín
c/Ramón Llull 11, 08504
Sant Julia de Vilatorta, Barcelona

Tel	+34 938 888372
Fax	+34 938 888374
Email	hoteltorremarti@yahoo.es
Web	www.hoteltorremarti.com

El Jufré

The hilltop villages of this part of Cataluña rival those of Provence. And the drive up to Tavertet, past craggy limestone outcrops and stands of forest, is an adventure in itself. El Jufré is perched over a craggy ledge and the views are superb; get up early and watch the sun rise. Wonderful to stay with Josep and sweet Lourdes in this very old house; rebuilt in the 1600s, some parts date back as far as 1100; Josep's family have been in residence for over 800 years. The style is rustic and bedrooms are simple and attractive, marrying ancient beams and exposed stones. We liked best the big room with the iron bedstead and the mountain-drop view. Glory in more views as you linger on the terrace over an aperitif, distant cowbells signalling the end of the day. The food is another reason to come: good, simple dishes make full use of their own organic beef, pork and vegetables. The village, though tiny (residents in the village number 50), has three restaurants, an 11th century church and a museum. El Jufré is for lovers of high places and utter tranquillity. Hikers will be in heaven.

Price	Half-board €95–€100.
Rooms	8: 7 doubles, 1 single.
Meals	Half-board only. Wine €5–€6.
Closed	22 December-7 January; 1-15 September.
Directions	From Vic C-153 for Olot & Roda de Ter to L'Esquirol & Santa Maria Corco. Here, right to Tavertet. House on left as enter village.

Josep Roquer & Lourdes Rovira
08511 Tavertet-Osona, Barcelona
Tel   +34 938 565167
Fax   +34 938 565167
Email   eljufre@gmail.com

Casa Rural Magnolia Blanca

For active families, this is perfect. Table tennis, games and a gorgeous pool here, and the Parque Natural de Montseny beyond, with its great rivers and sweeping forests of pine. The elegant house was built in 1934, a cool retreat for wealthy Catalans. A stone arch and a wooden gate open to three outdoor levels rampant with magnolias, roses and vines, stone statues, hammocks and secret ponds – lovely, peaceful, charming. Inside are large African paintings and bright Mediterranean colours; Helena and her family promise a happy, bright and welcoming home. Guests have a charming, high-ceilinged sitting room, its windows roundly arched, its furniture comfortably minimalist, all natural fabrics and big pale sofas. The kitchen is rustic, tasteful and self-contained; the dining room has one long table. Bedrooms are less spacious but equally polished, up in the loft with a simple, chalet-like feel. Bathrooms have large sinks and antique oval mirrors. If you're doing B&B, you'll be treated to homemade cakes and local *embutidos* at breakfast. But this is special all round.

Price	€75–€110. Singles €65–€90. Whole house €500–€617. Part of house €235–€407. Prices per night.
Rooms	7 twins/doubles (2 sharing bathroom). House available for self-catering.
Meals	Restaurants in main square.
Closed	Never.
Directions	From Girona on C-25; exit 202 on GI-543 to Viladraú. In town follow signs to hotel.

Elena Cardenal & Luis Salinas
Avda. Marcos Redondo 5,
17406 Viladrau, Gerona

Tel	+34 938 849495
Email	info@magnoliablanca.com
Web	www.magnoliablanca.com

Xalet La Coromina

Viladraú is an aristocratic, elegant little town close to the stunning Parque Natural de Montseny – known for the best drinking water in Spain! Woodlands are grandiose, water flows and falls, rare plants flourish, and the climate is delightfully cool in summer. This building dates from the 1900s when wealthy Catalans started to build summer retreats away from Barcelona; the building has kept its elegant exterior. Inside is unexpectedly formal. Turn-of-the-century furnishings are sober, the immaculately tiled and sofa'd sitting room has its original fireplace (lit in winter) and bedrooms combine paintings of pastoral scenes with a smart Seventies' décor. Bathrooms are white, with good showers. The rooms vary in size but we would choose the suite, for its terrace. New owners Salvador and his wife Belen are full of enthusiasm for their new venture. He is an experienced chef and there are Michelin standards to live up to, so you may expect the best. Outside are gentle gardens and a pretty hexagonal, stone-riveted pool. *A Rusticae hotel.*

Price	€120–€140. Singles €95–€105. Suite €195–€205.
Rooms	8: 7 twins/doubles, 1 suite.
Meals	Lunch €30. Dinner €30–€35.
Closed	Rarely.
Directions	From Girona C-25, exit km202 marker, then GI-543 to Viladraú. In village towards Vic: hotel on right after 50m. From Barcelona on AP-7, then C-17; exit to Seud/Viladrau.

Salvador Casaseca Almaraz
Ctra. de Vic 6, 17406 Viladrau, Gerona

Tel	+34 938 849264
Fax	+34 938 848160
Email	xaletcoromina@xaletcoromina.com
Web	www.xaletcoromina.com

Mas Vilarmau

Delightfully idiosyncratic: that sums up Pep and Pilar's approach to interior design. They've added individuality and fun to a secluded 12th to 18th-century farmhouse that was already crammed with character. Bedrooms are simple, wonky-floored and each has its own theme; bathrooms are generous and modern with beautiful floral tiles and colourful towels. An informal and slightly ramshackle cosiness spreads through this house; on each floor is a sitting area with old wooden beams and planked floors, stone walls and an open fire. Make the most of the remoteness and tranquillity – no phones, mobile signal or cash machines. You're on the edge of the mountainous Parque Natural de Montseny, a rambler's paradise and yours to discover, once you've pulled yourself away from the garden hammock. Heaven for children too, what with swimming pool, chickens and ducks, and games and toys galore. And, at the end of the day, delicious fresh regional dishes are lovingly prepared by Pep … with a great bottle of red straight from the cellar. *Minimum stay two nights at weekends. Near Gerona Airport.*

Price	Half-board €70 p.p.
	Full-board €80 p.p.
Rooms	9: 8 twins/doubles, 1 family room for 4-5.
Meals	Half- or full-board only.
Closed	Never.
Directions	From Barcelona C-17 for Seva. Through Viladraú; right direction Santa Fe del Montseny then second left signed Cami de Vilarmau. Follow for 3km.

Pep Bochaca & Pilar Masmuntal
Ctra. de Sant Marçal s/n,
17406 Viladrau, Gerona

Email	info@masvilarmau.com
Web	www.masvilarmau.com

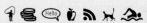

Catalonia

Mas Vinyoles

A cork farmer built this smart 1950s farmhouse for his bride; now Katerin lives here, amid the soft hills and pretty villages. The two self-contained apartments echo her character and Swiss origins: happy, open, generous. Expect dazzling walls, long sofas, modern lighting. In the bedrooms (almost all are en suite), bright walls come stencilled, beds are big and comfy, and windows open to sun and birdsong. Kitchens gleam, each sociably set into the cosy lounge. Pick at will from an abundant organic garden, buy in local markets or ask Katerin if she'll cook a meal; breakfast, too, can be on request. Wander the garden visited (at night) by badgers, perfumed by citrus trees and herbs; find shade under a cork tree or splash in the pool. There's a terrace for a breezy beer and a cosy fireplace for winter. Your conscience is as clear as the air outside, with heating from solar panels and water from a nearby well. Gerona lies one way, the Costa Brava the other, and in between are easy walks linking perfect villages; in summer, there's a fiesta every weekend. A fabulous tranquil spot, a delightful hostess.

Price	Apartment for 4, €645–€840. Apartment for 6, €967–€1,260. Prices per week.
Rooms	2 apartments: 1 for 4, 1 for 6.
Meals	Breakfast €6–€12. Restaurants 3km (Gerona 12km).
Closed	Rarely.
Directions	AP-7 exit 7; C65 for Costa Brava. Past Quart, left to GI6641. Continue for 7km; 700m past 'Sant Mateu de Montnegre' sign, left for Mas Vinyoles (also signed). Follow right-hand track for 50m.

Kathrin Schmidhauser
Mas Vinyoles, Quart,
17242 Sant Mateu de Montnegre,
Gerona

Tel	+34 972 468051
Email	info@masvinyoles.org
Web	www.masvinyoles.org

Ethical Collection: Environment; Community. See page 412.

Hotel Sant Roc

The Costa Brava remains a stunning stretch of coastline and this quiet little hotel in a pretty little village could restore your faith in seaside holidays in Spain. It's a family affair – not only family-run but a place where guests are treated like old friends. Many return. The setting is marvellous: a perch at the edge of a cliff, surrounded by pine, olive and cypress, the sea ever present. Its colours change with every hour, and from the dining rooms and terrace are delightful views across the bay: bobbing boats, hillsides, the village beyond. The best rooms have seaward terraces and all are gradually being modernised. We like them all, so light and pretty, and the older ones with sweet hand-painted headboards. Bathrooms are new. Dining is casual or formal and you can expect something good from the kitchen; fish is a speciality and the good wines are fairly priced. A path from the hotel winds down to the beach and there are longer walks around the bay. Young Barbara and Nicholas keep their good humour, even in high season! Their hospitality permeates this exceptional, family-friendly hotel.

Price	€112–€131. Sea view rooms half-board only: €222–€309; suites €280–€362.
Rooms	45: 42 doubles, 3 suites.
Meals	Breakfast €13. Lunch & dinner €26–€40. Wine €15.
Closed	End November to mid-March.
Directions	From Barcelona A-7 north to exit 6 (Girona Norte); signs for La Bisbal via Palamos, then on to Palafrugell; then Calella. Hotel signed. Parking.

Barbara Hallé
Plaça Atlàntic 2,
17210 Calella de Palafrugell, Gerona

Tel	+34 972 614250
Fax	+34 972 614068
Email	info@santroc.com
Web	www.santroc.com

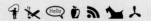

Hostal Sa Rascassa

Pungent pine on the nose and glimpses of rocky shores send you spiralling down to a cove. What immediately strikes you as a really old establishment was in fact built in 1916 by an eccentric millionaire. Forget the unpacking, make a beeline for that special little table and chairs on a pine-needled carpet and gaze out to sea. Scuba divers are in paradise, as are walkers following the spectacular Costa Brava coastline. So unfold the maps on offer and let Oscar 'walk' you through them with his boundless enthusiasm. At the end of the day, it's an easy path up to simple and pretty bedrooms with russet or sea-blue walls and creamy white armchairs. The whole feel of this charming little hotel will win you over, and if you're lucky, the prickly local rock fish, rascana, will make an appearance at dinner. The food is the best of Catalan: rock mussels, sardines, cockles. As light fades, easy music wafts through the bar and beyond; 'chilled' is the word – until the flamenco hits the terrace on a sultry summer night. Peaceful and quiet in low season, the pace hots up in July and August.

Price	€75–€105.
Rooms	5 twins/doubles.
Meals	Lunch & dinner with wine, €35–€40.
Closed	November–February.
Directions	From Begur 3km to Aiguafreda. Straight on at first crossroads towards Aiguafreda & Las Terrasses. Parking 800m ahead & hotel beyond.

Oscar Górriz Bonhora
Cala d'Aiguafreda 3, 17255 Begur,
Gerona

Tel	+34 972 622845
Email	info@hostalsarascassa.com
Web	www.hostalsarascassa.com

Hotel Restaurant Aiguaclara

Back from a shoreline once awash with pirates lies a treasure. Down a chic, cobbled street, behind a time-worn façade, waits a civilised hotel. The moment your feet hit the cool old Catalan floor tiles, you begin to wind down. Keeping faith with the past, there's an old fireplace and many original features – a reflection of the sympathetic nature of the owners. Local coves lend their names to ample bedrooms and up a floor, elegant double doors lead you through to another fine bedroom. The setting is beautiful – from Aiguaclara's grand old terrace of urns, you peer down to the village and up to the crumbling castle. Bathrooms are in simple retro style, not massive but charming, and there's WiFi throughout. You can almost smell the sea from here, and from nearby villages comes today's tantalising catch – given a deliciously modern twist and served up in the colonial restaurant, or under a 100-year-old cherry tree on the walled patio. After dinner, allow yourself a little nightcap from the honesty bar, sink into a deep leather sofa and let the classical music wash over you – or explore the new chill-out zone.

Price	€95–€145. Suites €120–€170.
Rooms	10: 8 doubles, 2 suites.
Meals	Tasting menu €43. Plus VAT at 7%.
Closed	January.
Directions	AP-7 Barcelona-Girona; exit 6 Bisbal/Palafrugel. Begur signed before reaching Palafrugell. Hotel can be seen from square by the church.

Clara Dato & Joan Lluis
St Miguel 2, 17255 Begur, Gerona

Mobile	+34 619 253692
Fax	+34 972 623286
Email	aiguaclara@aiguaclara.com
Web	www.aiguaclara.com

Aigua Blava

It's something of an institution in Cataluña, this large hotel next to the parador of the same name – but, thanks to exceptional management and clever design, manages to feel as intimate and as welcoming as the best B&B. Bedrooms are individually decorated and ranged on several terraced wings that look out across gardens to a delicious hidden cove; breathe in deeply the sweet pinewoods. Run by the same family for four generations, the hotel has a long history of personal attention. Two dynamic young Catalan chefs produce fabulous food and expert waiters advise – enjoy lobster straight from the cove as views sail from immaculate tables to sparkling waters beyond. So many places to unwind; the pub-like bar, the trellised terrace, the parasoled garden, the beach bar just below… or just bask beside the pool; for kids there's a well-equipped playground. Round off the day by dancing the night away in the popular nightclub. The village is one of the prettiest on the rugged Costa Brava and close to the medieval towns of Pals and Palafrugell. Coastal Spain at its best – light-years from Benidorm.

Price	€172–€256. Singles €114–€155. Suites €202–€312. Half- or full-board only in summer. Apts €188–€240 per night.
Rooms	85 + 10: 62 twins/doubles, 2 singles, 21 suites. 10 apartments for 2-6.
Meals	Breakfast €16. Lunch & dinner €39.
Closed	November-February.
Directions	From Gerona C-255 to Palafrugell. From here, GE-650 to Begur. Signed on entry to village.

Josep María de Vehí Falgás
Platja de Fornells, 17255 Begur, Gerona
Tel	+34 972 624562
Fax	+34 972 622112
Email	hotelaiguablava@aiguablava.com
Web	www.aiguablava.com

El Recés de Corçà

Pick this cosy B&B for rustic comfort and owners with infectious smiles. Their home is two old village houses stitched together: past studded cattle doors lies a warren of well-lit staircases and large pleasant rooms. Thick stone walls and flower-filled alcoves keep bedrooms warm and private, while modern lighting and super beds further spoil. As for bathrooms, pure luxury: rugs vie with towels for fluffiness; one shower has a glass-bottomed floor. You'll feel at home sipping tea amid the comfy rugs, sofas and leafy pot plants; you can even have a full English breakfast ferried to your room. Corçà is a tiny medieval cluster of stony houses, huddled roofs and clanging church bells; climb up to the sunny sitting room and terrace for the view. Golfing pros (like Jane) choose the Costa Brava; you can turn to her for lessons and advice on reduced rate green fee packages for local championship courses. Others can explore the coast, Gerona or Barcelona; your hosts can help you with car hire and timetables as well. An English home in the heart of one of the Costa Brava's most delightful villages.

Price	€88–€110. Extra beds €20.
Rooms	4: 3 twins/doubles, 1 family. Extra beds available.
Meals	Restaurants 5-minute walk.
Closed	Never.
Directions	From Gerona C-66 for La Bisbal d'Empordà. At Corçà traffic lights, left into old village; right-hand fork onto c/Major. El Recés 50m on left. Park on road.

Jane Fernley
Carrer Major 31,
17121 Corçà, Gerona

Tel	+34 972 630361
Fax	+34 972 630361
Email	info@elreces.com
Web	www.elreces.com

Mas Pons

Hidden in a tiny hamlet, a solid ivy-covered farmhouse with a delightful family feel. Décor changes with Cinta's caprice, but her urban style shines through: smooth panelled floors, linen-shaded spotlights, flowers in alcoves, bold contemporary art. Warm sun pours through the vast sitting room window while solid pine trunks support a sloping ceiling. Lovers share a limewashed bedroom with a four-poster bed – and a roll top bath on the mezzanine. Another room glows in warm sienna and tea-green, while families have an atmospheric den downstairs. On the romantic terrace is a telescope for stargazing, and a hammock in which to dream. Kids can muck around in the grassy garden amid geese, horses, dogs and Vietnamese pig; tidier pursuits include swimming pool and swings. Crunchy cocoa bread is served at scrumptious breakfasts – on a table that was once a dance floor. No lunches or dinners here, but lots of favourite restaurants to try. The Costa Brava's sandy coves beckon, and you return to fields and trees. Country chic with a hint of theatricality – and a truly charming hostess.

Price	€120. Family €170.
	Extra beds €22 child, €50 adult.
Rooms	3: 1 double, 1 twin, 1 family.
	Extra beds available.
Meals	Restaurants 2km.
Closed	Never.
Directions	From Gerona, C-66 for La Bisbal d'Empordà. Right for Cassa de Peiras/Puból; left at junction for Planils. After 30mph sign in village, road bends to left; right, up dirt track for 100m (unsigned).

Cinta Fernández
Veinat Planils 10,
17121 Corça, Gerona

Tel	+34 972 630755
Email	info@maspons.net
Web	www.maspons.net

Can Massa

This old peasant farmhouse is not swanky but charming. Outside are plants, urns and an old cart, a nod to 50 years ago when Josep's father worked the land. The sound of youngsters is never far off here; the warmth of strong family ties permeates this ramshackle place. The family have recently moved out of the main building to free up two more bedrooms for guests; unobtrusive hosts, they are extremely helpful and kind – walking books, maps, bikes, table tennis, toys: yours to share. Bedrooms are traditional, comfortable, unexceptional and well-priced. 'Chestnut' is the parents' old bedroom and just as it was; 'Blue' has a large terrace with views; 'Green' sports a fine antique bed and a mezzanine for two singles. Bathrooms are simple and small. After a day's walking in the green countryside, return to an *aperitivo* on the covered terrace – or to a winter sofa, log fire and dominoes. The medieval village of Pubol is a marked walk away – famous for Dali's Castillo Gala and gardens. We love the simplicity of this place.
Minimum stay two nights weekends, one week peak season.

Price	€48-€68. Triple €58-€68. Quadruple €68-€88.
Rooms	6: 3 twins/doubles, 1 triple, 2 quadruples.
Meals	Breakfast €6.
Closed	Rarely.
Directions	A-7 exit Gerona Nord; signs for Pálamos. At km15 marker, right to La Pera; house signed just past phone box.

Josep Massa Roura
c/Vell s/n, 17120 La Pera, Gerona

Tel	+34 972 488326
Fax	+34 972 488326
Email	canmassa@canmassa.com

Casa Migdia

The chunky stone-built house was the old village rectory, but there are no sermons now: Sébastien and Marie's quirky décor and easy manner mean you can really put your feet up here. Cosy and cave-like, Casa Migdia is a maze of wonky steps and vaulted ceilings, low doorways, nooks, crannies and cosy corners. Lovely old tiled floors are from Morocco while bright colours and fabrics stand out among reclaimed wooden pieces: a happy, hippy feel. With French owners you can expect gorgeous aromas from the kitchen, so book in for tasty market cooking with a Moroccan or Vietnamese twist. Eclectically furnished and homely bedrooms have free-standing baths in large tiled bathrooms and the occasional shocking colour scheme; ask for 'La Carmen' with its sunny private terrace and hammock. If not, spill out onto the small L-shaped lawn and olive-shaded patio – there's a hammock to swing in there too. Between historic Gerona and Figueras, with the Costa Brava a short drive, this sleepy village is perfect for a stopover or short escape. It's especially good news for families.

Price	€65–€150.
Rooms	5 doubles.
Meals	Dinner €25. Wine from €12. Restaurant 5-minute drive.
Closed	Never.
Directions	From Barcelona, AP-7 exit 5 L'Escala. Right after toll booth; left onto GIV-6234 thro' Viladasens. At junction, left on GI-633 to Sant Jordi Desvalls. In village, left (signed Centro Urb); right (signed Ajuntament). House 30m on left.

Sébastien Preignan
Carrer Migdia 4,
17464 Sant Jordi Desvalls, Gerona
Tel   +34 972 798909
Fax   +34 972 798909
Email   info@casamigdia.com
Web   www.casamigdia.com

Hostal Empúries

You couldn't be closer to the beach. A hundred years ago, this was a snack bar; then a vast Roman necropolis was discovered in L'Escala. Archaeologists flocked and rooms were added. Today, the once-modest Hostal Empuries is a boutique beachside hotel with a shabby-chic style all of its own; the atmosphere is relaxed, cool and contemporary. Don't be put off by the approach down a potholed track; once you're on that terrace overlooking the sands, the view is unforgettable; the bay glitters and you can smell the sea. Inside, fresh flowers stand out against the pale walls and subtle décor; there are dashing floor tiles, generous sofas and chairs dressed in linen, scattered with bright cushions. Bedrooms feel personal and special; sunlight streams in and plain fabrics are brightened with vibrant warm stripes. There's a wood-burning stove in the big sitting room, and the dining room and terrace overlook the beach; listen to the waves lapping the shore. The food is local, unpretentious and extremely good, and Cristina and her smiling young staff make you feel instantly at home. Finest out of season.

Price	€90–€145. Singles €85.50. Suite €100–€155. Half-board extra €33 p.p.
Rooms	38: 27 twins/doubles, 10 family, 1 suite.
Meals	Breakfast €10. Lunch & dinner €33 à la carte.
Closed	Rarely.
Directions	From Gerona AP-7; exit 5 (GI-623) for L'Escala. At L'Escala follow signs for Ruines de Empuries. Hotel on right on beach (follow signs for Platja); private car park.

Cristina Palomer
Platja Portitxol s/n, Apartado Correos 174,
17130 L'Escala, Gerona

Tel	+34 972 770207
Fax	+34 972 982936
Email	info@hostalempuries.com
Web	www.hostalempuries.com

Can Navata

Hospitable Joan (Catalan for John) and Marta worked in the hotel business before they decided to start a new life together in Can Navata. Enter a warren of living areas through a shady porch – cool, arched and colourfully decorated. The upstairs bedrooms are cool and calming, their slate floors topped with rugs and small dark wooden beds; the brighter downstairs rooms are more luxurious (with bigger beds). Bathrooms are functional, and family heirlooms and kitschy touches abound. Dinner is cooked by Joan and served at a long table in the vaulted basement; dishes are delicious and hearty, ingredients are locally sourced, breakfast preserves are homemade and eggs come from the hens in the garden. Families can truly unwind: there's a playroom on the ground floor, and a lovely sunny inner patio. Outside is a garden with pool and swings, upstairs a large sunny terrace. Comfortable sitting and reading rooms provide quiet refuges. Can Navata and its delightful owners, adorable children and enthusiastic dog are as friendly and as Catalan as it's possible to be. Come to walk, cycle, ride.

Price	€75-€88. Half-board €99-€112.
Rooms	6 twins/doubles.
Meals	Dinner, with wine, €13.
Closed	Rarely.
Directions	From Figueres N-II, then C-31 for L'Escala. After 4km, right for Siurana. On right 1km past Siurana.

	Joan & Marta
	Baseia 2, 17469 Siurana d'Empordà, Gerona
Tel	+34 972 525174
Email	turisme@cannavata.com
Web	www.cannavata.com

El Molí

Here is an inviting new farmhouse, a happy home, set among fields of barley and wheat, modelled on the traditional Gerona *mas*. Big bedrooms have rustically tiled floors, wafer-bricked and ochre-washed walls, floaty curtains, king-size beds, super showers and views across the garden to the fields and woods beyond. And there's a beautifully furnished terrace. María and Josep's welcome is warm; simple Spanish farmhouse style food is good value. Vegetables, chicken and beef come straight from the farm – pigs grunt, hens scratch – accompanied by a good local red wine and a *hierbas* infusion to finish. For breakfast there are organic eggs, salamis, tomatoes, watermelon and homemade jams. This would be a great place in which to break the journey travelling north or south, and smiling María, who speaks excellent English, will help you plan your trips. Choose between the Roman ruins at Empuries, the pretty fishing village of Cadaqués, the Dalí Museum at Figueres or the beach at San Pere Pescador, a 20-minute drive.

Price	€80–€85. Suites €90–€95.
Rooms	6: 4 twins/doubles, 2 suites. Extra beds available.
Meals	Dinner with wine €15.
Closed	One week in January.
Directions	AP-7 exit 4 for Figueres on N-II. After 2km, right on 3rd roundabout to Vilamalla; there, signs for Siurana & then hotel.

Ethical Collection: Food.
See page 412.

María Sanchís Pages
Mas Molí, 17469 Siurana d'Empordà, Gerona

Tel	+34 972 525139
Fax	+34 972 525139
Email	casaelmoli@teleline.es
Web	www.elmolidesiurana.com

Mas Falgarona

This helpful, professional couple spent years searching for Mas Falgarona and what a find it is. Built from golden stone, the 11th-century farm is said to be the oldest in the region. The restoration is an uplifting blend of ancient and new: light, modern colours, and a passion for old things. If the interior is bright and sparkling, the cypresses, olives, palms, aquamarine pool and stunning views over the Pla d'Estany are the gilding on the lily. Dominated by beautiful arched ceilings, lounge and dining room have cool, neutral tones; good, plain fabrics blend with old flagstones and terracotta tiles. Bedrooms and bathrooms are exquisite, their walls dotted with photographs taken by an artist son. There is a small, chic and cosy bar; in summer you eat under the stars. The a la carte menu, based on aromatic herbs and olive oil, is inventive and Mediterranean; vegetarians, too, are looked after. Wines are delicious, some local. From the moment you pull up in the immaculate courtyard you'll feel seriously pampered. Golf, horse riding and bike hire are close by – if you can bear to tear yourself away. *A Rusticae hotel.*

Price	€180–€198. Suites €250–€335.
Rooms	11: 5 twins/doubles, 6 suites.
Meals	Dinner with wine, €29–€58. Restaurant closed Monday & Tuesday.
Closed	January.
Directions	From Figueres N-260 for Besalú & Olot. After 5km, right to Avinyonet; signed on left 1km past village. Parking.

Severino Jallas & Brigitta Schmidt
17742 Avinyonet de Puigventós, Gerona

Tel	+34 972 546628
Fax	+34 972 547071
Email	email@masfalgarona.com
Web	www.masfalgarona.com

Hotel Torre Laurentii

Through the ancient iron gateway of a sweet medieval town lies a haven of cool sophistication – and a delightful family. Rebuilt from a 1600s ruin, the old farmhouse gleams with new life and laughter while flaunting its past: one suite sits in the town's defence tower. In the sunny inner courtyard, water tinkles in a mosaic fountain while inside, soft shapes, alcoves and gently vaulted ceilings harbour peace. Rooms run off a terrace overlooking the neat lawn, perfect for tea and chiming church bells. Stephan (from Miami) knows exactly which buttons to press in terms of comfort: huge sofas, a modern lift, gorgeous bathrooms with every trimming, acres of space in the contemporary suites. Tasty gourmet meals are cooked up by Cristina in the swish, cool restaurant, atmospheric with its marble floors and arched stone walls; the olive oil comes from her parents' organic farm. Hiking trails cross the Pyrenees and link sleepy Catalan villages, and historic Figueras and Gerona are a short drive away. Come for a fabulous blend of authentic Spanishness and stylish living. *A Rusticae hotel.*

Price	€125–€260. Singles €83–€110. Suites €175–€235.
Rooms	7: 2 doubles/twins, 1 single, 4 suites.
Meals	Half-board extra €25 p.p. Lunch & dinner with wine, €30–€35.
Closed	January to first weekend in March.
Directions	From Figueras, N-11 for La Jonquera. After 15km, GIP-5107 to Llers; GI-510 to Terrades; then GI-511 to Sant Llorenç de la Muga. Hotel signed in village.

Cristina Múrio
Plaza Paula Armet 2,
17732 Sant Llorenç de la Muga, Gerona

Tel	+34 972 569350
Fax	+34 972 193564
Email	info@torrelaurentii.com
Web	www.torrelaurentii.com

Mas Salvanera

In a blissfully quiet corner of the wooded Pyrenean foothills this solid, semi-fortified farmhouse has been transformed into a small luxury hotel. Beneath high old darkening beams are colourful fabrics and antiques, many of which Ramón has restored himself: furniture which has stood the test of time and will stand it for many more; It's a place where Spanish nobility of centuries ago would feel at home. The guest bedrooms are named after signs of the zodiac and are large and elegant. Bathrooms are generous and lovely. The main building has open hearths, exposed stone, an authentic country feel and delightful Ramón makes sure that guests have quiet corners to escape to with a book. The dining room, where local artists exhibit their work, is in the old cowshed and spills out onto the sunny poolside terrace. Everyone eats at the same time and food is fresh and seasonal, generally Catalan in style, with local game and meat featuring heavily. Outside, a peaceful walled garden and a big sculpted pool beneath the olive trees. Culture is within easy reach: the Dali museum at Figueres, and Besalu and Olot.

Price	€125. Half-board €179.
Rooms	9 twins/doubles.
Meals	Dinner €27. No meals July-Sept. Restaurant in Beuda, 1.5km.
Closed	Never.
Directions	Barcelona AP-7 Gerona. Exit 6 Gerona Norte; C-66 to Banyoles & Besalú. Right on N-260 Figueres; left for Maià de Montcal. Follow signs to Beuda; 1.6km to hotel.

Ramón Ruscalleda & Ana Degollada
17850 Beuda, Gerona

Tel	+34 972 590975
Fax	+34 972 590863
Email	salvanera@salvanera.com
Web	www.salvanera.com

Mas el Guitart

Toni and Lali are young, friendly hosts; they left creative careers to restore this old dairy farm. Thanks to their hard work and good taste they have succeeded in creating one of Cataluña's very best *casas rurales*. We loved the luxurious brand new spa and the honeymoon suite above; rooms in the main house are each decorated in a different colour with Lali's stencilled beds to match; there are wooden floors and old rafters, window shutters and washstands, little rugs, decent bathrooms, good views. The two sitting rooms are decorated in a similar vein. No meals, but two fully-equipped kitchens and a washing machine are available. Gaze on the gorgeous green pastures from the hammock, drift off by the safely fenced pool, explore the surrounding mountains. Delightful Toni knows everything: restaurants, walks, history, and is an experienced therapist – why not book a treatment? Swings, slides and a mini football pitch in the garden, cows, kittens, ducks and hens – it's heaven for families. A gastronome's paradise, too: a trio of Michelin starred restaurants are within driving distance. *Minimum stay two nights.*

Price	€57.50 (min. 2 nights). Suite €170. Apartments €110. All prices per night.
Rooms	5 + 2: 4 twins/doubles, 1 suite. 2 apartments for 4. Extra beds.
Meals	Restaurant 2km. Guest kitchens.
Closed	Rarely.
Directions	From Gerona, C-66 to Besalú. On to Castellfollit de la Roca. Here, signs for Camprodón on C-26. Follow signs La Vall de Bianya; left after traffic lights in L'Hostalnou de Bianya; signed.

Lali Nogareda Burch
& Antoni Herrero Perez
Santa Margarida de Bianya,
17813 La Vall de Bianya, Gerona

Tel	+34 972 292140
Email	guitart@guitartrural.com
Web	www.guitartrural.com

Rectoria de la Miana

Not for those looking for luxury – but poets, romantics and history buffs will love it. In the middle of a vast stand of beech and oak, at the end of three miles of rough, winding track, a former rectory in a fabulous setting. History is ever present: in the eighth century there was a fortified manor; in the 1200s a monastery was built, complete with escape tunnel and chapel. It took courage and vision for Frans to embark on the restoration – and from the ruins has emerged an unusual and simple hostelry. Flagged floors and undressed walls have been left intact; old sepia photographs are touching in their directness (a group of locals marvelling at the first radio to arrive at La Miana). Spartan bedrooms, some with bunk beds, vary in shape and size; all have high ceilings, stone walls and floors, and one, a terrace with views. Shower rooms are tiny. The food is regional/international and innovative, served in a vaulted dining room with century-old pews. Watch the sunset from the sitting room terrace, drink in the history and the peace. Best visited in summer – unless you are decidedly hardy!

Price	Half-board €90. Under 8s half-price.
Rooms	8: 5 twins/doubles, 3 family rooms, half sharing showers.
Meals	Half-board only (wine included). Picnic-style lunch €10.
Closed	Rarely.
Directions	Figueres N-260 to Besalú & Sant Jaume de Llierca. Left into village, 2nd left into c/Industria. 6km track to house following signs. Just past Can Jou farmhouse.

Frans Engelhard & Adriana Westerlaken
17854 Sant Jaume de Llierca, Gerona

Tel	+34 972 190190
Email	rectoriadelamiana@yahoo.es
Web	www.lamiana.com

Can Jou

You won't forget your arrival at Can Jou: as you drive up the three-mile track – an adventure in itself – you feel you are leaving the world behind. Round the final bend you catch sight of the farm, high on a hill, overlooking miles of forest of oak and beech – what a spectacular location. No wonder Mick and Rosa were inspired to revive this old place in search of the good life for themselves and now grown-up family. The 15 bedrooms are basic with a mix of old and new and lively colour schemes; six come with balconies. It's a favourite with riders and hikers and a great place for a family holiday: the horses are ideal for beginners, with marked forest bridleways, and children will enjoy scrambling up the rocky path to the little spring-filled pool. Take advantage of the treatments Rosi has to offer, from massage and shiatsu to sacro-cranial osteopathy. Watch the sun go down and shoot the breeze while you enjoy a drink from the honesty bar. Rosi's twin sister Libe prepares wholesome hearty food and dinners are friendly affairs around one vast table. Recommended for those looking for nature without luxury.

Price	€88. Half-board €62 p.p. Full-board €75 p.p. Half-price for under 8s. Plus VAT at 7%.
Rooms	15 twins/doubles.
Meals	Lunch & dinner, with wine, available.
Closed	Rarely.
Directions	From Figueres, N-260 to Besalú & Sant Jaume de Llierca. Left into village; 2nd left into c/Industria. 6km track to house; signed.

Rosi Linares & Mick Peters
La Miana,
17854 Sant Jaume de Llierca, Gerona
Tel   +34 972 190263
Fax   +34 972 190110
Email   canjou@canjou.com
Web   www.canjou.com

San Bartomeo de Torres

It's easy to settle into a lush Catalunyan foothill of the Pyrenees, easier still in a 13th-century Benedictine priory. Views of La Garrotxa's volcanic hills are best considered from the courtyard or during a patio breakfast by the peaceful pool. The original fortified *masia* was bequeathed to Guillem de Torres in 1212 after a successful bash in the Holy Land, where one of the spoils was a thorn plucked from Christ's crown. Steve tells how he covets it for his party trick, but it's Bea who puts on the real show with her sleight of interior design, creating an open-plan marvel of kitchen and living space. Whether you B&B (September to May only) or self-cater, you will be delighted by sculptures, couches, rugs, Steve's photography on the walls, a snooker table... all warmly framed between terracotta and wooden beams. Each mezzanine bedroom has its distinguishing features: an African statue here, an Indian wardrobe there, pewter lamps, a stone bath, graceful mosquito nets. The hardest thing to do is hand back the keys. *B&B September to May only (minimum stay two nights).*

Price	€120 (min. 2 nights). Whole house (sleeps 12) €4,800–€8,000 per week.
Rooms	2: 1 double, 1 twin. House available for self-catering.
Meals	Restaurant 5-minute drive. Chef available for self-caterers.
Closed	June–August for B&B.
Directions	Directions on booking.

Bea & Steve Garforth
17833 Fontcoberta, Gerona

Tel	+34 972 576264
Email	info@sanbartomeo.com
Web	www.sanbartomeo.com

La Pedra Remença

Nature and tranquillity bless this fairytale cottage, a new-build of superb quality and eco-friendly design. Inside, hand-glazed brick floors, sloping beams and old wooden furniture beautifully restored by Natalia create an air of rustic authenticity. As for the fittings, they're modern and faultless, the leather armchairs exude style, the compact kitchen blends in seamlessly and the home entertainment fights for attention with the views. Two cosy, classic bedrooms share a shower room with a stunning carved stone sink replete with fossils – surely the most historic basin in this book! Food tastes wonderful in the open air – savour it and the views from the sweet dining terrace overlooking the valley. And when you've polished off the contents of the hamper, stock up on produce from the farmers' cooperative. In the lush natural garden the lovely salt water pool is a godsend on a hot day; underwater lighting may tempt you to swim under the stars. Easy walks and bike trails link pretty villages, the Costa Brava's unspoilt beaches beckon and lovely, generous Natalia lives up the road. *Minimum stay two to seven nights.*

Price	€900–€1,350 per week.
Rooms	House for 4 (2 twins/doubles).
Meals	Restaurants 2km.
Closed	Never.
Directions	From Gerona, GI-531 thro' St Gregori & Sant Martí de Llémena. On to km22.5 marker; right to Les Carreres. On for 1km; iron gates to house on left.

Natalia Guillamet Casas
Les Carreres 7,
17154 Sant Esteve de Llémena, Gerona

Tel	+34 972 449899
Email	nguillamet@yahoo.es
Web	www.pedraremensa.com

Cal Pastor

Ramón and Josefina are gentle, friendly folk whose families have farmed this valley for generations. Bedrooms are simple, not cosy but spotless, with tiled floors, modest Spanish fabrics and comfortable beds: those in the attic have a warmer feel and bigger windows. Fling open the wooden shutters in the morning and the sunny valley bursts into the room. The dining room is slightly soulless but summer meals are taken on the terrace with the valley spread out below; there's eggs and bacon at breakfast – just ask – and Josefina's dinners are hearty and delicious; don't miss her *croquetas*. She's happy to cook vegetarian dinners too, with veg from the garden, and there's a little restaurant you could also visit next door. The trans-Pyrenean, Mediterranean-to-Atlantic footpath runs right by the house and you may feel inspired to do part of it, or go trout fishing in the hills. This is a good place to come back to – unpretentious, authentic, peaceful – and the hamlet is delightful and friendly. Be sure to visit the Museo del Pastor – a testimony to the work of four generations of Ramón's farming family.

Price	€48-€60.
Rooms	6: 3 twins/doubles, 3 triples.
Meals	Breakfast €8. Dinner €14.
Closed	Rarely.
Directions	From Vic, C-17 then N-260 to Ribes de Freser. On to Planoles; at km144 marker, left down to Fornells; house opposite junction.

Josefina Soy Sala
c/Palos 1,
17536 Fornells de la Muntanya-Toses,
Gerona

Tel	+34 972 736163
Fax	+34 972 736008
Email	apartrural@hotmail.com

Entry 123   Map 7

Can Borrell

This rambling old Pyrenean farmhouse of granite and slate is set high up in the tiniest of tightly clustered mountain villages, with meadows to the front and conifer-clad mountains behind. Wood is all about, while slate floors mirror the building's exterior. Dyanmic and welcoming Laura is at the helm and it still retains a real family feel; it is not over-prettified but has a delightful intimacy. And there are board games for families and paintings on the walls. There's a stunning new modern suite and bedrooms in the main house are inviting with polished floors, fabulous views and excellent beds. They vary in size, following the idiosyncrasies of an old house, and are simple and characterful; family rooms are split level, suitable for older children. The restaurant is a real local institution; you can expect an eclectic mix of Catalan and French dishes and families come for special celebrations. Uniformed waiting staff add an incongruous note for such an off-the-beaten-track sort of place. There are waymarked walks to neighbouring hamlets and cycle trails aplenty.

Price	€73–€145. Singles €61–€67.
Rooms	9: 6 twins/doubles, 3 family.
Meals	Lunch & dinner €24. À la carte from €33. Wine €7–€125.
Closed	Weds in November; Tues/Weds December to April (open daily Easter).
Directions	From Barcelona, A-18; C-1411 to Berga. Through Tunel del Cadí, then dir. Andorra. After 5km, right for Puigcerdá on N-260; left at Ger to Meranges. Signed in village.

Laura Forn Solé
c/Retorn 3, 17539 Meranges, Gerona

Tel	+34 972 880033
Fax	+34 972 880144
Email	info@canborrell.com
Web	www.canborrell.com

Casa Guilla

A matchless position, a magical place. As you climb ever higher to the hamlet perched on a rocky crag – an astonishing drive – you can only marvel at the tenacity of Santa Engracia's earliest inhabitants. Richard and Sandra Loder, who have a head for heights, fearlessly restored the old buildings two decades ago. A fortified Catalan farmhouse, parts of which go back 1,000 years, the labyrinthine dwelling twists and turns on multi levels... all feels deliciously organic. There's a large sitting room with an open hearth, a library on the mezzanine and bedrooms that are plainly but comfortably furnished: terracotta tiles, heavy beams, low ceilings, en suite showers. Tuck into big breakfasts with home-baked bread and four-course dinners – hospitable feasts at a big table. Outside, two beautiful terraces, one big (with pool), one small, both with those incomparable views. Geologists, lepidopterists, ornithologists and botanists will be in their element, as will anyone seeking stunning seclusion in a fascinating part of Cataluña. A large but waggy dog is part of the family too.

Price	Half-board €148. Singles €74.
Rooms	4: 2 twins/doubles, 2 family.
Meals	Half-board only (wine included). Packed lunch €7.50.
Closed	November-February.
Directions	From Tremp, C-13 direction Pobla de Segur for 1.5km, then left to Santa Engracia. 10km to village; left then right down to end of rough track (signed).

Richard & Sandra Loder
Santa Engracia, Apartado 83,
25620 Tremp, Lérida

Tel	+34 973 252080
Email	info@casaguilla.com
Web	www.casaguilla.com

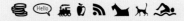

Entry 125   Map 7

Casa Pete y Lou

Crystal clear air, snug farmhouse, heady views – Pete and Lou serve up an intoxicating mix at their home high in the foothills of the Pyrenees. Every day a tough decision: trekking, rock climbing, whitewater rafting, horse riding or swimming in cascade ponds? Pete will help you, with maps and routes, transport and his own good company. But there's nothing to stop you staying put, enjoying the breathtaking views and the carpets of poppies, spotting a griffon vulture or short-toed eagle. The stone-built house, surrounded by relaxing gardens and terrace, is warmly rustic inside and full of Lou's imaginative decorative touches (she's a TV set designer). The simple bedrooms have beamed ceilings, rugs on wooden floors and extra heavy blankets; the shower is shared. In the bright kitchen it's all too easy to linger over one of Lou's wholesome suppers; tuck into home-grown seasonal organic veg, and homemade bread and jams at breakfast. Warm, friendly, laid-back and ultra-green, Pete and Lou make you feel at home the moment you arrive. *Minimum stay two nights.*

Price	€50.
Rooms	3: 2 doubles, 1 twin, all sharing bathroom.
Meals	Dinner €12-€15. Packed lunch available.
Closed	December-February.
Directions	A-2 Barcelona-Lleida (Lérida) to Tarrega:C-14 to Agramunt: on to Artesa de Segre: L-512 for Tremp: at Col de Comiols, left for San Salvador; after 6km, past bridge over river, left track for 1km. Signed Tolo then Casa P&L.

Peter Dale & Lou Beaumont
Toló, San Salvador de Toló, 25638
Tremp, Lérida

Tel	+34 973 252309
Fax	+34 973 252309
Email	lou@casapeteylou.com
Web	www.casapeteylou.com

Can Boix de Peramola

Ten generations of the Pallarés family have lived and worked at Can Boix; three of them have turned this seductively sited hotel into something of an institution. It is well-loved and well-run, with a distinct buzz. The restaurant is busy, fun and popular with Spanish families, and the menus are a celebration of what is locally grown or raised. The food is brilliant, the presentation superb, the wine list long and the accompanying views are fabulous. As for the bedrooms, they're big, immaculate and awash with modern comfort: air conditioning, DVDs, snowy towels and jacuzzis. Those in the main building have a small balcony or terrace, those in the annexe a large terrace overlooking gardens, plus direct access to the sauna and solarium. There's an ornamental garden by the swimming pool, which is lovely and large and surrounded by views; the ridge that towers above is typical of the sublime scenery of the Pyrenees. The décor may not be the most original but this is an immensely friendly place and confidently caters for all: business travellers, outdoorsy people, families. *A Rusticae hotel.*

Price	€103.50–€144. Singles €82.50–€115.20. Half-board €86.75–€150.20 p.p.
Rooms	41 twins/doubles.
Meals	Breakfast €12. Lunch & dinner €23. À la carte €60–€70.
Closed	2 weeks Nov/Dec; 4 weeks Jan/Feb.
Directions	Barcelona-Lleida (Lérida) on A-2. Exit Cervera & on through Cervera to Ponts; there, right on C-14 to Oliana. 3km after bridge, left to Peramola. 4km to hotel.

Joan Pallarès & Teresa Alba
Can Boix s/n, 25790 Peramola, Lérida

Tel	+34 973 470266
Fax	+34 973 470281
Email	hotel@canboix.cat
Web	www.canboix.cat

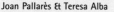

Can Cuadros

Arriving in the dreamy silence of siesta time, you'd never imagine the hamlet of Palouet could contain such a remarkable place as Can Cuadros. The labyrinthine 900-year-old castle is more museum than hotel, each room a step back in time. Young, English speaking, Catalan owners Roger and Isabel are seeking to relive the traditions of this corner of Cataluña and not even the shower rooms escape the hand of history – each has beams and antique fittings – while bedrooms, darkish yet appealing and mercifully cool in summer, have fine old beds, good mattresses, interesting curios and drawings. Ancient stone walls and uneven stone steps, no air con, no TV... no luxurious comforts but the place is soaked in character. There's a living room of antique armchairs, books and unusual CDs (flamenco, old blues, ragtime) and a dining room in the cellar (once a prison!) with a wine press for a fireplace, illuminated at night. For summer suppers there's a patio; Roger's in charge in the kitchen and what they offer is outstanding: peach jams at breakfast, local game in winter, black pasta, organic Catalan wines. Amazing.

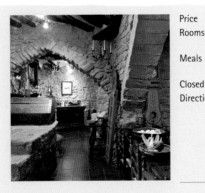

Price	€75. Singles €50. Family €80.
Rooms	7: 6 twins/doubles, 1 family, with separate shower rooms.
Meals	Breakfast €5.50. Lunch & dinner €24. Wine from €15.
Closed	Rarely.
Directions	From Barcelona N-II to Cervera. Here, right to Guissona; right to Massoteres; follow signs to Palouet.

Roger Puiggròs & Isabel Navascués
c/Major 3, 25211 Palouet-Massoteres, Lérida

Tel   +34 973 294106
Email   info@cancuadros.com
Web   www.cancuadros.com

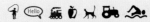

Hotel Rural Cal Rotés

Down a narrow street in colourful Linyola is a sweet 1750s townhouse and welcoming small hotel. Fine original features remain – an olive oil tank, a glazed-over sunken well, rustic ornaments and studded wooden doors. Abundant light, space and comfort combine with charming manager Maite and her staff's personal service to make you feel at home. Bedrooms are cosy with modern fittings and a nod to tradition; bathrooms blend lovely patterned tiling and marble sinks with super showers and fluffy robes. Snuggle round the fire in the restful sitting room, or lounge on the sunny rooftop terrace overlooking Linyola's jumbled rooftops; peacefulness surrounds you. Hidden in the wine cellar is a wood-decked swimming pool with jacuzzi and spa for massages and treatments. Behind beautiful modernist doors lie a sociable dining room and an open kitchen where you can watch the cooks rustle up tasty home-style meals. Come for bird-watching, horse riding, pitch and putt, local bodegas for wine tasting and meals, and Lérida, 25 minutes away. A delicate blend of quaint rusticity and modern comfort is Cal Rotés' winning recipe.

Price	€150.
Rooms	6: 4 doubles, 2 twins. Extra beds.
Meals	Lunch & dinner with wine, €25-€35, on request. VAT 7%.
Closed	Never.
Directions	A-2 Barcelona-Lleida (Lérida), exit 487 to Linyola. After 8km, exit Linyola Sud at r'bout. Continue into town; white signs to hotel. Park in street.

	Maite Macián
	c/Isabel II 19, 25240 Linyola, Lérida
Tel	+34 933 637660
Fax	+34 933 637666
Email	reserves@calrotes.cat
Web	www.calrotes.cat

Hotel Rural Les Vinyes

Josep has transformed a former roadside hostel into a hotel of imagination and personality. A quirky candelabra light is the first of many surprises, while each delicious-smelling bedroom is unique, with colourwashed walls inspired by the name: reds and greens for La Vinya, warm yellows for El Sol… Handmade soft furnishings and lampshades have been added, prettily painted antique furniture and ethnic touches, making each room very special. Bathrooms are brilliant, with marble basins and powerful showers; the high standards carry through to the elegant but comfortable dining and sitting rooms. Pamper yourself in the stunning new Wellness Centre, or cosy up in the rustically raftered and romantic new suite: big waterbed on the mezzanine; wood-burner, candlelight and dining corner below. Make the most of the all-Spanish dishes, and the wines: such tiny vintages that each bottle is numbered. Although on a main road, you're in the heart of a small wine-making community and vineyards surround you. If you want to explore or go riding, all will be arranged by your very friendly hosts. *No children.*

Price	€130–€150. Suites €180–€220. Plus VAT at 7%.
Rooms	8: 4 twins/doubles, 4 suites.
Meals	Dinner €35 à la carte. Wine €9–€34.
Closed	Rarely.
Directions	AP-2, exit 11 onto C-51 to Vendrell. After 2km, in hamlet on left.

Josep Ruiz Camps
c/Vilardida 13,
43812 Vilardida-Montferri, Tarragona

Tel	+34 977 639193
Fax	+34 977 639193
Email	info@lesvinyes.com
Web	www.lesvinyes.com

Cal Mateu

Staying at Cal Mateu is like rediscovering a long lost relative; guests have been known to shed tears when they take their leave! Carmen and her delightful daughters-in-law Montse and Merce have created a warm and happy home in the remote little medieval village of La Bisbal de Falset. Cal Mateu is of more recent construction but has the spirit of an older building. Its sitting room, dining room and kitchen are cosily rustic, spotlessly clean; two more sitting rooms are on the upper floors and the little bedrooms take their decorative cue from the rest of the house: rough plaster walls, simple iron and wooden beds, red- and mint-checked fabrics. Basic bathrooms (shared) have showers or sit-up-and-beg baths. The downstairs sitting room and four of the bedrooms have splendid views of the Montsant, a region known for its canyons and dry-stone terraces. The whole house breathes an air of unaffected charm, and meals are tasty and wholesome. The sleepy village produces prize-winning olive oil – take some home. Extraordinarily good value and the most *simpática* of hostesses. *Self-catering option.*

Price	€35. Singles €25.
Rooms	6: 4 twins/doubles, 2 family, all sharing bathrooms.
Meals	Breakfast €6. Lunch & dinner with wine, €15.
Closed	Rarely.
Directions	From Reus N-420 to Falset; there, right on T-710 to Gratallops then La Vilella Baixa. On via Cabaces to La Bisbal de Falset. House on right at dead end of main street, past church.

Merce Rubio Navarro
& Montse Gil Calabera
c/Mayor 27,
43372 La Bisbal de Falset, Tarragona

Tel	+34 977 819003
Email	casapagesmateu@terra.es
Web	www.calmateu.es

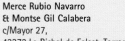

Venta de San Juan

Wonderful – not the sort of place you are likely to chance upon in this vast Spanish countryside. But if you begin your search in Batea you will be in benign mood, for it is a beautiful little town. There is a long rocky track up to the solid old house, deserted among the fields and woods, but full of life thanks to Jorge and Clotilde. They inherited it from a grandfather who made his fortune in Cuba but returned home after Independence… if you love dusty, faded old houses you'll love it here. The entrance is full of colourful clutter, flagstone-floored with doors leading into ancient rooms still dressed in flock wallpaper, just as they were when first sparked into life. Some might focus on the scarce electricity and poor showers; others will love the authenticity. The food especially makes the trip worthwhile and much of the produce (olives, almonds, vines) comes from the farm. Jorge and Clotilde are young and charming; they live in Barcelona but love nothing more than to welcome guests – and often friends – to this chaotic old house. *Advanced booking required (fax best). Minimum stay two nights. No cheques, cash only.*

Price	€48. Singles €40. Apartment €90 per night, €500 per week.
Rooms	4 + 1: 3 twins/doubles sharing bath. 1 apartment for 4.
Meals	Breakfast €4. Dinner with wine, €12.
Closed	December-Easter.
Directions	Barcelona-Valencia on AP-7, exit 38 onto C-44 to Móra, N-420 dir. Alcañiz. After Gandesa, right on C-221 to Batea, P-723 dir. Nonaspe. At km7.3 marker, 50m before boundary sign for Zaragoza, left on unsigned track. Through vineyards for 2km, bearing left.

Clotilde de Pascual
Ctra. P-723 Batea-Nonaspe km7.3,
43786 Batea, Tarragona

Mobile	+34 649 644724
Fax	+34 934 143854
Email	clotildepasqual@hotmail.com
Web	www.ventadesanjuan.es

Casa Pio

Against a backdrop of craggy mountains and olive fields is this sweet and eco-friendly stone farmhouse. Home improvement experts from their barge life in Bristol, Philippa and Iain have done it all magnificently, using reclaimed wood and lots of imagination. The cosy little apartment hugs the house, its sunny courtyard entrance flanked by shuttered windows. Don't expect five-star comforts, just a kitchen/living room simply painted in white and shades of blue, lovely snug bedrooms to one side, a sofabed for kids and a shower room that sparkles. Riches are found here on a simple scale: pickings from the organic kitchen garden, the star of the show – just pay when you leave – and fresh eggs from the hens. Dog and cats doze, chickens roam, sun and wind provide the energy, a swimming pool asks for a splash in the sun. Wild flowers pepper the grounds, olive trees are harvested for oil. It's fun, simple, wholesome, homespun – life lived happily in the slow lane. Walk in the mountains, fish on the Ebro, visit nearby beaches; Tarragona's Roman ruins are under an hour's drive. Lovely. *Minimum stay two nights.*

Price	€50–€60 (€250–€650 per week).
Rooms	Apartment for 2-6.
Meals	Dinner €25, by arrangement (Fri/Sat only).
Closed	Rarely.
Directions	From Barcelona C32 & A-7 Tarragona/Reus. junc. 39 then N340 El Perello. Right onto TV3022. At km12.5 marker; left onto track. House 200m on right.

	Philippa Bungard
	Polygon 13, Parcela 46-47,
	43513 Rasquera, Tarragona
Tel	+34 977 265208
Email	philbungard@yahoo.co.uk

Ethical Collection: Environment; Food. See page 412.

Tancat de Codorníu

Families will love this young, laid-back, fuss-free hotel, with its pretty rural backdrop and its proximity to the Delta d'Ebra – full of bird life, paddy fields and wide, empty, sandy beaches. At the end of an impressive palm-lined driveway, past a hidden crazy-golf course, you arrive at the vast, lovely, 150-year-old castle-style house – fantastically revamped by a Barcelona architect. Run by María, the hotel feels fresh, quirky and fun. There is a huge swimming pool, and another for children, and the garden backs on to working farmland – source of organic fruit and vegetables for the restaurant. If you step out to dine you'll find seafood restaurants nearby, serving fish straight from the Delta. The hotel's bedrooms announce the best of new, from walk-in hydromassage showers with wooden decking to designer products and robes, striking contemporary art and metal-wired spotlights illuminating walls. Some bedrooms have private saunas, jacuzzis and terraces with views over the sea. There's also a comfortably rustic living room, and a big summer house for celebrations. *A Rusticae hotel.*

Price	€120-€200. Suites €200-€350.
Rooms	15: 12 twins/doubles, 3 suites.
Meals	Breakfast €9-€12. Lunch & dinner €38.
Closed	November.
Directions	A-7 exit 41 towards Les Cases d'Alcanar. Right at port; hotel signed.

María Llasera Ramos
Ctra. 340 km1059,
43530 Les Cases d'Alcanar, Tarragona

Tel	+34 977 737194
Fax	+34 977 737231
Email	info@tancatdecodorniu.com
Web	www.tancatdecodorniu.com

La Pastorella

Light, space and airiness, inside and out. High up, on a corkscrew mountain road, this smart Finnish-pine chalet gazes out on Andorra's lofty peaks, while charming La Massana snuggles in the valley below. Ground floor, games room and garden are all yours, simple, practical and spotless with a touch of luxury: Villeroy & Boch china, a hot tub under the stars. Bedrooms take the mountains as their theme – 'Skier' has wooden skis, 'Fisher' has Mark's dad's ancient rod and net. All share sumptuous beds and unbroken views over pristine forested mountains. Cook for yourself in the small modern kitchen, barbecue on the sunny slate-floored terrace, or fill up on hearty meals in nearby restaurants – vital fuel for tackling the peaks and the parks. Multilingual, worldly and gentle, Mark, who lives upstairs, is a qualified mountain guide and sub-directs a ski school nearby; he will happily book you tours, lessons, adventures… and steer you towards the prettiest mountain flowers. The chalet is cosy and warm, airy and light. *Daily cleaning included.*

Price	€720–€1,180 per week.
Rooms	Chalet for 2–6.
Meals	Restaurants 10-minute drive.
Closed	Never.
Directions	From Andorra la Vella, signs for La Massana thro' Escaldes-Engordany. At r'bout, right to Anyos. 100m past church, right (unsigned); follow for 2km, keeping right.

Mark Crichton
Ctra Els Cortals d'Anyos,
AD400 Anyós, La Massana

Tel	+376 835603
Email	la-pastorella@la-pastorella.com
Web	www.la-pastorella.com

Ethical Collection: Environment.
See page 412.

Entry 135   Map 7

Castile and León

Posada del Marqués

Never mind the ordinariness of the town, there are few places to stay in Spain as special as this pilgrim's hostel. Pass through the fine portal to a pebbled cloister and exquisite gardens with a gurgling canal, a big old yew and walnut trees: not unlike an English rectory garden, with its high walls, hedges and rambling roses. Come for kind and erudite hosts and the most peaceful and beguiling of settings. Sober and charming bedrooms are set around a gallery on the first floor and are filled with family heirlooms: stunning Portuguese canopied beds, seductive oil paintings, tapestries and walnut dressers. History abounds. One room has a terrace over the cloisters for summer, there are big old radiators to tackle the winter months, and marble bathrooms are generously sized. The sitting and games rooms downstairs are similarly furnished – antique Castillian doors, carved chests, comfy armchairs and an English sofa in front of the hearth; the snooker table doubles up for ping-pong. Next door is a Cistercian nunnery and daily Gregorian chanting at 9am – don't miss it. A wonderful place. *Balloon flights available.*

Price	€76–€102.
Rooms	11 twins/doubles.
Meals	Restaurants in town.
Closed	10 November-15 March.
Directions	AP-71 (León-Astorga) exit 23 to Hospital de Orbigo; cross old N-120 for La Madalena on LE-420; Carrizo de la Ribera on km16 marker. In Carrizo, past playground on right,1st left, follow monastery wall to Plaza Mayor; left thro' arch.

Carlos Velázquez-Duro
Plaza Mayor 4, 24270
Carrizo de la Ribera, León

Tel	+34 987 357171
Fax	+34 987 358101
Email	info@posadadelmarques.com
Web	www.posadadelmarques.com

El Caminero

On the pilgrims' route to Santiago, there's jousting in June – in front of the amazing 13th-century bridge. The house, built 200 years ago to store tobacco, has undergone a complete restoration. Floors, doors and windows are mostly new but the old well remains – now a wine-cooler! – and the bread oven still works a treat. The food – wholesome dishes from Leon province spiced up with contemporary ideas – is excellent value: chickpeas with wild mushrooms, fresh tuna rolls, a delectable curd pudding, 'tocino de cielo'. Around a central colonnaded patio five peaceful bedrooms lie, some up, some down, each furnished with an illustrated travel guide to the Orbigo region. The rooms are simple and rustic but comfortable and homely. A charming antique wardrobe, a fine wrought-iron bedstead, a quirky settle for a child, all set off by white plaster walls and colourful patchwork. In reception is a tempting display of local chocolate and wines – a nice touch; the owners, with degrees in tourism, are eager to please. There are two stunning cathedrals within a short drive, at Leon and at Astorga.

Price	€60. Suite €70-€80. Singles €45.
Rooms	5: 4 twins/doubles, 1 suite for 3.
Meals	Lunch & dinner €15.
Closed	15-28 February.
Directions	From Madrid A-6, dir. Coruña, exit in La Bañeza. LE-420, dir. La Magdalena exit at km17 marker. From Leon N-120 exit for Hospital de Orbigo at km336 marker.

Carmen Fernández Turienzo
C/Sierra Pambley, 56,
24286 Hospital de Orbigo, León
Tel   +34 987 389020
Email   info@elcaminero.es
Web   www.elcaminero.es

Camarga

Your chance to discover this unjustily overlooked corner of Spain, where once the enigmatic Maragatos thrived. Over a century ago they developed an idiosyncratic culture of Christian rites with a pagan twist. Marga, your bilingual host, restored this 1890 house following the Maragato architectural style: dry stone walls, terracotta brickwork, traditional colours of mustard yellow, burnt sienna and cobalt blue 'añil'. Walk through the vaulted wooden doors into the cool courtyard, full of birdsong, where wicker furniture invites you to rest after a day of discovery in Castilla. Rooms, overlooking the courtyard, have refined touches: embroidered bedspreads, English linen, lace curtains made by Marga's mother. Impressive rusticity survives in the living areas – impossibly large flagstones and dignified old beams. The restaurant still has its bread oven; robust chains from the ceiling support its structure. You'll relish Marga's cooking, which blends local specialities and produce with a modern creative touch. If you have a sweet tooth, don't miss Astorga's chocolate museum and the many sweet shops in town.

Price	€70. Singles €59.
Rooms	9 twins/doubles.
Meals	Breakfast €3.50–€7.50. Lunch & dinner €19. Wine €7.50–€20.
Closed	8–31 January.
Directions	Madrid A-6 for Coruña; exit 326 signed Morales de Arcediano. Padt Morales; at km9 marker there is church. Street 4th on left.

Margarita Quintana Boza
c/La Ermita s/n,
24732 Santiago Millas, León

Mobile	+34 656 395158
Email	info@camarga.es
Web	www.camarga.es

Casa Zalama

In a farming village in a little known area of northern Spain, the wonderful Casa Zalama is a place in which to linger. María, originally from the Basque country, and her partner Graeme, uprooted from Brighton in search of a guest house, and found this. Maria's attractive furnishings in the carefully converted house are matched by Graeme's green fingers, and the landscaped garden is dotted with Graeme's wood sculptures. Beamed bedrooms have comfortable beds and lovely earthy colours; those with balconies have stunning views of the hills. Dinners, served in the chunky-raftered dining room (once the stables) are country Spanish and delicious: local sausage, home-grown veg, pear tart. Opposite the house there is a cosy and colourful self-catering cottage, perfect for couples or a small family. Your hosts are hugely helpful about where to go and what to do, and set you up with wholesome and hearty breakfasts. The views are bucolic, the birdwatching is brilliant, and the Ojo Guareña Nature Park is nearby. Wonderful value, just an hour from Bilbao and Santander.

Price	€50–€60. Suite €78–€82. House €100–€110 (€580–€680 per week).
Rooms	6 + 1: 5 twins/doubles, 1 suite. House for 4.
Meals	Breakfast €6. Dinner €18.
Closed	2 weeks in January/February.
Directions	From E-70 for Bilbao, exit km173 marker for Colindres. N-629 up over Alto de los Tornos. At Aguera, left for San Pelayo. Past church, on left.

Maria Cruz Totorika & Graeme Hobbs
c/La Fuente s/n,
09569 San Pelayo Merindad de Montija, Burgos

Tel	+34 947 565961
Email	info@casazalama.com
Web	www.casazalama.com

El Prado Mayor

The impressive façade of the 16th-century Prado Mayor is concealed behind a solid arched gateway. Via a small garden with a columned terrace – lovely for summer breakfasts – you enter a warm home. The cream-coloured stone gives the house a sheltered and peaceful air while the stylish understated décor is in perfect harmony with the architecture. Wooden-floored bedrooms are rustic and inviting: expect period antiques, rocking chairs, colourful blankets, dried flowers, pretty country cabinets under basins, ornate framed mirrors, and two stunning suites on the top floor. Breakfast is a must: your gentle hostess (who has a wicked sense of humour!) serves homemade cakes, biscuits, fruits, local bread baked in a wood oven. Lunch and dinner are superb affairs with organic home-grown vegetables and good local meats; the rabbit stewed with thyme is excellent. The lush landscape is one of Spain's best-kept secrets, breathing culture and history; the Ojo Guareña cave system, from where you can trace humanity's religious expression from Paleolithic times, is one of the biggest in the world. Readers love this place.

Price	€67–€75. Singles €55–€60. Suites €94–€102. Plus VAT at 7%.
Rooms	8: 6 twins/doubles, 2 suites.
Meals	Breakfast €8.50. Dinner, with wine, €24. Packed lunches available.
Closed	Rarely.
Directions	Burgos N-623 Santander. At Cilleruelo de Bezana, BU-654 for Soncillo. At Soncillo follow BU-526; village 7km before Espinosa de los Monteros. Left at entrance of village; on for 500m to fountain. Right at no. 52, 50m to hotel.

Olga Fernández
Quintanilla del Rebollar 53,
09568 Merindad de Sotoscueva, Burgos

Tel	+34 947 138689
Email	info@pradomayor.com
Web	www.pradomayor.com

Posada Molino del Canto

A shame to stay only a night. This jewel of a place lies in a primeval Eden-like valley, lapped by the river Ebro. It is a 13th-century millworkers' home, restored by young owner Javier, and the simplicity of the façade is reflected inside; all is authentic and exquisite. From the dim little entrance hall – cool for summer, warm for winter – you enter a chunky-beamed, stone-walled sitting room scattered with country furniture, and a kilim, a sofa, a crackling fire. Then to bedrooms upstairs, each a splendid surprise: a cosy, delightful sitting room downstairs with a sofabed for children, and a double on the mezzanine (hot in summer?). There are antique wrought-iron beds, large classic wardrobes, white-and-terracotta bathrooms, sky windows to gaze at the stars… and you drift off to the sound of the river. Breakfast is a fine start to the day and the dinners, fresh and seasonal, are memorable. On a promontory down by the river is the watermill, 1,000 years old; the old flint wheels spin into action still when the sluice gate is opened. Spot otters and fish in the river. Exceptional owners, heavenly place.

Price	€83. Singles €71. Plus VAT at 7%.
Rooms	6: 3 doubles, 3 twins. Extra beds.
Meals	Tapas-style lunch €5–€10. Dinner, 4 courses, €25. Wine €9–€30. Plus VAT at 7%.
Closed	Rarely.
Directions	From Burgos N-623 for Santander. North of Quintanilla de Escalada, at km66 marker, right for Gallejones. On for Villanueva Rampally. There left for Arreba. Posada signed to right after 2.6km.

Ethical Collection: Environment; Food.
See page 412.

Javier Morala & Valvanera Rodríguez
Molino del Canto s/n, Barrio La Cuesta,
09146 Valle de Zamanzas, Burgos

Tel	+34 947 571368
Fax	+34 947 571176
Email	molinodelcanto@telefonica.net
Web	www.molinodelcanto.com

La Gándara

The noisiest noise around here is cicada hum – and birdsong. The road stops at the village; remote, rustic, charming. This is a place of simple pleasures – canoeing on the river, forest walking, exploring Romanesque churches, visiting the spectacular gorge at Palancas. The old farmhouse reflects this rusticity but there are deep comforts too. Floors are oak, stairs creaky, windows shuttered, walls a pleasing mix of stone and plaster. The beamed bedrooms are furnished in elegant country style – authentic bedheads, embroidered covers, muslin curtains, warm colours, a walnut wardrobe, an antique wash stand. Two delightful bedooms tuck themselves under the eaves and the top-floor suite is heaven: spot deer from the windows, gaze at the stars from your tub. In the early evening, glass in hand, spot vultures from the long wooden balcony that overlooks the lush garden and hills. Gentle owners Javier and Isabel serve lovely meals with produce from their organic garden, and join their guests for supper. With no television, conversation lingers well into the night. Special.

Price	€54-€58. Suite €75-€80. Apartment €90-€100. All prices per night.
Rooms	6 + 1: 5 twins/doubles, 1 suite. Apartment for 2.
Meals	Breakfast €6. Dinner with wine, €18.
Closed	6-31 January.
Directions	From Santander N-623; left at km70 marker for Arreba & Manzanedo; on for 4km. Left; 1km to Crespos. House 1st on right.

Javier Moyano & Isabel Villullas
c/La Paloma s/n, 09572 Crespos, Burgos

Tel	+34 947 573184
Email	lagandara@teleline.es
Web	www.lagandara.com

Molino de la Ferrería

In a clearing in a wood, a delicious weekend bolthole for Madrileños: a river setting for summer, a ski resort (La Pinilla) for winter. Just outside the village of Villacorta, this smartly renovated flour mill, active until the 1970s, has become a stylish small hotel. Naturally the river flows right by, and the great old grinding stones are still at the heart of the place, perfectly preserved. Be welcomed by this charming young couple who lived and worked in Madrid before they swapped city buzz for a place in the country. The restaurant is a delight, with its chunky stone walls, circular white-clothed tables and friendly country furniture. A treat to dine in, it's packed at weekends and Mónica does most of the cooking. Peaceful bedrooms, some in the old mill, others on the ground floor of the new (but traditional) wing, all pristine and with every mod con, manage to be rustic and cosy. Be charmed by old bedsteads, new mattresses, chic lampshades on energy-saving bulbs (it's an eco-friendly place) and aromatic touches in super bathrooms.

Price	€98–€113.
Rooms	12 twins/doubles.
Meals	Dinner €18. Wine €7.50.
Closed	Rarely.
Directions	From Madrid N-I for Burgos. At km103 marker follow signs for Soria-Riaza. At Riaza take lane on right between church & main square; this links with SG-V-1111. Continue to Villacorta; follow main road; right after village; hotel signed.

Mónica Otero & Alejandro Mújica
Camino del Molino s/n,
40512 Villacorta, Segovia

Tel	+34 921 125572
Email	info1@molinodelaferreria.es
Web	www.molinodelaferreria.es

Posada del Acebo

Prádena sits snug in the lee of the Sierra de Guadarrama, the high chain of mountains just north of Madrid. Its older houses are surprisingly grand, built in an age when villagers were granted royal privileges for the quality of their sheeps' wool. You enter through the small dining/sitting room, with its rustic bench seating, scents of seasoned timber, small open fire and family photographs of semi-nomadic shepherds. Ramón will usher you up the fine old banistered staircase to your rooms, passing a charming collection of working antique clocks on the way. Vintage washstands, wrought-iron bedsteads and old lamps fill the rooms – named after places special to the family – while central heating and double glazing keep the fearsome winters of the Meseta at bay. There are mountains outside the door, the mighty Duratón river gorges to explore on foot or by canoe, and Romanesque churches and the medieval town of Sepúlveda to visit. Then back to dinner in that cosy dining room. Rooms and food are excellent value, and if you're missing eggs and bacon at breakfast, just ask!

Price	€54–€64. Singles €40.
Rooms	8: 7 twins/doubles, 1 single.
Meals	Dinner with wine, €15, by arrangement.
Closed	Rarely.
Directions	From Madrid, N-1 for Burgos. At km99 marker, exit onto N-110 for Segovia. After 12km, right into Prádena. House off main square.

	Ramón Martín Rozas
	c/Rafael Matesanz 11,
	40165 Prádena, Segovia
Tel	+34 921 507260
Fax	+34 921 507260
Email	acebo@tursegovia.com
Web	www.el-acebo.com

Hospedería de Santo Domingo

You could find your way to the village with your eyes closed, such are the aromas! Hilltop Pedraza has 14 restaurants, three churches and one castle. The hospederia was the house of the priest of the nearby Santo Domingo; now it holds 17 generously-sized, elegantly contemporary rooms. Exquisitely integrated into its Unesco-listed surroundings, this polished new inn is a welcome antidote to history and rusticity – and there's enough of scenic and cultural interest here to keep you busy in the region for days. Ask for a room with a balcony and a stork-nest view (they arrive in January and stay still until late summer!)… though all are cleverly put together, understated and delightful. So too are the open-plan reception/sitting area and small bar. Take a deckchair to the garden to fully appreciate the hotel's position, perched on the hillside above the road (some traffic noise, but not in the rooms). However, it is not just the town, the position and the comforts that guests remember: the staff too are lovely. The mood is set by Señora Alvaro, a whirlwind of professionalism and energy. *A Rusticae hotel.*

Price	€120. Suites €145–€177.
Rooms	17: 14 doubles, 3 suites.
Meals	Breakfast €12.50.
Closed	24 December.
Directions	From Madrid A-1; exit at km99 marker. N-110 to Segovia until Arcones. Turning to Pedraza, hotel 9km on.

Belén Álvaro Contreras
c/Matadero 3, 40172 Pedraza, Segovia

Tel	+34 921 509971
Fax	+34 921 508683
Email	info@hospederiadesantodomingo.com
Web	www.hospederiadesantodomingo.com

La Tejera de Fausto

The stone buildings of this rustic homestead stand a mile from the nearest village, close to the banks of the Cega river. The roofs, of course, are terracotta: *tejas* were made here, hence the name. The bedrooms, in an outbuilding, have a mix of old and new pieces while the cosy two-level suite has a four-poster bed and a hunting lodge feel. No phones, no TVs, just views. The decoration is warm, simple and appealing but it is the hostess, the restaurant (and Teja the German shepherd dog!) that set this place apart. In a series of snug, interconnecting rooms where fires blaze in winter, guests tuck into the very best of regional cooking – there's a much-loved gazpacho, and a delicious white fish cooked with pine nuts and sultanas. The gardens are lovely, too, with trees for shade. Close by is a Romanesque chapel whose foundation stones were pillaged from a Roman villa. This is a remote corner of Castille: a fertile valley in the lee of the jagged Guadarrama mountains that cut like a scimitar between Madrid and the Meseta: Castillian to the core. Note that wedding parties are held on some weekends.

Price	€105. Suites €145–€190.
Rooms	9: 7 twins/doubles, 2 suites.
Meals	Dinner from €27 à la carte. Wine €12.
Closed	Rarely.
Directions	From Segovia, N-110 for Soria to La Salceda. Then left for Pedraza. Hotel on left, after Val de San Pedro, by km7 marker.

	Jaime Armero Ctra. La Salceda-Sepúlveda km7, 40173 Requijada, Segovia
Tel	+34 921 127087
Fax	+34 915 641520
Email	reservas@latejeradefausto.com
Web	www.latejeradefausto.com

Saltus Alvus

Once a stopover for the Romans crossing the Sierra de Guadarrama, Sotosalbos was – still is – prime hunting territory. Begoña grew up here, then returned to settle. This holiday house and its annexe, newly built on land owned by the family, have a reassuringly traditional feel and an exquisite position: opposite an austerely beautiful Romanesque church. Generous windows make the most of the mountain views and let in plenty of light to big, delightful rooms with lovely rafters and thick stone walls. Every last detail has been finely considered and all is brought together with style and panache, and yet the effect is homely and rural. The annexe is equally fine. Bedrooms have glowing terracotta tiles and rich pine ceilings, firm beds and comfortable armchairs or a sofa, kitchens are fabulous, the walled garden is a delight; birds trill from morning till night. Begoña and Víctor who live next door are a friendly and erudite couple with a young son and have a great love for the area, listed for 'ecological interest'. There's a super restaurant nearby – ask Begoña to book you a table.

Price	€750–€2,000 per week.
Rooms	House for 6-8. Annexe for 2.
Meals	Restaurant in village.
Closed	Rarely.
Directions	From Segovia N-110 for Soria. After 18km, Sotosalbos on left. At restaurant Las Casillas, sharp left up track. 2nd right ('residents only' sign); house opp. church on left.

Begoña del Barrio Martín
& Victor Lopez
c/Tejadillo 1, 40170 Sotosalbos,
Segovia

Mobile   +34 639 891220
Email   saltusalvus@terra.es
Web   www.saltusalvus.es

Posada Fuenteplateada

Here is a young hotel constructed from reclaimed materials, serving seasonal food and run by the nicest people. It's the sort of place that would appeal as much to couples looking for a quiet weekend in the country as business folk planning a brainstorming session. The delightful owner Maria is from the area so, if you're a walker or a history buff, make the most of her knowledge. After a day in Segovia (a 15-minute drive), how nice to return to a massage in the spa and a scrumptious dinner in the restaurant (or at their sister restaurant down the road). Followed, perhaps, by a nightcap in the living room, so cosy at night. There's a modern, rustic feel here, thanks to exposed stones and chunky terracotta, along with great attention to detail: mosaics set into the reception's stone floor, sweeping peachy fabrics, woven-rush dining chairs. Bedrooms come with king-size beds and pillows to suit every whim, plus spacious sitting areas in the bedrooms; the largest even gets a garden. Outside is a garden, a play area for children and a pretty terrace for breakfast. *Ask about painting & cookery courses.*

Price	€105. Suites €120-€230.
Rooms	11: 3 twins/doubles, 8 suites.
Meals	Lunch & dinner €9-€18. Second restaurant in village run by owners.
Closed	Rarely.
Directions	From Madrid on A-6 to La Coruña. Just before Segovia, A-1 for Soria. At Collado Hermoso take track between church & bakery leading to the hills & hotel.

María Jesús Martín
Camino de las Rozas s/n,
40170 Collado Hermoso, Segovia

Tel	+34 921 403087
Email	info@fuenteplateada.net
Web	www.fuenteplateada.net

Entry 148   Map 11

Casa de Hechizo

Alfredo couldn't have chosen a better name for his hotel: it will indeed leave you 'spellbound'. A chunky adobe exterior, fronted by young, natural gardens, contains a refreshingly light interior. Enter a modernist mix of straight lines, smooth surfaces and polygon shapes, crisp white walls, immaculate wafer bricks and creamy open stones. Soothing taupes and splashes of red are the colours in characterful bedrooms, where Venetian blinds frame windows and beds are vast. The lighting is striking – alter the room's mood at the touch of a switch – while dark polished hardwoods reach from floors to bathrooms and radical flat-topped basins; some bathrooms are in alcoves, some blend into sleeping areas, others are divided by sliding doors. Our favourite rooms are those at the back: catch the sunsets from your bed. And then there's the spa – built directly under the roof and encased in glass, it is 'drenched' in Castillian light. Sink into the sauna, stoke the stove, slip into the jacuzzi, gaze at the stars (there's a telescope for that). The restaurant offers fresh, creative, imaginative food. Intimate, stylish, special. *A Rusticae hotel*

Price	€164–€201.
Rooms	8 twins/doubles.
Meals	Lunch & dinner €35. Wine €12.
Closed	Rarely.
Directions	N-110 Segovia-Soria; at km172 marker, left for Sotosalbos. Continue 7km to Carrascal. House on right on exit of village; signs for Barrio de Abajo.

	Alfredo Oneto
	Co. de Torreiglesias s/n, Barrio de Abajo, 40181 Carrascal de la Cuesta, Segovia
Tel	+34 915 584658
Fax	+34 916 617278
Email	info@hotelesconhechizo.com
Web	www.hotelesconhechizo.com

Caserio de Lobones

The Marques de Castellanos – eminent 17th-century aristocrat – could scarcely have imagined that his countryside retreat would, at some stage, open its doors to all. Take an extraordinarily aristocratic Castillian farmhouse and add landscape gardeners, clock makers and curators from the Royal Palace of La Granja; spare no expense on furnishings; and add the spark and conviviality of an Andalucían host. Back in 1847, an encyclopeadia gave a lengthy description of this exclusive rural retreat. Nearly two centuries on, Rocío and Jaime have created a series of sophisticated interiors without a hint of ostentation. Magnificent antique pieces rub shoulders with religious oil paintings and German architectural prints. Rooms flaunt fabrics in bold checks and elaborate florals. Massive mirrored wardrobes are unfazed by vast, high-ceilinged spaces; one wardrobe is genuine Louis XVI. Outside is as lovely, the interior walled garden a formal maze of lavender and box, while Sevilla roses grace romantic corners. The landscape encourages riding, walking and fishing, and monumental Segovia is five miles away. *A Rusticae hotel.*

Price	€121–€142. Singles €95.
Rooms	10: 9 twins/doubles, 1 single.
Meals	Breakfast €11. Dinner €40, by arrangement. Wine €10.
Closed	Rarely.
Directions	From CL-605 exit km5.5 marker for Valverde del Majano & Hontanares de Heresma. Follow signs to hotel.

Jaime Pujadas & Rocío Morales
Ctra. CL-605 km5.5,
40140 Valverde del Majano, Segovia

Tel	+34 921 128408
Fax	+34 921 128344
Email	info@lobones.com
Web	www.lobones.com

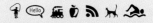

Posada de Esquiladores

The granite exterior and rush blinds at the windows do not suggest the treats within. Enter a big inviting sitting room with a huge granite-fronted hearth and an exquisite restoration. In the lovely mountain village of San Esteban, the 18th-century posada was a village shop until 1989; some of the original goods are still on display. Today's interior is a harmonious and contemporary mix of stone, terracotta and serenely lovely fabrics; bedrooms are dreamy, bathrooms spotless. Ask María José, your charming hostess, to show you the old vaulted cellars below; they contain row upon row of ancient clay vats once used for storing the local red, Pitarra. If you book dinner you'll taste many of the dishes that have made Castillian cuisine famous. You can explore the wild villages of the region from here; there's a twice-yearly festival in honour of St Peter Baptist, the Franciscan missionary martyred at Nagasaki (whose skull rests in the church), and an annual horse race, El Vitor, in which riders race bareback from the square to the cemetery. A delicious retreat, run by lovely people. *A Rusticae hotel.*

Price	€74.90–€139.10.
Rooms	12 twins/doubles.
Meals	Lunch & dinner, with wine, €24. À la carte from €28.
Closed	Rarely.
Directions	From Madrid, N-V/E-90 for Talavera de la Reina. At km123 marker, right on N-502 for Avila to Ramacastaños. Here, N-502 for Mombeltrán. At entrance of village, right for San Esteban. In village, right at 'Ayuntamiento' to square & hotel.

Maria José Quintanilla
c/Esquiladores 1,
05412 San Esteban del Valle, Ávila

Tel	+34 920 383498
Fax	+34 920 383456
Email	posada@esquiladores.com
Web	www.esquiladores.com

El Milano Real

Surrounded by the Gredos mountains, this has the feel of a smart Swiss chalet, with shutters on all sides and the constant trickle of water in the oh-so-neat garden at the front. Inside, all is comfort and ease. Bedrooms are colour-coordinated and a good size, and include several rather plush suites. One is Japanese, stunning with futon and low furniture; another resembles a Manhattan penthouse; another is country English, with wall-to-wall carpeting and four-poster; and the Nordic room has its very own sauna. There are two lounges with matching sofas and armchairs, one up under the eaves, and a library and an observatory. The owner Francisco ('Paco'), is a keen astronomer, happy to share his passion with guests. But the dining room is the biggest draw, the food winning a mention in many guides; there's also a tempting wine list. Paco and his wife Teresa, outdoor enthusiasts both, have compiled their own walking guide: 20 GPS-referenced walks that take you into the heart of Gredos, one of Spain's best-kept secrets. *A Rusticae hotel.*

Price	€107–€152. Singles €89. Suites €196. Half-board €94–€135 p.p.
Rooms	21: 13 twins/doubles, 8 suites.
Meals	Breakfast €15. Lunch & dinner €35–€58 à la carte.
Closed	Rarely.
Directions	Directions on booking.

	Yolanda Domínguez
	c/Toleo 2, 05634 Hoyos del Espino, Ávila
Tel	+34 920 349108
Fax	+34 920 349156
Email	info@elmilanoreal.com
Web	www.elmilanoreal.com

El Canchal

No Ritz, but perfect for walkers, who come for some of the most memorable routes in central Spain. Arenas de San Pedro, topped by a medieval castle and sculpted into the southern flank of the Sierra, is in the heart of the trails. This nobleman's residence – bang in the middle of the old quarter, not easy to find – dates from the Middle Ages; Isabel knows the history. She is the perfect innkeeper: unflappable, flexible, friendly. The feel is of an old travellers' inn, the furniture is darkly Castillian, the ceilings are low and all is spacious and cool. Multi levels lead to bedrooms, each named after a variety of mushroom – the area is popular with gatherers – and grandmother-cosy. There are antique beds and dressers, lace-edged curtains, antique washstands and dark beams. The lounge and dining room feel similarly homely, with their books, sofas, old tiles, beautiful rafters, ancient hearth. Enjoy meats, pastries and homemade cake at breakfast and eat in at least once: smokers may rule but meals are simple and great value and the house red is good. Don't miss the labyrinthine cellars deep below.

Price	€60–€64.
Rooms	6 twins/doubles.
Meals	Breakfast €4. Lunch & dinner €18. Wine from €7.
Closed	Rarely.
Directions	In town, before castle, left into c/Isabel La Católica. Follow signs for 'Ayuntamiento', clockwise round church to limited parking. Walk up c/Cejudo 100m; right at x-roads; 50m then left at fork; 20m, on left.

Isabel Rodríguez
c/de La Fuente 1,
05400 Arenas de San Pedro, Ávila

Tel	+34 920 370958
Fax	+34 920 370958
Email	reservas@elcanchal.com
Web	www.elcanchal.com

Posada Rincon de Alardos

A secluded microclimate where cool mountain air meets the warmth of the plains, and orange and fig groves bow to forests of chestnuts and oaks. Jagged crests tower behind you...the Gredos is an ornithologist's dream. Susan, the vivacious British-Argentinian owner, said it was love at first sight. Not just for her, for this former tobacco-drying barn seduces anyone lucky enough to drift its way. Two huge tobacco leaves by the entrance pay homage to a once thriving industry. Rincon de Alardos has that rare quality, where you feel you're not staying in a house but in a home. Stone floors and ancient wooden beams lead to bright and spacious rooms, all of which ooze atmosphere, elegance and style: solid carved wardrobes, antique chests of drawers, polished bureaus. Our favourites are the two balconied rooms with breathtaking views over the mountains. As you sit on the vine-shaded terrace sipping spring-water lemonade, you may mull over whether to venture beyond the garden and explore the nearby Celtic village, or go walking in the Parque Natural de Monfragüe.

Price	€80.25–€101.65.
Rooms	5 twins/doubles.
Meals	€12 tapas-style dinner. Wine €7–€25.
Closed	Rarely.
Directions	A-5 from Madrid to Oropesa; continue to Candeleda, C-501 to Madrigal. Left to El Raso immediately after river. Follow track for 2km; signed on left.

Susan Reed
Finca las Planas, El Raso,
05489 Candeleda, Ávila

Tel	+34 920 377075
Fax	+34 920 377129
Email	clientes@rincondealardos.es
Web	www.rincondealardos.es

La Casa Inglesa

Many guests are Spanish: they come for the food, the company and to escape the capital. 'The English House' is both home and retreat, tucked away on the mountainside in a pretty part of Bejar, in a chestnut wood from which El Castañar takes its name. Outside, a lush wild garden. Inside, a warm eclectic feel – a hotchpotch of antique drop-leaf tables, oriental vases and crystal decanters, books and candelabras, Moroccan lamps and plush sofas. Bedrooms have knick-knacks and chintz, bathrooms are spacious but dated. Gregarious Anna loves the good things of life so expect candles at dinner, classical music at most times and imaginative food: in the 60s she ran restaurants in London and fed the Rolling Stones. She is no typical ex-pat, and her cooking looks both west and east, with a good choice for vegetarians. Pure spring water runs throughout the house. Dinners have an oriental slant and she will happily serve you a cooked breakfast – on the terrace in summer. A charming hostess and a laid-back home; stay a couple of nights and visit the exceptional village of Candelario up the road.

Price	€50–€60.
Rooms	5: 4 twins/doubles, 1 triple.
Meals	Lunch €25. Dinner €20. Wine €10.
Closed	Rarely.
Directions	From Salamanca for Cáceres & Béjar. In Béjar pass 2 petrol stations, left for El Castañar. 2km, then immed. opp. Hotel Los Duques, sharp left down cobbled track. At 3rd hairpin bend, sharp left to black gate. Ring bell.

Anna Antonios
c/Rodeos del Castañar 25,
37700 Béjar, Salamanca

Tel	+34 923 404499
Email	owl2pooh@yahoo.co.uk
Web	www.casainglesabejar.com

Hotel Residencia Rector

In a city of ineffable loveliness, one of western Spain's most perfect small hotels. Señor Ferrán likes things to be 'just so' and examples of his care are found in every corner. There are two eye-catching stained-glass windows in reception, and wood is used to meticulous effect: sparkling parquet floors in the public rooms, inlaid tables and writing tables in the bedrooms; all is immaculate. You may not need the phone in the bathroom or the fax point in the bedroom but you'll be glad of the double glazing (you're in the centre of town), the deeply comfortable beds, the embroidered bed linen – and the iPod bases on request! Quietly lavish bathrooms in silvery marble have underfloor heating and Bulgari soaps. Superb standards at buffet breakfast too, where the staff are unfailingly courteous and helpful, and the spread lavish. Leave your car in the small hotel car park and head out on foot to explore: the cathedral is two minutes away. Close too is the interesting Casa Lis, a museum dedicated to Spanish Arts Nouveau and Deco. A small, charming and much-loved place. *Parking bookable in advance.*

Price	€120–€190. Suite €170–€210.
Rooms	13: 12 twins/doubles, 1 suite.
Meals	Breakfast €13.
Closed	Rarely.
Directions	From Madrid on N-501, 1st right at 'Centro Ciudad'. At r'bout, left into P. Rector Esperabé. After 300m, hotel in front of two walls, by museum. Drop off bags; hotel will direct you to car park (€16 per day).

	Julian Almaraz
	Paseo Rector Esperabé 10,
	37008 Salamanca,
Tel	+34 923 218482
Fax	+34 923 214008
Email	info@hotelrector.com
Web	www.hotelrector.com

Posada Real La Vadima

If it is Old Spain you're seeking, come here – to a former convent on a farm that raises bulls. The timbers and old granite lintels embrace you and there is Castillian antiquity at every turn. And kindness, from a hostess who cherishes her guests. Amalia's is a long-established Castillian family, and her love for this place gives life to every nook and cranny. The sitting room, with its checked sofas, trophies and roaring fire, has the feel of a hunting lodge – only grander; the atmospheric kitchen with original inglenook and implements is almost a museum. Ask for one of the rooms with a recently refurbished bathroom (some are dated); the suite, superb for families, flourishes matching Deco furniture and a 1900 washstand from Paris; the downstairs double is austerely beautiful, and tranquil; another room has a library of rare books. Doors are carved and heavy, curtains handmade, ceilings solid chestnut. There's a small lawned garden at the front and a superbly elevated pool at the back, with views. The wines and the cooking – whatever Amalia decides to produce that day – are as enjoyable as all the rest.

Price	€85–€97. Singles €70–€77. Suites €120-€135.
Rooms	10: 7 twins/doubles, 1 single, 2 suites.
Meals	Breakfast €10. Lunch & dinner, with wine, €25.
Closed	10-31 January.
Directions	From Salamanca cross Rio Tormes. Follow signs for Valladolid/N-620. Exit onto SA-300 for Ledesma. At bridge, right on SA-311 for Almeida/Miranda do Douro. After 7km, on right.

Amalia Casanueva
Ctra. Ledesma-Bermillo km7,
37100 Ledesma, Salamanca

Tel	+34 923 570230
Fax	+34 923 570329
Email	info@lavadima.com
Web	www.lavadima.com

Madrid & Castile–La Mancha

Abalú

Bang in the city centre – an innovative and affordable alternative to luxury hotels. The eye-catching 50s-style cafe-cum-breakfast bar, the funky lipstick-pink and black velvet armchairs and freeform sofa as you walk in the door give a mere hint of what is to come. Young and enterprising, Antonio and Carlos have transformed their parents' *hostal* and they have done it in great style. You are welcomed in off the bustling streets behind Gran Vía by cheerful staff and introduced to the box of delights which is the Abalú. Each individual bedroom is Antonio's homage to modern urban design – very of-the-moment, all clean lines, rich colours and personal touches. Walls become artworks, with gentle florals and bold prints, and every space bathes in mellow lighting – and each has its own cinema screen, sound and projection system. Bathrooms too have succumbed to the Antonio treatment – stone walls and floors, walk-in showers, rolltop baths, sleek basins, jacuzzis, even a plunge-pool bath. Perfect for a long weekend in this buzzy city that never sleeps. Walk your socks off, then retire to your cool, classy 'pad'.

Price	€75–€119. Singles €55–€105. Suites €120–€250.
Rooms	16: 9 twins/doubles, 1 single, 6 suites.
Meals	Breakfast €10. Restaurants nearby.
Closed	Never.
Directions	Metro: 'Noviciado' or 'Pza. de España'. From 'Noviciado' take exit for 'Ministerio de Justicia'. c/Pez is opposite as you come out of station. Hotel 100m up road, on right.

Carlos & Antonio Fernández
c/Pez 19, 28004 Madrid

Tel	+34 915 314744
Fax	+34 915 214492
Email	info@hotelabalu.com
Web	www.hotelabalu.com

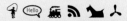

La Posada de Tamajón

A house with a colourful history: from wine store to 16th-century inn to Guardia Civil headquarters – and back to village inn. During the War of Independence the resident priest would hide religious artefacts from Napoleon's troops; the gracious Spanish family who live here now have unearthed many during their lengthy restoration. Now the house has reverted to its former status of posada. The owners, fond of local traditions, have also salvaged old farming implements and displayed them in the entrance hall. And they have a penchant for good antiques. (Some furniture is for sale – do ask.) The feel is of a rather grand manor house – at times ostentatious, at other times charming and homely. Shiny marble and brass, glittering silver, polished furniture and vibrant fabrics manage to co-exist. There are four bedrooms, one for each season, the most sumptuous being Invierno (Winter). It has marble and terracotta floors, lace bedcovers on a wrought-iron bed, a bathroom with luxurious brass basins, antique taps and jacuzzi, and a sunny private patio for breakfast. Quite a place.

Price	Half-board €200. Suite €350.	
Rooms	4: 3 twins/doubles, 1 suite.	
Meals	Half-board only. Restaurant in Tamajón.	
Closed	Rarely.	
Directions	From R-2, exit for Fontanar onto CM-101. Continue to Humanes; here, CM-1004 to Tamajón. Posada on main square, next to 'Ayuntamiento'.	

Javier Gamo Ruiz
c/Enmedio 35, 19222 Tamajón,
Guadalajara

Tel	+34 949 211739
Fax	+34 949 212934
Email	info@laposadadetamajon.com
Web	www.laposadadetamajon.com

Hotel & Spa Salinas de Imón

Prize-winning salt is still produced at Imón: you see the crystallising beds as you arrive. Just beyond is a tiny square and the Hospedería. This serene and elegant house began life as a convent, then became a salt warehouse. The heavy studded door now opens onto a second conversion: an unusual and exquisite mosaic of different styles. A sitting room hums with fresh flowers, bright sofas, antiques and ornaments, old dolls and books, framed prints and huge repro paintings by Luis Gamo Alcalde; his art enhances the whole house. Up the colourful stairway to bedrooms historically themed. One has musical scores and signed photographs of musicians, another a Louis XVI-style cradle; 'Carlos III' is graced by Empire beds and family photos; bathrooms are beamed and subtly lit. Right at the top, a cosy log-fired library leads to a patio and a stunning garden where the two towers of the original building rise... a secluded pool blends in. There's a fine spa close by — and furniture restoration and painting courses in three languages. Highly likeable, deeply cultural, and run with a personal touch. *Internet access.*

Price	€85–€135. Suites €195.
Rooms	13: 10 twins/doubles, 3 suites.
Meals	Breakfast €9. Dinner €25.
Closed	Rarely.
Directions	From Sigüenza take the CM-110 for Atienza; right turn into Imón after 14km. Hotel in main square of village.

Jaime Mesallés de Zunzunegui
c/Real 49, Imón, 19269 Sigüenza,
Guadalajara

Tel	+34 949 397311
Fax	+34 949 397311
Email	info@salinasdeimon.com
Web	www.salinasdeimon.com

Cardamomo Sigüenza

Wallow in the luxury of it all – but leave the young ones at home. This is a grown-up place that oozes velvets, raw silks and designery touches. At the top of a steep narrow road, peacefulness and wide open spaces surround you. Inside is lushness at every turn, from the moss and aubergine hues of the sofa'd sitting room to the teak seating on the cool shady terrace and the chic – but tiny – pool. Bedrooms are exemplary, as the price demands. King-size beds, feather duvets and springy carpets on parquet floors are standard, there are uber-stylish rococo wallpapers and linen cushions fringed with feathers, and the priciest rooms get the best views. The suites in the loft are huge, astonishing, one with a mosaic'd whirlpool bath in a corner, another with lighting dramatically projected from behind the bed; both have doors painted metallic gold. No concessions to vernacular architecture here: Cardamomo is determinedly 21st century. Polish the day off with a serious dinner: a mix of regional dishes and sophisticated specialities. The sleepy village lies just below; Sigüenza is a ten-minute drive. *A Rusticae hotel.*

Price	€110–€135. Suites €160.
Rooms	13: 11 doubles, 2 suites.
Meals	Breakfast €12. Dinner à la carte €25–€30. Wine €12–€25. Plus VAT at 7%.
Closed	Never.
Directions	From Madrid N-1 to Sigüenza; exit km104 marker. In Sigüenza, CM-110 for Atienza. After 7km left for Palazuelo. After 1.5km, right for Carabias; into village, past church on right. Up steep narrow road & down to square. Park; 50m walk to hotel.

Fernando Mateos Galvañ
Cirueches 2, Carabias,
19266 Guadalajara

Tel	+34 902 883108
Fax	+34 949 828600
Email	hotel@cardamomosiguenza.com
Web	www.cardamomosiguenza.com

El Molino de Alcuneza Hotel Spa

The quintessence of rural charm and fine taste: El Molino is proof of just what can be achieved when love and energy are present in great measure. Little remained of the 400-year-old mill when Juan and Toñi fell in love with it and this swathe of delicious greenery. The rushing millrace still offers respite from the baking summers of Spain's vast Meseta. Originally it was to be a weekend bolthole for the family but the idea of a hotel was mooted and Juan was hooked. Every last detail of the interior decoration has been carefully considered: pine floors beneath dark beams; rich fabrics; a glass floor under which flows a rivulet of crayfish and trout; fine linen at beautifully lit tables. Our favourite rooms are Nos. 3 and 4 but all are special. Dinner is a feast of local produce: partridge with chickpeas, trout baked in Albariño wine, mushrooms from the forest; breakfasts are hearty, picnic hampers can be arranged. Siguenza and Atienza, two great medieval villages nearby, are a cultural must; reinvigorate your senses with an a la carte massage in the newly opened Spa. *A Rusticae hotel. Minimum stay two nights.*

Price	€108-€220. Singles €72-€90.
Rooms	18: 17 twins/doubles, 1 single.
Meals	Breakfast €12. Dinner €33.
Closed	Rarely.
Directions	From Sigüenza towards Medinacelli. Molino well signed before you reach Alboreca, on right.

	Blanca Moreno
	Ctra. de Alboreca km0.5,
	19264 Siguenza-Alcuneza, Guadalajara
Tel	+34 949 391501
Fax	+34 949 347004
Email	info@molinodealcuneza.com
Web	www.molinodealcuneza.com

Posada de San José

Cuenca is a town that astonishes and engraves itself on the memory. Perched on the rim of its unforgettable gorge, this is an inn to match. Behind the magnificently crumbling portal is a nondescript reception area that opens to a fascinating rabbit warren of rooms, spaces and twisting staircases, and terraces with breathtaking views. What is even more unusual is that bedrooms range from spartan to palatial, the most luxurious with a balcony, a terrace or a canopied bed. All have fresh white walls, uneven floors and are furnished with old country pieces and decorative flair. The best and quietest are at the back and have views to make the spirit soar, but all of them are worth a night and the choir boy wing is being completely redeveloped. There's a little dining terrace perched right on the cliff face, whose end table is the most coveted – if you don't suffer from vertigo you get a view worth crossing the Meseta for. Cuenca is fascinating though parking is tricky, but you can park 150 metres away. The Posada bustles with walkers of all ages, and the food is good. *A Rusticae hotel.*

Price	€40–€157. Singles €28–€62.
Rooms	31: 16 twins/doubles, 4 suites, 2 singles; 5 doubles, 3 singles,1 triple each with shared bath.
Meals	Breakfast €9. Children €5.
Closed	Rarely.
Directions	From Tarancón, A40 to Cuenca; from Motilla del Palancar N320 to Cuenca. Follow signs to Casco Antiguo. Posada 50m from cathedral; 1st street on right (past steps). Unload; secure parking 150m or park in Casillo area, avoid Plaza Mayor.

	Jennifer Morter
	c/Julián Romero 4, 16001 Cuenca
Tel	+34 969 211300
Fax	+34 969 230365
Email	reservas@posadasanjose.com
Web	www.posadasanjose.com

El Jardín de San Bartolomé

Here are the vast, historic landscapes of the Spanish Reconquista, backdrop to battles between Christians and Berbers. In the library of this imposing 19th-century house, caressed by the warmth of a crackling fire, you'll recall the history. A monastic air pervades this place, in contrast to the witchcraft that prevailed here 500 years ago. There's even a prayer room – with confessional should you need one! The light-drenched inner courtyard, the heart of the house, conceals an ingenious smoke-heating system under the floor, devised to mitigate winter rigours; this is a land of climatic extremes. Vintage photographs and 19th-century manuscripts decorate the walls of the grand stone staircase, telling stories of prosperous times in Cuba. Beamed ceilings, 'hydraulic' floor tiles, flower-patterned bedspreads and curtains – a labour of love by Francisco's mother-in-law – add to the restrained comfort of the rooms. This is a cool and airy retreat to come back to after trips to Cuenca's 'hanging' houses and Segóbriga, one of the best-preserved Roman remains in Europe. Both are a day trip.

Price	€40-€85. Quadruples €60-€120.
Rooms	7: 5 twins/doubles, 2 quadruples.
Meals	Breakfast €6. Lunch & dinner, with wine, €18, by arrangement.
Closed	Rarely.
Directions	From Valencia/Madrid on A-3; exit for Saelices-Segóbriga. Just before Sealices, take road for Carrascosa del Campo-Huete. Here, hotel on left opposite church. Park on road behind hotel.

Francisco de Diego
& Carmen Sarmiento
c/Juan Gavala 2,
16830 Carrascosa del Campo, Cuenca

Tel	+34 969 124186
Fax	+34 969 124186
Email	fdediego@sudistrito.com

Hostal del Cardenal

Toledo is quintessentially, gloriously Spanish, having absorbed the richest elements of Moorish and Christian Spain. Tempting, then, to stay at the Cardenal, built 700 years ago, later inhabited by the Cardenal Lorenzana, down on the city walls. Toledo's character and charm is reflected within its cool, dignified Castillian interior, and the gardens are stately: fountains and ponds, geraniums and climbers. Go through the elegant main entrance to discover patios, screens, arches and columns... and rooms whose walls glow with fine old oils and *mudéjar* bricks. A hushed mantle lies softly over it all, to the background tick-tock of the grandfather clock. Wide *estera*-matted corridors, a domed staircase and numerous stairs lead to formal, somewhat dated bedrooms, with gleaming parquet floors and sombre furniture. Bathrooms are small, some are opulent. Choose between several small dining areas, one under the trees, and feast on stewed partridge. (Breakfasts are less impressive.) No views, church bells at 5am, but delicious roasted meats and the El Greco museum the shortest of strolls.

Price	€100–€129. Singles €63–€80. Suites €130–€165.
Rooms	27: 23 twins/doubles, 2 singles, 2 suites.
Meals	Breakfast €9. Lunch & dinner €35.
Closed	Rarely.
Directions	From Madrid A-42 or AP-41 to Toledo. On arriving at old town walls & Puerta de la Bisagra, right; hotel 50m on left, beside ramparts.

Luis González Gozalbo
Paseo de Recaredo 24, 45003 Toledo,

Tel	+34 925 224900
Fax	+34 925 222991
Email	cardenal@hostaldelcardenal.com
Web	www.hostaldelcardenal.com

Castile-La Mancha

Hotel Villa Nazules Hípica Spa

On the plain in Spain, in a sea of olives under a vast blue sky and fringed by distant mountains, this smart new hotel has a charm all of its own. The low, modern building is a favourite with visiting horse riders; fine thoroughbreds reside in the stables and stud farm next door, where national competitions are held. But this place also spells pampering. Space and light abound: huge terraces, gardens, a patio bar .... relax in the delightful spa with every treatment imaginable or cool off in the little spring-fed infinity pool. There's a tennis court, too – and 'padel', a cross between tennis and squash. Buffet breakfasts are delicious and generous, while nouvelle cuisine with a regional twist is served in the restaurant – the maître d' will advise on wine. There's tapas in the café/bar, which spills outside in summer. As night falls, retire to ultra-modern rooms, each different, each generous with subtle colours and good fabrics. Robe and slippers come as standard, as does every comfort; friendly José and his team of lovely staff think of everything. Toledo is 20 minutes away and dreamy castles abound.

Price	€74–€124. Suites €100–€167. Plus VAT at 7%.
Rooms	14: 12 doubles, 2 suites.
Meals	Breakfast €12. Lunch & dinner €35.
Closed	Never.
Directions	From Toledo CM-42 dir. Madridejos; exit 14, then immed. right at r'bout, signed Villa Nazules. Follow road past gravel pits, then right to hotel (signed).

José Hernández
Ctra. De Almonacid de Toledo a Chueca
s/n, 45420 Almonacid de Toledo, Toledo

Tel	+34 925 590380
Fax	+34 925 590304
Email	correo@villanazules.com
Web	www.villanazules.com

Hotel Rural

Set among the windmills Don Quixote took for giants is a small hotel in sweet Consuegra. The heart of this 19th-century farmhouse is its sunny inner court, bright and cool with cushions, plants and bold friezes. Upstairs are functional, air-conditioned bedrooms, with antique tiled floors and shutters for night-long sleep. Plain walls are hung with local art (for sale); some rooms have a microwave and fridge. There's no garden here but there are huge umbrellas to sit out under while the children frolic in the pool – or play in the games room. In winter, sink into deep armchairs in the fire-warmed lounge or choose the card table for bridge; there are concerts, pilates and painting classes too. You can sample local specialities close by (saffron and olive oil are big business here) or stroll to tapas bars and a bit of nightlife. Warm, friendly Paula cares about the environment as well as her guests; a biomass converter and solar panels provide energy. Toledo's flat landscape is great for bikes, so grab a free one and explore. A super stopover or a short escape.

Price	€65-€82. Singles €55-€67. Family rooms €71-€88.
Rooms	9: 4 twins/doubles, 1 single, 4 family rooms.
Meals	Restaurant 500m.
Closed	11 January-12 February.
Directions	From Madrid A4; exit 119 dir. Toledo, then CM42 exit 53. From C.Real N40, then 1st exit for Urda (approx.18km).

Paula Gutierrez
c/Colón 2, 45700 Consuegra, Toledo

Tel	+34 925 480609
Fax	+34 925 480609
Email	info@lavidadeantes.com
Web	www.lavidadeantes.com

Hotel Rural Antigua Casa de la Bodega

From the dusty-hot streets of Manzanares, slip through handsome doors into a shuttered peacefulness of polished tiles and rich furniture. This 19th-century former bodega has all the slow unhurried charm of a mature wine; one that demands you slip off your shoes, sink into a sofa and drink deeply. Isabel and Rafael spent three years lovingly restoring the house, giving it a swaggering exterior of white walls, wrought-iron balconies and gay awnings; the interior is formal traditional. Be soothed by plump upholstery, antiques, fine porcelain, bowls of fruit and acres of fabulously ornate floor tiles. The high-ceilinged bedrooms are all lace curtains, brass bedsteads, cool walls and dark wood. Elegant touches work their magic: monogrammed bed linen, a pretty glass chandelier, a petite writing desk, a cosy window seat. And always flowers. In one room, tiled steps lead up to a low-beamed love nest. Bathrooms sparkle whitely. Beyond the shady, plant-filled breakfast terrace, a small pool is tucked into the high-walled garden. All this, and owners who are as charming, kind and refined as their house.

Price	€80.
Rooms	6 doubles.
Meals	Restaurants nearby.
Closed	February.
Directions	From Madrid N-IV south; 1st exit (171) for Manzanares. At r'bout follow signs for 'Centro Ciudad'; through tunnel; hotel on left.

Isabel Blanco & Rafael Bermejo
c/Clérigos Camarenas 58,
13200 Manzanares, Ciudad Real
Tel   +34 926 611707
Email   info@antiguacasadelabodega.com
Web   www.antiguacasadelabodega.com

La Casa del Rector

An ornate jewel in the heart of Spain's hot, dry, central plain, Almagro was once tipped to become home to the next Spanish university. It never happened, and the Casa del Rector, a charming collection of 16th-century houses on the edge of town, passed into private hands. Some years ago, Juan Garcia, a restaurateur of some repute, bought the old place and, with the help of local craftsmen, gave its ashen features a rosy, healthy glow. Behind the sandstone façade are a number of originally furnished rooms and suites opening onto a galleried central atrium full of antiques and interesting paintings where water flows – a lovely place to unwind. Choose your bedroom before you arrive: Spanish traditional or rustic chic. Most have sofas, wood-burning stoves, smallish windows and adventurous (even open-plan) bathrooms, perhaps a sauna/shower or a massive mosaic hot tub. The young, friendly staff serve excellent breakfast with Manchegan cheese and charcuterie; for a Castillian dinner, look no further than the owners' brilliant restaurant. *A Rusticae hotel.*

Price	€85-€180. Singles €75-€100. Suites €200-€360. Half-board extra €35 p.p.
Rooms	16: 11 twins/doubles, 1 single, 4 suites.
Meals	Breakfast €10. Lunch & dinner €25-€45. Restaurant closed last week in July.
Closed	Never.
Directions	From Ciudad Real, CM-412 to Almagro. At 1st r'bout follow hotel signs; right, then 2nd on right.

Juan García
c/Pedro Oviedo 8, 13270 Almagro, Ciudad Real

Tel	+34 926 261259
Fax	+34 926 261260
Email	recepcion@lacasadelrector.com
Web	www.lacasadelrector.com

Hotel Albamanjon

In the heart of Albacete – land of windmills and Don Quixote – is this sleepy corner. By a crystal lake, surrounded by small beaches and elephant grass, the Albamanjón, its terraces and its gardens dropping down from a rocky headland, is blessed with an extraordinary site. Built in the 70s with some curious features (including a windmill frontage), its cosy spaces are filled with much-loved collectables. The place may appear a little frayed at the edges but it reflects the geniality of its owners and feels cared for. Bedrooms, in which the rock sometimes appears unannounced, reveal a hotch-potch of furniture and hydromassage baths; go for a room at the top. Raul's succulent cuisine (suckling lamb, roast ham in honey) is the draw and the terrace sparkles with fairylights in summer; there's also a cosy café. But the biggest reason to be here is the stunning ribbon of translucent deep-water lakes in the Ruidera National Park. Swim from the hotel jetty, or hire rowing boats, kayaks and mountain bikes and explore, pioneer-style. The wildlife is rich, the peace profound.

Price	€110–€150. Singles €88. Suite €152. Half-board extra €26 p.p.
Rooms	12: 11 twins/doubles, 1 suite.
Meals	Lunch & dinner €20–€55. Restaurant closed Tuesdays. Wine €6–€83.
Closed	Rarely.
Directions	From N-IV, exit Manzanares & N-430 for Albacete. At Ruidera, signs to lakes. Hotel signed from lakes.

Raúl Arés Espílez
Laguna de San Pedro 16, 02611
Ossa de Montiel, Albacete

Tel	+34 926 699048
Fax	+34 926 699120
Email	hotel@albamanjon.net
Web	www.albamanjon.net

Valencia & Murcia

La Casa Vieja

Old house, indeed, and peaceful, combining 450 years of old stones with a contemporary feel for volumes and shapes. There are nobleman's arches and columns, ancient floor tiles, twisty beams, an indoor well and… a small, square swimming pool in the verdant Moorish courtyard. The double-height sitting area faces an immense inglenook where leather sofas envelop you as you sip a welcome sherry before dining. Many of the antiques have been in Maris's family for ever – oil paintings and Persian rugs, a 16th-century grandfather clock, a carved mahogany table. Bedrooms, too, are stylish and homely, beds big and firm; the suite with its terrace would tempt any painter or writer, there are books and baskets of fruit and no TV. Views stretch to the orange-clad hillsides, summer meals are served among jasmine and candles and the fine food follows the seasons: fish, fruit and vegetables fresh from the market and interesting vegetarian alternatives. We enjoyed the grilled goat's cheese with fig and orange confit, and the excellent Spanish wines. A gem hiding in a back street of tiny Rugat.

Price	€70–€95. Singles €65. Suite €135.
Rooms	6: 5 twins/doubles, 1 suite.
Meals	Dinner €24. Restaurants in village.
Closed	15 December-15 January.
Directions	AP-7; from Valencia exit 60, from Alicante exit 61. N-332 exit onto CV60; 18km to exit 23. CV691, thro' Montechelvo, Rugat 2nd village on left. Hotel behind church.

Maris Watson de Andrés
Carrer del Forn 4, 46842 Rugat,
Valencia

Tel	+34 962 814013
Email	mail@lacasavieja.com
Web	www.lacasavieja.com

Hotel L'Estacio

The station for the old narrow-track railway is today a light, bright hotel, run by friendly Dutch cousins Sebastian and Mats. Reception is the station foyer, where an 'installation' of antique suitcases acts as a witty reminder of its history. Ultra-modern bedrooms, bathed in light from huge windows, have big comfy beds, elegant white blinds and a luxurious feel. The bathrooms match – generous and gorgeous. The large paintings you see everywhere are the work of Sebastian's talented mother. A vast building with vaulted ceilings – once the carriage shed – now houses a glass-roofed café/bar and a white-walled dining room, where you feast on regional dishes that make best use of local produce, flavoured with Mariola herbs grown in the garden. Wines are local and excellent. Stroll round the lovely medieval town of Bocairent, see the Sierra Mariola from a hot-air balloon, pop down to the coast – or simply unwind in the glass-canopied lounge or palm-lined, shady gardens, with pretty pool. The dark-chocolate sofas in the library make a cosy retreat in winter months. A stylish bolthole, a treat for all ages. *A Rusticae hotel.*

Price	€78-€130.
Rooms	12 twins/doubles.
Meals	Breakfast €9. Lunch €10. Dinner, with wine, €27.50. (Only à la carte at weekends, €27.50.)
Closed	Rarely.
Directions	From Alicante airport N-332. At Campello N-340 for Alcoi. There, take smaller road for Bocairent. Hotel to side of r'bout before town.

Mats Lodder
Parc de l'Estacio s/n, 46880 Bocairent,
Valencia

Tel	+34 962 350000
Fax	+34 962 350030
Email	reservas@hotelestacio.com
Web	www.hotelestacio.com

Mas Fontanelles

Light-flooded rooms, burnished wood floors, high raftered ceilings – it is rustic, contemporary, beautiful. The huge, peaceful, 200-year-old farmhouse overlooks the pine, olive and almond trees of Benijama valley, and has been lovingly restored by Isabel and Italian Roberto. Colours are ochre and blue, fabrics are creamy, furniture is restored-antique or sleekly modern – chic but not pretentious. Bedrooms, named after trees, have a light designer touch making perfect use of natural colours and materials: white cotton bedspreads, rush-seated chairs, antique chests of drawers. Some rooms have balconies, one a terrace and three have loft-style additions, brilliant for children. There's a cosy sitting room with board games and a living room with comfortably elegant sofas and vast paintings. And, everywhere, stunning views. Isabel and Roberto will help you plan your days; swim in the (unfenced) pool, bounce on the trampoline, walk, ride, quad-bike, paint, visit an Arab castle or two. Then back to a delicious freshly prepared supper, and a terrace from which to gaze, wine in hand, on a perfect southern sunset.

Price	€71–€77. Singles €59.
Rooms	8 twins/doubles.
Meals	Dinner €22. Restaurants in Biar, 4km.
Closed	Rarely.
Directions	From Alicante N-330 to Villena. Here, signs for Biar. Hotel 4km outside Biar on road CV804 to Bañeres.

Isabel Aracil & Roberto Medoro
Ctra. Biar-Bañeres km4,
03410 Biar, Alicante

Mobile	+34 686 426126
Fax	+34 965 979166
Email	info@masfontanelles.com
Web	www.masfontanelles.com

Almàssera Vella

The village's old olive press still stands – in the dining room. Derelict when Christopher and Marisa arrived, the house is both a stylish and inviting home and a cultural centre. Spanish Marisa is an expert seamstress and interior designer, and cooks like a dream; Christopher is a prize-winning poet. Courses, run mostly during the spring and autumn, include writing, painting, photography, tapestry and mountain walking. The bright, airy living room is stuffed with books (3,000 at the last count), the dining room is homely. Also in the main house are four cosy, cottagey bedrooms with original artwork and photographs on the walls; two look over the terrace garden with pool and giant chess, and the valley with Moorish hilltop castle beyond. Opposite is a smaller house for self-catering – and an independent studio flat upstairs, an inspiring retreat for artists and writers. Not every room has its own but there are plenty of bathrooms in both houses. A wonderfully creative place for adults with an interest in culture, history and the Arts to think and relax. *Minimum two people in cottage & studio high season.*

Price	€75. Cottage & studio €35–€40 p.p. (from €150 p.p. per week).
Rooms	4 + 2: 4 twins/doubles. 1 cottage for 6, 1 studio for 3.
Meals	Dinner, with wine, €20.
Closed	Rarely.
Directions	From exit 66 on A-7 (Villajoyosa); right (inland). After Orcheta, left to Relleu. Down street opp. main door of church; last property on right: "The Blue House".

Christopher & Marisa North
Carrer de la Mare de Deu del Miracle 56,
03578 Relleu, Alicante

Tel	+34 966 856003
Email	christopher@oldolivepress.com
Web	www.oldolivepress.com

Hotel la Serena

You are in the centre of the old town of Altea – a typical whitewashed seaside town – near beaches, restaurants and station. But this is a quiet, contemporary and well-designed hotel for grown-ups, painstakingly restored; relish the old tiles, reclaimed doors and architectural features. The sun-drenched poolside terrace is dotted with pretty pots and artist-painted glass panels, and in the basement is a sparkling hammam – yours to use for an hour a day; massages, too, are available. Sophisticated it may be, but, thanks to the owners, the mood is relaxed: you could play the piano or pull out a board game in the chic sitting room (toasty, with a wood-burner in winter) then wander through to the airy, intimate restaurant, open to non-residents too. Here the chef executes an exotic and delicious menu. Bedrooms are light and stylish with good bed linen, a music centre and state-of-the-art showers; fluffy towelling robes are yours to float around in and two bedrooms at the top get private terraces and fabulous sea views. Altea has a bewildering variety of restaurants, all an easy walk.

Price	€150–€200. Plus VAT at 7%.
Rooms	10: 9 doubles, 1 family.
Meals	Lunch €15. Dinner €30. À la carte €45.
Closed	Never.
Directions	AP-7 for Valencia (from south); exit for Altea onto N332. Right at 1st set of lights; signed La Serena. Detailed directions on hotel website.

Elia Albert Pava
c/Alba 10, Bellaguarda, 03590 Altea, Alicante

Tel	+34 966 885849
Fax	+34 965 840158
Email	info@hoteleslaserena.com
Web	www.hoteleslaserena.com

Finca el Tossal

Peace and tranquillity and spectacular views – at the top of a precipitous track! The house was built by the remarkable Sonia and Thorsten from Germany, who, have succeeded in making the impossible come true. From the wiring and plumbing to the bricks and mortar, Thorsten eco-built this himself – and with great style and taste. Now the plan is to develop the kitchen garden that already bursts with fresh organic produce. Friendly beds have firm mattresses and down duvets, arches are Arabic, floors are tiled; counterpanes come in subdued colours, modernity comes in iPod players and satellite channels. This is the great outdoors and the reason for coming, so fling open those shutters and be inspired. The garden has terraces and a beautiful pool, and the mountain breezes are a blessing; you can see the coast but not feel the clamour. Altea still keeps its charm, and a half mile away are the waterfalls of the Algar – an aqua park with springs, a magnet to the Spanish at weekends. Breakfasts are wholesome and tasty, restaurants are a mile away, back down that track, but plans are afoot for dining in.

Price	€79–€89.
Rooms	7: 6 doubles; 1 double with kitchenette. Extra beds available.
Meals	Restaurants 2km.
Closed	Never.
Directions	AP-7/E-15 exit 64 for Altea. CV-755 for 9km to Callosa d'En Sarrià. At r'bout, 1st exit onto CV-715 signed Bolulla/Tárbena. After 3km, right by ceramics factory, signed Fonts de Algar. Park in 'La Cascada' restaurant car park; owners will meet you.

Sonia Herrmann
Partida la Foya 5, 03518 Bolulla,
Alicante

Tel	+34 965 972183
Email	Info@finca-el-tossal.com
Web	www.fincaeltossal.com

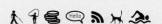

Refugio Marnes

A shepherd's refuge and a Bedouin tent in a valley ringed by mountains. This is for those who demand off the beaten track; there are dozens of paths to explore but none are signed – not even on the map! Dutch Willem and Richard bought both finca and forested land several years ago. With no mains power or utilities (still none) and an intermittent water supply, modernising was a challenge. They've done it all themselves – brilliantly – in cool eco style. From the parking area it's a 200m walk down a steep donkey track to the cottage and tent. La Ruina is cosy, compact and simply stylish, with a mezzanine for an extra bed and a private terrace. La Jaima, 100m away, a structure tried and tested by nomadic tribes for two millennia, is huge, theatrical and great fun, with modern plumbing and solar-generated electricity. Outside, a hammock swings from the branch of an ancient tree; the shared pool is unfenced and – delicious. You're utterly remote here, though the owners are unobtrusively available. The night skies are the clearest you're ever likely to see. *B&B rooms due to open 2009.*

Price	La Ruina €341–€694. La Jaima (tent) €418–€588. Prices per week.
Rooms	Cottage for 2-4; bedouin tent for 2-4.
Meals	Breakfast €9.50, by arrangement. Restaurant 5-minute drive.
Closed	La Jaima: October to March.
Directions	AP-7/E15 exit 63; thro' Benissa on N-332 for Calpe. After Benissa, right on CV-750; left fork onto CV-749, signed Pinos. On for 1km, over little blue bridge; immediately right up steep hill. Signed.

Ethical Collection: Environment.
See page 412.

Willem Pieffers
Pda Marnes 20115, 03720 Benissa, Alicante

Tel	+34 637 063003 (mobile)
Email	info@refugiomarnes.com
Web	www.refugiomarnes.com

La Madrugada

Your first reaction is to wonder if you've arrived at the right place: the impression is more 'swish home' than 'small hotel'. Only the discreet name plaque by the entrance gives it away. The villa, with its cool marble floors and sweeping staircase, was built for the Brightman family (soprano Sarah is one of the daughters) and has undergone a superb conversion from new owners. Everything – from fabrics and wallpapers to monogrammed towels – is top notch. The furniture is a successful mix of period and modern, and the bathrooms ooze quality (the one attached to the suite is particularly spectacular!). Bedrooms look out across to the sea at Calpe, where a rocky outcrop, the Peñón de Ifach, soars skywards. In the pretty garden, splashed with bougainvillea, you can play tennis, loll by the pool or curl up with a book in the thatched arbour. Dutch Irma and Theo, who manage the hotel, are brilliant at their job and between them speak a flurry of languages. Breakfast on the terrace is a lovely affair, and snacks and light lunches are always available – but to get anywhere, restaurants included, you need a car.

Price	€95–€135. Suite €240–€270. Plus VAT at 7%.
Rooms	8: 7 doubles, 1 suite.
Meals	Breakfast €12. Restaurant at sister hotel Casa del Maco, 5km (closed Tues). Half-board extra €46 p.p. Plus VAT at 7%. Wine €14.40.
Closed	February.
Directions	AP-7/E15 exit 63. Thro' Benissa on N-332. After km174 marker U-turn in forecourt on right of 'La Estancia' building then sharp right down narrow track; 700m on left.

Bert & Lieve de Vooght
Partida Benimarraig 61b, 03720 Benissa, Alicante

Tel	+34 965 733156
Fax	+34 966 489649
Email	info@lamadrugada.es
Web	www.lamadrugada.es

Casa del Maco

It's described as a rustic farmhouse but it's grander than that. An imposing paved terrace, statuesque trees and Lloyd Loom loungers around the pool give the Casa a gracious air. The 18th-century rooms, their beamed ceilings and deeply recessed windows betraying finca origins, are similarly special, the décor revealing flair and restraint. The restaurant, too, is sophisticated rather than rustic. One chef is Belgian (as are the owners), the other Moroccan and the food and wines, served by an impeccable staff, are delicious. Bedrooms are not huge but are romantic, and bathrooms luxurious; four have views (of mountains or sea), one has a terrace. The remote valley setting is stunning, the gardens overlook vineyards, olive groves and almond orchards; behind, a bare shoulder of rock juts through the pine-covered hills. Excellent walks lead from the door; from Calpe, you can hike up to the flat top of the Peñón de Ifach. Either way, you'll get great views of the saltpans, the mountains and the precipitous coastline to Cape La Nao. If you long for the sea and can face the crowds, the Costa is a short ride. Heavenly.

Price	€84–€111. Singles €72–€87. Plus VAT at 7%.
Rooms	5 twins/doubles.
Meals	Breakfast €9. Lunch/dinner from €40 à la carte. Plus VAT at 7%. Restaurant closed Tuesdays.
Closed	January.
Directions	Leave AP-7/E-15 at exit 63. Drive through Benissa on N-332 for 8km. Just past km170 marker on steep, sharp, LH bend turn right into narrow, partly paved road. Hotel 1km, signed.

Bert & Lieve de Vooght
Pou Roig 15, 03720 Benissa, Alicante

Tel	+34 965 732842
Fax	+34 965 730103
Email	macomarcus@hotmail.com
Web	www.casadelmaco.com

Caserío del Mirador

Verdant mountains swoop around Johnny and Sarah's dream home with staggering views, some stretching to the sea. Splash amongst the hills in the fantastic pool, chat in comfort to your young, generous, humorous hosts under the bamboo canopy. Crisp, charming B&B bedrooms are bathed in whites and browns; solar-lit shower rooms display minimalist lines. Two spacious open-plan apartments (above which live the owners) are equally rustic-contemporary; the rest are self-contained. And you can tell that Sarah is a cook because your kitchen has absolutely everything you need (except, of course, for Sarah, to fill it with the delicious aromas of her tapas). Enjoy conversational dinners brimming with local produce and wine (made by the mayor himself); tempting to eat in every night. Families will love it here: the sandy coast is a breathtaking drive, there's a donkey sanctuary nearby, bustling Jalón (true Spain) is five minutes away, and there are fantastic walks in the hills. Best of all are the lazy days spent here, at this charming and happy home, in the company of Johnny, Sarah and their three young children.

Price	€85–€145. Apartments €650–€1,450 per week.
Rooms	2 + 5: 2 twins/doubles sharing shower. 5 apartments: 3 for 2; 2 for 4. Cots & extra beds.
Meals	Breakfast €7.50. Lunch/picnic €15. Tapas €15–€20. Dinner with wine, €20–€30.
Closed	Rarely.
Directions	Directions on booking.

Johnny & Sarah Robinson
Apdo. 180, 03727 Jalón, Alicante

Tel	+34 965 973024
Email	enquiries@villajalon.com
Web	www.villajalon.com

Hotel Rural Almasera

Painted in bright and happy colours, Casa Almasera is collection of houses and a former olive mill, high in the mountains of Alicante province; its proud aim is to make you feel good in body and spirit. Masses of relaxation therapies are on offer here, but even more popular are the guided walking, hiking, mountain biking and birding tours led by energetic Michael through the spectacularly beautiful valleys and mountains that surround the *casa rural*. The area is full of natural limestone gorges; you can swim in secret lakes formed millions of years ago, explore caves and fascinating medieval villages, even visit a herb centre. The Almasera's rooms are light and airy, with beamed ceilings, simple, comfortable furnishings and fine new mattresses; outside is a tiled terrace with sunloungers and views. Michael's food is good and wholesome, most organically grown; this, the mountain air and the silence will soon heal body and soul. For culture, visit Cocentaina: once capital of a vast earldom, it has a 15th-century palace, a Clare convent and a Renaissance church. Beautiful beaches are a 30km drive.

Price	€60-€70. Apartments €350 per week.
Rooms	5 + 4: 5 doubles. 4 apartments for 2.
Meals	Lunch & dinner available. Wine €15-€20.
Closed	Never.
Directions	From Valencia, N-332 to Oliva. Exit Pego. In Pego, right at 1st lights, following signs for Cocentaina & Adsubia. Approx. 8km after Alpatró, left for Margarida.

	Michael Vietze
	c/Abadía 12-20,
	03828 Margarida-Planes, Alicante
Tel	+34 965 514314
Fax	+34 965 514314
Email	info@almasera.eu
Web	www.almasera.eu

La Casota

On a clear day you can see to Ibiza. The old farm is perched on the mountain side and has sensational views. Buildings ramble, flowers and herbs burst from pots, a big rectangular stone shades the fish pond, olive groves spread as far as the eye can see. Joaquina, friendly and kind-hearted, speaks excellent English, runs the farm on organic lines and has a team of girls to help look after the guests. It's a warm and inviting little place, simple, rustic, relaxing. Joaquina gives you four charming rooms in the *riu rau* where raisins were once stored, opening to a garden, and a delightful living area in another building, shared by all guests – comfy sofas, modern paintings and old farming implements on the walls, and glorious open fireplace in the corner. Self-caterers have an equally rustic studio-apartment and a two-storey house, the latter with a Moorish oven and all mod cons, both with a wood-burning stove for chilly nights. The food is a wonder – eggs from the hens, salads from the garden, fresh sorbets, homemade pastries, gilthead bream – and the pool overlooks the sea.

Price	€65-€75. Singles €45-€55. House €150-€170. Studio €85-€110. All prices per night.
Rooms	4 + 2: 4 twins/doubles. 1 house for 6, 1 studio for 4.
Meals	Breakfast €6. Picnic-style lunch €6. Dinner €17.50. Wine €8.
Closed	Rarely.
Directions	From Alicante on AP-7 for Valencia; exit 62 Ondara. CV-725 for Orba; here, signs to Vall de Laguar. Left on track just past signed entrance to Fleix. Hotel signed.

Joaquina Garrido
03791 La Vall de Laguart, Alicante

Tel	+34 965 583646
Email	info@lacasota.com
Web	www.lacasota.com

El Capricho de la Portuguesa

You are tucked away down a maze of narrow streets in a small village deep in a valley of orange groves and ancient olive trees. The jolly owner, Juan, requires you to relax, so bob in the jacuzzi with a gin and tonic and a good book – this is a retreat for sybarites. Peckish? Drinks and light snacks are served by friendly, helpful staff. Weary-limbed? Beside the two underground plunge pools lurks a masseuse at weekends. Sleepy? Your bedroom is decorated with fabulous attention to detail and great flair, from the glorious chandeliers to the comfy beds with white linen and fluffy robes. Bathrooms are spacious, spotless and crammed with lotions and potions. All is sumptuous here, high-ceilinged, wood-panelled, stone-floored and just a tad quirky; old cobbled steps invite you to a small courtyard garden for more lazing, the public rooms are alive with hugely colourful and joyous paintings by Spanish artist Luisa Mora and Juan chooses rather good music. More active souls can enjoy fabulous walking, or explore the village – there are five good restaurants within walking distance.

Price	€107-€137.
Rooms	7 doubles.
Meals	Breakfast €6. Dinner €25.
	Wine €15-€30. Restaurants nearby.
Closed	Rarely.
Directions	Detailed directions on hotel website.

Juan Jose Gimeno
c/Trinquet 7, Beniali,
03787 Vall de Gallinera, Alicante

Tel	+34 966 406674
Fax	+34 966 406554
Email	laportuguesa@senntire.com
Web	www.elcaprichodelaportuguesa.com

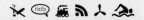

Xaymaca

Who would not love this old former olive mill in a sleepy village surrounded by almond and orange groves? An impressive wooden front door gives way to a spacious open-plan living area divided by a central kitchen, overlooking a plant-filled courtyard. Pass the fountain and climb the lamp-lit stone staircase to a charming hidden garden with panoramic views, pool and shaded barbecue area by an orchard – bliss on long warm days and sultry nights. Inside, all is vibrant and fun: happy colours, natural fabrics and bright paintings. Exposed stone walls and lofty beams add to the homely mood, and there's cosy seating in two living rooms with log fires. High-ceilinged bedrooms have big comfortable beds and private terraces or balcony. The friendly, attentive owner lives close and provides a little welcome pack. Discover safe sandy beaches and *parques naturales* nearby, perfect for walkers and birdwatchers. Wine and gastronomic tours too. There's also El Sequer, a bright and comfortable cottage for 4 close by; a sweet and serene place, full of light and colour and with a delightful garden. *Minimum stay two to seven nights.*

Price	€1,280-€1,850 per week. B&B rooms (low season) €46-€66 per night. El Sequer €50-€70 per night (€715-€1000 per week).
Rooms	House for 8 (2 doubles, 2 twins). El Sequer for 4.
Meals	Restaurant 2-minute walk.
Closed	Rarely.
Directions	AP-7 from Valencia/Alicante, exit 62; signs for Ondara. Take CV-732 for Beniarbeig, follow signs for Benimeli.

Jennifer Pilliner
c/Pou 9, 03769 Benimeli, Alicante

Tel	+34 966 424056
Fax	+34 966 424056
Email	jpilliner@telefonica.net
Web	www.mediterraneorural.com

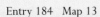

Hotel Chamarel

Within a short walk of this friendly atmospheric hotel you can be nosing around the 12th-century castle, watching the fishermen down on the quay, or quaffing a beer at a street café. The house was a nobleman's residence until the 1900s, and has been restored in a style that mirrors the era. The owners, from Valencia, are a lively pair with a background in art and design: note the wall hangings and the quirky paintings. Original teak and tiled floors glow, elaborate lamps hang from high ceilings, wood-panelled windows retain their shutters. Bedrooms range from a starkly elegant single to a velvety decadent suite: take your pick. Bamboo baskets spill aromatic lotions and the best views are over the courtyard, enticingly strewn with creepers and ferns. The other main public space is the shining all-wood bar, with zebra print armchairs and crouching cheetah mural. You could spend the rest of your life here… reading the morning away in shady corners, signing up for pilates or yoga, strolling into town. There are rollaway beds and table tennis for children – and all the bright beaches of the Costa Blanca.

Price	€75–€105. Suites €115–€124.
Rooms	14: 5 doubles, 4 twins/doubles, 1 family, 5 suites.
Meals	Tapas only. Wine €25. Not Sundays. Restaurants 2-minute walk.
Closed	Never.
Directions	E-15/AP-7 exit 62; CV-725 for 8km, signed Dénia. At 5th r'bout (Glorieta de Mahon) take 2nd exit. At T-junc. bear right; 2nd left; 2nd left again. Park & unload. Right onto Carrer Dels Cavallers; hotel 20m on right. Hard to find.

Eugenia V. Fuks
c/Cavallers 13, 03700 Denia, Alicante

Tel	+34 966 435007
Fax	+34 966 435600
Email	info@hotelchamarel.com
Web	www.hotelchamarel.com

Hostería Mont Sant

The Arab castle towers above; the views sweep dramatically over town and country way below. Terraced gardens glisten with orange trees and 1,000 young palms wave over fascinating archaeology... Iberian and Roman shards, Moorish fortifications, Cistercian walls. A Moorish irrigation system has guaranteed year-round water since the 12th century and the mountain streams are channelled into a vast cistern under the garden. Javier Andrés Cifre is proud of his old family house, including the relics he has uncovered. The natural unmanicured gardens are full of nooks, corners and canvas parasols. Cool, beamed living areas have intimate alcoves; bedrooms (tiny and dark in the attic) have antiques, good bathrooms and great views. Ten large, slightly dated, pine-clad cabañas (with deck, air conditioning, TV, DVD) are dotted among the pines, one of them a suite has its own pool. Mont Sant is renowned for its food: tuck into elaborate Valencian dishes from state-of-the-art kitchens, and, should you over-indulge, recover in the sauna, small pool or jacuzzi. *A Rusticae hotel. Used for big receptions.*

Price	€95-€140. Suite €260-€320. Half-board extra €45 p.p.
Rooms	17: 16 twins/doubles, 1 suite.
Meals	Breakfast €12. Lunch & dinner available.
Closed	7-20 January.
Directions	From Valencia A-7 for Albacete. Xátiva (Játiva) exit; follow signs for 'Castillo'. Signed. From Alicante to Madrid then A-7 to Valencia.

Javier Andrés Cifre
Ctra. del Castillo s/n, 46800 Xátiva, Alicante

Tel   +34 962 275081
Fax   +34 962 281905
Email   mont-sant@mont-sant.com
Web   www.mont-sant.com

El Jardín Vertical

Vilafames is a gorgeous hilltop village of red tiled roofs, turrets and towers, and a stunning museum of contemporary art. El Jardin Vertical is *the* place to stay, with its rambling, enchanting layout and views that sweep across cherry and almond groves (a feast in early spring) to the mountains beyond. It's a 400-year-old house, a rustic-chic hideaway that's been exquisitely styled. Floors are thick terracotta or 1920s cement-tiled, walls are open-stone or colourwashed plaster, and paintings and pottery, wicker chairs and Moroccan mosaics pepper the cool, serene reception area and the sitting room with its open fire. Madrileño pizzaz and panache extend to the patio and the big bedrooms; the suite in the attic (hot in summer) has sensational views and a winter fire; a spiral stair links the two levels of the family room (with private patio). Pale tiled floors reflect warm colours, the bed linen is the finest, the paintings are by Gloria's daughter. Double-glazing and shutters mute village street noise. And Gloria – to crown it all – is a fabulous cook. *A Rusticae hotel. Minimum stay two nights at weekends.*

Price	€135–€155. Family €175. Suite €185.
Rooms	8: 6 twins/doubles, 1 family room (with sofabed), 1 suite.
Meals	Breakfast €15. Lunch & dinner €30.
Closed	Rarely.
Directions	From Barcelona A-7 exit 'Castellón Sur'. After toll to Benicassim, exit for Borriol onto CV-10; on for San Mateo. Exit 38 to Vilafames; at village entrance, right to hotel. Park by 'Ayuntamiento'; hotel at far right of square.

Gloria Diaz–Varela Parada
Carrer Nou 15, 12192 Vilafames,
Castellón

Tel	+34 964 329938
Fax	+34 964 329938
Email	casarural@eljardinvertical.com
Web	www.eljardinvertical.com

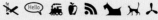

Hotel Cardenal Ram

You will never forget the dramatic approach to this magnificent old fortress town – and reach for your camera the minute it comes into view. It's even better close up, though best out of season: traffic-free, cobbled and 14th-century, with one of its grandest mansions, as medieval as the rest, now housing this hotel. Through the colonnade, beneath the Ram coat of arms, and into the vaulted entrance hall – spectacular in its scale and wall-encompassing tapestry, lowly in its well-worn leather sofas – to be greeted by the genial Jaime Peñarroya and his staff. A granite stairway sweeps up to the variously sized and definitely ungrand bedrooms. Despite fridges and tellies, one might hear echoes of medieval austerity in the bare white walls, dark mahogany furniture and dim lighting – a nod towards the monastic frugalities beneath the pageantry of Popes and cardinals? Then a new bright white bathroom, some with jet showers or hydromassage baths, will bring you back to the present. Food is good, truffles and sweet tarts are specialities – but Morella will stay longest in the memory. A good overnight stop.

Price	€70. Singles €45. Suites €80. Half-board extra €20 p.p. Full-board extra €35 p.p.
Rooms	19: 16 twins/doubles, 1 single, 2 suites.
Meals	Breakfast €6. Lunch & dinner available.
Closed	Rarely.
Directions	Into old town thro' P. de San Miguel; follow road round town until hotel signs. 200m from cathedral. Unload & park by P. de los Estudios, outside city walls.

Jaime Peñarroya Carbó
Cuesta Suñer 1, 12300 Morella,
Castellón

Tel	+34 964 173085
Fax	+34 964 173218
Email	info@cardenalram.com
Web	www.cardenalram.com

Casa Pernías

This place will grow on you. The hotel is modern, its raw lines to be softened by newly planted shrubs, but it's designed to be deliciously cool on hot summer days. The overriding impression is one of immaculate minimalist sophistication; the bedrooms are big and elegantly stark, the bathrooms serene. You'll enjoy lawyer Javier's company. His family has owned the land here for generations and he's charming, witty and very knowledgeable about all things Murcian. When he's working in Madrid, the place is run by Maria, whose mum makes the jam served at breakfast; she is helped by her friendly staff. Dinner is in the big formal restaurant and is open to all so you'll need to book. Dine off elegant white china on Spanish standards like gazpacho, and traditional Murcian dishes. This is open, rolling, farming country, framed on all sides by distant sierras, populated by vultures, eagles, partridge and wild boar. The GR7, an EU long-distance medieval track that begins in Albania and finished at Cape St Vincent, runs through part of the estate… or stay put, by sleek sofas and cool pool.

Price	€115–€160. Suites €160.
Rooms	16: 12 doubles, 4 suites.
Meals	Lunch €30–€35. Dinner €25–€30. Plus VAT at 7%.
Closed	24/25 December.
Directions	From Murcía C-415 West, becomes C-330 after Caravaca de la Cruz. Continue to Barranda; right on MU-702 for El Sabinar. Shortly after 22km marker, property signed on right.

Javier Ruiz de Assin
Ctra. Barranda-El Sabinar km23,
30441 Moratalla, Murcia

Tel	+34 968 726311
Fax	+34 968 726313
Email	info@casapernias.com
Web	www.casapernias.com

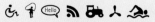

Molino del Río Argos

Remote and beautiful, the fruit and walnut farm hides beside an ancient canyon cut by the Argos – paleontologist heaven. Its abundant waters explain why grain was milled here for centuries… now Carmen and Scandinavian Jan have restored the 16th-century mill and created an award-winning place to stay and produce artisanal organic beer. The peachy colour-wash and dyes for doors and beams are natural, the floor tiles are handmade according to an ancient technique, and organic orchards and veg gardens clothe the terraces. In earlier times peasants came to exchange goods for flour; now people come for a perfect night's sleep in a rustically simple apartment or room, lulled by the sound of fountains and streams. Murcian dishes, occasionally Scandinavian, are seasonal and delicious, with wild meat a speciality. Patios, pergolas and outdoor pool, river walks and birdwatching, a cool room to contemplate the impressive mill machinery; the 'health and culture centre' offers therapies and courses (check dates). Caravaca, the fifth holy city, and the Ethnological Music Museum, are nearby. *Ask about courses.*

Price	€56-€70. Apartments €106-€120. Special prices for groups available. All prices per night.
Rooms	1 + 6: 1 double. 6 apartments for 2-6.
Meals	Breakfast €6. Lunch & dinner €18-€25. Wine €12-€20.
Closed	Rarely.
Directions	From Alicante A-7 for Murcia, then C-415 to Caravaca de la Cruz then C330 signed Andalucia. Thro' Barranda, right onto MU702, hotel signed after 5km.

Carmen Alvárez
Camino Viejo de Archivel-Benablón,
30400 Caravaca de la Cruz, Murcia
Tel +34 968 433381
Fax +34 968 433444
Email molinodelrio@molinodelrio.com
Web www.molinodelrio.com

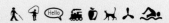

Hospedería La Mariposa

In the old days you climbed the winding road to stock up on flour, eggs and baccy. Now the old place has become a super family-run activity hotel, overseen by welcoming, hard-working Mark and Sam, who moved here in 2004. But what a site, on the edge of the Sierra Espuna Regional Park: supreme hiking country. Let Mark guide you on the quad bikes, visit the old ice houses and the famous dinosaur footprints; squeeze in some rock climbing, too. If nature won't tempt you then stay put by the pool. From the patio you can drink in the spectacular – almost lunar – landscape: there are binoculars and two telescopes to help you. Wrapped around a central courtyard, the eight bedrooms are nicely uncluttered and a very good size, with ceiling fans for summer and big radiators for winter; insect screens keep beasties at bay. The dining room is open for breakfast and the dish of the day; Sunday roasts are popular with visiting ex-pats. Take a cool drink to the courtyard, listen to 'golden oldies' in the cosy English bar. Water is recycled, solar power used, and much of the fruit is home-grown.

Price	€39–€65. Family €75–€90.
Rooms	8: 6 twins/doubles, 2 family.
Meals	Lunch & dinner from €9. Wine €10.
Closed	Never.
Directions	From Alhama follow signs for Mula & Gebas. Hotel on right on entering Gebas.

Mark Langton
Casa del Estanco 67, Gebas,
30840 Alhama de Murcia, Murcia
Tel   +34 968 631008
Fax   +34 968 632549
Email   info@hotellamariposa.com
Web   www.hotellamariposa.com

Casa el Azahar

A residential backstreet, a pair of white metal doors. Step in… to a soothing oasis a step from the sea. Katrine, multi-lingual and raised in Paris, owner of a friendly young boxer dog called Kila, has a relaxed manner and a warm open smile. She gives you pastries and orange blossom honey ('azahar') at breakfast, runs two restaurants and is an accomplished cook: just try her sea bream. The setting is chocolate-box resort; the house, a holiday home built in 1978, is a soporific hideaway with an exotic garden and a peaceful air. On opposite sides of a cobbled courtyard with an elegant palm are two bedrooms comfortable and bright, with a small fridge each and a spotless shower. Later, find a shady arbour and doze off with a book, or pop out the back gate and splash in the sea. This inland lagoon has its own microclimate, so for beach lovers and watersporters this is hard to beat. If it's shops, bars and ice cream parlours you're after, they're a two-minute pedal away; Katrin has bikes. She also loves to tailor-make tours – try a boat trip to the Isla de Baron for breakfast and a leisurely swim.

Price	€85-€100.
Rooms	2: 1 double, 1 twin.
Meals	Dinner, 3 courses with wine, €45, by arrangement. Restaurants 5-minute walk.
Closed	November to mid-March.
Directions	AP-7/A-30 thro' La Manga; 6km to petrol station on left. Next traffic lights, right-hand lane & left. Down to sea & left. House 50m past main road.

Katrine Duerinckx
297 Camino de Sotavento,
30380 La Manga, Murcia

Tel	+34 968 141035
Fax	+34 968 141035
Email	katrine@terra.es
Web	www.casaelazahar.com

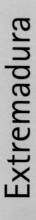

Extremadura

Casa Manadero

What's so thrilling about Spain are these vast, untamed parts of its interior. All-but-unknown Robledillo lies at the heart of the Sierra de Gata, yet is still within easy reach of Salamanca and Portugal. This village – one of the region's prettiest – makes much use of the local slate: *arquitectura negra*. The tiny restaurant has heavy old beams, subtle lighting and excellent regional food – "one hundred per cent natural products," says young Caridad, who has pillaged the family recipe books for your benefit. There's plenty for vegetarians to get excited about, too, while Cervantes himself was fond of the local wines. The apartments, on three floors, vary in layout following the dictates of the original building; all are cosy yet airy and lofty, with kitchenettes and Caridad's cheerful décor. Outside is a basic, low-ceilinged cabin for two, with a geranium-strewn balcony for summer; views stretch over tiled roofs and endless vegetable gardens. You are surrounded by forests of oaks, olive groves and vineyards – marvellous for riding and biking. And there's a natural swimming pool close by.

Price	€55–€80 p.p. Half-board extra €14 p.p. Full-board extra €29 p.p. All prices per night.
Rooms	1 studio for 2-3; 4 apartments for 2-4; 1 cabin for 2-3.
Meals	Breakfast €6–€7.95. Lunch & dinner €10–€15. Set menu weekdays only.
Closed	Never.
Directions	Through village of Descargamaría, right for Robledillo; 2km, left & down into village. Beware steep narrow roads. Contact owner re access.

Caridad Hernández
c/Manadero 2, 10867 Robledillo de Gata, Cáceres

Tel	+34 927 671118
Fax	+34 927 671173
Email	info@casamanadero.com
Web	www.casamanadero.com

Finca El Cabezo

Across the rolling hills and cork forests of Cáceres: eagles above, the road to yourself – it's awe-inspiring and remote. You're headed for a working farm (9,000 olive trees, 300 head of cattle) but don't expect a scruffy old ranch. As you pass through the gates of the ivy-hung building you enter a magical inner courtyard of rambling creepers and massed potted plants. The big, eminently comfortable rooms, some in the eastern wing, some above the kitchen, have much elegance: antiques on parquet and ancient terracotta, warm colours and modern art, chunky rafters, carved shutters, fabulous bathrooms. The sitting room deserves a feature in an interiors magazine: slate floors, granite walls, warm fabrics, interesting paintings. Feast on organic eggs fried in olive oil, goat's cheese and homemade cakes at breakfast; at dinner, drop into a cheerful little restaurant in San Martín or a book into the Michelin-listed treasure down the road. Miguel can advise on walks and hikes; this may be in one of Spain's furthest flung corners but it is worth a long detour and you couldn't hope to meet a more charming host.

Price	€85. Suites €101.
Rooms	6: 5 twins/doubles, 1 suite.
Meals	Restaurants nearby.
Closed	Rarely.
Directions	From Salamanca for Ciudad Rodrigo. Here, towards Cáceres; once over mountain pass 'Puerto de los Perales', right for V. del Fresno on EX-205. House on left at km22.8 marker. Signed.

Miguel Muriel
Ctra. Hoyos – Valverde del Fresno km22.8,
10892 San Martín de Trevejo, Cáceres

Tel	+34 927 193106
Fax	+34 927 193106
Email	correo@elcabezo.com
Web	www.elcabezo.com

La Vaquería Cantaelgallo

Play lord of the manor: rent the house (breakfast, laundry and maid service included, private cook available), install your friends in the cottage next door and pretend the estate is your own. Reached by an unmade track and in rolling, wooded countryside – with glimpses of the Gredos mountains – this has a secret, hideaway feel. As for the house, it oozes such luxury and style it's hard to believe it was once a barn: Soledad and Iago spent three years reshaping it. Be delighted by cosy red armchairs, toile de Jouy curtains, a real log fire, a veranda with two irresistible hammocks. The gardens, too, are a joy: six hectares of holm oak and chestnut trees, cherries, apples, oranges, peaches, figs, olive and madroño: pluck what you will from the kitchen garden. Rural sounds are provided by the 'Chicken Palace' – source of fabulous new laid eggs – and frogs tuning up on the nearby pond. House and cottage share the prettily set (though unheated and unguarded) swimming pool. A hotel is being built on the estate a ten-minute walk away, and its facilities will be open to you. *Can collect from Madrid airport.*

Price	House €240–€300 (€1,500 per week). Cottage €900 per week.
Rooms	House for 6-7 (3 doubles). Cottage for 4 (2 doubles).
Meals	Breakfast included. Dinner with wine, from €12. Restaurants 2km.
Closed	Never.
Directions	From Plasencia EX-203 to Jaraiz de la Vera (30km). Thro' town; right immediately after small park on right. Follow for 2km (becomes rough track). House signed.

María Soledad Pidal Ochoa
10400 Jaraiz de la Vera, Cáceres

Tel	+34 913 103248
Fax	+34 914 422532
Email	info@vaqueriacantaelgallo.com
Web	www.vaqueriacantaelgallo.com

La Casa de Pasarón

Young, friendly and energetic, Susana is so proud of the 1890s village house in which her grandparents once lived that she has embarked upon major improvements. A terrace and pool, a big meeting room-cum-sports bar with a giant public screen and a new bodega/restaurant are being added, behind the elegant portal of carefully dressed sandstone. Inside, the lounge mixes old and new furnishings – cushioned sofas, brass chandelier, photographic portraits and Impressionist prints – while the vaulted dining room feels welcoming with its sprinkling of attractively laid tables and the original marble-topped dressers; start your day here with oven-warm bread, local cheeses and fruit compotes made by the family. Dinner is excellent value, and delicious; perhaps soup followed by meatballs or kid stew. Bedrooms are reached via a heavy granite staircase: most are on the first floor, four are in the attic with skylight windows. They are simple, spotless and quiet. At the back, a garden full of walnut and lemon trees. The quaint and pretty village is a gem in this very lovely corner of Spain and the hiking is fabulous.

Price	€100. Twins €80.
Rooms	13: 4 doubles, 9 twins.
Meals	Dinner €18.
Closed	10 January–1 February.
Directions	From Plasencia EX-203 dir. Jaraiz de la Vera. Cross Tejeda del Tiétar, fork left at km24 marker to Pasaron, 1st left on entering village. Signed.

Susana Ayala
La Magdalena 18,
10411 Pasarón de la Vera, Cáceres

Tel	+34 927 469407
Email	pasaron@pasaron.com
Web	www.pasaron.com

Delacava

One visitor used this tiny fairytale cottage for meditating; another, a wildlife photographer, took it as his 'hide'. Whatever your interests, the bodega, once used for wine-making, provides an invigoratingly simple and isolated place to stay. Set in six acres of oak trees and overgrown vineyards, it's three miles (some on unmade track) from the nearest town – but the backdrop of the mountains is stunning. Park the car in a clearing among the trees and introduce yourself to the casita. In the bed-cum-sitting room are a coat stand for a wardrobe and a very comfortable bed. Kitchen and bathroom are simple and well-equipped, beamed ceilings and herringbone-pattern brick floors give a pleasingly rustic air, there are books, magazines and DVDs. Most of the electricity comes from solar panels, so don't expect air con, just thick stone walls to keep you cool and a wood-burner and heaters for winter. Emma and César live with their young daughters a stroll away. They're hard-working and enthusiastic potters, more than happy for you to visit their studio and have a go. *Breakfast on 1st day & hamper provided.*

Price	€80 (€390 per week).
Rooms	Cottage for 2.
Meals	Restaurants 5km.
Closed	July & August.
Directions	A-5/E-90 from Madrid; exit 148; CM-5102. In Madrigal de la Vera left onto EX-203 for Villanueva. Left after 74km marker & garage, signed Vega de la Barca. After 750m right onto unmade road; continue 2km; signed.

Emma Mier Neele
Apdo. de Correos 29,
10470 Villanueva de la Vera, Cáceres
Tel   +34 927 198576
Email   mierivas@hotmail.com
Web   www.delacava.es

Entry 197   Map 10

Casa de la Plaza de Moritos

Up twisting, cobbled streets into the heart of the medieval town, you slip through a simple door... and enter, magically, another world. Wrapped around by gardens, this conquistador's mansion towers over town and countryside. Unexpectedly grand, restored from 1970s' ruins, its rooms sweep you up with old-fashioned country-house style: lush drapes, soft lamps, large fireplaces, rich rugs. Entertain royally in the marble-floored drawing room with its plump sofas, big table (it seats 12) and decorative furnishings. Eat in the vaulted dining room or on the shady terrace, sprawl in the comfy sitting room with sofas and card tables, flaunt your cooking skills in the super-duper kitchen. Guest room style bedrooms are formal and comfortable, their bathrooms brisk and unfussy. Rooms across the terrace are cosier – good for peace-seekers or children. The owners, charming and courteous, live nearby and are experts on Trujillo's rich history; ask them too about walking, birdwatching, fishing. Or just unwind in the secluded, terraced gardens with pool, shady nooks and fabulous sunsets. *Daily maid service Mon-Fri (3hrs).*

Price	£1,550–£2,200 (sterling) per week.
Rooms	House for 8.
Meals	Restaurants 5-minute walk.
Closed	December–February.
Directions	From Madrid E-90/A-5; exit 253 onto EX-208. After 1.5km over x-roads; signs for Centro Ciudad/Plaza Mayor. Diagonally across Plaza; left after 200m, signed Castillo/NH Hotel. Past hotel, under arch; right; immed. left. House in square.

Juan Garton
Plaza de Moritos, 10200 Trujillo,
Cáceres

Tel	+44 (0)20 7381 6000
Email	garton@alderney.net
Web	www.trujilloespana.com

Casa Rural El Recuerdo

Extremadura is a land that is embracing and wild, one of vast, open landscapes, big skies and ancient stones. The Kelseys, recently returned from charitable work in India, were moved by the magic of the place – and its birdlife, which is exceptional. They happened upon a former 'lagar', a farm where wine was made, and, after some serious renovation, created a home of simple, solid comfort, the whole made spicier thanks to a quantity of furnishings and prints brought back from the East. The house's most memorable feature is its wafer-bricked, vaulted dining room where the wine was once made. You may be lucky and share dinner with Martin and Claudia, whose dishes are inspired by the recipe books of Spain, India and South America. There is high vegetable quotient and much of it fresh from the garden. Find time to take coffee in the square in nearby Trujillo, or laze beneath the willow beside the pool, perhaps perusing one of Martin's many books on birds (he's a professional ornithologist). Bedrooms are spotless, peaceful, traditional, just right for this type of rural retreat.

Price	€70.
Rooms	6 twins/doubles.
Meals	Dinner, with wine, €20, by arrangement.
Closed	Rarely.
Directions	From Trujillo EX-208 towards Guadalupe. After 11km, right for San Clemente. Signs to house.

Martin & Claudia Kelsey
Pago de San Clemente, 10200 Trujillo,
Cáceres

Tel	+34 927 319349
Email	info@casaruralelrecuerdo.com
Web	www.casaruralelrecuerdo.com

Finca Santa Marta

Lost in a semi-wild Spanish landscape – yet linked by a brand new motorway to Madrid – these two fincas have been transformed by Marta Rodríguez-Gimeno into a bucolic retreat. Bedrooms vary in size and design but each has been newly redone, each with a character of its own; there are country antiques and a smart new suite. The main hotel space has been transferred to the Santa Teresa farmhouse on the other side of the (very peaceful) road; now there are two sitting rooms, one in the vast, vaulted olive press, the other in the old wine cellar. Be charmed by subtle lighting and a mix of pieces collected from time spent overseas; your much-travelled host was Dutch Ambassador to Kuwait, Peru and Korea. The fincas are surrounded by 30 hectares of olive groves, almond orchards and vineyards – and birds: the area is an orthnologist's delight and the hotel is popular with nature lovers, who have been heading here for years. In summer, the extended garden and super new pool are a boon. An enchanting spot, where peace wraps itself around you and sleep is deep. *A Rusticae hotel.*

Price	€85–€120.
Rooms	14 twins/doubles.
Meals	Dinner, with wine, €30.
Closed	Rarely.
Directions	From Madrid, A-5 motorway to Trujillo, then Ex-208 dir. Guadalupe. After 14km, on right, in front of winery, where you see eucalyptus trees with storks' nests (km89 marker).

Marta Rodríguez-Gimeno & Henri Elink
Pago de San Clemente, 10200 Trujillo,
Cáceres

Tel	+34 927 319203
Fax	+34 927 334115
Email	henri@facilnet.es
Web	www.fincasantamarta.com

Hotel Casa Escobar Jerez

Steeped in 500 years of history, the casa wraps around you like the pages of a beloved book. A joint crusade by José and Susana, it took six years to peel away dirt and rotting timbers and restore the fabric to its original magnificent proportions: granite walls and oak doors, flagstone floors, vaulted ceilings, and a spiral stone staircase leading to the roof terrace. There are panoramic views over the town and Portuguese border and you're well-placed for golf, walks, riding (the hotel has a ranch), and medieval Albuquerque with its market and bars. Bedrooms overlook the tiny street or inner courtyard – peaceful apart from the clacking of the storks (beware the mating season!). Cool and restful with raftered ceilings, rugs on tiled floors and limewashed or elegant papered walls, the décor is handsome and restrained. Big beds, volumes of space – in the bathrooms, too. Plenty of spots to enjoy the sun or shade, be sociable or escape, plus a small spa (steam room, massage pool) to revive. Everyone smiles, food is simple and seasonal, and you can raise a glass to the stars. *New rooms, lift & spa planned for 2009.*

Price	€90–€180. Suites €220–€300. Half-board €30 extra p.p.
Rooms	9: 4 doubles, 5 suites.
Meals	Dinner €27, by arrangement. Wine €10–€75.
Closed	1 June–15 July; Christmas.
Directions	From Cáceres N-521; exit km140 marker for Valencia de Alcántara. 150m past petrol station, right onto Paseo de San Francisco. Onto c/Duquesa de la Victoria; right onto c/Alfacar. Hotel on right. Park in Plaza Mayor.

Susana Lorenzo
c/Alfacar 13-15,
10500 Valencia de Alcántara, Cáceres

Tel	+34 927 668139
Fax	+34 927 581205
Email	recepcion@casaescobarjerez.com
Web	www.casaescobarjerez.com

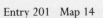

Dehesa Tres Riveros

The countryside is gorgeous rolling *dehesa*: open oak woodland dedicated to grazing Iberian pigs, cattle and sheep. This cluster of newly converted holiday cottages lies at the heart of a 400-hectare estate, within the boundaries of the national park that straddles the border between Spain and Portugal, the Rio Tajo. After an exhilarating drive, be greeted by the kindly farm manager, Eduardo. The cottages appear somewhat rectilinear from the outside but their unforgiving lines are softened by abundant greenery. Inside the feel is much more welcoming: warm colourwashes in sitting rooms and bedrooms, attractive stencilling and some unusual rustic Mexican furniture. Given the remoteness of the place – the nearest restaurant is eight kilometres away – you'll appreciate the well-equipped kitchens, while the makings of a simple breakfast are delivered to your door each evening by Eduardo. If you love a remote setting, and look forward to days spent hiking, riding, mountain biking and birdwatching, this is a superb place to stay.

Price	House for 5, €91-€115. House for 6, €110-€135. House for 8, €146-€180. All prices per night.
Rooms	3 houses: 1 for 5; 1 for 6; 1 for 8.
Meals	Self-catering includes breakfast. Restaurant 8km.
Closed	Rarely.
Directions	Cáceres N-521 Valencia de Alcántara; right for Cedillo. After 18.5km right for Herrera de Alcántara. After 4km, right for Santiago de Alcántara. Signed on left after 2km; 3km track to house.

Gabriel Hernández García
10512 Herrera de Alcántara, Cáceres

Tel	+34 923 238185
Fax	+34 923 257895
Email	agroturismo@losbayones.com
Web	www.losbayones.com

Andalusia

Hotel Alminar

Hotel Alminar stands in the heart of graceful, characterful Seville. And because it gives onto a tiny pedetrianised street it is generally quiet too – a treat in a city of 4am dust carts and midnight mopeds. Young staff take great pride in their work and could hardly be more helpful with tips and recommendations. This new renovation of a handsome townhouse opened in 2005 with a stylish sprinkling of rooms, the nicest being at the top; numbers 31 and 32 have their own small terraces and bird's-eye views of the Giralda. They are plainly minimalist in style, with cream walls, clean lines, sober furniture in neutral shades, and fabulous bathrooms in immaculate mosaics. All feels spotless and well cared-for. There's no lounge, space at breakfast time is limited and breakfast is a modest buffet. But who cares where there are so many enticing bars so close to hand; it feels good to start the day with the locals over a *café con leche*. Soulful Seville lies at your feet. If you visit nothing else, visit the exquisite Moorish palace of Alcazar, and its oasis of a garden.

Price	€90–€155. Singles €60–€95.
Rooms	12: 10 twins/doubles, 2 singles.
Meals	Breakfast €6. Restaurant close by.
Closed	Never.
Directions	Hotel 50m east of Cathedral. Best to park in c/Albareda car park next to Plaza Nueva, then walk.

Francisco Naranjo
c/Alvarez Quintero 52, 41004 Sevilla

Tel	+34 954 293913
Fax	+34 954 212197
Email	reservas@hotelalminar.com
Web	www.hotelalminar.com

Casa Numero 7

The owner, an aristocrat from Jerez, has a fondness for Britain and the British; the result: a touch of Chelsea in the heart of Seville. Perhaps it was memories of England's country houses that inspired his conversion of a fine Moorish townhouse into an award-winning small hotel. A mood of privileged intimacy prevails, with six bedrooms – very quiet for the centre of town – grouped around a central courtyard. And there's a roof terrace from which you can gaze on the Giralda. Bedrooms are regal affairs, every one different; ask for the Yellow Room with its 'Juliet' balcony or the Blue Room next to the roof terrace. All is immaculate, fabrics, furniture, lighting; beds are sumptuous and large. Yet there's a delightfully at-home feel, thanks to fragrant fresh flowers, books (*Who's Who!*), magazines and photos of the owner's famous forebears. The cool and elegant drawing room is the perfect spot for a glass of sherry – from the family's Jerez bodega, of course – and breakfasts are perfectly English, served by butlers in white gloves. Alejandra is the ever-helpful manageress, and Seville lies outside the door.

Price	€177–€275.
Rooms	6 twins/doubles.
Meals	Restaurants nearby.
Closed	Rarely.
Directions	Park in Aparcamento 'Cano y Cueto' at junc. of C/Cano y Cueto & Menendez Pelayo (next to Jardines de Murillo). Tell attendant staying at Casa No. 7. From here 5 minutes' walk to hotel.

Gonzalo del Río y González-Gordon
c/Virgenes 7, 41004 Sevilla

Tel	+34 954 221581
Fax	+34 954 214527
Email	info@casanumero7.com
Web	www.casanumero7.com

La Casa del Maestro

You may feel compelled to dance a flamenco inside this classic Sevillian townhouse. It was once the home of the maestro guitarist, Nino Ricardo. Photographs of his handsome face and passionate playing cover its walls, evoking the heady days of the 1900s. The house has kept that era's gracious style while carefully introducing 21st-century comfort. The focal point is the central covered courtyard with its stunning mosaic floor, elegant chairs and tables and double tier of wrought-iron balustraded galleries. The upper galleries lead to the bedrooms: stylishly classic with creamy stucco walls, rugs on tiled floors, noble bedheads and embroidered linen. Antiques, fresh flowers and glossy magazines add a warm, homely feel; bathrooms are sumptuous with delicious toileteries. Breakfast is served by charming staff in the courtyard, on the rooftop terrace or in your room. After a day's exploring the fascinating old Jewish quarter of Santa Cruz, return to sunset-watching from the rooftop terrace. This place captures the intimacy and romance of Seville, and our readers love it. *A Rusticae hotel.*

Price	€105–€260.
Rooms	11 twins/doubles.
Meals	Restaurants nearby.
Closed	Some days in August.
Directions	In Sevilla S-30 for Córdoba, exit S. Justa. At S. Justa station, 1st right; 1st left; right for P. de Osario. Right on c/Escuelas Pías, pass church, 1st left. Straight to Plaza S. Leandro; turn into c/Francisco Carrión Mejías; 1st left.

Patricia Zapardiel
c/Niño Ricardo 5, Antigua Almudena, 41003 Sevilla

Tel	+34 954 500007
Fax	+34 954 500006
Email	reservas@lacasadelmaestro.com
Web	www.lacasadelmaestro.com

Casa el Marqués

The dukes of Seville came to this area to escape the blistering heat. You might be tempted to do likewise; you'll still be a bus ride from Spain's sultriest city – birthplace of Carmen. There is a strong sense of being hidden away here, tucked behind the high wall of the Casa de Cultura, in the grounds of a former olive mill. This sweetly elegant holiday home belongs to Juan and Macarena, whose knowledge of Seville's palaces, museums and green spaces will set you on the right track. Via a small courtyard (your hosts live opposite) you enter a smartly furnished house, cool with white walls and tiled floors and stairs. Furniture is mostly antique (Macarena ran a shop in Seville). The two bedrooms, one with a balcony that overlooks the courtyard, are clean and uncluttered. Downstairs are the bathroom and living room, and chairs on the cobblestoned patio so you can spill into the sun. There are flashes of colour from the pots outside. Those escaping the noise and dust of the city will be very happy here, and if you tire of self-catering, there are a number of restaurants a stroll away.

Price	€90–€180 per night.
Rooms	House for 2-4.
Meals	Restaurants close by.
Closed	Rarely.
Directions	Sevilla-Huelva A-49. At km3 marker, exit Castilleja. At 1st r'bout, exit for Centro Comercial. Straight over 2nd r'bout; at 3rd r'bout, left. Just pass Supercor right at sign 'Casa de Cultura'. Take 2nd right, house on left.

**Macarena Fernandez-Palacio &
Juan Castro**
c/Enmedio 40,
41950 Castilleja de la Cuesta, Sevilla

Tel	+34 629 791188 (mobile)
Email	informacion@casaelmarques.com
Web	www.casaelmarques.com

Cortijo Aguila Real

Aguila Real is every inch the classic, whitewashed cortijo. You are surrounded by fields of cotton, sunflowers and wheat, yet are no distance at all from the charms of Seville (catch a glimpse of the Giralda tower from the gardens). Passing under the main gate you enter a vast inner courtyard, where bougainvillea romps and an old dovecote and water trough are reminders that this was a working farm. The public rooms, the best with beautiful barrel-vaulted ceilings, are decorated in ochres and terracottas with a smart mix of modern sofas and heavy antiques and the odd painting and hunting trophy on the wall. Dinner in the purpose-built dining room and on the elegant summer terrace comes with silver cutlery and classical music; the food is regional, the wine list long. Bedrooms, set around the inner courtyard, are traditionally Spanish, with huge beds and lots of space, some with terrace; bathrooms have double sinks, and the tower room has views. The palm-filled garden where doves coo is subtly illuminated at night – and there's a pretty pool. Stay for a night or two and soak up the authentic atmosphere.

Price	€70–€136.40. Suites €120–€215.65. Plus VAT at 7%.
Rooms	15: 10 twins/doubles, 5 suites.
Meals	Breakfast €13.20. Dinner from €29.90 à la carte. Wine from €23. Plus VAT at 7%.
Closed	Never.
Directions	Sevilla ring road SE-30 to Merida A-66. Exit 798 towards Guillena (SE-460). In Guillena, right at 2nd lights. Hotel on Guillena-Burguillos (A-461) road; signed.

David Venegas
Ctra. Guillena-Burguillos km4,
41210 Guillena, Sevilla

Tel	+34 955 785006
Fax	+34 955 784330
Email	hotel@aguilareal.com
Web	www.aguilareal.com

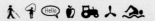

Las Navezuelas

A place of birds and natural beauty, a 16th-century olive mill set in 136 hectares of green meadows, oak forest and olive groves; you are in some of Spain's loveliest countryside and the place is an ornithologist's dream. Water streams down from the Sierra, often along Moorish-built channels, swallows and storks nest, boar and deer roam, sheep bells jangle and pretty Cazalla is two miles away. The house and converted outbuildings are pure Andalucía with a beautiful stepped central patio and the garden a southern feast of palms and orange trees, wisteria, jasmine and pool for lazing – admire the amazing views. You will find the most characterful of the variegated bedrooms in the rambling main house; all are whitewashed and well-lit, with old bits of furniture and a homespun, occasionally faded feel. Apartments are attractive though minimally supplied. There are two sitting rooms and two dining rooms, the oldest aromatic with log fires in winter, and the menu includes good local dishes and produce from the farm – in smallish portions. The town is a five-minute drive – good news for self-caterers.

Price	€59–€63. Singles €45–€55. Studios €86–€90. Apartments €110–€140. All prices per night.
Rooms	6 + 6: 4 twins/doubles, 2 suites. 3 studios for 2; 3 apartments for 4–6.
Meals	Lunch & dinner €20. Wine €21. Lunch in summer only.
Closed	7 January–25 February.
Directions	From Sevilla 8006 to Cantillana. Here, A-432 for Cazalla. Pass km43 marker; after 500m, right at sign.

Luca Cicorella & Miraló Tena
Ctra. A-432 km43.5, Apdo. 14, 41370
Cazalla de la Sierra, Sevilla

Tel	+34 954 884764
Fax	+34 954 884594
Email	navezuela@arrakis.es
Web	www.lasnavezuelas.com

Los Pozos de la Nieve

Once the hacienda was an ice factory for Seville – note the ice pit's frescos, and the old smokery's blackened beams. The history and fabric of this prize-winning restoration captured our imagination, along with the enthusiasm of the Dutch owners. They give you breakfast on the first morning; if they cannot greet you (they live some way away), the caretaker will. After a drive through beautiful countryside it is a treat to approach this glorious classical façade, behind which lie two rustic-chic apartments with white walls and masses of light. Moroccan rugs warm terracotta floors, exposed stones and beams add character. Cream linen curtains dress new windows, simple kitchens have stylish mod cons, there are great big beds with fat mattresses, stainless steel lamps, country wardrobes and scatterings of white cushions. Discover a metal staircase here, a wood-burner there, and lovely bathrooms – shared in one apartment, baths in the bedrooms of the other. Organic olive groves to roam, bikes delivered to the door, restaurants a five-minute drive, a new pool to come home to. A big treat for a small party.

Price	€700–€1,200 per week.
Rooms	2 apartments for 4–6.
Meals	Restaurant 300m; Constantina 5-minute drive.
Closed	Never.
Directions	From Sevilla, E5 dir. Cordoba, exit 506 dir. Lora del Rio, through Lora, dir. Constantina, through Constantina, dir. Cazalla; Pozos de la Nieve on right just before roads splits to Cazalla & Alanis.

Dirk Winderickx & Dominique De Bock
Ctra. de Constantina–Cazalla de la Sierra
km4, 41450 Constantina, Sevilla

Tel	+34 955 669266
Fax	+34 955 669266
Email	constantina@lospozosdelanieve.com
Web	www.lospozosdelanieve.com

Hotel Rural El Olivo

Chances are you won't have heard of Puebla de Los Infantes. It hides in the furthest corner of Seville province, on a quiet back road that cuts up from the Guadalquivir valley to the foothills of the Sierra Morena – the sort of place where a foreign number plate might turn heads. The sturdy white building, a labour of love for the Sáenz family, stands on a small square edged with citrus trees, and the owners are proud of what they have achieved. The décor is as Andalucían as can be: marble and tiled floors, sugary prints of flowers on white walls, wrought-iron ballustrading and window grilles galore, potted palms and aspidistras and all is new and shiny. The sole communal space is a tiny sitting area by reception furnished with rattan chairs. However, the simple bedrooms, each named after a variety of olive, are so spruce and such brilliant value that you won't mind a bit. It might be nice to break the journey here, en route from Seville to Córdoba, and get to grips with that fabled 'real Spain'.

Price	€50-€60.
Rooms	10: 7 twins/doubles, 2 singles, 1 suite.
Meals	Restaurants in village.
Closed	Rarely.
Directions	From Sevilla A-4 towards Madrid; exit for Carmona/Lora del Río. Continue to Lora del Río then on Via Ermita de Setefilla to La Puebla. Hotel on left of 1st square.

	Miguel Sáenz
	Pza. Virgen de las Huertas 1,
	41479 La Puebla de los Infantes, Sevilla
Tel	+34 954 808103
Email	reservas@casaruralelolivo.com
Web	www.hotelruralelolivo.com

Palacio de los Granados

Push the boat out and treat yourself to this beguiling baroque palace where every guest feels like a prince or princess and charm oozes from heavy tasselled fabrics, deep sofas and thick rugs. Arches, lanterns and brassware, reflecting the city's Arabic past, add an exotic touch. It's design-mag worthy. The courtyards are magical: one has pillared archways, soothing fountains and glossy ferns; the other, with an elegant pool and 120-year-old palm, is scented with orange and pomegranate trees: sheer delight at breakfast. The high bedrooms are grand in every detail: queen-size beds, jewel-bright fabrics, exotically coloured walls, mosaic-tiled bathrooms. Some have chandeliers, others Moorish alcoves, or draped beds straight from *The Arabian Nights*. The utterly indulgent menus change daily – a mix of Andalucían and South American. Explore ancient Écija, fascinating for its Roman remains and baroque churches, return to a nightcap by that lovely little pool. Owners Pablo and Francisco, cultured and charming, may tell the restoration story, their staff are totally gracious; you will be hopelessly spoiled.

Price	€145-€177. Suites €177-€220.
Rooms	14: 10 twins/doubles, 4 suites.
Meals	Lunch & dinner, with wine, €40-€65.
Closed	Rarely.
Directions	From Sevilla on A-4; exit for Écija & Osuna on A-351. At r'bout follow signs for 'Centro urbano, Ayuntamiento, Palacio de Granados'. Hotel at end of c/Emilio Castelar, on right (parking spaces next door).

Pablo Ojeda O'Neill
c/Emilio Castelar 42, 41400 Écija,
Sevilla

Tel	+34 955 905344
Fax	+34 955 901412
Email	info@palaciogranados.com
Web	www.palaciogranados.com

Cortijo Alguaciles Bajos

Bed and breakfast in the rolling wheatlands of the Sevillian hinterland, where the only passing traffic is the tractor from the next village. Arrival is up a palm-lined drive, then into a cobbled courtyard where beautiful whitewashed walls are offset by ferns, geraniums and jasmine. The housekeeper greets you (very much in Spanish!) and shows you to your quarters in the old grain stores, where furniture and paintings form part of the collective memory of the Mencos family, who live in Madrid for most of the year. Our favourite is the Naranjo room whose bathroom is the size of a studio in London or Paris, but all are roomy, comfortable and full of original and interesting features. Water, as so often in Spain, is solar-heated. No meals in the Cortijo, apart from a rudimentary breakfast, but for dinner there is an authentic *venta* (a roadside restaurant) a short drive away. Silence surrounds you, perhaps the odd barking dog at night... you will feel closer to understanding real Spain. You may also find yourselves here alone. But it is both enchanting and good value, a refreshing antithesis to chain hotels.

Price	€60. Singles €48.
Rooms	8 twins/doubles.
Meals	Two restaurants nearby.
Closed	1-15 August; 1-15 September.
Directions	N-IV Sevilla-Cádiz to Cabezas de San Juan. There, at crossroads left on A-371 for Villamartín; 6.5km; left again on A-8128 for Montellano. Farm on left after km3.3 marker.

	Simon Carrero
	Ctra. A-1828 km3.3, 41710 Utrera, Sevilla
Mobile	+34 630 561529
Fax	+34 915 641071
Email	alguaciles@alguaciles.com
Web	www.alguaciles.com

Entry 212   Map 20

Hacienda de San Rafael

The hacienda lies in glorious isolation amid the undulating farmlands of Seville's hinterland, half a mile of olive-lined drive leading to its sunny façade. Andalucía! The views are vast, golden with sunflowers in summer. You'll be greeted by one of San Rafael's staff with an iced drink – and will continue to be pampered at every turn. San Rafael has been in the brothers' family for nearly 150 years, and is lovelier than ever. Stunning bedrooms – split-level, stone-floored, with their own verandas and gorgeous bathrooms – give onto the exquisitely cobbled central patio, the inner sanctuary of any true cortijo. Geranium, jasmine and bougainvillea romp. In the gardens are three thatched casitas, beautifully furnished in a mix of country antique and modern, with a piece of terrace each and sharing an infinity pool. There are two elegant drawing rooms where oriental furnishings and prints collected on trips to the East blend with local pieces, and a thatched dining area in the garden for summer meals; the cooking is superb. There's even a little shop selling local blankets and Indian jewellery.

Price	€240. Casitas €480. Prices per night, plus VAT at 7%.
Rooms	11 + 3: 11 twins/doubles. 3 casitas for 2.
Meals	Lunch from €25 à la carte. Dinner, with wine, €55.
Closed	15 December–1 March.
Directions	From Sevilla south on N-IV, San Rafael is 1st turn on right-hand side after km594 marker, before Repsol petrol station.

Anthony & Patrick Reid Mora-Figueroa
Ctra. N-IV (km594),
41730 Las Cabezas de San Juan, Sevilla

Tel	+34 954 227116
Fax	+34 955 218414
Email	info@haciendadesanrafael.com
Web	www.haciendadesanrafael.com

Finca Buen Vino

After 30 years in this divinely isolated spot of wild natural beauty, hidden among the thick oak and chestnut woods of the Aracena mountains, Sam and Jeannie have been made honorary citizens of their local town. Buen Vino was built in the early 1980s but many of the materials used were ancient, shipped in from far corners of Spain; the panelled dining room, the arched doors and the wooden staircase have a seductive, timeworn patina. All is being refurbished for 2009 but currently the house's decoration is unaffected and elegant, and the bedrooms are cosy, with our favourites up in the attic. There are easy chairs and cushions, cheery oil paintings, books and family memorabilia, comfortable beds and good linen, perhaps a bath tub with a view. Outside is a fabulous infinity pool. There are also three independent cottages to rent, hidden away on the edges of this bucolic estate, each with a wood-burner (it gets cold from October to March) and a private pool. The owners aim to encourage small groups and parties – up to 12 in the main house – and Jeannie, a fine baker and cook, will be offering cookery courses too.

Price	€120-€150. Cottage details on request.
Rooms	4 + 3: 2 twins/doubles; 2 twins/doubles each with separate bathroom. 3 cottages for 4.
Meals	Lunch €20, by arrangement (summer only). Dinner, with wine, €40.
Closed	Christmas & New Year.
Directions	From Sevilla, north on A66/E803 direction Merida. N4333 direction Portugal. Bypass Aracena & Los Merinos. Right at km95 marker; through gates.

Sam & Jeannie Chesterton
Ctra. CN-433 km95, 21208 Los Marines, Huelva

Tel	+34 959 124034
Fax	+34 959 501029
Email	sam@fincabuenvino.com
Web	www.fincabuenvino.com

Molino Rio Alájar

Rustling leaves and birdsong: it is as bucolic as can be. Come for the peace, or for the famously delicious ham or, in November, for the mushrooms. This gentle complex of self-catering stone cottages seems as much part of the natural scenery of this secret valley as the cork trees that surround it. Each has its own terrace, and each is finished to a high standard by the Dutch owners, Peter and Monica. Peter, who once walked from Amsterdam to Santiago de Campostela, has written a guide to local walks – you will not be left to wander aimlessly. The larger houses have underfloor heating, rafters and log fires, and steep stairs to the upper sleeping area; the smaller house is open-plan and has no kitchen (but you can cook in the reception building). Each dwelling is beautifully modern: tiles from Seville, woven rugs, painted ironwork beds, warm colours... and a welcoming bottle of wine. Blissful for families: a pool, donkey rides, trees to climb, and restaurants in cobbled Alájar, up the lane. Portugal is over the border – but you may not wish to venture far. *Spanish courses & flamenco guitar lessons available.*

Price	€665–€980 per week.
Rooms	6 cottages for up to 6.
Meals	Restaurants 1.5km.
Closed	Rarely.
Directions	From Sevilla, N-630 for Mérida; N-433 to Aracena. Left on HU-8105 to Alájar. After Alájar, at km20 & 19 marker, left; follow signs.

Peter Jan Mulder
Finca Cabezo del Molino s/n,
21340 Alájar, Huelva

Tel	+34 959 501282
Email	molinorioalajar@telefonica.net
Web	www.molinorioalajar.com

Hotel Rural Posada de Alájar

Alàjar, one of Andalucia's loveliest small villages, is dominated by the craggy, wooded peak of Arias Montero and its chapel; simply stunning – and it has some of the province's very best walking and birdwatching on its doorstep. You'll need it to work off your over-indulgence at this mouthwatering *posada*! Lucy and Angel's cooking, using excellent local produce, is irresistible – *ajo blanco* (garlic soup), pork loin in sweet chestnut, layered apple pie – and all is as eco-perfect as can be. The 18th-century inn feels welcoming and warm the moment you step into the slate-floored, log-fired living room. As if by magic, you are drawn to the tiny bar beyond, then into the cosy, buttercup yellow dining room with its country tablecloths and Angel's collection of olive oils. The low-beamed bedrooms make the most of limited space and are decorated in breezy colours with simple furnishings. Front rooms have balconies overlooking the street while those at the back are the quietest, but all assure a good night's sleep. Genuine warmth, a friendly welcome, loads of information and a great mountain position.

Price	€60. Family suite from €120.
Rooms	9: 8 twins/doubles, 1 family suite for 2-7.
Meals	Dinner €20. Wine €10-€20.
Closed	Rarely.
Directions	From Sevilla, A-66 towards Mérida; N-433 towards Portugal & Aracena. At Aracena continue towards Portugal; left for Fuenteheridas. Left at r'bout (signed Alájar & La Peña). At T-junc, right, then left into village. Hotel on left, just before main square.

Lucy Arkwright & Angel Millán Simó
c/Médico Emilio González 2,
21340 Alájar, Huelva
Tel   +34 959 125712
Email   info@laposadadealajar.com
Web   www.laposadadealajar.com

Posada Finca la Fronda

On a plateau in Spain's stunning Sierra de Aracena, hugged by cork and chestnut trees and reached by a steep track, this elegant new hotel comes with views that stretch to distant points of the compass. U-shaped with open cloisters around a chequered Andalucian patio, Charles and Maria's early retirement project blends solar panels, spring water and top quality (often organic) food with a real care for guests' comfort. Generous bedrooms are smartly furnished with huge beds and pretty sitting areas; there are double basins in bathrooms and private terraces. Laze by the poolside, pick mushrooms and chestnuts on the 25-acre farm or enjoy the fire in the spacious lounge, bright with pictures by local artists. You can pop into whitewashed Alájar for dinner or ask for a simple meal or sandwich – the best jabugo ham is reared nearby and homemade jams and bread appear at breakfast. Hike in the Parque Natural de Picos de Aroche, uncover layers of history in Aracena or join in with local festivals. It's as secluded as can be in this rural retreat, but there's no lack of life round here.

Price	€105.
Rooms	7: 6 doubles, 1 twin (2 rooms can interconnect).
Meals	Dinner €10–€15. Restaurants 1.5km.
Closed	Rarely.
Directions	From Aracena, HU–8105 (ex A-470) direction Alajar. Signed on right at km22.4 marker.

Ethical Collection: Environment.
See page 412.

Charles Wordsworth
Finca la Fonda, 21340 Alájar, Huelva

Tel	+34 959 501247
Email	info@fincalafronda.com
Web	www.fincalafronda.com

Casa Noble

In little whitewashed Aracena: a jewel. Behind the tall white and blue Art Deco façade is a houseful of riches and light, orchestrated by Melanie who arrived with a burst of LA stardust. Enter the elaborate arched portico: the effect is dazzling. To the left is the dining room, painted in shades of light blue and gold, with frescoes on the walls… then a sitting room with a chequerboard of green and white tiles and a wood-burning stove, big white sofas and sparkling mirrors, and a music system that plays around the whole house. Steps lead down to a plush, intimate cellar bar; outside are elegant terraces with views of rooftops, castillo and cathedral. Out here the best of local tapas are generously laid out every night; bliss, too, to relax in the outdoor jacuzzi with a glass of champagne. As for the suites, all are vividly different and delightful – stylish sofas and chairs, patterned tiled floors, tables to write at, dramatic art on white walls, perhaps a beamed ceiling or a terrace. Choose 'Nobleza' for its presidential balcony, Castillo for its view. Amazing, welcoming, huge fun. *Unsuitable for children.*

Price	€195–€260.
Rooms	6 suites.
Meals	Tapas on the house. Dinner available. Restaurants in town.
Closed	Occasionally mid-July to mid-August.
Directions	From Sevilla A66 N for Merida 35km; exit 782 Venta de Alto & Aracena, left at r'bout, 200m. At junc. left under m'way; N-433 to Aracena. In Aracena, over 1st r'bout for Portugal; 2nd r'bout exit 'centro', past church, right after 50m at fork, house on right.

Melanie Denny
c/Campito 35, 21200 Aracena, Huelva

Tel	+34 959 127778
Fax	+34 959 127778
Email	enquiries@lacasanoble.net
Web	www.lacasanoble.net

Hotel Chancilleria

Step through the door into this super little hotel in the heart of hot Jerez – famous for its sherries. Designed around feng shui principles, restored with natural materials and accessible to all, this eco-friendly building is the successful weaving together of two townhouses. Minimalist chic wins out in the bedrooms, where bright fabrics jazz up neutral walls and good quality furniture. Stuccoed bathrooms (some with wet-room showers) offer robes and lush lotions. Take breakfast on the upper terrace and gaze across Jerez's hotchpotch roofs; for dinner, let the up-and-coming chef in the small, popular restaurant ply you with a tasting menu and the region's best wines and sherries; there are also tapas at the bar. There's a grassy garden fringed with climbing plants and hugged by 17th-century town walls, a library, and a slick sitting room for disappearing with a book. Moorish baths, a fortress and riding school lie outside the door among Jerez's fun shops, restaurants and flamenco dancers… unspoilt beaches are a short drive, and Joana and her staff are ever-friendly and helpful. *Made-to-measure stays.*

Price	€90.
Rooms	14: 8 doubles, 4 twins, 2 singles.
Meals	Dinner, with wine, €40–€45.
Closed	Never.
Directions	Exit A4 Jerez ringroad for Parque Empresarial; signs to Centro Ciudad. Through 8 sets of lights, then left by church into Calle Porvera; 1st right; hotel 200m on left.

	Joana Francis
	c/Chancilleria 21,
	11403 Jerez de la Frontera, Cádiz
Tel	+34 956 301038
Fax	+34 956 329747
Email	info@hotelchancilleria.com
Web	www.hotelchancilleria.com

Casa Viña de Alcántara

The owner is linked to the Gordon-Byass sherry dynasty – which means they serve a very decent glass of fino. A fervent anglophile, Gonzalo, who divides his time between the family estate and his hotel in Seville, is a charming man with a gift for gracious living. Great-grandfather's 1890 hunting lodge has an instant allure and is equally appealing inside. First it was gutted, then exquisitely restored: polished limestone downstairs, parquet upstairs made from aromatic old sherry boards. Bedrooms have refined elegance *and* warmth, thanks to fine family furniture and Gonzalo's mother's paintings. His daughter Maria del Rio now runs the hotel. All is perfection, from beautiful gardens to terracotta-tiled pool, taps to towels, fresh flowers everywhere, and the bathrooms are some of the best. Breakfast – English, with southern Spanish touches – is served by a white-gloved butler. The Casa is fringed by a small forest of palms and pines and surrounded by the vine-braided hills that nurture the palomino grape. Jerez, an architectural gem, is ten minutes by motorway; beaches are not much further.

Price	€160–€310.
Rooms	9 twins/doubles.
Meals	Dinner by arrangement.
Closed	Rarely.
Directions	From Jerez A382 for Arcos de la Frontera, 1st exit 3. At r'bout follow signs to La Cueva. Hotel is 1km on, on right, surrounded by trees.

Gonzalo del Río y González Gordon
Autovía A-382, salida 3,
11400 Jerez de la Frontera, Cádiz

Tel	+34 956 393010
Fax	+34 956 393011
Email	info@vinadealcantara.com
Web	www.vinadealcantara.com

La Casa de Bovedas

In Moorish times, one side of this 1780 Jesuit house was part of the old town wall and it still keeps its own lip of pavement, which you drop down onto through a lovely arched wooden door. From a central open patio the wooden walkway ascends, wonderfully connecting all the levels and offering several inviting spots to curl up with a book. Cleverly designed for both summer and winter, the house can be fully opened up via a retractable awning in the glass-covered roof to let the breeze flow in from the Sierra de Garazalema, or else battened down and warmed by the large wood-burning stove below. The huge old lemon tree dominates a lower terrace bursting with plant life; the upper level offers warm terracotta views over the town as you breakfast on homemade treats. The downstairs suite once kept the animals, and curves toward a vaulted ceiling; now a niche with a platform bed couldn't be more snug. Further up, another lovely room lies under muted blue beams and sports its own Juliet balcony. Multi-lingual Cecilia is a charming hostess, happy to share her family home.

Price	€65–€75. Suites €75–€95.
Rooms	6: 3 doubles, 1 twin, 2 suites (with sofabeds).
Meals	Restaurants 5-minute walk.
Closed	Rarely.
Directions	From Plaza del Cabildo 200m to hotel.

Cecilia Lozano
c/Bovedas 9,
11630 Arcos de la Frontera, Cádiz

Tel	+34 956 705154
Fax	+34 956 705154
Email	reservas@lacasadebovedas.com
Web	www.lacasadebovedas.com

Boticas 19

Imagine… a steel-sheathed kitchen up floating glass steps, Colombian bedcovers on big funky beds, Casablanca fans and Moorish arches. The charming French owners have taken an architectural gem in the centre of Arcos and added their own urban-chic stamp; now just the 17th-century façade remains, its doors serenaded by a stone-carved coat of arms. An English-Spanish couple in the village do the meet and greet, and invite you in to a minimalist's dream: a ten-metre plunge pool and floors of black slate, a grey felt banquette lined with silk cushions, an electric dumb waiter linking kitchen with roof terrace. No sitting room but two terraces, loads of books and satellite TV in each seductive – even lavish – bedroom – and views that sweep over Arcos's churches to the Grazalema National Park. Two cobblestoned alleys away is the Plaza Boticas with its bodegas and bars, perfect small market and closed-order convent that serves freshly baked magdalenas. Precariously perched Arcos is one of Andalucia's most loved 'pueblos blancos'… and the river winds through the plain 100m below. Special.

Price	€300–€726 per night.
Rooms	House for 6 (3 twins/doubles).
Meals	Restaurants close by.
Closed	Never.
Directions	From Sevilla airport to Arcos. Through Arcos dir. Paradorwich on Cabildo Square. Boticas is a one way street in the Old Town.

Sophie Darcet
c/Boticas 19,
11630 Arcos de la Frontera, Cádiz

Tel   +34 686 099515 mob
Email   contact@casaboticas19.com
Web   www.boticas19.com

La Casa Grande

La Casa Grande nudges right up to the very edge of wonderful old Arcos – spectacular. At night, from its roof terrace, you gaze onto two floodlit churches and mile after mile of surrounding plain. The house is almost 300 years old and many of its features have survived to tell the tale. In true Andaluz style, a central, colonnaded, plant-filled patio is the axis around which the house turns; vaulted rooms lead off to all sides, nooks and crannies appear at every turn. A cosy lounge doubles up as a library with thousands of books – some of them written by delightful, elegant Elena. The decoration of the house reflects her eclectic, bohemian taste: tiles from Morocco, blankets from Grazalema, a Deco writing table topped by a designer lamp, wickerwork and watercolours and a poem for each room. Music gently plays. Guest bedrooms (one with a door-free bathroom, two below street level but with balconies and views) are full of antiquey bits and pieces, with double glazing to protect you from night-time hum. Then wake to breakfast on that unforgettable terrace. One of our favourites. *A Rusticae hotel.*

Price	€70–€91. Singles €59 (low season only). Suites €81–€159.
Rooms	8: 6 twins/doubles, 2 suites for 4.
Meals	Breakfast €9. Small tapas menu in evening.
Closed	7 January–7 February.
Directions	In Arcos follow signs to Parador. Park in square in front of Parador & walk to end of c/Escribano (just to left of Parador). Right, past Hotel El Convento, then left. House on right.

Elena Posa Farrás
c/Maldonado 10,
11630 Arcos de la Frontera, Cádiz

Tel	+34 956 703930
Fax	+34 956 717095
Email	info@lacasagrande.net
Web	www.lacasagrande.net

Cortijo Barranco

Grand Barranco stands alone, high on a hillside, within viewing distance of Arcos de la Frontera. Getting here is an adventure yet this is every inch the classic olive mill-cortijo, the private quarters and former stables wrapped around a central courtyard; and the olive oil is certified organic. The guest rooms are comfortably rustic with their terracotta floors, wrought-iron bedsteads, heavy linen curtains and hand-crocheted bedspreads; ask for the double with the terrace and huge views. Scattered self-catering casitas are charmingly authentic and mostly open plan. The communal sitting room is beautifully raftered, has a friendly red-checked sofa and room for a billiard table; the dining room is lofty, with warm wood tables and an open hearth at one end, and the huge vine-clambered patio is a haven on hot days. A beautiful pool overlooking the Sierra de Grazalema completes the picture. Stroll out after dinner and abandon yourself to the beauty of the sun dipping behind the hills… later, let the owls hoot you to sleep. Heavenly.

Price	€57–€87. Singles €47–€67. Family rooms €77–€107. Casitas €84–€159. All prices per night.
Rooms	15 + 6: 13 twins/doubles, 2 family rooms. 6 casitas: 1 for 2, 4 for 4, 1 for 6.
Meals	Lunch & dinner €21–€25, by arrangement. Wine €7–€16.
Closed	Never.
Directions	From Arcos de la Frontera, A-372 El Bosque. After 5.7km marker, at end of long straight section, left at sign onto paved track; 2km to farm.

Maria José & Genaro Gil Amián
Ctra. Arcos-El Bosque (A-372) km5.7,
11630 Arcos de la Frontera, Cádiz

Tel	+34 956 231402
Fax	+34 956 231209
Email	reservas@cortijobarranco.com
Web	www.cortijobarranco.com

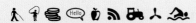

El Batan de Lara

They used to make blankets here, at the old wool mill on the gushing Majaceite; the sound of the river will lull you to sleep. This is a fabulously lush and well-watered spot, in the lee of the Parque Natural de Grazalema. As you approach, you find a terraced garden, a verdant orchard and an old irrigation tank, now a pretty pool; then the mill below, blending in beautifully with the greenery. Open the old wooden doors to discover a large open-plan living area drenched with light, and warmly inviting: deep red walls, thick overhead beams, an open fire. The bedrooms are on the lower floor, darkish, cool, cosy, each with its own entrance, each rurally charming: walls gently colourwashed, bathrooms simply tiled. The kitchen too has a sweet simplicity, with its old floor tiles and blue ceiling beams. There's a creative hand at work here, and the art on the wall is for sale. Birds sing, cicadas chirrup, water flows – from irrigation channels, streams and natural springs. In the village: a water museum and several good little restaurants. The walking is wonderful; the caretaker lives at the top of the track.

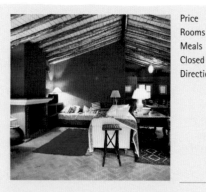

Price	€1,000–€1,300 per week.
Rooms	House for 6.
Meals	Restaurants in Benamahoma.
Closed	Never.
Directions	From El Bosque A372 signed Grazalema/Benamahoma. Left after 4km, signed Benamahoma. Cottage 1st on left; continue thro' gates to end of track (about 300m).

José Antonio Portillo
c/Ribera s/n,
11679 Benamahoma-Grazalema, Cádiz

Mobile	+34 639 157011
Fax	+34 956 805135
Email	info@huertasdebenamahoma.com
Web	www.huertasdebenamahoma.com

Hostal El Anón

In the heart of Jimena, five wonderful old townhouses have been amassed into a catacomb of beamed and low-ceilinged rooms on a myriad of levels and intimate terraces: a cosy little corner of authentic Spain. American-born Suzanna has lived here for years, knows the people and country like her own, and always has time for tea and a chat. She can also organise riding, painting, birdwatching, walking and flora-spotting expeditions. The countryside has treasures galore and the best views are from the little saltwater pool on the rooftop; they reach all the way to Gibraltar. Enjoy the cool peace of the arched main courtyard and the exotic banana and custard-fruit trees, and the mishmash of bits and pieces collected over the years – wall hangings, paintings, model trains; then join the (many) ex-pats for excellent spare ribs and veggie dishes on the verdant terrace, or in the bustling restaurant and English-pubby bar. Rooms – and plumbing! – are basic, with the quietest at the back. Come for quantities of Spanishness and an unusually laid-back B&B. Jimena throbs with its jazz festival in July.

Price	€64–€74. Singles €39. Extra bed €25.
Rooms	11 + 1: 5 twins, 2 singles, 2 triples, 2 quadruples. Apartment for 2.
Meals	Lunch & dinner from €25 à la carte.
Closed	2 weeks June; 2 weeks November.
Directions	From Málaga, AP-7 dir. Algecíras; exit Sotogrande/Castellar. Thro' Valderrama, cross railway bridge, then right onto A369 to Jimena. Head up through village, then turn left & follow signs to El Anon. Parking tricky.

Gabriel Delgado & Suzanna Odell
c/Consuelo 34-40,
11330 Jimena de la Frontera, Cádiz

Tel	+34 956 640113
Fax	+34 956 641110
Email	reservas@elanon.net
Web	www.andalucia.com/jimena/hostalanon

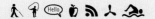

Entry 226   Map 20

Casa Julio Verne

Cross the sleepy square to Rose and Sagi's house, unmissable with its smartly painted exterior and tumbling geraniums. Inside is stylishness at every turn. The living area has luscious linen sofas, Moroccan lamps, books and games, while against the neutral palette are vivid flashes of colour – a bowl of scarlet gerberas on the breakfast table, a magenta bougainvillea bloom gracing white bathroom towels. All the bedrooms are lovely here, particularly the capacious, light-filled Nemo suite with its double jacuzzi, soaring beams and wood-burner. Down in the courtyard is a hammam; up on the roof terrace, views that stretch all the way to Africa on a clear day, the great rock of Gibraltar in between... a stunning spot to sit and relax over a drink from the honesty bar. Your young hosts are great fun, and they'll tell you all about the area over a breakfast spread (Sagi's lavender-infused orange juice is inspired). But why is it called Casa Julio Verne and why are there copies of the great man's books in 'Nautilus', 'Nemo' and 'Lidenbrock'? Book in and find out! *Minimum stay two nights April-October.*

Price	€85-€90. Suites €90-€120. Whole house (sleeps 6-8) €1,350-€1,950 per week.
Rooms	3: 1 twin/double, 2 suites. House available for self-catering.
Meals	Restaurants nearby.
Closed	Rarely.
Directions	Málaga A-7/E-15; exit 119 San Roque & Gibraltar. Right at bottom of slip road; right again after bus stop. Over r'bout; 1st first left to top of hill into Plaza Espartero. On left in c/Sagasta.

Rose Favell & Sagi Ifrach
Plaza de las Viudas 9,
11360 San Roque, Cádiz

Tel	+34 956 782623
Email	enquiries@casajulioverne.com
Web	www.casajulioverne.com

Monte de la Torre

Puzzling to come across this Edwardian building in the very south of Spain – it was built by the British when they were pushing the railway through the mountains to Ronda. This commingling of northern architecture and southern vegetation and climate is as seductive as it is unexpected. The house stands alone on a hill, surrounded by resplendent gardens; bask in the shade of the trees, gaze onto the Bay of Gibraltar, dip into the pool. Quentin's family has farmed this estate for generations. The drawing room is panelled, the dining room elegant, there are masses of books, family portraits, a grandfather clock, dogs… this is a home, not a hotel. The bedrooms (reached by a grand staircase) are high-ceilinged, decorated with family heirlooms and have period bathrooms – a festival of tubs and taps. Each is different, all lovely in an old-fashioned way. The self-catering apartments are in the former servants' quarters, and the garden is a birdwatcher's paradise. Sue and Quentin are charming hosts, and there are many good restaurants within easy reach. *Children welcome in apartments.*

Price	€110-€130. Apartments €550-€950 per week.
Rooms	3 + 2: 3 twins/doubles. 2 apartments for 5.
Meals	Picnic lunch, with wine, by arrangement. Restaurants & tapas bars 1km.
Closed	15 December-15 January; July & Aug.
Directions	From Hotel Montera Plaza in Los Barrios, pass petrol station on left; left at r'bout. Cross river, signed CA9206 (km4 marker). After 0.8km, entrance on right (before bridge).

Sue & Quentin Agnew Larios
Apdo. de Correos 66,
11370 Los Barrios, Cádiz

Tel	+34 956 660000
Fax	+34 956 634863
Email	montedelatorre@gmail.com
Web	www.montedelatorre.com

Cortijo La Hoya

Two miles of challenging tree-fringed track deliver you to the farm and Fabiola's casitas, tucked among the eucalyptus and cork oaks in an exquisite corner of the Alcornocales Park. Their chicken-shed origins are hard to credit. Charming, intelligent Fabiola has decorative nous; her colour schemes are inspired by the earthy washes of the Mahgreb, her patterned fabrics are lovely. Kitchenettes are well-equipped and there's central heating for winter. The wonderful garden, full of intimate corners, all created by Fabiola, leads to a sensationally situated 'infinity' pool where the water of the pool merges with that of the Straits of Gibraltar, above which rises the Moroccan Rif, its colours changing as subtly as the iridescent coastal light. Fabiola is mindful of guests' privacy, but, should you ask, will tell you all you need to know. And then there are the dogs... four of them, of all shapes and sizes, ever ready with a wag. Do note her recommendations about where to eat in Tarifa. This ancient town pulsates on a Friday and Saturday night, and its white sand beaches are superb. *Minimum stay two to seven nights.*

Price	€90–€130 per night.
Rooms	3 casitas for 2-3.
Meals	€30 hamper, with wine, by arrangement. Restaurants in Pelayo, 3km.
Closed	Rarely.
Directions	From Algecíras, N-340 for Cádiz. Through Pelayo; at youth hostel, U-turn & head back. 100m past km96 marker, sharp right onto track. Follow signs for 3km.

Fabiola Dominguez Larios
Ctra. N-340 Tarifa-Algecíras, km96,
11280 Tarifa, Cádiz

Tel	+34 956 236070
Email	bookings@cortijolahoya.com
Web	www.cortijolahoya.com

Dar Cilla Guesthouse

As you laze on the roof terrace you gaze on Morocco: Zoe's spiritual home. With energy and flair, English Zoe has created a corner of Morocco in Tarifa. Handsome, 100-year-old Dar Cilla (once a ruin) was built against the 12th-century town wall and wraps itself round not one but two patios. These studios and apartments are truly lovely: wafer bricks, sienna-washed plaster, polished stucco, illuminated nooks and crannies and kilims on terracotta; the finishes are superb. You get bedrooms and dining/sitting areas, shower rooms and kitchenettes in a fashionable, but low-key, Arab-Andaluz style, dotted with decorative features and fabrics that Zoe has picked up on trips to Tangier. Instead of a lounge, that amazing roof terrace, cosy and convivial with loungers, shower and fridge for drinks. No meals, but cafes for breakfast and a good restaurant are practically on the doorstep. Surf the golden beaches of the wind- and kite-surfing capital of Europe, gallop in pine forests, dip into the many bars of the old, labyrinthine town – or do that ferry hop to Morocco. *Two new apartments planned for 2009.*

Price	Single studio €50–€65. Apartments for 2, €90–€150. Apartment for 4, €195–€240. All prices per night.
Rooms	1 studio, 5 apartments for 2, 1 apartment for 4.
Meals	Breakfast €3–€5. Restaurants 5-10 minute walk.
Closed	Rarely.
Directions	N-340 Algeciras-Cádiz; 1st exit for Tarifa. Dar Cilla 1km, on left.

Zoë Ouwehand–Reid & Martina de Rijke
c/Cilla, 11380 Tarifa, Cádiz

Mobile	+34 653 467025
Fax	+34 956 627011
Email	info@darcilla.com
Web	www.darcilla.com

Huerta Las Terrazas

Climb up the cork oak shaded path through honeysuckle, mimosa, oleander, cypresses to reach the cool, blue pool. Turn and gaze southwards to the exotic outlines of the Moroccan mountains. The three-acre terraced gardens, dizzy with scent and colour, are the draw of this white casa, teetering below the foothills of the Sierra de Ojen, on the edge of the Parque Natural de Alcornocales. In the bedrooms – choose La Casita for a self-contained hideaway – the young English owners have blended cool modern design with traditional furnishings. Seagrass matting, white walls and soft bed linen mixes with dark wooden furniture, rich cushions and hints of Morocco. The sitting and dining rooms are emboldened with warmer colours, lamps and candles. Breakfasts are from their organic fruit and veg garden while their own spring feeds the pool as well as the taps. But don't forget this is the countryside: neighbouring dogs are not always quiet. Swim, surf or ride on the beaches, explore cosmopolitan Tarifa, enjoy one of Amy's expert treatments or birdwatch; the house is under the African migration route. Fabulous. *Minimum stay two nights.*

Price	€85–€120.
	Cottage €550–€800 per week.
Rooms	2 + 1: 2 doubles. 1 cottage for 2.
Meals	Light lunch €12. Dinner €30.
	Wine €12.
Closed	Rarely.
Directions	From Algecíras, N-340 for Cádiz. Pass km97 marker, under footbridge; 150m, right. On uphill; 2nd left after yellow wall. Follow road to green gates at top.

Alistair & Amy Farrington
c/Sierra de Lucena, Pelayo,
11390 Algecíras, Cádiz

Tel	+34 956 679041
Email	alandamy@huertalasterrazas.com
Web	www.huertalasterrazas.com

Hotel Restaurante Antonio

A short walk to the laid-back fishing village of Zahara, with gardens that lead straight onto one of the least spoilt beaches on the southern coast, these sister hotels share a stunning spot. We prefer Antonio Mota's first, smaller, family-run affair, popular with the Spanish. The newer venture is modern and four-star. Both are southern in spirit, with some uninspiring prints on the walls (romantic swans, bullfights) – but you're here for the site, which is superb. Choose dinner in the 'old' restaurant: lobster fresh from the tank and excellent local wine; breakfasts with eggs, cheeses, hams and loads of fresh fruit. Bedrooms in the new hotel are a good size and come with balconies, somewhat basic furnishings and air con; ask for a view of the sea. Older rooms have more character; go for a terrace room overlooking the palms and the breakers crashing 100 metres away. There's a lovely pool, a beach bar too, and horses for hire – ride along the beach to Bolonia, hunt out Roman ruins and restaurants. Note that this stretch of coastline is unlikely to remain unspoilt for ever!

Price	€69–€155. Singles €40–€77.50. Suites €83–€163.
Rooms	66: 22 doubles, 3 singles, 5 suites. New hotel: 18 doubles, 16 family, 2 suites.
Meals	Lunch & dinner €21. À la carte from €35. Wine list available.
Closed	November–January.
Directions	Algeciras E-5/N-340 to Cádiz. 25km after Tarifa left to Barbate; Zahara on left after 10km. Signed.

Antonio Mota Pacheco
Bahía de la Plata, Atlanterra km1,
11393 Zahara de los Atunes, Cádiz
Tel   +34 956 439141
Fax   +34 956 439135
Email   info@antoniohoteles.com
Web   www.antoniohoteles.com

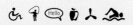

Hotel La Casa del Califa

No fewer than eight village houses are woven into the fabric of La Casa del Califa, and their gradual union has created a seductively labyrinthine structure: the antithesis of the made-to-measure hotel. Parts of the building are ancient and have seen occupation since the time of the Moors, so corridors and rooms follow the twists and turns of the building, and bedrooms have oodles of character. There are vaulted ceilings and beamed ones, some private terraces, and some original, geometric-tile floors. Expect brightly coloured cushions and bedspreads, interesting lamps, contemporary paintings and a stylish debt to all things Moroccan. Best of all is the courtyard bar and restaurant with its *A Thousand and One Nights* buzz, thrilling on spring nights when the lamps are lit and the citrus trees are in blossom. The menu offers a delightful change from the look-alike menus of so many of Andalucía's restaurants: interesting salads, Islamic flavours and an interesting selection of wines. Califa is one of the most seductive of Spain's small hotels; it shouts 'romantic break for two'!

Price	€70–€110. Suites €120–€170.
Rooms	20: 16 twins/doubles, 4 suites.
Meals	Lunch & dinner €25–€30.
Closed	Never.
Directions	From Algeciras E-15/N-340 towards Cádiz. Take 2nd turning left for Vejer at km36 marker. Up hill, then follow signs for 'Ayuntamiento' to Plaza de España. Casa del Califa on left.

James Stuart & Regli Alvarez
Plaza de España 16,
11150 Vejer de la Frontera, Cádiz

Tel	+34 956 447730
Fax	+34 956 451625
Email	reservas@lacasadelcalifa.com
Web	www.lacasadelcalifa.com

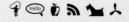

Tripería no.1

The diminutive Plaza de España is the neural centre of old Vejer. Its swaying palms, beautiful ceramic-tiled fountain and lively bars and restaurants can't fail to put you in that 'I'm on holiday' mood. Tripería, just a few steps down from the square, is, in essence, an annexe to the neighbouring Casa de Califa. An unassuming door on the street takes you through to the inner patio and the large swimming pool, a bonus in the sweltering centre of town. Bedrooms are big on space and have been decorated in the same Andaluz/Moroccan style as that of the sister hotel, with the same excellent mix of eastern artefacts and contemporary art. It all feels light, airy, clean and welcoming. From the private terrace of your room you can feast on a vista that sweeps across the rooftops to the distant pines of the Parque Natural de Las Marismas, cutting a delicious green swathe between Vejer and the ocean. There is a basement kitchen where you can prepare your own breakfast – but it's much nicer to eat next door in Casa de Califa's leafy, lovely courtyard restaurant.

Price	€69–€103. Suites €84–€121. Family suite €126–€158.
Rooms	6: 1 double, 2 twins, 2 suites, 1 family suite for 4.
Meals	Breakfast (included) served next door, at Casa del Califa. Lunch & dinner €25–€35, at Jardín del Califa.
Closed	Never.
Directions	From Algeciras E-15/N-340 towards Cádiz. Take 2nd turnng left for Vejer at km36 marker. Up hill then follow signs for 'Ayuntamiento' to Plaza de España. Tripería on left.

James Stuart & Regli Alvarez
Plaza de España 16,
11150 Vejer de la Frontera, Cádiz

Tel	+34 956 447730
Fax	+34 956 451625
Email	reservas@lacasadelcalifa.com
Web	www.grupocalifa.com/triperia

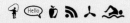

El Sueño

When summer's heat hits Andalucía's 'Coast of Light', you'll relish a siesta in these stylish country cottages just 15 minutes inland, near whitewashed Vejer de la Frontera. On eight acres of ecologically managed estate – some of it down on the river flats – three white open-plan casitas sport cool terracotta floors, warm wood stoves and bright kitchen tiles under high ceilings – and all you need to keep children amused. If you're feeling flush, rent the master house instead, luxurious with its two smart sitting rooms, four-poster beds and double-ended baths. Swim in the safely fenced pool, barbecue in the shade of trees and climbing vines, stroll the Citrus Walk or relish the heady breath of ornamental herb gardens. The main house has its own panoramic pool, bar and terrace gazing down to a water meadow teeming with nature. Tear yourself away to unspoilt beaches and golf courses, hire a horse or take a dolphin-watching tour; you can even pop over to Morocco. Friendly and enthusiastic, Tanya and Sean are happy to help; ask about childminding, catering and more. A place as dreamy as its name.

Price	€395–€795 per week.
Rooms	3 cottages: 1 for 2; 1 for 4; 1 for 6. House for 8 (2 doubles, 2 twins).
Meals	Restaurants 500m.
Closed	Rarely.
Directions	From Vejer, N340 direction Tarifa; at km41 marker, right signed El Soto; after 250m, left into village. House on right, after 500m.

Ethical Collection: Environment.
See page 412.

Sean & Tanya Macrae
El Soto 64, 11150 Vejer de la Frontera, Cádiz

Tel	+34 956 450240
Fax	+34 956 450240
Email	relax@elsueno.net
Web	www.elsueno.net

Casas Karen

Recline among the broom and mimosa in your hammock on one of the last wild coastlines of southern Spain. Casas Karen feels like a mini village hidden in a wild expanse of garden between pinewoods, sand dunes and beach, the sort of place to meet friends for life. While the overall feel is rustic, all the houses have their own privacy and are cosy and comfortable, with bright flowing fabrics and stylish local touches; local here means Andalucían and Moroccan – the high mountains of the Magreb are visible on clear days. Many have open fires for winter and the airy and environmentally friendly 'chozas' – houses made of thatch – are sweet and romantic. The place attracts an interesting clientele (artists, lawyers, surfers) and the atmosphere is totally laid back – like Caños itself, a celebrated hang-out for hippies until its 'discovery' two decades ago, and now rather shabby around the edges. Perfect for the more adventurous traveller: massage, yoga and other therapies and coaching can be arranged and there's walking, riding, biking and so much more too. Creative Karen and her team are happy to advise.

Price	€40–€80. Houses €55–€155. Thatched houses €45–€130. Studios €45–€110. All prices per night.
Rooms	1 double; 4 houses & studios for 2-4; 2 houses for 4-6; 2 thatched houses for 2-4.
Meals	Restaurants 5-10 minute walk.
Closed	Never.
Directions	San Fernando–Algeciras A-48, exit 36 for Vejer; r'bout right for Los C A-2230. 8km to next r'bout; left A-2233. 4.5km left into Calle Levante. 400m, right at sign; 50m, on left.

Ethical Collection: Environment.
See page 412.

Karen Abrahams
Camino del Monte 6, Los Caños de Meca,
11159 Vejer de la Frontera, Cádiz

Tel	+34 956 437067
Fax	+34 956 437233
Email	info@casaskaren.com
Web	www.casaskaren.com

Casa de Medina

House-hunting in the town's oldest quarter, the Bistons stumbled upon an ancient dwelling, fell in love with it and, 24 hours later, bought the place. A year of renovation followed and now they have the guest house of their dreams. The old building wraps itself around an inner patio where wafer-bricked columns support drop arches, and potted palms and jasmine add splashes of green to floors of sandy marble. You could breakfast here, or in the dining room to one side, but the temptation would be to grab a tray, clamber up to the roof terrace and drink in the view – of Cádiz, the Atlantic and, on a clear day, the mountains of the Moroccan Rif. The decked plunge pool above the terrace gives blessed relief in summer. Bedrooms are fresh, inviting and hugely comfortable: white walls, marble floors, excellent linen, feather pillows, Casablanca fans to keep the heat at bay. There are several lively tapas bars around the main square, a short stroll away: easy to make new friends. Then back up the hill to Gary and Kirsty, your good-humoured hosts who look after you brilliantly.

Price	€60–€125.
Rooms	5: 4 twins/doubles, 1 triple.
Meals	Occasional dinner, with wine, €25. Restaurants nearby.
Closed	Rarely.
Directions	From Jerez A-381 for Los Barrios; exit 24 Medina Sidonia. Signs into town & 'Iglesia Mayor - Sta María de la Coronada'. Park on square; walk down hill, terraced gardens on left; 1st right onto c/Tintoreros. Or call hotel for pick-up.

Gary & Kirsty Biston
c/Tintoreros 5, 11170 Medina Sidonia, Cádiz

Tel	+34 956 410069
Fax	+34 956 410069
Email	info@andaluciahideaways.com
Web	www.casademedina.com

Cortijo El Papudo

There's a good feel to this authentic old farmstead in the fertile valley of the Guadiaro river, where fruit trees flourish: everything from citrus to custard fruit, pomegranates to avocados. A number of plant nurseries have sprung up and the Harveys have one of their own too; it's become an obligatory shop-over for the coastal ex-pat community. They are, of course, highly knowledgeable about all things botanical. Their own lovely garden, an exotic, multi-coloured ode to southern flora with a charming rill and plenty of sitting corners, laps up to the high, solid old cortijo. The bedrooms are simple and pleasing if a little dated: their original timber ceilings give character, there are Casablanca-style ceiling fans for summer and central heating for the colder months. All have views of the garden and across the farm to the surrounding orange groves; one has a balcony onto the flower-fringed pool. You will find a handsome flagged floor, a wood-burner and even an honesty bar in the rustic breakfast room and there's a small kitchen for picnics or barbecues. The beach is a 15-minute drive.

Price	€75. Singles €50.
Rooms	11 twins/doubles.
Meals	Restaurants 2km.
Closed	Rarely.
Directions	A-7 Málaga-Cádiz; exit 133 Sotogrande/Torreguadiaro on A-2102 towards San Martín del Tesorillo. Drive through Secadero, turn right just before bridge. 1.5km; then up hill for 50m; sharp left for hotel.

Michael & Vivien Harvey
11340 San Martín del Tesorillo, Málaga
Tel   +34 952 854018
Fax   +34 952 854018
Email   papudo@mercuryin.es
Web   www.andalucia.com/gardens/papudo

Andalucia Yurts

Few places sit in such natural seclusion – astonishing that you are only ten miles from the Costa del Sol. Sited by a river so clean you can drink from it (with otters and wild boar as fellow guests – heaven for swimming), the place is engulfed by cork and pine plantations against a backdrop of sheer soaring peaks. With only one building in sight – the castle in Gaucín – it is the sort of wild escape nature lovers crave. The B&B centres on a pretty cottage, sensitively restored using old wooden beams and sustainable materials. Its nerve centre is the veranda, which is covered in long concrete benches, comfortably decked in exotic Indian fabrics. Your bedrooms are under canvas, but don't worry – these yurts are spacious, airy and utterly private, tucked away in different corners of the smallholding. The Hoggs – tree surgeons by trade – are engaging people, and passionate about the environment. Fellow guests may include yogis, birdwatchers and writers. As well as being an organic farm, water is pumped from the river and solar panels are de rigeur. The African Bush comes to Spain – hurrah!

Price	€35 p.p.
Rooms	2 yurts for 2-4.
Meals	Dinner, with wine, €20.
Closed	Winter.
Directions	A-377 from Manilva to Gaucín. At km21 marker turn right after bridge. Follow track for 3.8km; second right is La Huerta.

Ethical Collection: Environment.
See page 412.

Penny Hogg
La Huerta, 29480 Gaucín, Málaga

Tel	+34 952 117486
Email	hoggs@vsatmail.com
Web	www.andaluciayurts.com

La Herradura

Unforgivable not to make the most of a panorama like this. And the designers of the little pink-washed house have done just that: house, terrace and pool are perfectly positioned for maximum effect. Behind and to either side is wild, green mountainside; ahead, breathtaking views to Africa. La Herradura, owned by Sally next door, has been newly built in an unobtrusive, rustic style, while flair and imagination have created an effect of rural simplicity tempered with sophistication inside. Pastel colours – pinks, blues and golds – glow gently against creamy pink walls. In the airy, open-plan living room, a big woven rug, burnished old floor tiles, original artwork and lots of books; a squashy sofa and armchairs are grouped companionably around. The ceiling is chestnut-beamed and slopes down towards two sets of double doors that open onto the terrace. There are fireplaces in the living rooms and in the attractive kitchen/dining area, too – but you'll want to eat outside whenever you can. Outside: the jacuzzi and a gorgeous pool, poised on the very edge of the hillside; beyond: those unbelievable views.

Price	€1,200–€1,800 per week.
Rooms	Villa for 4.
Meals	Restaurants in village, 5-minute walk.
Closed	Never.
Directions	AP-7 to exit 142; on to Gaucin. Right into village at T-junc.; sharp right onto road marked 'Camino de Gibraltar'; 1km downhill on left.

Sally von Meister
Camino Romano, 29480 Gaucín, Málaga

Tel	+34 952 151303
Fax	+34 952 151083
Email	elnobo@telefonica.net
Web	www.elnobo.co.uk

El Nobo

The gardens are tremendous, showing clearly what a dozen and more years in Spain can produce. And the organically shaped pool – its views stretching to Gibraltar and the mountains of Africa – is magical. Gaucín has long been popular among the more adventurous of the ex-pat community and Sally lives in one of the area's most charming homes. At the end of a dusty old track, anchored to a rocky hillside... a Moorish courtyard, a Spanish villa, two stone cottages, one fountain and several sun terraces; impossible to believe that a shepherd's hut once stood here. The drawing room pays full homage to that view-of-views thanks to enormous French windows and is an enchanting spot for breakfast and dinner. Gregarious Sally runs the place with aplomb, has created a colourful mix and match décor, cooks confidently (two nights a week) and adores her dogs. The bedrooms at El Nobo are relaxed spaces, comfortably flamboyant; bathrooms have mosaics and Moroccan mirrors. As for precariously perched Gaucin, it has the best views in all Spain.

Price	€130. Suite €150.
Rooms	3: 2 twins/doubles, 1 suite.
Meals	Dinner with wine, €35, twice a week.
Closed	July & August; Christmas; New Year.
Directions	AP-7 to exit 142; on to Gaucín. Right into village at T-junc.; tricky turns, then sharp right onto road marked 'Camino de Gibraltar'; 1km down hill on left.

Sally von Meister
Aptdo. 46, Camino de Gibraltar,
29480 Gaucín, Málaga

Tel	+34 952 151303
Fax	+34 952 151083
Email	elnobo@telefonica.net
Web	www.elnobo.co.uk

La Casa del Arriero

No fewer than three of Andalucía's most beautiful *parques naturales* are on your doorstep. The Guadiaro valley is criss-crossed with ancient drovers' paths and these young owners know its loveliest corners. The house takes its name from the muleteer who once lived here and the equine tradition continues: Mel, a rider all her life, can organise full or half day rides. They also have route maps of all their rambles and can help plan a walking holiday. They've given new life and a twist of style to this traditional village house – all yours – with a roof terrace that looks to the church tower and across the rolling pastures of the valley. Things within work beautifully: an open-plan kitchen and diner, a small plant-filled patio for summery meals, a cosy lounge with a wood-burning stove. There are two bedrooms, one vast with its own sun terrace, the second much smaller but fine for kids. There's lot to do but if you're feeling idle, this is the place to recharge your batteries. Buy veggies fresh from the market, rub shoulders with the locals in any number of bars, get a taste of that fabled 'real' Spain.

Price	€400–€490 per week.
Rooms	House for 2 + 2 children.
Meals	Restaurants in village.
Closed	Never.
Directions	From Málaga E-15 for Algecíras; exit for Gaucín. A369 direction Ronda. Left to Cortes de la F. Down high street. Right after Bar Monteros. Up hill to top.

Melanie & Tiger Templer
c/Cantón 8, 29380 Cortes de la Frontera,
Málaga

Tel	+34 952 153330
Email	enquiries@casaarriero.com
Web	www.casaarriero.com

Entry 242   Map 20

The Hoopoe Yurt Hotel

Under the shade of cork and olive trees, these authentic Mongolian, Afghani and Maimani yurts sit in splendid Andalucían isolation. On raised wooden platforms, the felt-lined white circular tents are reinforced with arching roof poles that support a domed crown; wicker baskets, ethnic furniture, sheepskin rugs and bold colours create a rustic and romantic mood. The charming and well-travelled young owners have made the yurts stylish while maintaining a 'back to nature' feel, and there's a compost loo and solar-heated water in the lovely bamboo-walled shower rooms. Indeed, the whole camp is run on solar power. Wonderful views of the soaring mountains are best enjoyed from a hammock slung between two cork trees or on a bamboo sun bed beside the freshwater pool. The staff are wonderful; even massage is possible. Wake to birdsong, cowbells and the distant rumble of trains; at night, tiptoe your way to bed past twinkling lights in the trees. Henrietta uses the best local and organic ingredients and the food is delicious; the village, one of the most organic in Spain, is a 20-minute walk. Bliss. *Minimum stay two nights.*

Price	€130.
Rooms	5 yurts for 2, each with shower.
Meals	Sandwiches/paninis €5. Dinner with wine, €30.
Closed	Mid–October to end April.
Directions	After Benaojan, cont. for C. de la Frontera; there, 1st left after fountain. Before petrol station, left on track, then left at fork; after 1km, right onto track before white house.

Ethical Collection: Environment; Food.
See page 412.

Ed & Henrietta Hunt
Apartado de Correos 23,
29380 Cortes de la Frontera, Málaga

Tel	+34 951 168040
Email	info@yurthotel.com
Web	www.yurthotel.com

Los Castaños

You will be charmed the moment you step through the huge studded door. The Moorish influence seduces so easily: water trickles in a little tiled fountain, arches beckon, geraniums splash the dazzling walls with colour. There's a fireplace, too, for the nippier months. Climb to the next floor and you'll find cool, airy bedrooms – four with balconies; windows frame the loveliest mountain views. Handmade beds, old Spanish rocking chairs, low tables, Moroccan lights and super bathrooms add to the sense of well-being. Go up again and emerge onto an entrancing roof terrace, benignly presided over by the white tower of next door's church. Set among pillars and pierced terracotta screens is a sweet plunge pool for instant cooling. A pampering, grown-up place, where Di and her partner John, smiling and generous, know how to soothe and spoil. The food is delicious; the village is tiny, charming and deeply quiet, and there are good walks to villages glimpsed through the trees – the chestnuts are stunning in the autumn...

Price	€80–€130. Apartment €45. All prices per night.
Rooms	6 + 1: 5 twins/doubles, 1 single. Apartment for 2.
Meals	Dinner €30 (not Sunday). Wine from €12.50.
Closed	Rarely.
Directions	From San Pedro to Ronda on A-397. 10km before Ronda, left after petrol station to Cartajima. After recycling bins bear right, then 1st hard right; park by phone box. On right.

	Di Beach & John Walker
	c/Iglesia 40, 29452 Cartajima, Málaga
Tel	+34 952 180778
Fax	+34 951 160236
Email	reservations@loscastanos.com
Web	www.loscastanos.com

Molino del Santo

The owners moved south in search of the good life, and restored a century-old mill surrounded by national park. The setting is delightful: water tumbles past flowered terraces, under fig trees and willows and into the solar-heated pool. (When it comes to things environmental, these owners are top greenies.) Pretty rooms and restaurant wear warm local garb – terracotta tiles, beams, carved beds, rush-seated chairs. Fresh flowers are everywhere and the Molino's reputation for good Spanish food is established – organic and free-range. Quite a few guests are British yet loyal locals often descend, to enjoy regional hams and sausages, rabbit, fish and imaginative vegetarian. The staff are exceptional, generous with advice on walks from the door, and other trips: take the sleepy train to Ronda, or visit some of the white villages of Andalucia. There's good info on restaurants and birdwatching routes, too. The Molino, one of the Sierra's most enjoyable small hotels, has achieved the perfect balance between warmth and professionalism. Pay extra for a superior room with a terrace – and book in advance.

Price	€85–€140. Suites €100–€180. Half-board extra €29 p.p.
Rooms	18: 15 twins/doubles, 3 suites.
Meals	Lunch & dinner €25. Wine from €8.50.
Closed	Mid-December to mid-February.
Directions	From Ronda, A374 Sevilla; after 2km, left for Benaoján on MA-505. After 10km, having crossed railway & river bridges, left to station & follow signs.

Ethical Collection: Environment.
See page 412.

	Pauline Elkin & Andy Chapell
	Barriada Estación s/n,
	29370 Benaoján, Málaga
Tel	+34 952 167151
Fax	+34 952 167327
Email	info@molinodelsanto.com
Web	www.molinodelsanto.com

Cortijo Las Piletas

The peace restores your soul, here among 100 hectares of wheat and sunflower fields, oak woodland and cattle grazing. This sprawling cortijo, with its brilliant white walls and tomato-red shutters, is a fine example of an Andalucían country estate; it's been in the family for 200 years. Lovely light-filled bedrooms have elegant wardrobes, coloured and carved bedheads, soft white curtains and private terraces; flowers and plants add a country touch. The farmhouse hall has become a sitting room enriched with tapestries, oil paintings and antiques; a crackling fire and an honesty bar add to the home-from-home feel. The beamed dining room – with terrace for summer meals – is small and cosy, its tables set with pretty china. This is terrific walking country: three *parques naturales* are on the doorstep. Return to a dip in the pool (your children may join theirs) and binoculars for birds – charming Pablo and Eli adore the wildlife. From the gardens, watch the sun set over Grazalema, glass of wine in hand… Pablo is a superb cook and keeps a fine cellar. All this ten minutes from Ronda.

Price	€90–€96. Singles €74–€80.
Rooms	8: 7 twins/doubles, 1 family.
Meals	Dinner €30. Picnic-style lunch €9.
Closed	November & January.
Directions	From Ronda A-374 for Sevilla. Ignore first turn to Benaoján/Montejaque. On towards Sevilla; left for Montejaque on MA-8403. Las Piletas is 1st farm on the left, with red windows.

Elisenda Vidal & Pablo Serratosa
Apdo. 559, 29400 Ronda, Málaga

Tel	+34 952 004095
Fax	+34 951 230603
Email	info@cortijolaspiletas.com
Web	www.cortijolaspiletas.com

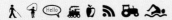

Finca La Guzmana

You'll want to stay here for at least a week – such a lovely, relaxed place to be. The house, a 150-year-old, single-storey Andalucían cortijo, is surrounded by five acres of olive and fruit trees and vines and, apart from the occasional train, or the put-put of the tractor as Peter works his organic fields, it's truly peaceful. At the heart of the Finca are a tiled courtyard, wrapped around by the three whitewashed wings of the house, and a huge lounge with soaring ceilings. A dappled terracotta roof juts forward to provide cloister-like shade; vivid geraniums spill from supporting pillars; dogs scamper and cats doze. Breakfast out here by the lion fountain is a delicious way to start the day. The pleasant bedrooms, with square, deep-set windows and lots of light and space – and the open-plan kitchen that guests are free to use – open off the courtyard. Outside is a superb, 20m salinated pool where you can swim and gaze up at the mountains. There's masses to do in the area, and Peter is happy to recommend places to eat nearby. For dinner, good food can be found at the *venta* at the end of the track.

Price	€70–€90. Weekly rates available.
Rooms	7 twins/doubles.
Meals	Restaurant 300m.
Closed	Never.
Directions	Ronda-El Burgo road to km4 marker. Take track ('Carril Privado') opp. La Venta; 300m.

Peter McLeod
Apdo. de Correos 408,
29400 Ronda, Málaga

Tel   +34 952 114912
Email   info@laguzmana.com
Web   www.laguzmana.com

Alavera de los Baños

A rather fetching small hotel on the edge of the old Tanners Quarter – peaceful sheep-grazed pastures to one side, steep ascents to Ronda on the other. *A la vera de* means 'by the side of' – your hotel is next to the first hammam of the Moorish citadel. The new building is in keeping with the Hispano-Moorish elements of its surroundings: thus terracotta tiles, wafer bricks and keyhole arches outside and, in the cosy little bedrooms, a softly oriental feel: kilims, mosquito nets, colour washes of ochres, blue and yellow. Shower rooms are compact but charming. Book one of the more peaceful terrace rooms if you can; at the back, on the ground floor, they lead to a lush little garden and a delicious little pool (popular in high summer) with views. The dining room is lily-filled and candlelit, cut across by an arched central walkway leading to the rooms at either end. Breakfasts are different each day; dinners have a Moorish slant: lamb is the speciality and there is tasty veggie food too, much organically grown. But come out of season for the Alavera as its best; even in winter it's lovely.

Price	€85–€105. Singles €65–€75.
Rooms	10: 9 twins/doubles, 1 single.
Meals	Dinner €22–€25. Wine €15–€20.
Closed	December & January.
Directions	In Ronda, directly opp. Parador hotel, down c/Rosario. Right at end & down hill to Fuente de los Ocho Caños. Here left; 1st right to Arab Baths; hotel next door. Park here.

Christian Reichardt
c/San Miguel s/n,
29400 Ronda, Málaga

Tel	+34 952 879143
Fax	+34 952 879143
Email	alavera@telefonica.net
Web	www.alaveradelosbanos.com

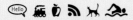

Entry 248   Map 20

Baraka

Anahid is a vital mix of Armenian Lebanese with a good shaking of Anglo Californiese, which means she's practical, funny, hugely enthusiastic… and a touch enigmatic. With the renovation complete of this 18th-century townhouse in the former Arabic district of Ronda, she cooked a large Lebanese meal for the tearfully grateful local builders; groups of six or more can order the same treatment. Pass through Arabian Nights doorways with the recurring theme of a turban arch painted above them to find an intimate plant-filled patio with fountain and two round mosaic tables where breakfast takes place, enhanced by tasty local 'molletes' (Arabic flat buns) and 'labne' (salted, drained and minted yogurt). The scent of jasmine follows the metal stairs all the way to the top terrace and a rooftop panorama accompanied by church bells and birdsong. Traditional bedrooms appear on different levels, with artistic touches in flower murals and decorative curls on metal-frame beds; the bathrooms are ordinary. 'Safra' is a favourite, painted yellow and graced by a lovely alcove window seat with table and wicker chairs.

Price	€50–€75. Suite €100.
Rooms	3: 1 double, 1 twin, 1 suite.
Meals	Dinner (min. 6) by arrangement. Restaurant 5-minute walk.
Closed	Mid-December to mid-January.
Directions	From Grenada, to historic centre. Before bridge, last right turn, Calle Santo Domingo, downhill; road forks at fountain on right; pedestrianised Calle Ruedo Doña Elvira on right, uphill; house on right.

Anahid Nazeli
c/Ruedo Dona Elvira 16,
29400 Ronda, Málaga

Tel	+34 952 872843
Fax	+34 952 872843
Email	anahid@barakaronda.com
Web	www.barakaronda.com

La Alcantarilla

The Moors turned this corner of Ronda's Llano de la Cruz valley into a lush paradise. Named after the water course ('alcantarilla') they installed in the 8th century, this smallholding proves their legacy, its five acres of orchards and aqueducts functioning to this day. The house speaks the local vernacular with a little help from its generous English owners, an artist, whose striking works decorate the rooms, and a writer. They have preserved most of its features, from the pantile roofs to the window grilles and doors. Inside is an oasis of calm, with cool stony hues and stylish décor downstairs, more colour and exotic textures in bedrooms. Outside, a choice of private patios, one a formal rose garden, its pergola decked in wisteria, its views to distant, shimmering mountains. Across a bridge, hidden by walnut trees, is the simple 13-metre pool and engagingly unkempt garden. Expect a fridge full of local products (perhaps some plums, figs or pears from the garden) and an excellent fully functioning kitchen. Central heating is extra; logs come free. *Massage, yoga, hair, hands... by arrangement.*

Price	€650–€1,300 per week. Main house also for rent in summer.
Rooms	House for 6.
Meals	Meals by arrangement. Wine from €5. Restaurant within walking distance.
Closed	Never.
Directions	Directions on booking.

	Gabriella Chidgey
	Apdo. 504,
	29400 Ronda, Málaga
Tel	+34 951 166060
Email	enquiries@alcantarilla.co.uk
Web	www.alcantarilla.co.uk

Hotel Molino del Puente

Slip out of the main door of the hotel, and just down the road is the hotel's secret riverside garden – resplendent with figs, quinces, pomegranates and vines, visited by kingfishers and the occasional otter. There's a small waterfall, too – bliss with a book and a chilled rosé. As for the 300-year-old mill, it has been radically revamped by Ian and Elaine, with two courtyards and a colonnade overlooking a pool; the millstones remind you of its origins. Five minutes from lovely old Ronda, it stands beside the Gaudalcobacin river in a tree-screened valley. The bedrooms are understated and newly tiled, with big wrought-iron beds and solid wooden desks, simple rugs and raw silk covers. Bathrooms lean towards the luxurious. Elaine and Ian ran a restaurant in Cabopino, Marbella before taking to the hills; lovely enthusiastic people, they organise adventure weekends. Chef Ian's style is eclectic: fresh bass with a peanut crust; confit of duck with cointreau and raspberry sauce… both restaurant and central bar are very popular with locals and tourists alike. A happy place.

Price	€70–€100. Suite €110–€135.
Rooms	10: 7 doubles, 2 twins, 1 suite.
Meals	Dinner, 2 courses, €25. Wine €10.50.
Closed	December & January.
Directions	From Ronda, A374 to Sevilla. After 7km, right at Don Benito Hotel. Follow road, bear left at fork. Mill's car park directly in front of you.

	Elaine Love
	Fuente de la higuera 7 bajo,
	29400 Ronda, Málaga
Tel	+34 952 874164
Email	info@hotelmolinodelpuente.com
Web	www.hotelmolinodelpuente.com

La Fuente de la Higuera

The Ronda mountains wrapped Tina and Pom in its spell and they realised their dream: a blissful retreat encircled by olive groves, ten minutes out of town. Tina is the 'spark', a charming woman who has decorated the area's first boutique hotel with cool, understated elegance. Pom is born to the role of host: a raconteur by nature and a connoisseur of wine. The conversion of their old mill has been accomplished with local expertise, smooth plastering and planked floors adding to the immaculate furnishings and the stylish feel – a change from the more usual beam and terracotta. Each lovely suite has an open fire for cosy winter stays; Indonesian beds, muslin drapes, lamps, chairs and tables add a touch of exotica. Bathrooms are generous. An honesty bar, books and a vast collection of CDs add to the relaxed and laid-back feel. The focus is poolwards; beyond, groves of olives and the changing colours of the mountains – a blissful backdrop to your sundowner. Feast on regional food that gets better and better, matched by fabulous Andalucian wines. *New sister hotel nearby.*

Price	€89–€148. Suites €179–€280.
Rooms	11: 3 twins/doubles, 8 suites.
Meals	Dinner €42. Wine €16–€40.
Closed	Rarely.
Directions	Bypass Ronda on A-374 towards Sevilla. Pass turning to Benaoján; right at sign for hotel at km28 marker. Under bridge, left at 1st fork; over bridge; left after 200m.

Pom & Christina Piek
Partido de los Frontones,
29400 Ronda, Málaga

Tel	+34 952 114355
Fax	+34 952 165609
Email	info@hotellafuente.com
Web	www.hotellafuente.com

El Tejar & Dar Hajra

From a high terrace near Ronda you contemplate a panorama of oak forest, almond and olive groves and the distant Grazalema mountains. Guy stumbled across El Tejar, once a tile factory, when out walking over 20 years ago and turned it into a deliciously labyrinthine series of spaces built up and down steps and steep stairs. Its décor is inspired by his travels in the East and Andalucía's Moorish past: Kashmiri rugs, Rajastani throws, carved Moroccan mirrors, beautiful pots from Fez. It definitely feels like home, thanks to books and magazines, paintings and Guy's shots of exotic lands. But best of all are those views through the greenery of the terraced areas, stretching southwards to the peaks. The four airy bedrooms look south too, and have excellent beds, big wardrobes, CD players and cooling fans. Francisca, your friendly housekeeper, cleans and tidies each morning (if that's what you'd like) and can prepare meals. If you're looking for a smaller place there is Dar Hajra ('House of the Rocks') higher up; sculpted around a limestone outcrop, it has an infinity plunge pool and more sublime views.

Price	El Tejar €1,350-€1,785. Dar Hajra €1,150-€1,350. Prices per week.
Rooms	El Tejar for 6-8. Dar Hajra for 2-4.
Meals	Dinner by arrangement.
Closed	Never.
Directions	From Ronda A374 for Sevilla 20km. Right into Montecorto; cobbled track opp. church; at end, right. Pass left of no. 54; at last house, right up track to El Tejar & Dar Hajra.

Guy Hunter-Watts
c/Nacimiento 38,
29430 Montecorto, Málaga

Mobile	+34 616 057184
Email	info@rondatejar.com
Web	www.rondatejar.com

Molino de las Pilas

The lofty, atmospheric dining hall of the Molino, liberally adorned with restored farm machinery from the 1880s – the decade in which it was built – is one of the best places to eat in the interior of Andalucía. The hotel next door is equally charming. The old mill was in ruins when gentle Pablo found it, and the restoration took three years. Simply but comfortably furnished in an elegantly rustic style, bedrooms have excellent beds, fine bathrooms and log-burning stoves, and there's a big sitting room that's cosily beamed. In summer you'll want to be outside, in the courtyard – a riot of bougainvillea and honeysuckle – or on the terrace at the back, where views soar across rolling fields of olives and wheat to the Serrania de Ronda. In the restaurant the old workings are in place: great grindstones for mashing the olives, a massive beamed press, and huge *tinajas* set in the floor to store the oil. Equally remarkable is Esmeraldas's cooking: superb fish, fabulous marinaded partridge, salads a delight – all at amazingly reasonable prices. The Molino gets better and better.

Price	€80.
Rooms	6 twins/doubles.
Meals	Lunch & dinner from €25 à la carte.
Closed	3 weeks in January.
Directions	From Málaga, A-357 for Campillos. After Ardales, cross bridge at lake, left at km11 marker to Teba, on MA-5404. After 6km, right at petrol station, up hill. 1km, signed on left.

Pablo Moreno Aragón
Ctra. Vieja de Ronda km1,
29327 Teba, Málaga

Tel	+34 952 748622
Email	info@molinodelaspilas.com
Web	www.molinodelaspilas.com

Casa Isabella

You won't get closer to 'real' rural Spain than this charming white olive presser's house, hiding in a mountain village, hugged by exuberant nature. Enter a sitting area with white walls, terracotta tiles and warming log stove, brightened with fire-red armchairs and a rustic imagination; one table is an old window. Wooden doors lead to a dining room for four and a homely kitchen with a well-stocked dresser. Upstairs, the bedrooms are separated from another snug sitting area by just a head-height wall, and have linen curtains for doors. The furnishings themselves are lovely: brass beds, a sofa to recline on, rustic wardrobes under high rafters. Tapas bars abound in El Burgo but it would be a delight to cook in the kitchen, complete with the old animal byre, and eat out on the shady cobbled patio. Be sure to buy some of the local mountain ham, goat's cheese and honey – so delicious. In summer, you can swim in the village pool or the rivers close by; the owners (and the neighbours!) will give you all the info. Come for authenticity and peace, and the Sierra de las Nieves on your doorstep.

Price	£300-£350 (sterling) per week.
Rooms	1 cottage for 4 (1 double, 1 twin).
Meals	Restaurants close by.
Closed	Never.
Directions	Directions on booking.

David & Sarah Tolhurst
c/las Laderas 3, 29100 El Burgo,
Málaga

Mobile	+34 689 824038
Email	sarah@casaisabellaspain.com
Web	www.casaisabellaspain.com

Hotel Cerro de Híjar

On a clear day you can see – well, if not forever, at least to the sea. It has a remote and unrivalled position, this hotel, on a bluff 700 metres high. From the sleepy Arab village of Tolox (known for its old-fashioned spa), you follow the winding road up and up… to a new hotel built with rare vision. Inside: a terrific sense of light and space, creamy stucco walls, bright rugs and pleasing furniture, a winter fire and Andalucían paintings on every wall. Bedrooms range from big to massive, each with its own stylish lighting, a designer bathroom, colourwashed walls, tapestries from Morocco. You'll eat and drink wonderfully well: Martín's cooking is traditional Andalucían with an inspired touch, while the excellent buffet breakfast is laid out with care and served on bone china. Martín, Guillermo and Eugenio run the place in an eco-friendly manner (every guest is given a sapling to plant before they leave) and manager María is a gem. The Málaga valley reaches out before you; closer are the peaks of the Sierra Nevada, snow-capped until March. The walking is magnificent, the place is a treat.

Price	€73-€88. Singles €53-€62. Suites €90-€118.
Rooms	18: 14 twins/doubles, 4 suites.
Meals	Breakfast €8. Lunch & dinner €24 each. Wine €12-€30.
Closed	Never.
Directions	From Málaga, to Cártama. Filter right to Coín, then onto A-366 for Ronda. Left to Tolox, through village to Balneario (spa); right up hill for 2.5km to hotel.

Guillermo Gonzalez, Eugenio Llanos
& Martín Jerez
Cerro de Híjar s/n, 29109 Tolox, Málaga

Tel	+34 952 112111
Fax	+34 952 119745
Email	cerro@cerrodehijar.com
Web	www.cerrodehijar.com

Ethical Collection: Environment.
See page 412.

Albero Lodge

A private villa reborn as a romantic beach hotel. Young trees stand sentinel in front of the modern, ochred exterior (*albero* describes the sandy colour of the bull ring) lending it a ceremonious air. The interconnecting dining room, sitting room and bar are similarly formal. The bedrooms, by contrast, are triumphantly, stylishly individual, each inspired by a different city: Florence, Deauville, Berlin, Dover, Ronda, Madras, Djerba, Fez and New York. Those with an eastern theme are especially luscious. Walls are colourwashed, every room gets its own patio, Djerba is peaceful and Fez's bathroom oozes rustic chic. The gardens are similarly groomed, resplendent with palm trees, jasmine, hibiscus, plumbago. Living areas have stylish wicker sofas and chairs, the terrace a delicious pool, and charming staff serve breakfast until 12. Albero Lodge is part of a smart development of villas fairly close to the N-340; from outside there's a distant hum, but indoors the insulation is good. 'Secret' footpaths lead you to the beach, Gibraltar is a short drive to the west, and Morocco is a day trip away.

Price	€85–€120. Suites €105–€155.
Rooms	9: 4 twins/doubles, 5 suites.
Meals	Breakfast €9. Restaurants nearby.
Closed	10 January–10 February
Directions	From Málaga, A-7 for Estepona; exit Selwo. Back on A-7 for Málaga. After sign for Guadalmansa Urb. follow service road; right into Park Beach Resort.

Myriam Pérez Torres
Urbanización Finca la Cancelada,
c/Támesis 16, 29689 Estepona, Málaga

Tel	+34 952 880700
Fax	+34 952 885238
Email	info@alberolodge.com
Web	www.alberolodge.com

Amanhavis

There's a real warmth to this place, thanks to Burkhard, Leslie and staff, and you sense it the moment you enter. The mountain village of Benahavis has long been known for its string of restaurants, the most renowned of which is surely this intimate restaurant-hotel. Make the most of Burkhard's "creative Mediterranean cuisine": fresh tiger prawns, fillets of monkfish, raspberry cream cake, mountain cheeses... no wonder the Marbella set flock. Bedrooms, radiating off the pretty inner courtyard with plunge pool, are lavish and a decent size – nine flights of fantasy with themes that refer to Spain's Golden Age (the Astonomer's Observatory, the Spice Trader's Caravan) – and equipped with every modern treat. Bathrooms have a Moroccan slant and luxurious towels. A perfectionist's attention to detail is evident throughout, from the snugs in the suites to the aromatic oils. In summer you dine by the little pool; indoors is a convivial bar. This excellent place is five kilometres from the sea and all those golden beaches – a romantic escape for two.

Price	€99–€159.
Rooms	9 twins/doubles.
Meals	Breakfast €11. Dinner €39.90. Wine from €12.95. Restaurant closed Monday in low season & Sunday all year (open for Sunday lunch).
Closed	7 January–12 February.
Directions	From Málaga for Cádiz. Just past San Pedro, right for Benahavis. Hotel on far side of village, signed.

Leslie & Burkhard Weber
c/El Pilar 3, Benahavis,
29679 Marbella, Málaga

Tel	+34 952 856026
Fax	+34 952 856151
Email	info@amanhavis.com
Web	www.amanhavis.com

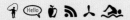

The Town House

Maria is eager for people to discover the simple elegance that is the real Marbella and there couldn't be a better launch pad than this. Plaza Tetuán is a lovely square in the very heart of the old town and close to the beach. It's not on any through route, so is surprisingly quiet (except during the Feria in the second week of June). The house is a rare and striking place to stay, with a peachy marble entrance at the corner of the building and a charming little roof terrace. Originally an old family house – seven brothers lived here – it has been gradually restored. Inside, Moorish and Modern have been married to arresting effect; the whole place has an air of supremely chic and tasteful decadence! The small but luxurious bedrooms are decorated in neutral colours or lustrous pastel shades and furnished with restraint: sumptuous beds, fine mirrors, the occasional superb antique… Each room is different; all are marble floored and subtly lit, with exuberant plants and suitably sybaritic bathrooms. You'll have to eat out but that should be a pleasure, with the fine array of good restaurants close by.

Price	€95–€130.
Rooms	9: 6 doubles, 3 twins.
Meals	Restaurants nearby.
Closed	Never.
Directions	From Málaga airport for Cádiz; exit for Marbella 'Centro Urbano'. On for 2km; right at junc.; follow signs for Hotel Lima. Last exit at r'bout into Avda Nabeul. On c/Najera to Plaza Tetuán. On corner.

Maria Lundgren
c/Alderete 7, Plaza Tetuán,
29600 Marbella, Málaga
Tel   +34 952 901791
Fax   +34 952 901791
Email   info@townhouse.nu
Web   www.townhouse.nu

El Oceano Hotel & Beach Club

One of the best on the Costa del Sol. El Oceano may not be particularly Spanish, but it is as spoiling as can be, and the people who run it are delightful. Mooch around all day in a white bathrobe in the spa, get your nails polished, your hair done, then slip into something fabulous for dinner. Double bedrooms look onto the mountains, suites face the ocean; several have terraces, a few have outdoor jacuzzis, and the newest are truly stylish. There's a hint of Florida in the lounge/bar and a touch of the Far East in the outdoor pool, lush with palm trees and thatched bar – glide up for a generous measure of pink gin. The restaurant is one of the best around and the cuisine, accompanied by fine wines and live music, is international and delicious. In warm weather you dine on a terrace overlooking the sea. Beyond the pool: a long sweep of ocean; the blue water shimmers, waves lap onto the rocks and the beach feels as though it's yours. Yes, you are off the N-340 and close to Marbella's sprawl, but El Oceano sits on its own rocky outcrop with clean, empty and stunning beaches nearby.

Price	€140. Suites €195-€260. Studios €160.
Rooms	39 + 15: 15 twins/doubles, 24 suites. 15 studios for 2-3.
Meals	Lunch €12.50. Dinner €30-€50 à la carte. Wine from €16.
Closed	Winter months.
Directions	From Málaga, N-340 for Marbella. Exit Riviera del Sol. At r'bout, left under m'way, back onto N-340 for Fuengirola. Under footbridge, take 1st exit. Hotel on right.

John Palmer
Ctra. N-340 km 199, Urbanización Torrenueva,
29649 Mijas, Málaga

Tel	+34 952 587550
Fax	+34 952 587637
Email	info@oceanohotel.com
Web	www.oceanohotel.com

The Beach House

Marlon Brando was once photographed by the pool... alongside which the Mediterranean splashes and sparkles. An arresting spot: you may be sandwiched between the devil (the N-340) and the deep blue sea, but once you've negotiated the slip road, it's easy to forget the devil. In a previous life, this was the ritzy villa of a wealthy Arab. Now the Swedish Westerbergs are the owners. This boutique hotel has a zen-like calm and is a haven of special touches – from the orchid floating in a bowl by your bed to the music on the hotel's compilation CD. Staff are professional and charming, serving you breakfast, a fine-looking buffet, on the decked terrace in summer. The whole beautiful place exudes a Nordic chic – buckskin rugs in reception, baskets brimful of magazines – yet is irresistibly inviting. It is like staying in a friend's exquisite villa. The pool is heated all year, the (beautiful) beach waits below, and Marbella, spiritual home to Europe's *nouveaux riches*, is a shake away. Ask for one of the quieter rooms in the main villa.

Price	€125-€175.
Rooms	10 twins/doubles.
Meals	Snack bar nearby.
Closed	Mid-December to mid-February.
Directions	From Málaga N-340 Cádiz. Keep on N-340; past km202 marker, exit Cala de Mijas. Follow signs Fuengirola & Málaga; back onto N-340. Keep hard right; past 1st footbridge, slip road to right. On right after 250m.

Irene Westerberg & Carina Anderson
Urbanización el Chaparral,
CN-340 km203, 29648 Mijas Costa,
Málaga

Tel/fax	+34 952 494540
Email	info@beachhouse.nu
Web	www.beachhouse.nu

Rancho Sentosa

A few miles inland from the Costa del Sol, hilltop Mijas keeps its Spanish charm. Its web of cobbled streets, the prettier the higher you go, are stuffed with tiny shops and traditional bars, while donkey-taxis line the main square. Rancho Sentosa hides in a leafy glade just below, the last villa in the road. Ex-London restaurateurs Vanessa and Slawek, in search of seclusion, fell in love with the place. Now, after several years of hands-on restoration, they have created both a home for themselves and two fabulous guest apartments. Living/dining rooms are airy and generous, bedrooms are immaculate with king-size beds, chic kitchens and mosaic'd shower rooms sparkle, and a brimming welcome hamper gets you off to a flying start. Modern art sits serenely with traditional beams and tiles. Masses of space outside too, with terraces for each bedroom and another for the shared pool – a lush and lovely spot with a sundeck, covered barbecue and rustic dining area. Vanessa and Slawek may join you but are mindful of your privacy; lovely hosts, they want you to go home with happy memories. *Minimum stay four nights.*

Price	€115–€145 per night.
Rooms	2 apartments for 2.
Meals	Restaurants 1km.
Closed	December–February.
Directions	From Málaga N-340 take A-7/E-15; 2nd exit for Mijas/Fuengirola at km213 marker. Up hill towards Mijas on A-387; just before Bellini restaurant, right; signs down hill to Rancho Sentosa.

Vanessa Schon & Slawek Bolesta
Ctra. de Mijas, La Alcaparra 7,
29650 Mijas, Málaga

Tel	+34 952 590755
Email	info@ranchosentosa.com
Web	www.ranchosentosa.com

Santa Fe Hotel-Restaurante

The old farmhouse sits among the citrus groves of the Guadalhorce valley, to one side of the road from Marbella up to Coín; traffic is audible, but not intrusive. The transformation from farm to guest house has been faithful to local tradition, while the small and basic bedrooms and bathrooms are soon to be upgraded. There are terracotta floors, rustic furniture and stencilled walls; rooms with small windows are darkish in winter. Outside are a big garden and pool, and a terrific little pool-side restaurant, popular with the locals – Spanish or Costa-cosmopolitan. Delightful new Dutch owners, Marige and Jaap, both worked at the Santa Fe for 4 years before taking over in 2007; he was the highly acclaimed chef and continues to rustle up the likes of maigret of duck and salmon and turbot carpaccio; delicious vegetarian dishes too, and wines. No sitting room but a dining room with a log fire and a cosy conservatory and bar. But most of the year you dine beneath the huge and ancient olive tree. Note that they cater for wedding parties sometimes. A relaxed atmosphere, delicious meals and late breakfasts reign.

Price	€70–€75. Singles €60–€65.
Rooms	3 twins/doubles.
Meals	Lunch & dinner €25–€40 à la carte. Not Tuesday.
Closed	2 weeks in November; 2 weeks in February.
Directions	From Málaga on N-340 for Cádiz. 1km after airport A-366/C-344 for Coín. Nera Coín on A-355 for Monda & Marbella; take exit Coín signed A-7102. Hotel 500m, on left.

Marije Veugen & Jaap Schaafsma
Ctra. de Monda km3, Apartado 147,
29100 Coín, Málaga

Tel	+34 952 452916
Fax	+34 952 453843
Email	info@santafe-hotel.com
Web	www.santafe-hotel.com

Rancho del Inglés

Now the children have flown, David and Miyuki have transformed their old rambling ranch into a quirky, fascinating place to stay. While the farmhouse itself is from the 1860s, complete with cobbled floor and fireplace, the rest is a fabulous cornucopia of building materials 'salvaged' from Europe to Asia and furnished with some apocryphal pieces. A shelving unit from a Surrey post office, an ancient Salamanca door, the headrest of a raised-iron Punjabi bed, a shower room open to the elements. No two rooms are alike and yet there are constants: in the beautiful old *barro* tiles and the arched shuttered windows that give onto delicate balconies. Various living areas have large log-burning stoves and huge dining tables; loggias have space and views; the citrus trees glow. Few British couples in Spain come more interesting than David and Miyuki. He a former advertising mogul, she a designer, they now market their own avocados and grow mountains of bougainvillea to defend their three-hectare oasis of charm from the inexorable sprawl of Alhaurin. *15 minutes from airport. Cook available.*

Price	€60–€80. Houses £215–£1,500 (sterling) per week.
Rooms	4 + 3: 4 twins. 1 house for 2; 1 house for 4–6; 1 house for 6–8.
Meals	Breakfast €10. Restaurants in Alhaurín, 3-minute drive.
Closed	Rarely.
Directions	A-366/A-404; exit Parador del Golf/Churriana onto A-366. Thro' Alhaurín to BP-petrol. At r'bout, exit Málaga/Coín; at 2nd r'bout, onto A-404; 1st right after 100m; on left before road bears right.

Miyuki Taylor
Camino del Convento,
29130 Alhaurín de la Torre, Málaga

Tel	+34 952 410692
Email	info@ranchodelingles.com
Web	www.ranchodelingles.com

Cortijo Padre Avilés

If it's solitude you're after, Padre Avilés is one of the quietest, remotest and most relaxing spots in Andalucía, up in the hills 20 minutes from Málaga – and only half an hour from the airport. It's a converted 17th-century convent steeped in history. And behind its walls lie two excellently equipped and spacious apartments, each with its own front door and private terrace. From one you slip straight out through French windows to the pool. Rooms have a nautical bent; the owners are super-keen sailors. And ideal hosts, very much around should you need them. Everything is shipshape: bedrooms light and airy, bedding crisp and white, mattresses orthopaedic; bathrooms have decent sinks and pretty mosaics; the cabin-style kitchen-diners have immaculate white sofas. Familes will not want to leave: there are two separate play areas, tennis courts, hammocks and a big pool. Take a well-worn path round the 180-acre estate scattered with olive and almond trees, or make for the national park just up the road. Views out to sea are awesome; on a clear day you can see Africa.

Price	€850–€1,150 per week.
Rooms	2 apartments for 5.
Meals	Choice of restaurants within 7km.
Closed	Rarely.
Directions	From Málaga airport towards town; exit for Motril/Almería onto A-7. After 20km & 3 tunnels, exit 246B dir. La Cala del Moral/Olías on M-24. Exit 5 for Olías; right at T-junc; house gate 6.5km, after telephone posts.

Claire & David Parish
Ctra. de Olias km 7.5,
29197 Padre Avilés, Málaga

Tel	+34 952 294242
Fax	+34 952 294242
Email	dave_claireparish@yahoo.co.uk
Web	www.padre-aviles.com

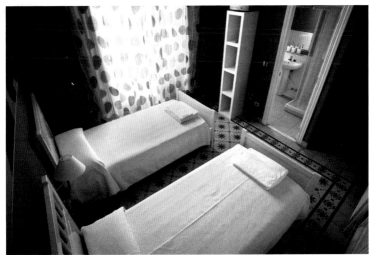

Las Acacias

The funky sea-blue and white exterior gives a clue to the up-for-a-good-time feel of this hostal. On Malaga's beachside outskirts, one of a 19th-century terrace, this welcoming and colourful place is for the young-at-heart. From the tiny bar reception through to the bedrooms you're hit by brilliant, breezy colours: sky blue, burnt orange, custard yellow, fiery red… Furnishings are fresh and simple – wooden or wrought-iron beds, little tables, a sculptural twig arrangement – and pepped up with pop-art curtains, contemporary art and colourful original floor tiles. Roadside rooms may be a little noisy for some, so ask for garden-facing or splash out on the Garden Suite, tucked at the end of the terrace. Excellent breakfasts – until midday – and dinners are served on the shady garden patio, warmed by gas heaters if cool (or there's a small dining room full of photographs and art). Chef Nacho's menu announce fresh and modern regional cooking. With its fun atmosphere and helpful staff, its stroll from the beach, its ten-minute bus ride into town – Picasso Museum, cathedral, cobblestone streets – life here is a breeze.

Price	€59-€95. Singles €42-€79. Suite €96-€127.
Rooms	8: 5 twins, 1 double, 1 single, 1 suite.
Meals	Dinner à la carte €20. Restaurants 2-minute walk.
Closed	Never.
Directions	Around Málaga on Ronda de Málaga; exit 247 for El Palo. Head for sea; left after bridge, right at traffic lights onto Avda Juan Sebastioan Elcano. 3rd left onto Paseo de las Acacias; hotel on right at end of street.

José María Casero
Paseo de las Acacias 5,
29017 Málaga,

Tel	+34 952 200167
Fax	+34 952 200167
Email	info@lasacaciashr.com
Web	www.lasacaciashr.com

Los Limoneros

Drift off to sleep in Morocco, China or Japan. The bedrooms in this Andalucían farmhouse – half an hour inland, but a world away from the Costa del Sol – are globally themed. 'Japan' is neat with pale lilac walls, simple black furniture and pretty fans; 'Africa' has rich red walls, exotic prints and mosquito netting. Enfolded by citrus groves and with views to the Arab town of Álora and the mountains and valleys of Guadalhorce, this hotel is guaranteed to help you unwind. Furnishings in the beamed and tiled public rooms are rustic and simple, enhanced with second-hand finds. Anne-Marie looks after the cooking – menus are varied, flavoursome and cater for any need. Yvette, a complementary therapist, offers reflexology, massage and crystal healing, or come for a yoga or reiki week. They are easy, laid-back people who have created a happy, wholesome place to stay. Laze by the pool, in the shade of the bamboo-clad terrace, or the fragrant garden, with its lemon groves, fig and orange trees. Granada, Seville and Ronda are too close to ignore – and the walking and riding are magnificent. *B&B October-May only.*

Price	€90. Singles €60. Whole house (June-Sept) €1,500–€1,700 per week.
Rooms	8: 7 twins/doubles. 1 single. Extra beds. House available for self-catering.
Meals	Light lunch €7. Dinner €20. Wine €6–€10.
Closed	June-September for B&B.
Directions	From airport towards Málaga, then Motril. Exit on A-357 for Cártama. From A-357 exit on A-343 to Pizarra. Here, left; at km49 marker, right at sign 'Ermita de N.S. de la Fuensanta'. House 2nd on left.

Anne-Marie Walker & Yvette Winfield
Apdo de Correos 314, 29560 Pizarra,
Málaga

Tel	+34 952 484072
Fax	+34 952 484072
Email	loslimoneros@gmail.com
Web	www.loslimoneroshotel.com

Cortijo Jacaranda

The problem with holidaying with young children is that so few places answer your needs and theirs. This is different; Lorna and Lee's 16-acre farm in the bare southern hills is the perfect place for family holidays. With two good, purpose-built and simply styled cottages, each with its own terrace with great views, and an apartment, Lorna and Lee have made the whole place as family-friendly and relaxed as can be: the pool has a shallow area for kids, and toys, cots and baby gadgets galore. Add a big suntrap terrace, purpose-built play area, giant patio chess, videos and DVDs to rent, mountain bikes to borrow and loads more – tremendous fun for all. One evening a week is barbecue night, another paella, and your hosts are happy to provide a free babysitting service one evening during your stay, ferrying you to and from your chosen restaurant. Lorna can do all sorts of relaxing beauty therapies for deserving mothers, golf, riding, quad biking and archery can be arranged, and skiing is possible (a two-hour drive) between January and April. They'll even meet you at the airport and guide you to the farm.

Price	Houses €110-€120. Apartment €75-€85. All prices per night.
Rooms	2 houses for 4-6; 1 apartment for 2-4.
Meals	Restaurants in Alora.
Closed	Rarely.
Directions	From airport dir. Malaga, then Motril; exit A357 dir. Cartama; exit A343 dir. Alora. Pass sign to Alora, right at T-junc. after 0.7km, left at bus stop. After 1.5km right fork at stream bed. Continue 2.7km over top of hill, entrance at bottom of hill.

Lee & Lorna Rickwood
Apdo. de Correos 279, 29500 Álora, Málaga

Tel	+34 952 112703
Fax	+44 (0)20 8133 9005
Email	bookings@cortijojacaranda.com
Web	www.cortijojacaranda.com

Finca Las Nuevas

Since living the dream in the West Country, Jane & Mark have been deeply involved in the sustainable idyll. They've recreated it perfectly here in Spain, among the remote, rolling peaks of the untouched Alora region. This delightful pair have turned a 200-year-old ruined farmhouse into a magical hideaway – simple rooms, staggering setting. As the crow flies it's just five miles from Málaga, but in reality almost an hour's drive, worth every twist and turn. Self-catering it may be, but a cook is on hand to tempt you with lunch and dinner, or picnic baskets for days out in the mountains. The casitas are uncomplicated and rustic, just white walls, wooden beams and pine furniture; each has a living and kitchen area and some a wood-burning stove. Bathrooms are white-tiled and plain. Laze on the terraces under shady vines; dip in the pool with the housemartins. Reed beds, recycling, home-grown veg – the green credentials shine through. You're welcomed with a basket of food essentials and they'll do a weekly shop – there for when you arrive. Ask nicely and they may be able to babysit too.

Price	€350–€750 per week.
Rooms	4 houses: 1 for 6-8; 2 for 4; 1 for 2.
Meals	Lunch, dinner & hampers by arrangement. Wine €7.50.
Closed	Rarely.
Directions	Detailed directions on booking.

Jane & Mark Howlett
Apdo. Correos 171, 29500 Álora, Málaga

Tel	+44 (0)20 8144 1018
Email	jane@lasnuevas.co.uk
Web	www.lasnuevas.co.uk

La Finca Blanca

The sangria on arrival sets the tone. This is a happy and generous set up, thanks to Terry and Barbara who ran a great pub in Bath for 26 years. They live in one half of the main house with the independent units clustering around; one apartment stands by the pool. Kitchens are well-equipped, beds really comfortable and lounges spacious. The décor varies in style; an open-stone wall here, a wrought-iron four-poster there, bright scatter cushions and nice breezy curtains. The apartments have pretty views with either a balcony or terrace; for family parties some interconnect. But it is the shared facilities that shine – the saltwater pool, the tennis court, the boules pitch, the (free) mountain bikes. There are lemon groves and fruit trees all around, a high railway bridge close by (you're more likely to hear the two donkeys and the splashing fountain!), a lovely pecan tree shelters the front terrace and banana trees shade the barbecue by the pool. The mountain village of Alora and the Chorro Gorge are ten minutes away; the Ardales Lakes and Malaga airport an easy drive. *Minimum stay three nights.*

Price	Apartments for 2, €300–€550. Apartments for 4, €300–€650. All prices per week.
Rooms	3 apartments for 2; 2 apartments for 4.
Meals	Restaurants 10-minute drive.
Closed	Rarely.
Directions	Directions on booking.

Terry & Barbara Nash
Apdo. de Correos 13, 29500 Álora, Málaga

Mobile	+34 676 429805
Fax	+34 952 496683
Email	nashpulteney@hotmail.com
Web	www.lafincablanca.com

Fuegoblanco

This true Andaluz finca (half 1950s, half new) sits in its own nascent citrus grove, relishing the fruit-ripening sun that illuminates every corner of the house. Kenneth clearly saw the light by choosing the giant windows to embolden the entrance hallway and the large shared sitting room downstairs – a great space to be cool in in summer (or snug by the wood-burner) and an excellent reference library to plan hikes. Do ask Sarah for advice, she brings such energy to this enterprise. Otherwise, in a child-friendly garden, ruminate in a swing seat among the olive trees. Simply furnished in pine, with Indian hangings and Casablanca fans, each bedroom has its own spotless if slightly spartan bathroom and guests have their own entrance to the main house. Outside is lovely, dining at pretty individual tables on the patio, enjoying speciality vegetarian dishes or homemade Seville orange marmalade for breakfast. Above the house, the pool is a splendid place to flop amidst plants, bougainvillea and hillside views; similarly recline on rough-hewn wooden furniture that the very first lemon sale kindly provided.

Price	€73–€83. Singles €48–€53. Suite €100–€122.
Rooms	6: 2 doubles, 2 twins, 1 single, 1 suite.
Meals	Lunch €8. Dinner, 3 courses with wine, €22.50. Restaurants 5-minute drive.
Closed	Rarely.
Directions	A357 from Malaga, right to Alora; 2nd r'bout exit El Chorro; signed 2km on right.

Ethical Collection: Environment; Food.
See page 412.

Kenneth & Sarah Beachill
Partido los Aneales, 29500 Álora,
Málaga

Tel	+34 952 497439
Fax	+34 952 497439
Email	enquiries@fuegoblanco.com
Web	www.fuegoblanco.com

Cortijo Valverde

The land around Valverde is still farmed and the 1843 farmhouse has been sympathetically restored. Surrounded by a landscape of hills and rocky outcrops, you can gaze up at the Torcal range in one direction and Álora in the other. After a day spent discovering the glories of Granada or Córdoba, bliss to return to a drink on the terrace with beautiful views. Dinner, too, is something to look forward to — a house-party atmosphere and a menu based on fresh local produce. After aperitifs on the terrace, enjoy a convivial meal; Friday night is Spanish Night, when owners Caroline and Ali join guests for tapas and paella. Bedrooms in casitas are nicely private, light, airy and with every modern comfort: walk-in showers, private terraces, heating and air conditioning. Wander the scented gardens, take a dip in the big pool, or relax in the sitting room/bar with its winter woodburner. Guided walks and horse treks can be arranged, El Chorro and Ardales Lakes are a half-hour drive, and the hotel is the first carbon-neutral hotel in Andalucia. *Airport pick-up extra charge. Car hire can be arranged.*

Price	€96-€120.
Rooms	7 casitas for 2.
Meals	Lunch €3-€12. Dinner €25-€30. Wine €9-€15. No food Sunday.
Closed	Rarely.
Directions	From Málaga, A-357 for Campillos; A-343 to Álora. Don't go into village but cross river. At T-junc., by Bar Los Caballos, left for V. de Abdalajis. Pass km36 marker; sign to right; 300m; sharp left up to hotel.

Caroline & Ali Zartash-Lloyd
Ctra. Alora-Antequera km 35.5,
29500 Álora, Málaga

Tel	+34 952 112979
Email	info@cortijovalverde.com
Web	www.cortijovalverde.com

Hotel La Fuente del Sol

High up in the Torcal mountains, the little and aptly named village of La Joya ("the jewel") gazes towards Africa. Set against a teetering backdrop of national park and sheer rock, la Fuente del Sol is actually the spring that waters the grounds and burgeoning gardens. The epitome of rustic-deluxe, the hotel is surprisingly new, although there's little to distinguish it from the other century old white-walled cortijos in the area. Modern spaces come with authentic touches to the reconditioned beams, wooden doors and windows, even an 1879 Dodge City station clock that still seems to work. Siesta-inducing chaise-longues line the hallways in between the plants; and if you make it that far, a heated pool or massage is only a flop away. Ratchet up the tempo in the gymnasium. A young cook caters for the hungry in modern Andaluz style with excellent salads and dishes such as smoked salmon on a bed of spinach and pine nuts. Bedroom eyries with raffia rugs, neutral tones and quirky lamps let you spread your wings.

Price	€160–€275. Singles €120. Suites €220–€275.
Rooms	14: 11 twins/doubles, 3 suites.
Meals	Lunch & dinner €30–€40. Wine from €13.
Closed	January.
Directions	From Málaga exit 148 for Villanueva de la Concepción on to A-45. In Villanueva, signs for La Joya & hotel.

Luis Lozano
Paraje Rosas Bajas, La Joya,
29260 Antequera, Málaga

Tel	+34 951 700770
Fax	+34 951 232090
Email	info@hotelfuentedelsol.com
Web	www.hotelfuentedelsol.com

Posada del Torcal

The fruit of the owners' conversion from bustling Costa to harshly beautiful Sierra is this smart B&B, previously an award-winning small hotel. Inside and out feels thoroughly Andaluz, and the setting – not far from the Dalí-esque limestone formations of the Torcal Park – is sublime. Lavish bedrooms are dedicated to Spanish artists; the oils are local copies of originals, while many of the trimmings come from further afield – the beds, some brass, some gothic, some four-poster, were shipped out from England. The balcony rooms have the most outstanding views. Peace prevails, underfloor heating warms in winter, air conditioning cools... and there are open fireplaces and jacuzzis in some of the rooms. Optional half board includes a delicious *menu del día*, afternoon tea and cakes and unlimited house drinks. Terraced gardens run down to the pool, heated all year round, and there's tennis, sauna, mountain bikes and gym if you're feeling energetic – and outdoor activities galore. Karen and Geoffrey will point you in the right direction if walking, riding, skiing, ballooning or golf is your thing.

Price	€120–€155.
Rooms	8 twins/doubles.
Meals	Half-board supplement €45.
Closed	11-19 December.
Directions	Málaga N-331 for Antequera, exit 124 for Casabermeja. There, right for Almogía; next left to V. de la Concepción. At top of village, left at junc.; 1.5km, right for La Higuera. Hotel 3km on left.

Karen & Geoffrey Banham
Partido de Jeva,
29230 Villanueva de la Concepción,
Málaga
Tel   +34 952 031006
Email   karen@laposadadeltorcal.com
Web   www.laposadadeltorcal.com

Fountainhead

One of the hippest hotels to open in recent years, Fountainhead surveys Andalucía at its wildest – a mere 15 miles from Málaga. Sierra de Caramolos unfolds behind an unadulterated scene of olive groves and almond trees; the peace is incredible. A carob tree marks your entry onto the walled patio where a circular hole in the wall portals the cane covered walkway to your own casita, bordered by wild flowers and trim cacti. Just four – Indian, Sultan, Oriental, Arizona – they have been conceived with clean zen-like lines that belie Helen's fiesta of designer-savvy touches and glorious patterns. The fridge is packed full of goodies from manchego cheese to strawberries, while hot croissants and fresh bread are delivered to your door each morning. Architects by trade, Helen and Peter are your thoughtful hosts, zealous about organics and up for a laugh. They now produce their own olive oil, vegetables and delicious almonds. Unsurprisingly, the menu is local sophistication par excellence with staples of lemon grass and cumin soup and a salad of langoustine, orange and chicory. Even the wheelbarrows are stylish.

Price	€225.
Rooms	4 suites.
Meals	Dinner €30.
Closed	Mid-November to mid-December. Ask about weekend breaks.
Directions	Directions on booking.

Ethical Collection: Environment; Food.
See page 412.

Helen Bartlett & Peter Jewkes
Partido del Río el Terral,
Fuente la Camacha, 29180 Riogordo,
Málaga

Mobile	+34 696 183309
Email	info@fountainheadinspain.com
Web	www.fountainheadinspain.com

Hotel Humaina

Hotel Humaina is hidden deep in a forest of oak and pine, at the end of a mile of steep but solid unbeaten track. It was a hunting lodge before being reborn as a small hotel; the area's status as a Parque Natural means that today's rabbits, foxes and hares roam free. What strikes you when you arrive is the tranquillity, and the gentle greeting from your laid-back host. The dining room and bedrooms are plainly furnished and nothing special, but ask for one at the front for the best woody view. The cosiest space is the small lounge with its chimney piece and plentiful books on walking and nature; be sure to go on one of the three waymarked trails nearby, and don't be surprised if the resident dog joins you. This is an eco-aware hotel so water is heated by solar panels, then re-channelled into the garden, and organically grown produce comes from the veg patch. Try the meaty *plato de los montes* or one of several vegetarian dishes, followed by a glass of *vino de pasas*, the local raisin wine. Birds sing, wild boar nose by at dusk in this simple forest getaway.

Price	€71–€92. Singles €52–€56. Suites €106–€118. Half-board extra €30–€33 p.p.
Rooms	13: 9 twins/doubles, 2 family, 2 suites.
Meals	Breakfast €8.50. Lunch & dinner €25. Wine €10.
Closed	Rarely.
Directions	Málaga-Motril, exit 244 for Limonar. On for Camino Colmenar. After 15km onto C-345, at Fuente de la Reina, road on left for 3.8km.

Juan María Luna
Parque Natural Montes de Málaga,
Ctra. de Colmenar s/n, 29013 Málaga,

Tel   +34 952 641025
Fax   +34 952 640115
Email   info@hotelhumaina.es
Web   www.hotelhumaina.es

Entry 276   Map 21

Hotel Palacio Blanco

If you're a watcher of reality TV, you may know the story of Lesley and Nick's heroic struggles to transform this 400-year-old bishop's palace into a stylish, urban hotel. Others will be surprised: its sober white façade gives little away. But beyond the heavy wooden doors an elegant, colonnaded patio opens out with a sweep of staircase leading up to the bedrooms and, up another level, to a little rooftop spa pool and sunbathing terrace: no better place for a sun-downer gazing across the old town to the hilltop castle. The dazzling white walls are the backdrop for a series of richly-coloured paintings inspired by flamenco dance. Bedrooms are deeply comfortable with the best linen sheets, big beds stacked up with bright cushions and fabulous bathrooms. This is studied minimalism with splashes of rich golds and crimsons, and all the technical gadgetry you may want, or not. Breakfast is the time to chat to your lovely hosts; Nick does an early croissant run to the local baker's and Lesley – vivacious and fun – can help plan trips: the Picasso museum, Granada, a tram down to the beach, great walks.

Price	€85–€110. Plus VAT at 7%.
Rooms	8: 6 doubles, 2 twins.
Meals	Breakfast €8.
Closed	21-29 December.
Directions	From Málaga, A7 towards Motril, exit at junc. 272, bear left towards Vélez-Málaga. 1st r'bout straight across, 2nd r'bout right. 3rd r'bout 3rd exit into Calle Alcalde. Straight over next r'bout then immed. right. Bear right at fork by florists, up hill, hotel on left.

Lesley & Nick Vallance
Calle Felix Lomas 4,
29700 Vélez-Málaga, Málaga
Tel   +34 952 549174
Email   nick@palacioblanco.com
Web   www.palacioblanco.com

Hotel Paraíso del Mar

Nerja is one of the busiest resorts of the Costa del Sol. But the Paraíso has a great site, away from the main drag of restaurants and bars, and on the edge of a cliff looking out to sea. The main house was built in the Sixties by an English doctor (no lift, several stairs); the annexe is newer. All has all been thoroughly revamped thanks to charming Enrique and his wife Alicia, and an exotic, southern air prevails. Refurbished bedrooms have a sugary Andaluz décor but are super-comfortable with jacuzzis, fluffy bathrobes and good towels; ask for one facing the sea. From the best, a spiral stair leads you up to a private roof terrace, designed for sunset-watching, sunbathing or just gazing over the sparkling bay. Beneath the hotel are a sauna and a hot tub dug out of solid rock. Most remarkable perhaps are the hotel's terraced gardens that drop down all the way to the beach (a rare treat) — a lovely tumble of jasmine, palms, bougainvillea, bananas, morning glory and a washingtonia. You breakfast on the terrace overlooking the Med. Restaurants are a ten-minute stroll.

Price	€85-€140. Singles €75-€125. Suites €116-€170.
Rooms	17: 9 twins/doubles, 8 suites.
Meals	Restaurants nearby.
Closed	Mid-November to mid-December.
Directions	From Málaga A7 towards Motril. Exit at 292km marker. At junction with N340, left, then signs for Parador; Paraiso del Mar is next door. Limited garage parking.

Enrique Caro Bernal
c/Prolongación de Carabeo 22,
29780 Nerja, Málaga

Tel	+34 952 521621
Fax	+34 952 522309
Email	info@hispanica-colint.es
Web	www.hotelparaisodelmar.es

Hotel Rural Almazara

There's an unexpectedly rural feel to this new hotel, built above the coastal road in the vibrant resort of Nerja. After braving the beach or the shops, return to attractive grounds lined with palm trees and seating spots, decorative jasmine and acacia. The entrance is guarded by the olive press from which the hotel gets its name; the communal areas are comfortable in classic Spanish rustic style. And there's plenty of opportunity to splash: a pool on the terrace, perfect for families, and a plunge pool in the natural cave in the basement (extra charge, for couples only). There are also a jacuzzi and sauna. The restaurant, which has an adventurous menu and a good wine list, is a hive of activity in summer, and is considered one of the area's best. Dine outside with views of the sea. Spotless bedrooms have terraces and wicker chairs, and some traffic hum. Staff are friendly and helpful; take a copy of this guide and they will give you a 10% discount. It's worth staying at least a night: in spite of encroaching urban sprawl, the beaches are some of the best in the region.

Price	€69–€104. Singles €57–€76.
Rooms	22: 21 twins/doubles, 1 single.
Meals	Lunch & dinner €16.
Closed	Rarely.
Directions	From Málaga, N-340 for Motril. At Nerja (exit 292), MA-105 to Frigiliana. Hotel on right after 100m.

José Antonio Gómez Armijo
Los Tablazos 197, Ctra. Nerja-Frigiliana,
29788 Nerja, Málaga

Tel	+34 952 534200
Fax	+34 952 534212
Email	info@hotelruralalmazara.com
Web	www.hotelruralalmazara.com

La Quinta

Wrap-around views – high mountains, white villages, green foothills, a glimpse of the Mediterranean – make it hard to leave the terrace of La Quinta. And there's no need! Susi's generous breakfasts and dinners are served here, you can watch birds of prey soar and swoop, stroll to the pool for a refreshing dip, and sink into white-cushioned chairs to watch sunsets. On a bluff, two miles from the Moorish mountain village of Sedella, the villa combines Spanish cool with English charm: brick arches and terracotta floors, plump sofas and lavish curtains. White and creamy bedrooms are plush and comfortably furnished with soft lamps, crisp cotton and neat rugs. The double has a chaise longue and arched four-poster; the twin is smaller but nicely tucked away across the courtyard and with its own patio. The trim shower rooms, like the rest of the house, are shinily spotless. Susi and Chris welcome guests like family (nowhere is off-limits) and will help plan walks, visits to the 'pueblos blancos', coastal Nerja or day trips to Granada. Home-from-home warmth.

Price	€100. Singles €60.
Rooms	2: 1 double, 1 twin.
Meals	Lunch €15. Dinner with wine, €25. By arrangement.
Closed	Rarely.
Directions	From A7 exit 272, thro' Vélez; right for Sedella. After Canillas continue until 300m past km5 marker; right on track for Valverdes/Rubite. Left at fork; 300m on right.

Susi & Chris Rawlings
Loma Parra, 29715 Sedella, Málaga

Tel	+34 952 115507
Email	laquinta777@hotmail.com
Web	www.aplacetorelaxandenjoy.com

Finca El Cerrillo

From the delightfully sleepy square of whitewashed La Axarquía, a narrow road zigzags steeply down into the valley, crosses the river, then loops up to the old finca where olives and raisins were once farmed. When you reach the shady front terrace – with its heart-stopping view – you can't fail but slip into that 'I'm on holiday' mood. Everyone loves El Cerrillo, where bedrooms and living spaces are traditionally Andalucían and contemporary comforts have been integrated with style. Gordon was a set designer and has an eye for what works, in terms of colour and use of space. Bathrooms are tiled and gleaming, mattresses and linen are first class, and most rooms have wonderful views of the village and valley below. Add to this an enchanting garden, a spectacular pool, fabulous breakfasts and dinners, hiking in the sub-tropical valley, and relaxed and charming hosts. Indeed, it's all so lovely that we recommend you book for several nights. You could also reserve a place on one of their 'Arts at the Finca' events: painting, writing, ceramics – just ask.

Price	€100–€120. Singles €65–€90.
Rooms	12 twins/doubles.
Meals	Dinner €27 (4 days a week). Buffet lunch €12. Packed lunch €9. Wine from €10. Restaurants 1.5km.
Closed	Mid-November to mid-December.
Directions	Exit Algarrobo/Caleta, then signs towards Competa. Pass Sayalonga; left to Archez, dir. Sedella/Salares. Cross bridge, up hill; right at sign 'Fogarate'. On right before Canillas. Email for more details.

Sue & Gordon Kind
29755 Canillas de Albaida, Málaga

Tel	+34 952 030444
Fax	+34 952 030444
Email	info@hotelfinca.com
Web	www.hotelfinca.com

Casa el Bolinar

A narrow track loops its way through vineyards, almond and olive groves to the valley's southern flank. Here, walking distance from one of the prettiest villages in the Axarquia – lively Canillas – is Emma and Jocelyn's farmhouse. Named after the broom on the hillside, it stands in an intimate garden of palms and roses, jasmine and moon plants, its lovely pool screened by trellises. The very old, single-storey house has been transformed, and filled with books, kilims and gorgeous things. No key to the sitting room when the owners are away but a deep colonial veranda and a wonderful Andulaz courtyard with a river of cobbles and beds of lavender. Fresh beautiful bedrooms are in the new wing, their French windows opening onto the terrace: 'Yellow Room' with exotic birds painted by Jocelyn's great-grandmother, 'Mediterranean' with aqua-green hand-painted bedheads. Bathrooms are gorgeous. Breakfast is served – al fresco when possible – by Mercedes, the Spanish maid, and when the owners are (occasionally) here, you can dine with them: the food is fabulous, cooked by chef Colin. And the sea is an easy drive.

Price	€100–€150.
Rooms	2: 1 double, 1 twin.
Meals	Dinner, with wine, €60. Restaurant 1.5km.
Closed	Never.
Directions	A7 exit for Algarrobo. Head up mountain thro' Alagarrobo & Sayalonga; left to Árchez. Cross bridge; right for Sedella & Salares. Continue for 1.5km; right at sign.

Emma Cheape
29755 Canillas de Albaida,
Málaga
Mobile   +44 (0)7970 166649
Email   emtennant@hotmail.com

Casa de los Espejos

Comfortable, cosseting and eye-catchingly lovely inside, the 'House of Mirrors' snuggles into sweet Alhama, breathing an air of contentment. Owner Leonie gave the grand old village house a makeover and now it positively glows, with cushions, oriental weavings, exotic fabrics from distant lands – and mirrors of every shape, size and hue! Three bright first-floor bedrooms share a lovely retro shower room, temptingly stocked with goodies. The master double upstairs exudes luxury, with a huge bathroom and corner bath. Like the best family homes, the heart of this one is its kitchen, where a circular table and stunning instrumentalia make cooking a treat; eat by the wood-burning stove, or under the skylights in the dining room. You're yards from tapas bars in a lively square – yet blissfully free of the hubbub. From the terrace, gaze over jumbled rooftops to where mountains call walkers. Follow the gorge to healing hot springs, or jump in the car to Granada. An amazing place – immerse yourself in the simple pleasures of Andalucían life, surrounded by every imaginable comfort. *Yoga, massage, reflexology by arrangement.*

Price	€180–€300 per night.
Rooms	House for 8.
Meals	Restaurants nearby. Honesty bar in house.
Closed	Rarely.
Directions	Málaga A45 then A92 Granada. Exit km197 marker for Alhama de Granada on A7216. There, follow signs to 'Zona Monumental/Ayuntamiento' & park in Plaza de la Constitución. Walk up street from SW corner of square; house on right, at top.

	Lizzi & Graham Dunnett
	c/Arquillos 8,
	18120 Alhama de Granada, Granada
Tel	+34 958 363785
Email	info@los-espejos.com

Cortijo del Pino

Little-known Albuñuelas, a short drive from the Costa and 30 minutes from Granada – what a position – is a fetching little place surrounded by citrus groves. Approached by a steep road, El Cortijo del Pino sits high on a bluff, taking its name from the Aleppo pine that stands sentinel over house and valley. The sober lines of the building have an Italian feel and the sandy tones that soften the façade change with each passing hour. Perhaps it was the endlessly shifting light that attracted artist James Connel. His painterly eye and his wife Antonia's decorative flair have created a warm enveloping place to stay, an open house for guests and friends. Bedrooms are big and beamed, with antique Spanish beds and very good bathrooms. Outside, birdsong and church bells, roses and wisteria, a terrace with sweeping views, a gazebo overlooking the town below, a lovely, solar-heated pool… if you are inspired, grab a canvas and an easel and retire to James's studio. Art lovers be warned: his paintings are on every wall and you may be tempted to buy! The walking is wonderful. *House available for rent in summer.*

Price	€85–€110. Singles €65. Whole house (sleeps 9) €2,300 per week.
Rooms	5 twins/doubles. House available for self-catering.
Meals	Restaurants 5-minute walk (300m).
Closed	Rarely.
Directions	From Málaga dir. Granada; m'way to Motril, exit 153 for Albuñuelas. Opp. bus stop, right & follow steep road to house.

James Connel & Antonia Ruano
c/Fernán Núñez 2, La Loma,
18659 Albuñuelas, Granada

Tel	+34 958 776257
Fax	+34 958 776350
Email	elcortijodelpino@gmail.com
Web	www.elcortijodelpinolecrin.com

Alojamiento Rural Cortijo del Pino

Tranquillity ten minutes from Granada, and much character. Kind, artistic Concha and her mother make this place, and their grand old farmhouse, topped with tower and pigeon loft, hard to resist. The approach is marvellous, the beautiful trees creating a warm, out-of-time atmosphere, and this cooperative's cornfields are ecologically run. The apartments – the nicest two in converted cattle stalls and dairy – are supremely comfortable: one a nest for two, another for six, two for four. There are wood-burning stoves, underfloor heating and charming, well-equipped kitchens with lovely hand-made tiles. Furnishings are antique, the beds a delight; ceilings are high, walls thick and cool. There's no communal space, bar the pool and the large inner patio, and a wide circular path that links the apartments, each with its own furniture, but this is best in summer. You may even be offered products from the holding's own *huerta ecológica*. When you've had enough of home cuisine, there's an excellent *venta* nearby. *Minimum stay two to seven nights. Shared laundry.*

Ethical Collection: Environment.
See page 412.

Price	€68–€123 (€408–€861 per week).
Rooms	4 apartments for 2-6.
Meals	Restaurants 2km.
Closed	Never.
Directions	From Ronda de Granada, exit 129. At r'bout to 'Depuradora Aguas Residuales' & 'Campo de Golf'. Cross river to Churriana de la Vega. At r'bout to C. de la Vega. 1.4km; right for 'Camino Viejo de Cullar'. Follow signs.

Concha López
Cortijo del Pino s/n,
18194 Churriana de la Vega, Granada
Tel   +34 958 250741
Email   info@cortijodelpino.com
Web   www.cortijodelpino.com

El Nido & El Nidito

The gurgle of water, a secluded garden, cosy and colourful rooms – a place to relax and dream. These two sturdy cottages have a quirky offbeat charm that works magic. Sitting either side of Clare and Ainsley's house, they're close but prettily screened by gold and black bamboo, shrubs and fruit trees; views are of the Sierra Nevada. Snug with colourwashed walls, soft lights, ethnic throws, cushions and a jumble of paintings, books and games, the cottages exude homeliness rather than showhome polish. In El Nido the second bedroom is curtained off from the open-plan living area, making the layout suitable for families; El Nidito has two separate bedrooms. The kitchens are well-equipped – but note: Ainsley is a great chef! He once ran a restaurant with Clare (a reflexologist) and will make meals from their own organic produce, served by the pool. Friendly and laid-back, your hosts have 20 years of knowledge behind them on walking, birdwatching, riding, and trips to Granada and the beach. It's a ten-minute stroll to Órgiva – for cafés, market and New Age charm. Enjoy the bohemian vibe – and the hamper on arrival.

Price	Cottages €550–€750 per week.
Rooms	2 cottages for 5.
Meals	Dinner, 3 courses, €30, by arrangement. Restaurants 10-minute walk.
Closed	Never.
Directions	A44 exit for Lanjarón; signs to Órgiva. Left at BP petrol station & hotel Mirasol; follow narrow tarmac road which becomes a track. After 300m, houses signed (by ceramic tile).

Clare Sasada
Rio Chico Pago de la Tejilla,
18400 Órgiva, Granada
Tel   +34 958 784315
Email   reservations@elnido.co.uk
Web   www.elnidito.com

Ethical Collection: Environment; Food.
See page 412.

Los Piedaos

At the end of the long winding track, on a tree-covered ridge beneath the soaring Sierra Nevada, the multi-levelled farmstead has been renovated by its architect owner with shade, privacy and huge views in mind. Each white casita reveals old tiles and timbers, recycled shutters and doors and a colourful hotch-potch of terraces and furnishings: convivial dining tables, throws over sofas, simple bedrooms/bathrooms and plenty of novels. The owners – keen hispanophiles, welcoming but discreet – are passionate about the organic growth of the Orgiva area and are aiming for absolute sustainability. Roofs are painted white to reflect sunlight, grey water is channelled into pretty gardens, hot water comes from solar panels, the pools are cleansed by copper/silver purification, air conditioning is low energy, olives and oranges are organically grown. Trails lead to quiet spots, swallows swoop above ancient olives and a 40-minute walk brings you to popular Orgiva, one of Spain's hippy towns (yoga, tai chi, meditation). Exceptional peace, subtle architecture, soaring views. *Minimum stay five nights.*

Price	€325–€750 per week.
Rooms	4 cottages: 3 for 4, 1 for 2-3.
Meals	Restaurants in Orgiva, 3km.
Closed	Rarely.
Directions	Detailed directions & map on website.

Ethical Collection: Environment.
See page 412.

Shujata & David Dry
Las Barreras, 18400 Órgiva, Granada

Tel	+34 958 784470
Email	holidays@lospiedaos.com
Web	www.holidays-in-southern-spain.com

El Cielo de Cáñar

The road climbs up, the ground falls away until, suddenly, somewhere between the earth and the sky, you've arrived. This low-lying, Alpujarran slate cortijo seems to grow out of the stony southern slopes of the Sierra Nevada on which it is perched. The view is vast: Alpujarra mountains, white villages, Orgiva. Energy comes from the sun, water from the Sierra. Each bedroom, opening onto a private terrace, shares the panorama. Interiors are sharp and clean-cut (like the air) with a mostly white colour scheme that is spiked with bright Indian fabrics, Moroccan lampshades, modern art. Bathrooms are crisply contemporary. Simply chic, yet cool and restful, this is a place to recharge batteries. No TVs, no phones, just a spacious, terraced garden with a bounteous orchard, large pool and private corners to read or snooze. Feeling active? Hiking and riding are on the doorstep, Granada and the beach are an hour away. Return to excellent home-produced dinners, and stargazing from the terrace. Well-travelled English owners John and Orna fell in love with the area and now they happily share it.

Price	From €97. Price for whole house (sleeps 14) on application.
Rooms	5 doubles. House available for self-catering.
Meals	Dinner €24, by arrangement. Wine from €8.
Closed	Rarely.
Directions	A44 from Granada or coast to Lanjarón & Órgiva. At Órgiva take A4132 dir. Bubion & left at GR4201 ro Cañar. At Bar Piqui, hard left & follow road for 2km up hill to El Cielo de Cañar.

Ethical Collection: Environment; Food. See page 412.

	Orna Gorman
	Llano de Manzano 001, 18418 Cáñar, Granada
Tel	+34 958 953015
Email	enquiries@elcielodecanar.com
Web	www.elcielodecanar.com

Sierra y Mar

Take the blue door to paradise: a sunny, shady, leafy-walled garden and a world apart. Mention breakfast – a minor feast shared with others under the spreading mulberry tree. This is a gorgeous place run by two delightful people (Italian and Danish) who know and love Andalucía, and are relaxed, intelligent and 'green'. The ancient labyrinthine house has been extended with total respect for its origins, and is charmingly furnished with old rural pieces and natural materials for curtains and bedcovers, in simple, wholesome taste. Each room has its own shower or bath, and central heating for winter stays. Seppe and Inger organise walking tours, so make time for the half-day circular hike that begins and ends at the house. There's a well-equipped kitchen for guests and a great family-run restaurant you can walk to, also a couple of vegetarian restaurants nearby. The atmosphere is easy, the village is beautiful (you're right at the top of it) and your hosts know the Alpujarras like few others; just take a look at their library. Very special and loved by walkers – book well in advance. *Minimum stay two nights.*

Price	€62. Singles €42. Triple €84.
Rooms	9: 6 twins/doubles, 2 singles, 1 triple.
Meals	Kitchen for guests. Restaurants 1km.
Closed	December & January.
Directions	From Granada, A7 exit Las Alpujarras & Orgiva. In Orgiva, left for Pampaneira; 2km before Pitres, left to Mecina, then left to Ferreirola. Park in square.

Inger Norgaard & Giuseppe Heiss
c/Albaycín 3, 18414 Ferreirola,
Granada

Tel	+34 958 766171
Fax	+34 958 766171
Email	sierraymar@hotmail.com
Web	www.sierraymar.com

Alquería de Morayma

The owner built this fascinating, rambling, slightly shambolic hamlet-hotel in local style, recreating the nature of an Alpujarran village. The farm and the houses, one of which inhabits the old chapel, are set amid olive groves, vineyards and kitchen garden where everything is organically grown. Each room differs from the next, each feels cosy and characterful; there are antique brass bedsteads, Alpujarra bed covers, marble-topped dressers and photographs of the old farming days. Food is part of that celebration of all things local, from delicious organic olive oil to charcuterie to the semolina cakes typical of this region; with a little bit of luck you'll leave with a deeper understanding of the traditions of mountain village life. There are two restaurants, and wine from Mariano's beautifully tiled bodega in the cellars. See olives being milled during the winter, or muck in with the grape harvest: it's a laid-back sort of place. The walking is wonderful; Mariano has helped pen a long-distance walking guide, and there's 'ski de fond' in the winter. *Ask about reiki & relaxation courses.*

Price	€58-€66. Singles €46-€53. Apartment for 2, €66-€69. Apartments for 4, €88-€98. Plus VAT at 7%.
Rooms	19 + 3: 18 twins/doubles, 1 suite. 3 apartments: 1 for 2, 2 for 4.
Meals	Breakfast €3. Lunch & dinner, with wine, €12-€30.
Closed	Never.
Directions	From Granada, A44 south then exit for Las Alpujarras/Orgiva; A348 via Lanjarón, Órgiva & Torvizcón; 2km before Cádiar, signed on left.

Mariano Cruz Fajardo
Ctra. A-348 Cádiar-Torvizcón,
18440 Cádiar, Granada

Tel	+34 958 343221
Fax	+34 958 343917
Email	alqueria@alqueriamorayma.com
Web	www.alqueriamorayma.com

Casa Rural El Paraje

A short track through groves of almonds, past chestnut, olive and oak trees brings you to this old farmhouse. From the terrace – originally the threshing circle – are the most glorious views. And all around, superb walking country; one of the reasons Anita and Walter chose to settle here was to indulge their passion for walking. They're Dutch but completely at home in their adopted country – they spent many years exploring Spain and know it intimately. They are now experts on the sierra and will advise on walking or lend you mountain bikes. The farm covers about 20 hectares; the house was semi-derelict when they bought it and they did much of the restoration themselves. The simply furnished bedrooms are attractively austere but provide everything you need – and the underfloor heating is a major plus in the Alpujarran winter. Downstairs is a small bar and restaurant, and the food is a treat. Walter, a terrific cook, uses good, fresh produce and serves local wines. He and Anita are the kindest, friendliest hosts and the area is refreshingly tourist-free. An exceptional place. *Meals not available on Thursdays.*

Ethical Collection: Environment, Food.
See page 412.

Price	€40–€48. Apartment €60.
Rooms	4 + 1: 4 twins/doubles. 1 apartment.
Meals	Breakfast €4.50. Dinner €15. Wine €6–€15.
Closed	Rarely.
Directions	From Málaga, east on N-340. Pass Motril, then left on N-345 to Albuñol & Cádiar. Then A-4127 for Mecina; left on A-4130 to Bérchules. Here, at crossing, left for Trévelez. After 2km, right at sign.

Anita Beijer & Walter Michels
Ctra. Granada-Bérchules s/n,
18451 Bérchules, Granada

Tel	+34 958 064029
Email	info@elparaje.com
Web	www.elparaje.com

Hotel Los Bérchules

All that a walker could hope for: cosy, with good food and wine, and a great welcome from young Alejandro. The hotel sits just beneath the village of Bérchules, 1,322m above sea level – it's about as high as Ben Nevis. But things are on a human scale here: a small, pine-clad lounge bar with a brick hearth and masses of walking guides; a beamed dining room full of good things. Excellent home-cooked food – choose between à la carte and the good value *menú del día*; if you like rabbit, try Alejandro's paella. And you can stroll into the village for a beer and tapas before dinner. Guest bedrooms are sober and clean, pleasingly furnished with bright Alpujarra-weave curtains and blankets, with their own balcony-terraces and central heating for cool nights; the best views are from those at the front. The long-distance footpath that runs the length of the southern flank of the Sierra Nevada passes right by; the owners know every route, and will run you to and from your forays. An (unheated) pool has been added, open from April to October. Great value. *Ask about all-inclusive walking holidays.*

Price	€46–€55. Singles €33–€38. Apartment €75 (€450 per week).
Rooms	10 + 1: 10 twins. 1 apartment for 4.
Meals	Breakfast €5. Light lunches. Dinner €14–€22. Wine €12.
Closed	Rarely.
Directions	Málaga, east on N-340. Pass Motril, left to Albuñol. Just after Albuñol, right on GR-433 to Cádiar. Here, uphill 4km to junction; left, through Alcutar; cont. 500m, then left to hotel.

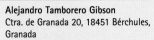

Alejandro Tamborero Gibson
Ctra. de Granada 20, 18451 Bérchules, Granada

Tel	+34 958 852530
Fax	+34 958 769000
Email	hot.berchules@interbook.net
Web	www.hotelberchules.com

Casa Rural Las Chimeneas

Modest Mairena is the unspoilt gem of a village at the eastern end of Sierra Nevada; here David and Emma, thoroughly green and integrated ex-teachers – David sits on the local Council – use produce from their own organic farm for their super 'Casa Moro'-touch Mediterranean food. Come to explore the little-trodden paths that radiate from the village: your hosts know them all. The old house has been restored with great sensitivity, you feel it the moment you enter. The guests' living room is light, lofty, serene: four rocking chairs round a wood-burning stove, rush matting to warm stone floors, plants, books and views across the terraced hillsides. A plant-filled terrace with a tiny plunge pool shares the view (glimpses of North Africa on a clear day). Bedrooms are artistically furnished with antique dressers and beds (and modern mattresses). Bathrooms are uncluttered, stylish, homespun – as are the self-catering studios nearby. Dinner and breakfast – inside or out – are in the new restaurant: the spirit of Las Chimeneas is relaxed and friendly. A perfect place for a long, restful stay.

Price	€70. Singles €45. Studios €50–€90 (€300–€500 per week).
Rooms	3 + 3: 3 twins/doubles. 3 studios for up to 4.
Meals	Packed lunch €5. Dinner €20. Wine €8.
Closed	Rarely.
Directions	From Laroles, 2nd right into Mairena, by willows. Park in square; down narrow street at south-east corner; 10m to house.

David & Emma Illsley
c/Amargura 6, 18493 Mairena,
Granada

Tel	+34 958 760352
Fax	+34 958 760004
Email	info@alpujarra-tours.com
Web	www.alpujarra-tours.com

La Almunia del Valle

Secluded terraces, soothing fountains, channels ferrying water everywhere: an *almunia* was a Moorish summer residence and there's a distinctly Moorish feel to this hillside garden. The house stands in its own orchards, its white lines softened by groves of chestnut, olive and fig trees, its interiors a masterly mix of period and modern – traditional slate floors and contemporary art, leather chairs and woven hangings – plus some arresting colours and masses of books. Beautifully finished bedrooms smell deliciously of cherrywood and are lavishly equipped; bright kilims and ceiling fans add to the understated elegance, the downstairs rooms have superb new terraces. From the vast sitting room, painted a warm rose, step out onto the wide terrace, take in the dramatic sweep of mountains and valley below, enjoy the jazz during an immaculately presented dinner: terrific food and good wines. A relaxed and competent couple, they run their house with intelligence and the love of a pair of gentle labradors. Perfect for sybarites, just 20 minutes from Granada yet rural, remote and tranquil. *A Rusticae hotel.*

Price	€106-€135. Singles €89-€118.
Rooms	9 twins/doubles.
Meals	Dinner €30-€36. Wine €16-€20.
Closed	13-30 November; 22 December-2 January.
Directions	Follow for Alhambra & Sierra Nevada on Ronda Sur ring road; exit 2 Monachil. Follow for Monachil & Casco Antiguo; through hamlet then at sign bear hard right & follow signs up to La Almunia.

José Manuel Plana & Patricia Merino
Camino de la Umbría s/n,
18193 Monachil, Granada

Tel	+34 958 308010
Fax	+34 958 304476
Email	laalmunia@infonegocio.com
Web	www.laalmuniadelvalle.com

Molino del Puente

The water that gushes from the high Sierras is the raison d'être for this old mill – and explains the greenery and birdlife. Dori and Francisco started off making organic biscuits and jams, now they run a successful restaurant with rooms. The two dining rooms have already made a name for themselves with the locals, and rightly so: the food is Andaluz, the meats chargrilled, the desserts wood-fired, the fruits, vegetables and liqueurs home-grown. Note that they can get tied up with parties at weekends and reception staff double up in the restaurant. Bedrooms are spotless and full of creature comforts, there are cosy rafters and Impressionist prints on rag-rolled walls, and shower rooms full of towels. The sound of rushing water is never far away, competing with the cars crossing the bridges to either side, so a first-floor room would be a wise choice during winter. The newest bedrooms are in a separate wing, but our favourite is room 102 – a waterfall plunges down outside the window. Come for the food and the setting – and there's good hiking up the Durcal gorge. Children will love the pool. *Best in summer.*

Price	€77–€128. Singles €59.
Rooms	12 twins/doubles.
Meals	Lunch & dinner €20–€30 à la carte. Wine €8–€35. Restaurant closed Mondays.
Closed	2 weeks in January; 2 weeks in November.
Directions	From Motril A44; exit km153 marker. At junction, right for Durcal; cross bridge, 1st right. Signed.

Francisco Maroto Caba
Puente de Durcal s/n, 18650 Durcal,
Granada

Tel	+34 958 780731
Fax	+34 958 781798
Email	reservas@elmolinodelpuente.com
Web	www.elmolinodelpuente.com

El Ladrón de Agua

Captivated by Granada in 1924, the Nobel prize-winning poet Juan Ramón Jiménez wrote *Olvidos*, a spiritual journey inspired by the water found throughout the city; one vast painting in the hall of the 16th-century building pays tribute to the poet. Raúl, the sympathetic manager of El Ladrón, hopes his beautiful, unusual hotel will be a source of inspiration too. The place fuses poetry, water, architecture, art, culture, luxury and friendliness in an irresistible blend; most memorable is its central patio. Slender columns of Tuscan marble support a graceful gallery, the fountain has been sculpted from a block of sombre marble. In the high-ceilinged bedrooms nothing has been stinted or forgotten: sumptuous beds, oriental rugs on terracotta floors, lovely writing desks… Each room has been named after a character or poem connected to Jiménez. Eight look across to the Alhambra hill; those at the front of the hotel are above a busy thoroughfare. You're right in the middle of old Granada, a short walk from the Alhambra itself (or take the bus); tapas bars and nightlife abound. *Alhambra tickets can be pre-booked.*

Price	€110–€237. Singles €83–€181. Half-board €35 extra p.p.
Rooms	15 doubles.
Meals	Breakfast €10.50.
Closed	Never.
Directions	In Granada head for city centre & Plaza Nueva. Here, drive up Carrera del Darro (parallel to river Darro). Park in any central car park & take a taxi.

	Raúl Lozano Ruiz
	Carrera del Darro 13, 18010 Granada
Tel	+34 958 215040
Fax	+34 958 224345
Email	info@ladrondeagua.com
Web	www.ladrondeagua.com

Gar-Anat Hotel de Peregrinos

Raúl is the man behind this conceptual project (his second hotel in Granada – the first is El Ladron de Agua) and his vision is poetic. On entering the central courtyard you enter a stage peopled by pilgrims – the hotel is sited on the Placeta de los Peregrinos – while the bedrooms, inspired by these travellers of old, echo their memories. In sympathy with the thespian theme, heavy drapes announce the entrance; the surrounding galleries, on three floors, remind one of an Elizabethan theatre. The 17th-century building sits in Granada's heart and the buses that whisk you up to the Alhambra are a short stroll... two top bedrooms catch splendid views of Granada. As for the interiors, each room reveals an uncluttered and warm minimalism. Expect huge beds, huge comfort, dramatic lighting, the odd flight of fantasy. The decoration is super-contemporary: white sofas, dark wood floors, Starck-like chairs, amazing rain showers. There's a sitting room with art and books, where modern-day pilgrims may forge friendships... and breakfast, in a superb vaulted dining room, is in convivial refectory style.

Price	€110–€237. Singles €83–€181. Plus VAT at 7%.
Rooms	15: 7 doubles, 8 twins.
Meals	Drinks & snacks available. Restaurants nearby.
Closed	Never.
Directions	From Granada ringroad, exit A129 for city centre. At Plaza Puerta Real, right to c/Ganivet, then left to c/San Matías, hotel 70m. Drop luggage & park in Puerta Real car park.

	Raúl Lozano Ruiz
	Placeta de los Peregrinos 1, 18009 Granada
Tel	+34 958 225528
Fax	+34 958 222739
Email	info@hoteldeperegrinos.com
Web	www.hoteldeperegrinos.com

Casa del Capitel Nazarí

At the heart of this 16th-century *palacete* is a superb Granadino courtyard. Slender marble columns, two of them Roman, surround the pebble mosaic. There's also the Nasrid carved capital which gave the hotel its name, and several carved ceilings; look skywards and you'll see the elegant, encircling galleries above. It is an attractive if slightly disorganised place, with pretty communal spaces but less impressive beds and bedrooms, some of which are on the small side, as are their shower rooms. Ask for one of the quieter rooms, away from the patio. Guests are well cared for by Angela and her willing young staff. Modest buffet breakfast is in the little dining room; in summer you spill into the courtyard, delightful with plants and wicker chairs. Restaurants, cafés, one of Granada's best tapas bars and Moroccan tea houses are just outside the door. Although parking is a taxi ride away, the position, in the Alabayzín, Granada's oldest quarter, is superb, 200 metres from the Plaza Nueva whence you can bus or walk (20 mins) up the wooded Alhambra hill to the palace. *Alhambra tickets can be pre-booked.*

Price	€72–€110. Singles €57–€88.
Rooms	17 twins/doubles.
Meals	Breakfast €8. Restaurants 50m.
Closed	Rarely.
Directions	A-44 exit 131 for Armilla–Palacio de Congresos. Follow signs to Parking Plaza Puerta Real (€18.50 per day). Taxi to hotel; hotel will reimburse with taxi receipt.

Angela Caracuel Vera
Cuesta Aceituneros 6, 18010 Granada

Tel	+34 958 215260
Fax	+34 958 215806
Email	info@hotelcasacapitel.com
Web	www.hotelcasacapitel.com

Muralla Ziri Boutique Apartments

You are in the heart of the historic Albayzin quarter where the Ziri clan founded the Kingdom of Granada – a short stroll from the tea shops, restaurants and tapas bars of the buzzy Plaza Nueva. The two houses that make up these family-owned apartments incorporate the 11th-century original city walls and the design is inspired by Andalucian architectural heritage – expect Moroccan-bright living rooms and tables once used to thresh corn, gleaming bathrooms with arches and moulded plaster, super smart kitchens… and, on upper floors, flower-decked balconies and a stunning penthouse with Alhambra views. Bedrooms are not huge but beautifully decorated; some rooms have a tub to splash about in and there's underfloor heating for cool nights. The feel is peaceful, cosy and inviting with books, magazines, candles. As well as the Alhambra there's the Cathedral to admire and live music in town – so much to do here, night and day. Pop back home, where the arched patio of the Casa Roja wraps itself around a plush hammam: steam yourself, get pummelled or just float in the jacuzzi. *Minimum stay two nights.*

Price	€80–€150 for 2 people. Extra bed €15. Penthouse €225–€265. Extra bed €33. All prices per night.
Rooms	12 apartments in 2 houses: 1 for 3, 10 for 4, 1 penthouse for 5.
Meals	Restaurants/bars close by.
Closed	Rarely.
Directions	Directions on booking.

Manuel Matés García
c/San Juan de los Reyes 7, Albayzín,
18010 Granada

Tel	+34 958 049851
Fax	+34 958 049858
Email	info@apartamentosmurallaziri.com
Web	www.apartamentosmurallaziri.com

Carmen del Cobertizo

Step through carved wooden doors into a timeless world of Spanish elegance. A rare example of a 'carmen' – a city house with a garden – it's full of neo-classical flourishes: polished floors, white walls, raftered ceilings, an inner courtyard with wraparound balconies. In the beautiful labyrinthine alleys in the heart of the Albayzin, a Unesco heritage site, this 16th-century house, gracefully furnished, with massed flowers and ferns, is rich but not overpowering. Quiet and deliciously comfortable bedrooms are plump with family treasures; bathrooms and shower rooms are luxurious with thick towels and hand-painted tiles; top-floor suites spoil with private terraces and Alhambra views. Lazy breakfasts are served amongst birdsong and greenery in the courtyard; dinners, too, if you book the whole house. And quiet corners abound in courtyard, library and on balconies. But the highlight is the jasmine-scented garden with fruit trees, flowering shrubs, murmuring fountain and water tank turned plunge pool, a blissful hideaway after a day soaking up the treasures. Massages are available, too… a delight. *A Rusticae hotel.*

Price	€148. Suites €168-€285. Whole house €4,300-€5,500 per week. Plus VAT at 7%.
Rooms	6: 3 twins/doubles, 3 suites for 2. House available for self-catering.
Meals	Whole house rental includes dinner. Restaurants close by.
Closed	Never.
Directions	Park in Plaza Puerta Real car park & walk/taxi to first bridge on river Darro; 1st right into narrow alley. Carmen del C. on left.

Ms Lorena Padillo
c/Cobertizo de Santa Inés 6,
18010 Granada

Tel   +34 958 227652
Fax   +34 958 229268
Email   info@carmendelcobertizo.com
Web   www.carmendelcobertizo.com

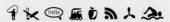

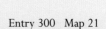

Andalusia
B&B

Hotel Santa Isabel La Real

Granada teems with hotels but it takes something special to tickle our fancy. This is very much in the grand house tradition, with a double tier of balustraded balconies wrapping round a central marble-floored courtyard, and the obligatory murmuring fountain and potted plants. The del Castillo family are delightful, and generous in their welcome. Young Elena will usher you to bedrooms she is right to be proud of, pretty with rugs, pictures, framed fabrics, antique bedsteads, latticed cupboards. The rooms get better as you go higher and the top ones gaze on the Alhambra. Breakfast is in the cellar (with windows), soft oriental music gets you in the mood. No garden but a sunny patio, and a gorgeous little sitting room bright with sofas, rugs and silk cushions, to which you may retreat for coffee and sandwiches. At the top end of the Albayzín the hotel is nevertheless well placed for tapas bars and restaurants. The family will book your Alhambra tickets, of course, but that's not all Granada has to offer: there are hikes in the Sierra Nevada, skiing in winter, and a Moorish *hammam* oozing luxury.

Price	€85-€145. Suite €165-€185.
Rooms	11: 10 doubles, 1 suite.
Meals	Restaurants 5-minute walk.
Closed	Never.
Directions	Park in Aparcamiento San Agustin or El Triunfo then taxi to hotel. Hotel has own car park (€14 per day). Call for directions.

	Elena del Castillo
	c/Santa Isabel la Real 19, Albaizyn, 18010 Granada
Tel	+34 958 294658
Fax	+34 958 294645
Email	info@hotelsantaisabellareal.com
Web	www.hotelsantaisabellareal.com

Casa Morisca

Imagine yourself outside a tall, balconied, 15th-century house on the south-facing slopes of the Albaycín. The street drops steeply away and opposite towers the Alhambra. You are in the old Moorish quarter of Granada and Casa Morisca is an exquisite example of the old style. Rescued and restored by Carlos, its architect owner, it won the Europa Nostra prize; easy to see why. A heavy door leads from the street to a galleried inner courtyard, where slender pilasters, wafer-brick columns, delicate mouldings and pool create serenity and space. The same subtle mastery of effect runs throughout. In one of the blissful bedrooms you lie on your bed and espy the Alhambra from a specially angled bathroom mirror. One top-floor room with astonishing views has been turned into the most romantic of eyries; another has a magnificent *mudéjar* ceiling, stripped of its plaster shroud. Bathrooms are ultra-chic. On a more prosaic note, the eateries of Acera del Darro are a step away – or you may climb the labyrinthine streets to the restaurants of Plaza San Miguel Bajo and rub shoulders with the Granadinos.

Price	€118–€148. Family €155–€198.
Rooms	14: 13 doubles, 1 family.
Meals	Breakfast €10.
Closed	Never.
Directions	Detailed directions on booking.

María Jesús Candenas & Carlos Sánchez
Cuesta de la Victoria 9, Bajo Albaycín,
18010 Granada

Tel	+34 958 221100
Fax	+34 958 215796
Email	info@hotelcasamorisca.com
Web	www.hotelcasamorisca.com

Cortijo La Haza

An old farmhouse lost in the olive belt that stretches from here north and eastwards across almost half of Andalucía. If you like olive groves (it helps) and little-known corners of Spain, stay here – and use it as a base for your visit to the glories of Granada and Córdoba, the famous beaches of the Costa del Sol, and Málaga, whose charming Old Town is often passed by. Owners Patriek and Bernadette have backgrounds in travel and tourism and are enthusiastically putting their stamp on this delightful small hotel. Opened seven years ago, the renovation feels new yet the 'rustic' air of a 250-year-old Andalucían cortijo has been beautifully preserved: walls have a rough render, old country pieces have been restored. Beamed bedrooms have Egyptian cotton sheets on wrought-iron bedsteads; bath and shower rooms are en suite. The sitting room and dining rooms are deliciously cosy with log-burning stoves, and in summer you spill into the white-walled courtyard. It is quiet, remote, friendly… and the pool and the garden share a spectacular view as far as the snow-capped Sierra Nevada.

Price	€80. Singles €65.
Rooms	5 twins/doubles.
Meals	Dinner €21. Wine from €11.
Closed	Rarely.
Directions	From Málaga airport, A-7 for Málaga; A-45 & A-359 exit 139. After 24km, exit 1 onto A-333 for Iznajar. After km55 marker, left on CV-9200 for 100m; left by small school for 2.6km. Signed on right.

Patriek Defauw &
Bernadette van der Heijden
Adelantado 119, 14978 Iznájar,
Córdoba

Tel	+34 957 334051
Email	info@cortijolahaza.com
Web	www.cortijolahaza.com

Casa Rural el Olivar

Christian and Kathleen – young, energetic, charming – have upped sticks from Belgium to live the dream. The views are sensational, the infinity pool beautiful and the approach is just over the hill – yet it feels a world away from the town. The Andalucian farmhouse was renovated in 2003, so chic-ly it has appeared in magazines. Now there are five ground-floor B&B rooms, all in a row, each with a different species of potted olive tree outside its door, each overlooking terraces, olive grove and lake. Wander down the oleander-lined path to this watery oasis of calm and 360 degree views of the landscape. The place is perfect for families, thanks to swings, sandpit, ping-pong, boules, mini-golf, and kayaks to borrow. There are grape vines for shade, an honesty bar, guest kitchen and gas barbecue, a herb garden to plunder, plants all around. The interiors are rustic chic, the sunloungers are wicker, the breakfasts are delicious, and three self-catering casitas lie over the (quiet) road. Interiors are simply furnished: white walls, tiled floors… and no air con but fans, in the eco spirit of this place.

Price	€89. Casitas €525 per week.
Rooms	5 + 3: 2 doubles, 3 twins. 3 casitas for 2.
Meals	Restaurants 5km.
Closed	Never.
Directions	A92 to Sevilla; exit 175 for Iznájar. 2nd right to access village, continue to Plaza de la Venta. In left corner of square, take c/Cuesta Colora; continue for 1km, over hill. Hotel on right.

Christian & Kathleen Van Calster-Dockier
c/Cierzos y Cabreras 6, 14970 Iznájar,
Córdoba

Tel	+34 957 534928
Fax	+34 957 534928
Email	info@casaruralelolivar.com
Web	www.casaruralelolivar.com

Cortijo Las Rosas

Two sisters, three cottages, and a fabulous olive-grove setting over the largest lake in Andalucia: let the peace enter your soul in this secluded rustic place. Marylynne and Gillian bought the old farmhouse as a retirement project after a whirlwind trot round the globe. Snug, simple and individual, each cottage has a private entrance and a courtyard, but the cluster can be linked for larger groups. One is open-plan and flooded with light, another has old low ceilings and an inglenook feel; Perdiz and Liebre, our favourites, sport Moorish sofas. All are charmingly dressed in terracotta tiles, white walls, bright fabrics, with modern en suite bathrooms. No neighbours detract from the rural peace, but you can stroll through olive groves to the local shop, stock up at farmers' markets and bring back your spoils to the barbecue. Bask on a wicker lounger by the pool – such views! – or play petanque on the sand court. Get off the beaten track on 'vías verdes' (old railway tracks that have been turned into pathways), borrow bikes, go rock climbing or riding, and take binoculars for the birds. A delicious retreat.

Price	Casita for 1-2, €65. Casitas for 1-4, €85. All prices per night, plus VAT at 7%.
Rooms	3 casitas: 1 for 1-2; 2 for 1-4.
Meals	Restaurant 2km.
Closed	Never.
Directions	From A333 exit at km48 marker for Iznajar. Follow winding road up hill to Fuentes de Cesna/Algarinejo. Follow signs to Cortijo Las Rosas, 8km from Iznajar.

Marylynne Morris & Gillian Purcell
Apartado de Correos 61,
14970 Iznájar, Córdoba

Mobile	+34 637 896357
Email	info@ruralaccommodationandalucia.com
Web	www.ruralaccommodationandalucia.com

Finca las Encinas

Maki, Japanese, introduces you to sherry and olive tasting tours. Clive, Welsh, offers guests cookery courses that are easy and fun. The house is higgledy-piggledy and 170 years old, rustic and charming. It stands on the side of a hill on the edge of a small Moorish village in the Parque Natural, an hour from Cordoba and Granada: what a position. Outside on sloping land are hammocks and picnic tables, figs, almonds, olives and vines, and a small upper terrace overlooking an inviting little pool. Inside, old doors have become headboards and the cool downstairs bedroom was once the pantry; now it has a sofa and opens to a terrace. All four bedrooms are cosy, darkish, simple and small, with delightful thick walls, modest beds, fluffy bathrobes, characterful touches. In the living room are books, antiques and modern art. Your hosts and their little boy Cei, who live in a separate house in the grounds, could not be friendlier or kinder. Pick fat tomatoes from the veg garden, buy fresh fish from the market; learn lovely new ways of cooking with Clive, then feast and have fun. Simply special.

Price	€55–€75. Suite €85–€95.
Rooms	4: 1 double, 2 twins, 1 suite.
Meals	Dinner, 3 courses, from €20. Wine €8–€20. Restaurant 10-minute drive.
Closed	Rarely.
Directions	Past Iznájar for Rute; right to El Higueral & Priego de Córdoba on A-333. After 5km left to Los Juncares. After 1km, 2nd left. Finca on right after 100m.

**Maki Murakushi Ridout
& Clive A Ridout**
c/Partido de los Juncares s/n,
14979 Iznájar, Córdoba

Mobile	+34 629 610783
Email	info@finca-las-encinas.com
Web	www.finca-las-encinas.com

Ethical Collection: Community; Food.
See page 412.

Hotel el Cortijo la Prensa

Not for shy souls or children. Alan and David have transformed an old country mansion and olive press into a buzzing boutique hotel with a hint of extravagance. Open, tolerant and self-consciously sleek, this is the place to top up an all-over tan in the naturist jacuzzi and sunning spot – or sweat in a sauna and dip in the deep pool. At siesta time, nip inside to large, stylish bedrooms kitted out with luxurious beds, sofas and every bell and whistle you might possibly desire. Tall windows open to balconies or a patio with fabulous mountain views; moody lighting adds atmosphere at night. The talented chef pushes back boundaries in the – not surprisingly – popular restaurant, and you eat al fresco in summer. Inside and out, this is designed for pure relaxation: a fountain'd central terrace and bar, a fire-warmed drawing room, and a boudoir-style bar in the cellar. There's a small gym and you can order massage and treatments. Surrounded by ten acres of olive grove, two rivers and a modern gazebo you could stay put all day; if not, ask the friendly, generous manager for a mountain bike, and explore.

Price	€89–€340.
Rooms	12: 10 doubles, 2 suites.
Meals	Lunch & dinner à la carte. Wine from €8. Restaurant closed Tuesday lunch & all day Monday.
Closed	Never.
Directions	A45/N331 dir. Cordoba, then right onto A344 Rute; left in Rute onto A331. Just past restaurant Atocha El Vado, right signed Cerrillo; right at next T-junction; hotel on right.

	Alan Seviour
	Arroyo de las Tijeras, 14960 Rute, Córdoba
Mobile	+34 606 313532
Fax	+34 957 724299
Email	info@elcortijo-laprensa.com
Web	www.elcortijo-laprensa.com

Casa Uno

The owners are English and charming and live in the village. Nicholas is a broadcaster, Fay is a photographer, both know the area well. Maribel, the caretaker, lives next door, a big plus: she rustles up a meal when you need one and her 'gambas al ajillo' are delicious! The house is fresh, spacious, airy and new, designed for outdoor living for most of the year. The village is a one-horse town: mini-market, bar (good tapas) and a bread lady who visits every day. Step in to the kitchen: enormous, well-equipped, inviting and the first room you enter, it opens onto a sitting room with a wood-burner and a colonnaded patio with a pool. The décor is bright and breezy – Andalucian plates on the walls, a fountain tinkling under the bougainvillea, good books on the shelves and squishy sofas on which to read them. Three simple bedrooms lie alongside the pool, the master bedroom is upstairs and the showers are en suite. Upstairs is a roof-top dining area too, with barbecue, handsome furniture and a canopy for shade. Carlota's shops and cafes are a ten-minute drive, Cordoba's treasures are almost as close.

Price	£700–£1,350 (sterling) per week.
Rooms	House for 8.
Meals	Packed lunch €12–€15. Dinner €20. Wine from €5.
Closed	Never.
Directions	From Córdba E5; exit 430. Right at r'bout; La Chica Carlota. After 3km marker, right at x-roads. Las Pinedas after 1km; Casa Uno in square.

Fay & Nicolas Tresilian
Plaza Andalucia 1, Las Pinedas,
14111 La Carlota, Córdoba

Tel	+34 957 300379
Email	fay@andaluciauno.com
Web	www.andaluciauno.com

Palacio de la Rambla

The old towns of Úbeda and Baeza are often missed as travellers dash between Madrid and the coast, yet they are two of the brightest jewels in the crown of Spanish architecture. At the heart of old Úbeda, the exquisite Palacio de la Rambla dates from the Renaissance and has never left the Orozco family. You enter through an ornate Corinthian-columned portal into the cloistered patio; opulently colonnaded on two levels, smothered in ivy and wonderfully cool on a sweltering day. Lounge, dining room and bedrooms are large to massive and a perfect match for their setting: antique beds, chests, trunks, lamps, pretty washstands, claw-foot tubs, religious mementos, family portraits, and native terracotta softened by *estera* matting. Young, bubbly, glamorous staff will serve you one of the best breakfasts in this book: eggs, toast with olive oil, baskets of fruit, cheese, charcuterie, homemade cakes and jams. Palacio de la Rambla has a long tradition of regal welcoming; King Alfonso XIII stayed here when he was in town. A delectable, peaceful retreat. *A Rusticae hotel.*

Price	€96–€140.
Rooms	8: 7 twins/doubles, 1 suite.
Meals	Restaurants nearby.
Closed	7-29 January; 13 July-7 August.
Directions	From Madrid south on N-IV. At km292 marker, N-322 to Úbeda. There, follow 'Centro Ciudad' until Palacio is in front of you, between c/Ancha & c/Rastro, opposite cafetería La Paloma.

	Elena & Cristina Meneses de Orozco
	Plaza del Marques 1,
	23400 Úbeda, Jaén
Tel	+34 953 750196
Fax	+34 953 750267
Email	hotel@palaciodelarambla.com
Web	www.palaciodelarambla.com

La Finca Mercedes

La Iruela's crowning glory is the castle fortress built by the Templars; make it to the top for a staggering view. La Finca Mercedes stands just outside the village: a simple rustic family-run inn. It takes its name from its bright and charming owner, who is ably helped by her three daughters. You are just next to the road so do ask (in Spanish!) for a bedroom at the back – not just for peace but for those views; they sweep across the olive groves and far beyond. In bitter winter the restaurant is as cosy as can be, with a fire crackling gently in the corner hearth throughout the day. Decorative flourishes include old copper saucepans, hunting trophies and piano; the food is simple, regional, flavoursome and good value (and Mercedes' husband hunts rabbit and deer!). Bedrooms are a standard size with stained pine furniture and good bathrooms (full-size baths are a treat in Spain). There's a small fragrant garden with a pool, and six larger bedrooms at the family's farmhouse, Cortijo Berfalá, a five-minute walk down the steep road. Brilliant for walkers, and those on a budget. *Advance bookings preferred.*

Price	€39–€42. Singles €24–€27. Suite €39–€42. Plus VAT at 7%.
Rooms	11: 8 twins/doubles, 2 singles, 1 suite. Cortijo: 6 twins/doubles.
Meals	Breakfast €3.30. Lunch & dinner €12.60. A la carte from €18.
Closed	Rarely.
Directions	From Cazorla into village centre; just before large square, left for La Iruela. Follow road for 1km round bottom of La Iruela; Finca just to left. Do not confuse with hotel next door!

Mercedes Castillo Matilla
Ctra. de la Sierra km1,
23476 La Iruela, Jaén

Tel	+34 953 721087
Email	info@lafincamercedes.com
Web	www.lafincamercedes.com

Cortijada Los Gazquez

The Beckmanns have joyfully restored five houses that make up this cortijada. The ceilings are lofty, the finish is perfect, the thinking is environmental, the family is delightful. There's Simon, artist and designer, Donna, illustrator, Solomon and Sesame, twins; they are completely dedicated to their restored family house and cannot wait to cook for and entertain their guests. Rooms weren't quite finished at the time of our visit but promise to be warm, simple and light, with a fun/funky twist. Olive oil soaps sit by cool concrete basins, pine logs furnish roaring fires, rainwater is harvested, and wind and solar power keep floors toasty and water piping hot. Reed beds eliminate impurities and the water irrigates the land; soon there will be a natural pool and a wood-fired sauna. And the landscape? The farmhouse sits magnificently and remotely in the *parque natural* surrounded by fruit, almond and olive trees... the view of La Sagra mountain is beautiful in every weather. Ramblers, artists, nature lovers will be very happy here. All you hear is the call of the eagle and the owl at dusk. *Minimum stay two nights.*

Price	€85.
Rooms	6: 3 twins/doubles, 3 doubles.
Meals	Dinner with wine, €18.
Closed	Christmas.
Directions	At Velez Blanco Visitors Centre (signed) 1st right, signed Las Almahollas. Left at fork, follow road for 8km. At junc. follow signs to Los Gazquez.

Ethical Collection: Environment;
Community; Food.
See page 412.

Simon & Donna Beckmann
Hoya de Carrascal, 04830
Velez Blanco, Almería
Tel   +44 (0)20 7193 6056
Email   info@losgazquez.com
Web   www.losgazquez.com

Cortijo el Ciruelo

You are just five minutes from the motorway yet all around are the hills and pine forests of the breathtaking Sierra Maria-Los Velez National Park. Even nearer is a nest of Booted Eagles, who soar away on the thermals at dawn and return at dusk. You might also see red squirrels, wild boar and genets dropping by for a feed. Walks start from the door – with the promise of a rescue in a 4x4 should it be needed. A former hunting lodge, the 300-year-old cortijo still has its original tiles and some of its beams; the rest is pretty new. The interiors are spic and span with comfortable matching furniture. Bedrooms are impeccably clean and share a well-stocked minibar (on the house). There are several set menus, which can be chosen in advance; meals are served at a lovely large table, they grow their own veg and Gillian bakes a fabulous almond cake. Packed lunches are also available for your jaunts around the region; don't miss the interesting town of Vélez Rubio, and Vélez Blanco with its famous castle, just ten minutes away.

Price	€50–€65.
Rooms	4 twins/doubles.
Meals	Dinner €18. Wine €6–€10.
Closed	Rarely.
Directions	From Granada on A-92-N. 9km after junc. 385, exit for 'Area Descanso Ciruelo Picolo'; left over motorway, left again following signs for hotel.

Gary & Gillian Williamson
04825 Chirivel, Almería
Mobile   +34 667 477673
Email   enquiries@elciruelo.net
Web   www.elciruelo.net

Cortijo Níspero

An unassuming, cosy home in a small hamlet surrounded by olive, lemon and almond trees and with uninterrupted views of the surrounding hills. Much-travelled Stephen and Vonney are friendly, generous and warm: find a small guest sitting room on the first floor with a wood-burning stove and board games, and airy and spotless bedrooms with comfortable extra large beds, crisp linen and an uncluttered feel. Greenies will like to know that water is from a local spring and heated by solar panels. Food is taken seriously: bread freshly baked, veg home-grown and all ingredients sourced as locally as possible; paella is a speciality of Vonney's. Meal times are fluid, there's a serene pool for cooling off in and a garden replete with hammocks, chickens, fruit trees and orange blossom scent carried on the breeze. The honesty bar reflects the easy-going nature of your hosts, but resist the temptation to stay put: there are beaches, galleries and restaurants nearby to explore and this is arduous walking country for those with heartier dispositions. *Reduction for 3 nights or more.*

Price	€60.
Rooms	3: 2 doubles, 1 twin/double.
Meals	Lunch €6. Dinner, 2-3 courses, €13.50-€17. Wine from €6.
Closed	Rarely.
Directions	From A334 Arboleas Junction, towards Arboleas over river bridge, left (signed Zurgena) at r'bout. After 600m right signed Arroya Aceituno. After 11.8km right at Cortijo Nispero sign, and immediately right into hamlet of Los Patrocinios. Second house on left.

Stephen & Yvonne Amore
Los Patrocinios 4, 04850 Cantoria,
Almería

Tel	+34 696 557983 mob
Email	info@cortijonispero.com
Web	www.cortijonispero.com

Hotel Tikar

A restaurant with rooms and a great stopover if you want to be near the beach in Almería. Don't worry that the Tikar is in a built-up area – wait and see what's inside. It's a gem, a hotel, restaurant and art gallery too, run with warmth and charm by Beatriz and Sean. The sitting room is cosy with modern sofas, small bar and wood-burning stove, and the bedrooms are large, cool and comfortable, their lively, even eccentric colours offset by dark parquet and teak. And paintings – dozens of them – on every wall. Children are welcomed and well catered for, too; Beatriz and Sean have two young sons of their own. Take a dip in the small pool with walled garden and fountains or relax on the rooftop terrace and watch the sea. But the main event is the food. Sean's Restaurante Azul gets a Michelin mention and has a devoted local following, the menu being an inventive mix of Californian (light sauces and seafood) and Spanish. Plenty of vegetarian dishes too, and a list of over 75 wines. Don't miss the lively afternoon fish market of Garrucha.

Price	€59–€130.
Rooms	6 suites.
Meals	Lunch €15. Dinner €25.50. Wine from €9.50.
Closed	December.
Directions	From N-340/E-15, exit 534 for Garrucha. Pass Vera & pass through outskirts of Vera. Straight on at r'bout. Hotel on right at entrance of Garrucha.

Beatriz Gallego & Sean McMahon
Ctra. Garrucha – Vera 17,
04630 Garrucha, Almería

Tel   +34 950 617131
Fax   +34 950 617132
Email hoteltikar@hoteltikar.com
Web   www.hoteltikar.com

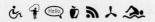

Hostal Mirador del Castillo

Its slogan is *el punto mas alto* ('the highest point'): the hotel stands alone at the very top of the white Andalucian village. On the ruins of a castle, it was originally built as the private home of a concert pianist; it is still, off-season, a venue for chamber music and jazz. The concrete fabric may be little frayed, the Sixties' interpretation of a Moorish fortification may not be to everyone's taste, but don't be put off: the setting, with vistas across mountains to the Med, is spectacular. Next to the bar is a small but cosy restaurant that serves gorgeous food; for late breakfasts (11am on), light meals and matchless sea views there's the terrace. Bedrooms are very charming, though due for some upgrading; each room has its en suite bath. Come for B&B, or make up a party of friends and rent the whole place; the owners are delightful and nothing is too much trouble. This would be fun for a party... a small pool, a vast salon, a kitchen, a grand piano, and, in winter, a Moroccan-style open fire. Mojácar is at its best out of season. *Bookings for whole house required three months in advance.*

Price	€70–€120. Whole house (sleeps 10-14) €2,800 per week.
Rooms	5: 1 double, 3 twins/doubles, 1 suite for 4. House available for self-catering.
Meals	Breakfast €6. Lunch & dinner, with wine, €18–€30. Café closed Wed afternoon & Thurs low season. Restaurants 80m.
Closed	November.
Directions	Directions on booking or detailed directions on website.

Juan Cecilio Cano Tello
Plaza del Mirador del Castillo,
04638 Mojácar Pueblo, Almería

Tel	+34 950 473022
Email	information@elcastillomojacar.com
Web	www.elcastillomojacar.com

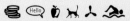

Cortijo Los Malenos

At any minute, Clint Eastwood could come riding over the hill. Perched above a canyon, encircled by barren hills and semi-desert, this is a gem. The low, white cortijo lies in one of Spain's most alluring, harsh and unexpected landscapes, with all the classic hallmarks of the Wild West. Guarded by stocky date palms, this 'ranch' flaunts its finer features – a rose patio, a double-fireplaced living room – while a warren of courtyards and rooms makes up the space. Drawing deeply on Spanish and Indian influences, bedrooms are beautifully designed, comfortable and serene. Neutral and natural is the look, and stunning images of the landscape pepper the walls. Borrow whichever sunhat takes your fancy and brave the sun. Cacti, palms and carobs find their natural home here, creating a perfectly adapted garden. Round each quiet corner you may absorb staggering desert vistas, then cool off in the saltwater pool. Hot flamenco concerts in summer, laid-back winter nights by the fire, delightful staff all year round. Reminiscent of the silver screen, this is even more extraordinary in real life.

Price	€80-€130. House €120-€190. Prices per night.
Rooms	8 + 1: 8 twins/doubles. House for 4.
Meals	Picnic €10. Dinner €20. Wine €11.
Closed	Rarely.
Directions	From Almería on E-15; exit 494 for Carboneras. 8km after exit, right to Agua Amarga. Cortijo 2km beyond, on left, opp. turn-off for Fernán Pérez.

Aurora Cacho Quesada
04149 Agua Amarga, Almería

Mobile +34 618 286260
Email contactar@cortijolosmalenos.com
Web www.cortijolosmalenos.com

Ethical Collection: Environment.
See page 412.

Entry 316 Map 22

La Joya de Cabo de Gata

She calls it her "miracle in the desert". Charo García discovered the landscape of Almería, the dry river beds and dunes, the dazzling white dwellings, the tough vegetation… and was captivated. So she built two farmhouses and imported a bedouin tent, added a hammock'd terrace shaded by roofs of scrub and heather, a beautiful little saltwater pool with great views, an open-air shower in a grotto… now her dream appears in glossy magazines. The farmhouses, run on solar energy and recycled water, are charming: whitewashed walls and rustic floors, Spanish antiques and stainless steel, DVDs and terraces that face east and north. Spacious and private, the *jaima*, set among olive trees and palms, has an ecological stove for winter, ventilation for summer – no fans! – a vast bed, a perfectly equipped kitchen and colourful Arabic décor. Breakfasts, based on "respect for the environment", are brought to you. Coves, inlets and empty beaches await, there's Garrucha for sea food, Mojacar for its hippy beach, Nijar for pottery. The stars are a joy at night, as are the illuminated paths, jacuzzi and pool.

Price	€130-€200 for 2; €225-€325 for 4. Tent €90-€150. All prices per night.
Rooms	2 houses for 2-4; 1 bedouin tent for 2.
Meals	Self-catering includes breakfast.
Closed	Never.
Directions	A-7/E-15, exit 494 for Carboneras. After 3.5km, right for Agua Amarga. Sign on right for La Joya de Cabo de Gata or Charo's House, 2km before Agua Amarga.

	Charo García
	Paraje La Joya, 04149 Agua Amarga, Almería
Mobile	+34 619 159587
Email	reservas@lajoyadecabodegata.com
Web	www.lajoyadecabodegata.com

Hotel Family

Marc's parents came to Agua Amarga on French leave; seduced by what was then a remote fishing village, they dreamed of moving here. They have given this little place their all, and now it is a modest, old-fashioned family affair, run by Marc with Michele and René's help. A small but busy street brings you to the hotel/restaurant and concrete-lined pool away from the centre of the village, yards from one of the area's most gorgeous beaches; this is the draw. Rooms are very simple, the newest on the first floor, but air-conditioned and with their own balconies. Those at the front have sea views. Come for Michele's food – huge portions, decent value – and breakfasts that are feasts: yogurts, fruits, tortillas, homemade jam. (Note, there is nowhere to eat outdoors.) There's the whole of the Parque Natural de Cabo de Gata to discover – the walking is wonderful and the beaches are some of Spain's loveliest. As for Agua Amarga, it's more developed than it was but remains an enchanting spot – particularly out of season. Suitable for families on a tight budget.

Price	€45-€120. Singles €40-€115.
Rooms	9: 7 twins/doubles, 2 family rooms.
Meals	Lunch & dinner with wine, €23. Lunch weekends only.
Closed	1 November-15 December.
Directions	From N-344 exit 494 Venta & Carboneras. On for Carboneras; right for Agua Amarga. Signed to right in village as you arrive.

Marc Bellavoir
c/La Lomilla s/n, 04149 Agua Amarga, Almería

Tel	+34 950 138014
Fax	+34 950 138070
Email	riovall@teleline.es
Web	www.hotelfamily.es

Cortijo el Saltador

Come for the absolute stillness of this remote farmhouse, entirely rebuilt by delightful Claudia – perfect for those who love wild surroundings and rare peace and quiet. There's a spiritual dimension to the smooth tiled floors, whitewashed walls, splashes of artwork and simple furnishings; guest rooms surround a light, open courtyard and in the main house there are kitchens for aspiring cooks (Claudia has plans for courses) and a good library – no chairs, just cushions and rugs and board games and books. The lazy can be looked after: breakfast is when you get up and where you want it, lunch and dinner are moveable feasts, from romantic dinners for two to a huge spread for groups. Chill in your bedroom: they are cool, sparsely furnished, spotlessly clean and exceptionally large – warm with underfloor heating and with fairly basic but brilliantly colourful bathrooms, with arty basins and natural textures. You may be seduced by the serenity and you have unbroken views of the mountains, but from here you can go caving, walking, riding, and the charming beach village of Aguamarga is just 20 minutes away.

Price	€50. Whole house (sleeps 10+) €375–€400.
Rooms	8 twins/doubles. House available for self-catering.
Meals	Lunch & dinner with wine or beer, €14. Restaurants 6km.
Closed	Never.
Directions	From Málaga/Almeria/Granada A92 to Tabernas, then 340A dir. Sorbas, then right to Lucainena de las Torres, follow winding road to Rambla Honda. Left to Polopos, after 1.4km follow track to house. Signed.

Claudia Scholler
04210 Lucainena de las Torres,
Almería

Mobile	+34 676 437128
Email	claudiascholler@yahoo.com
Web	www.elsaltador.com

Maxwells

Soak up rural Spain, in a sleepy Almerian town miles from anywhere; you overlook rooftops and church and the views are charming. This is self-catering at its best, and although the owner (a photographer/designer) is based in England, there's Phillippa in the village to welcome you. This is a completely renovated house, old on the ground floor, new above, without garden or pool but with two terraces, one up, one down, connected by stairs; bliss to come home to, and watch the sun set over the mountains. As for inside: oh joy! There are animal print rugs, new leather sofas, framed photographs of far-flung travels. The kitchen is large and well equipped, with an island in the middle, the dining room is simple but inviting, topped by rustic beams. The sitting room is upstairs, off the terrace, the bedrooms are down; on your comfortable new bed lies a welcome pack of suncream, tissues, postcards and bathroom smellies. Heaps of books and DVDs: worth the trip alone. There are shops, tapas bars and a summer pool in the village, and the nearest big town is a 35-minute drive. The coast is under an hour. Lovely.

Price	£350-£600 (sterling) per week.
Rooms	House for 6.
Meals	Cafes & bars 5-minute walk.
Closed	Mid-November to mid-March.
Directions	Directions on booking.

Steve Rolls
04279 Uleila del Campo, Almería

Tel	+44 (0)1903 854920
Fax	+44 (0)1903 854921
Email	steve@maxwellsworld.com
Web	www.maxwellsworld.com

Balearic Islands

Posada de Lluc

Pollensa, as old as the Middle Ages, is a charming town, long a favourite of painters; 21st-century galleries are mushrooming in the old town, and art furnishes many of this hotel's walls. The Posada has an interesting history. Built for a medieval nobleman it became a sanctuary for monks in 1459 – a handy place to decamp to after visiting the monastery at Lluc; today it is a more prosperous retreat. The hotel stands in a quiet, narrow street, so don't expect lavish views or acres of land. But do expect space: behind that inconspicuous façade lie an unexpectedly large, airy, cobbled entrance hall, eight immaculate bedrooms and an inviting pool. Furniture is antique Mallorcan, sofas are modern, chandeliers come from the glass factory in Campanet, and all is modesty and elegance, down to the chess set (do play). Joana ensures you get the best local produce at breakfast and is always happy to advise. The bedrooms are large, peaceful (particularly the poolside ones), uncluttered and cool, with beams, stone floors and white or open-stone walls. A quiet small-town hotel.

Price	€95–€185.
Rooms	8 twins/doubles.
Meals	Restaurants nearby.
Closed	December & January.
Directions	From airport for Palma; m'way for Inca & Alcudia. 20km after Inca, left exit to Pollensa. After 11km, left into Pollensa. Follow road left up Carrer Roser Vell.

Joana Vives Cánaves
Roser Vell 11, 07460 Pollensa, Mallorca

Tel	+34 971 535220
Fax	+34 971 535222
Email	info@posadalluc.com
Web	www.posadalluc.com

Son Siurana

You may be close to Puerto Pollensa and Alcudia but this stunning stone finca is enveloped by almond groves and sheep-grazed pastures. And few places are reached via such a long, sweeping driveway. In the family since 1748, the house is a long, low and graceful stone building, its doors and windows highlighted by light and elegant *marés*. Life in summer centres around a large terrace with wood-burning stove that looks onto a large and lovely swimming pool with a glorious view. Beyond, 100 hectares of ancient pines, lakes and a charming walled kitchen garden that supplies visiting chefs: guests can pick their favourite vegetables for the twice-weekly dinners. You stay in one of eight stylish self-catering cottages which have been slotted into the farm's outbuildings. The beautiful rooms are furnished with a rustic charm and have hand-painted tiles, terracotta or wooden floors, smart sofas and natural fibres, sisal carpets and country antiques. Breakfast is served in the main house, on the terrace or in your cottage. A very special place. *A Rusticae hotel.*

Price	Suite €105-€160. Cottages/apartments €114-€170.
Rooms	1 + 8: 1 suite. 5 cottages for 2; 1 cottage for 4; 2 apartments for 4. Extra beds available.
Meals	Breakfast €12. Lunch €12. Dinner €36 (Tuesday & Thursday only). Wine €8.50.
Closed	Rarely.
Directions	From Palma towards Alcudía. Left for Son Siurana, opposite km42.8 marker.

Sofia & Montse Roselló
Ctra. Palma-Alcudia km42.8,
07400 Alcudía, Mallorca

Tel	+34 971 549662
Fax	+34 971 549788
Email	info@sonsiurana.com
Web	www.sonsiurana.com

Agroturisme Son Pons

This beautifully restored and lovely cream stone farmhouse is several centuries old, set deep in a vast, organically run estate surrounded by woodland; an impressive palm tree, dwarfing the rough stone walls, stands guard. Sit on the wide terrace edged with stone water troughs, or in a wicker chair by the 16th-century well, and drink in the peace. Behind the house is a garden with lovely well-kept lawns, enticing patios and shady corners – perfect for watching the wildlife. Rabbits hop across the grass, exotic birds from the nearby nature reserve drop by. There's a large modern pool, too, beside a bougainvillea-swathed patio. The house is equally delightful inside, with its stone walls, beams and beautiful old Mallorcan furniture. The suites are comfortable, spacious and pleasing, each with intriguing features and original artwork, some with private terrace, fireplace or jacuzzi. Your hosts, an immensely friendly, multilingual family, ensure you get a fabulous breakfast and an excellent dinner five nights a week, and snacks are available if you get peckish during the day. The beaches are a 12-minute drive.

Price	€100–€200.
Rooms	6: 4 suites. Annexe: 2 suites.
Meals	Dinner €28, available 5 days a week. Snacks available every day.
Closed	Rarely.
Directions	From Palma dir. Alcudía; here, signs for Búger. From centre of Búger, take road to Sa Pobla (also signed Son Pons). Hotel 1.2km on left.

	Inés Siquier
	Ctra Búger-Sa Pobla, 07311 Búger, Mallorca
Tel	+34 971 877142
Fax	+34 971 509165
Email	finca@sonpons.com
Web	www.sonpons.com

Ethical Collection: Environment; Community. See page 412.

Entry 323 Map 23

Can Furiós

Can Furiós has always been one of the most upmarket of Mallorca's country house hotels; Adrian and Susy have made it even better. It sits in the hamlet of Binibona – no shops, three small hotels – on the stunning, sheltered eastern flank of the Tramuntana mountains. Impossible to believe that once the building was in ruins. Now small pebbled gardens planted with palm, olive and citrus trees fringe the outdoor pool and the smartly renovated 16th-century house. There's a lovely sociable terrace for pre-dinner drinks, while the dinners, served at formally dressed tables outside or in (the old farm's almond press makes an excellent dining room) are delectable; the menu changes every day and seafood is a speciality. The bedrooms are in the main house and the suites in the farmworkers' cottages have private terraces: all are traditionally comfortable, with oriental rugs on tiled floors, best English mattresses and patterned drapes. Extra touches include white bathrobes and Crabtree & Evelyn soaps – and torches for jasmine-scented strolls after dark. Adrian and Susy have thought of everything.

Price	€165-€230. Suites €190-€320.
Rooms	7: 3 twins/doubles, 4 suites.
Meals	Lunch €10-€14. Dinner €40. Wine €17-€80.
Closed	17 December-10 January.
Directions	From Palma, PM-27 N to Inca. There, signs to Selva & Binibona. From Selva, signs to hotel on small country roads; 1st hotel on left as you enter the hamlet of Binibona.

Adrian & Susy Bertorelli
Camí Vell de Binibona 11,
07314 Binibona-Caimari, Mallorca

Tel	+34 971 515751
Fax	+34 971 875366
Email	info@can-furios.com
Web	www.can-furios.com

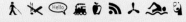

Finca Es Castell

One of the oldest fincas on the island has become one of the loveliest hotels. These 750 acres still yield olive oil and more; today a hammock also sways between the olives and a lazy pool beckons. The rambling farmhouse has been in the family for ever – along with a small mountain behind. Now it is rented to this welcoming young couple and has been infused with new life. A huge old olive press, a 12th-century fireplace, 17th-century wall parchments, ancient beams: old and modern meet in a glowing restoration. New are the chunky terracotta floors, the chestnut tables twinkling with night lights, the curly wrought-iron terrace chairs, the fresh bathrooms, the pretty beds, the African touches. The inner courtyard is rustically dotted with pots and overflows with green. You can't help but warm to this lovely place, and the setting is sensational: watch the sun dipping down over the Tramuntana mountain ranges as you dine (brilliantly) on one of three terraces. The old finca is surrounded by palms, pines, olives – and a grassed area where Pilates and Yoga classes are sometimes held (best to check). Mallorcan heaven.

Price	€110–€165.
Rooms	12 twins/doubles.
Meals	Dinner €33. Not Sunday. Wine €10–€15.
Closed	January.
Directions	From airport for Palma; exit 3 for Viá Cintura; exit for Inca. There, towards Lluc & Selva. After Selva, road on right for Es Castell; on for 3km. At entrance of Finca-Hotel Binibona, right; 0.5km.

Paola Cassini & James Hiscock
c/Binibona s/n, 07314 Caimari, Mallorca

Tel	+34 971 875154
Fax	+34 971 875154
Email	info@fincaescastell.com
Web	www.fincaescastell.com

Entry 325   Map 23

Ca'n Reus

Few villages in southern Europe have quite such a heart-stopping setting. Fornalutx is in the middle of Mallorca's rumpled spine, sandwiched between the craggy loveliness of the Puig Major and the Puig de l'Ofre. Artists, sculptors and writers discovered it long ago but the place has kept its charm. Light, elegant Ca'n Reus was built in faux-Parisian style by a returning emigrant – with none of the ostentatiousness that some of the *casas de indianos* display. The entrance hall is stunning and the bedrooms charmingly traditional with old tiled floors, 19th-century Mallorcan beds, crisp white bedcovers and mesmerising views. The garden room is the most peaceful and the most private. Owner Sue has introduced a delightful mix of Englishness and exoticism: deckchairs in the garden, candles up the stairs, orange trees by the lovely little pool. At breakfast, from 9am, local cheeses and sausages, homemade marmalades and tarts as you gaze on more loveliness. Sociable dinners cooked once a week by Sue and good restaurants in the village. It's friendly, peaceful, special, and great for walkers.

Price	€120–€170. Singles €100.
Rooms	8 twins/doubles.
Meals	Dinner €35 (Monday or Thursday only).
Closed	Rarely.
Directions	Round Palma on ring road; exit for Soller. Through (toll) tunnel, round Soller for Puerto de Soller. At 2nd r'bout, right at signs for Fornalutx. Park in village (ask about meters) & walk; Ca'n Reus in lowest street.

Susan Guthrie
Carrer de l'Auba 26, 07109 Fornalutx, Mallorca

Tel	+34 971 638041
Fax	+34 971 631174
Email	info@canreushotel.com
Web	www.canreushotel.com

Fornalutx Petit Hotel

Whether the nuns who lived here until the 1920s chose this spot for its setting we'll never know – but this is its trump card. Fornalutx is possibly the loveliest village in Spain and this peaceful designer hotel has inspirational views. (It's worth paying for a room with a view.) Inside are bright appealing rooms with a contemporary feel. Large, high-ceilinged bedrooms are simply furnished, colourful abstracts by local artists brighten pale walls, and one beautiful suite – white, crisp, minimalist – is in the chapel. A breakfast room in the cavernous cellar makes a charming wet-weather alternative to the al fresco version on the terrace. In the tranquil garden you may recline with a book in the shade of the citrus trees – source of the wondrous orange juices squeezed and served at breakfast by Isabel and her helpers. A small infinity pool and outdoor jacuzzi provide cool in high summer; there's a sauna, too. The cobbled cul-de-sac street (virtually traffic-free) is your departure point for the beautiful town of Soller just down the valley, and the pretty resort of Puerto de Soller lies a few miles beyond.

Price	€141–€152. Singles €77–€106. Suites €198–€247.
Rooms	8: 6 twins/doubles, 2 suites.
Meals	Snacks available all day. Restaurants nearby.
Closed	Rarely.
Directions	From airport ring road west; exit for Soller. After Bunyola through tunnel. At Soller towards Fornalutx. There, park in public car park after shops; head down towards river; c/Alba on right.

Patricio Roig Monjo
c/Alba 22, 07109 Fornalutx, Mallorca

Tel	+34 971 631997
Fax	+34 971 635026
Email	info@fornalutxpetithotel.com
Web	www.fornalutxpetithotel.com

Alquería Blanca

A long winding drive leads to a very grand mountain villa surrounded by olive groves, overlooking a plain that stretches to the bay of Palma – stunning. The house, in the family since 1902, has a French Provençal feel with its yellow shutters and statues, fountains and vines. It also has an extraordinarily beautiful and rambling interior, its public rooms both rustic and luxurious – in tranquil salons are sandy colours, wood-burners, paintings and sofas. The six bedrooms are in old outbuildings and stables whose mellow stones go back to the 13th century; each feels new, sparkling and spacious inside. There are tiled floors, white walls, modern art, perhaps a four-poster or a country antique, immaculate bathrooms, delicious soaps. Each room comes with a semi-private, unfurnished terrace. Best of all, perhaps, is the food – simple but stylish Mallorcan (frito, tumbet, tostades) served on request in a room lined with ancestral portraits – or, more fun, in the lovely old olive press. Local wine is on display in the honesty bar; outside is an exquisite pool, with views. Palma is 20 minutes down the road.

Price	€150–€200.
Rooms	6: 4 doubles, 2 suites.
Meals	Dinner €30, on request. Wine from €16.
Closed	16 November–1 March.
Directions	From airport for Palma-Sóller. Exit km13.6 marker. Turn left at sign for Alquería; drive on to blue barrier.

Cati Crespí
Crta. Palma-Sóller km13.6,
07110 Bunyola, Mallorca

Tel	+34 971 148400
Fax	+34 971 615525
Email	info@alqueria-blanca.com
Web	www.alqueria-blanca.com

Leon de Sineu

Hilltop Sineu is one of the most charming small towns of Mallorca – and one of the oldest: people have been coming to its market since 1214. (Don't miss it: it's on Wednesdays.) The bars and restaurants are another draw. The Leon is equally delightful, a bit scuffed around the edges perhaps, but welcoming, sensitively decorated and with a lovely symmetrical façade. The reception leads into a walled garden full of ponds and quiet corners, with a pool: a peaceful escape at the end of the day. From the Winter Room, a covered terrace, one can sit and enjoy it out of season. The bedrooms, opening off a balustraded staircase of wrought-iron splendour, have a mix of dark antiques and fresh white walls; the best have terraces and the suite has stupendous views. Hospitable Señora Gálmez Arbona manages to recreate the atmosphere of a Mallorcan home, and the terrace restaurant (serving good food from a Mallorcan chef) is charming. Breakfasts are traditional Mallorcan – cheese, salami, pâté, eggs, fruit, cake. Just the thing before you squeeze into your bikini and head for the cool pool – or the beach.

Price	€100–€140. Singles €80–€92.
	Suite €140–€162.
Rooms	8: 6 twins/doubles, 1 single, 1 suite.
Meals	Dinner €20. À la carte from €30.
Closed	Rarely.
Directions	Head for town centre. Hotel signed.

Francisca Gálmez Arbona
Carrer dels Bous 129,
07510 Sineu, Mallorca

Tel	+34 971 520211
Fax	+34 971 855058
Email	reservas@hotel-leondesineu.com
Web	www.hotel-leondesineu.com

Torrent Fals

The Tramuntana mountains appear in the distance, and the low, golden, 15th-century farmhouse is surrounded by vineyards and plains. The views are lovely – especially from the two suites with the roof terrace; inside is equally alluring. Pedro and his English wife Victoria have transformed a once-desolate ruin; now, airy spaces, lovely old stones and an understated elegance reign. In a striking and uniquely shaped sitting room (once the wine cellar!), the walls are of creamy stone and the high vaulted ceiling is striped with beams. Shapely arches lead from uncluttered bedrooms to spotless bathrooms of marble. Tastefulness and refinement notwithstanding, the whole place exudes comfort and warmth, thanks to Pedro's personality and energy. He is receptionist, gardener and cook all in one. Duck and fish are his specialities, fruits and vegetables come from the family allotment, and wines are from their vines. Your dynamic host can even be found at work cleaning the fabulous pool – designed to allow water to escape in a tantalising trickle at either end. Special. *A Rusticae hotel.*

Price	€145. Suites €165.
Rooms	8: 2 twins/doubles, 6 suites.
Meals	Dinner €30, by arrangement.
Closed	Rarely.
Directions	From Palma MA-27 for Inca/Alcudía. Right on MA-303 before Santa María for Sencelles. Torrent Fals on left short way up track, before Biniali. Look out for sign.

Pedro Cañellas Llabrés
Ctra. Sta. María-Sencelles km4.5,
Aptdo Correos 39,
07320 Santa Maria, Mallorca

Tel	+34 971 144584
Email	pjcanellas@terra.es
Web	www.torrentfals.com

Finca son Jorbo

Near "the most Mallorcan town in Mallorca" is this lovely old farmhouse, parts of which are three centuries old. At the end of a small lane, the finca sits surrounded by ten peaceful acres of olive, fig and carob, a small bird-trilled garden and a secluded pool. It has recently and stylishly been renovated by English owners, Martin and Annie. The set-up is B&B but what you get are four spacious apartments with their own kitchenettes. All lie within the main house, three have their own entrance; there are two tiled and airy reception/sitting areas with sofas and a wood-burner and several lovely wicker-furnished terraces for breakfast. The overall feel is of a friendly and intimate hotel. The apartments themselves are bright, light and contemporary, with new wrought-iron beds, prettily mosaic'd bathrooms, private sun terraces and art on white walls; pristine kitchens welcome you with a bottle of sparkling wine. Just one restaurant in pretty Porreres, but if you fancy taking a picnic to the beach at Estrenc (15 minutes away) your lovely, helpful hosts will provide a rucksack and a coolbox.

Price	€110–€140.
Rooms	4 apartments: 3 for 2, 1 for 3.
Meals	Restaurants 2km.
Closed	February & March.
Directions	Directions on booking.

Annie Sofiano & Martin Page
Cami de s'Olivar, Apt.65 Correos,
07260 Porreres, Mallorca

Tel   +34 971 181251
Fax   +34 971 574763
Email   info@fincasonjorbo.com
Web   www.fincasonjorbo.com

Entry 331   Map 23

Son Mercadal

If you are looking for kind hosts, delicious food and a secluded setting, head here. The family derive great pleasure from welcoming guests to their rambling, beautifully restored farmhouse; every last corner is a delight. The house is a 'painting', as the Spanish would say, a measured still life of things old and rustic; the grandfather clock, piano, old washstands, the engravings of Mallorca. José's son Toni's artistic eye has created a warm and harmonious mood. Most of the country antique pieces were already in the family: simple farmhouse bedrooms have balconies and views over the gardens; bathrooms are small. And the food is of the best the island has to offer: try the local specialities. Breakfast on the vine-shaded terrace on local sausage, cheeses, eggs from the farm, wonderful bread and one of Mama's 50 different jams; at dinner, on *tumbet* (the local meat-and-veg delicacy) and some of the island's very best wines. Most of what graces your table is straight from the farm, there are prize-winning dancing horses in the stable, amiable dogs, large and lovely gardens and a pool.

Price	€105. Singles €85.
Rooms	8 twins/doubles.
Meals	Lunch & dinner €30, by arrangement.
Closed	Rarely.
Directions	From Palma towards Santanyi. At Campos, left to Porreres. 1km before Porreres, right at sign 'Son Mercadal - Camí de Son Pau'. 2km track to house; tucked away on right.

José Roig Ripoll
Camino de Son Pau s/n,
Apartado de Correos 52,
07260 Porreres, Mallorca

Tel	+34 971 181307
Email	info@son-mercadal.com
Web	www.son-mercadal.com

Agroturismo Finca Es Passarell

Hidden up a mile-long track, its sprawling stone walls bedecked in bougainvillea and vines, this is a companionable place. The sunny, verdant garden has plenty of seats and shade, and a big sociable terrace. Es Passarell has been lived in for centuries, and while some of the spaces can feel dark and monastic, most are clean, light and airy. Joy and Spencer add a friendly English touch, and the rambling house is great for families. Bedrooms are big, cool and mostly on the ground floor, with attractive old beams and floors; expect bright rugs and cushions, lace drapes, dried flowers, intimate terraces. Apartments are simple, each with an extra sofabed and a private terrace. Breakfast is buffet and big – freshly made cakes, lemon curd, fresh orange juice and a cornucopia of fruit from their 60 organic trees – cherries, lemons, apples, figs, pears, plums, peaches, pomegranates and olives. Delicious dinners also feature their own organic vegetables and Spencer's desserts; the cellar is stocked with Mallorcan wines. *Spring / autumn guided cycling & walking tours.*

Price	€90–€150. Apartments €125–€160.	
Rooms	5 + 5: 5 twins/doubles. 5 apartments for 1–4.	
Meals	Lunch €6–€15, by arrangement. Dinner €22–€25.	
Closed	December & January.	
Directions	From Palma to LLucmajor, then on to Porreres; here, towards Felanitx. Between km2 & km3 markers, at sharp bend, right; after 2.5km, house on right, signed.	

Joy & Spencer Rennie
2a Vuelta No. 117, 07200 Felanitx,
Mallorca

Tel	+34 971 183091
Fax	+34 971 557891
Email	info@espassarell.com
Web	www.espassarell.com

Entry 333   Map 23

Es Pins

Unravel slowly in the peculiar charm of Es Pins within sight of pretty Porto Petro. Beautifully renovated, each room in the 18th-century manor has a history to tell, such as the separate suite with arched ceilings that sheltered a Republican soldier during the civil war. A system to feed him was adapted by means of holes, a dining etiquette that has since changed; feasting on fresh tumbet, a local speciality and favourite of the Filipino housekeeper/cook, is no hardship. The gardens are another delight. Stone paths lead from the huge raised pool, one through a sea of oleander, another into an olive grove and a short cross-country walk to the village. Enormous rocks surround a Japanese zen garden and vegetables grown on site are yours for the picking. Original terracotta and hydraulic tiles have been preserved with the old fireplace, while antiques from Lots Road in Chelsea – Harvey's favourite haunt – fill bedrooms without disguising their peachy afternoon glow. The farmhouse has a superb kitchen and all the electro-domestics you could need. Great for families. *Minimum stay one week in summer.*

Price	€1,500–€3,950 per week.
Rooms	House for 12.
Meals	Breakfast €10. Lunch €15. Dinner €30. Restaurants 10-minute walk.
Closed	Rarely.
Directions	Detailed directions on website.

Harvey Herrmann
c/Convento 35, Alquería Blanca,
07691 Santanyi, Mallorca

Tel	+44 (0)20 8747 1851
Fax	+44 (0)20 8995 0903
Email	harvey@mallorcancountrysideholidays.com
Web	www.mallorcancountrysideholidays.com

Ca'n Bassa Coll

The low-tiled roof, characterful windows, the pergola on its front terrace, the majestic mountain views – these were the reasons that Harvey, the urbane owner, fell in love with this place 20 years ago. Never mind the road that runs nearby, the 'home at the foot of the hill' is a delightful and rustic oasis. The old building and the ultra-modern annexe are joined by a palm and fountain walkway, making them ideal for two parties. Children will roam the grounds, surprising parents around hidden corners, before everyone settles down to lunch under the deep shade of the loggia tree. Take time to digest among a natural bounty of creeper, hibiscus, plumbago and cypresses, as you watch an abundance of lemon, níspero and grapefruit that seem to grow more ponderous with every thought. Uncluttered bedrooms clean the senses for sleep and three lead out to a peaceful terrace. Marble floors and inlaid mirrors reflect decently sized bathrooms. Whether you're relaxing in the garden, gazing out to sea or exploring the rugged coastline around Portopedro – this is Mallorca at its prettiest. *Minimum stay one week in summer.*

Price	€1,250-€3,150 per week.
Rooms	House for 11.
Meals	Breakfast €10. Lunch €15. Dinner €30. Restaurant 100m.
Closed	Rarely.
Directions	Detailed directions on website.

Harvey Herrmann
Ctra. Alqueria Blanca-Porto Petro 55.,
07691 Alqueria Blanca, Mallorca

Tel	+44 (0)20 8747 1851
Fax	+44 (0)20 8995 0903
Email	harvey@mallorcancountrysideholidays.com
Web	www.mallorcancountrysideholidays.com

Entry 335   Map 23

Finca Son Gener

Follow the winding drive to an architect-owned paradise on an olive-groved hill. The once-dilapidated farm buildings have become a sophisticated, understatedly elegant but extremely friendly small hotel, miles from the tanning crowds. Impeccable lawns and an organic vegetable garden frame the house with its gently luminous *maré* façade; there are palms, roses, bougainvillea, exotic trees. The interior is a celebration of light and form: old rafters, limestone floors, neutral natural colours and carefully selected sofas, plants and flowers. Art ranges from gentle-modern to rich mock-renaissance. It is soothing yet uplifting, each lofty bedroom being a cool haven in summer and as snug as toast in winter. Ground-floor rooms overlook the courtyard, upstairs ones get the views; each has fine Mallorcan linen and a private terrace. Some rooms have a more rustic mood, and their own fireplaces. The sauna and hamman, gym, spa and saltwater pools — one out, one in — share the same purity of style, and you breakfast and dine on one of many patios, each lovelier than the last. Exclusive, inviting, exquisite.

Price	€280.
Rooms	10 suites.
Meals	Lunchtime snacks. Dinner €50. Restaurant closed Tuesday.
Closed	1 December–15 January.
Directions	From Palma to Manacor. There, towards Artá; through Sant Llorenc; 2km before Artá, right on 403-1. Signed on left after 3km.

Aina Pastor
Ctra. Son Servera-Artá km3,
Apartado de Correos 136,
07550 Son Servera, Mallorca

Tel	+34 971 183612
Email	hotel@songener.com
Web	www.songener.com

Biniarroca Hotel Rural

Once a working farm, now a place of beauty. Sheelagh, a designer, once ran a guest house on the island, Lindsay is an artist and her light-filled paintings enhance the rooms. Together they have created something special on this hidden oasis of land that leads down to Menorca's southern coast. A solitary palm stands sentinel over the cobbled courtyard; to one side is an elegant pool. Plumbago and bougainvillea festoon the old farmhouse's façade, while the tamarisk-strewn gardens and shaded terraces are enchanting. Comfortable, traditional bedrooms have wide beds, pretty antiques, oil paintings and optional extras; the larger suites in the old stables have private terraces and a second pool. The restaurant is considered the best on the island – sophisticated dishes include fish fresh from the Mediterranean and organic fruit and veg from the garden. Breakfasts are a cornucopia of cheeses, breads, fruits, pastries. Peace reigns – apart from the cockerel's crow. Impossible to imagine a prettier or more peaceful little hotel – the perfect romantic getaway. *Massages by the pool. Unsuitable for children.*

Price	€120–€130. Singles €75.
Rooms	18 twins/doubles.
Meals	Light lunch €10.
	Dinner from €40 à la carte.
Closed	November–April.
Directions	From airport towards Maó, then to
	Sant Lluís. Here, follow signs on left
	for Es Castell. Biniarroca signed on left
	after 1.5km.

Lindsay Mullen & Sheelagh Ratliff
Camí Vell 57,
07710 Sant Lluís, Menorca

Tel	+34 971 150059
Fax	+34 971 151250
Email	hotel@biniarroca.com
Web	www.biniarroca.com

Hotel Rural Son Granot

Yachts line the quays of the port of Mahon – one of the longest and best natural harbours in the world. Es Castell is a charming 18th-century town close to the harbour entrance and the hotel, from its elevated position, has impressive views. This red colonial building is owned by a young, child-loving family who are passionate about its history and restoration. There's a cosy living room with board games and DVDs and a dining room with a modern-rustic feel; air conditioning and heating keep it comfortable all year round. In the sprawling grounds the family keep chickens and grow organic veg, there's a lovely parasoled terrace for delicious breakfasts and lunches, and a gorgeous pool flanked by teak loungers. The bedrooms in the main house have tiled floors, soft colours, shared balconies and the best of modern furniture; the suites, in another building, are bigger and have their own gardens – worth splashing out for. Dinners are candlelit and seasonal (lobster stew, mint flan, tomato soup with fresh figs) and there are good restaurants and lively waterfront bars in Es Castell.

Price	€98–€280. Suites €155–€320.
Rooms	11: 8 doubles, 3 suites.
Meals	Lunch €24. Dinner à la carte from €30. Wine from €16.
Closed	24/25 December.
Directions	From Mahon to Es Castell; thro' Es Castell for San Felipe. 500m after Es Castell, red house on right.

Carolina Hontoria
Ctra. Sant Felip s/n, 07720 Es Castell, Menorca

Tel	+34 971 355555
Fax	+34 971 355771
Email	hotel@songranot.com
Web	www.songranot.com

Can Lluc

San Rafael has kept its charms, and its restaurants are the best on the island. Can Lluc, surrounded by beautiful forested hills, is appealingly close (about a mile), but you do need a car. Everything smacks of perfection here, from the crisp cool gardens and startlingly modern pool to the rustic-chic interiors. The farmhouse itself is a beauty and the land produces almonds and vines. You could happily spend all day here, lolling under the palms, dividing blissful time between jacuzzi and saltwater pool. Most of the bedrooms are where the animals once slept – not that you'd know: the exposed stones and timbers gleam, the beds are of wood or wrought iron, the colours are restful, the bathrooms small but delightful. Some rooms have a jacuzzi, some a terrace, two a kitchenette. More rooms in the new building by the pool: some big, some small, all fabulous. There's a cosy sitting room with rural Ibizan touches, a dining room with wood-burners and modern art, shady terraces fringed with oleanders, a spa, a small gym. Scrumptious breakfasts display fresh figs, pastries and jams from the farm. *A Rusticae hotel.*

Price	€225-€600.
Rooms	12 twins/doubles.
Meals	Lunch & dinner €40-€60. Wine from €18. Restaurants 2km.
Closed	Rarely.
Directions	Ctra. Ibiza San Antonio; exit right at km7 marker for San Rafael. Ctra. St Agnes exit at km2 marker.

Lucas Prats
Ctra. a Santa Iñes km2,
07816 San Rafael, Ibiza

Tel	+34 971 190808
Fax	+34 971 190666
Email	info@canlluc.com
Web	www.canlluc.com

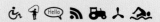

Canary Islands

Hotel Rural Las Calas

Hide in the hills, below the peaks of Gran Canaria. This is a relaxed and relaxing little hotel (friendly dogs, an easy feel), converted from a century-old building. Abundant wood, stone walls, warm colours and traditional Canarian furnishings are tempered by splashes of restrained modernism and Magüi's colourful paintings. The generously sized and comfortable rooms, each with its own personality, open onto the peaceful courtyard garden – most are traditional in style; two are ultra-modern and red-themed – ask for the style you'd prefer. Relax in the tented open-air sitting room, cool off in the little salt pool or scrump some fruit from the orchard and admire the abundant vegetable garden. When evening comes, you could dine in on some typical Canarian cuisine, around a table shared with other guests. Beyond the hotel lie the protected natural havens of the Cumbre de Tejeda and Pino Santo — you're up high here and it can be chilly in winter. Explore on horseback; there's an equestrian centre nearby. Vega de San Mateo is the nearest small town with a colourful cattle fair and farmers' market at the weekends.

Price	€86–€98. Singles €76–€86. Suites €120–€150. Half-board extra €20 p.p.
Rooms	9: 7 twins/doubles, 2 suites.
Meals	Dinner €18. Wine €12.
Closed	Rarely.
Directions	Airport Tafira; after Santa Brigida, Vega de San Mateo; follow sign at end of village for Tejeda; cont. to lane on left, signed La Lechuza; pass football field on left, turn left down lane (signed), hotel on right.

Magüi Carratala	Ethical Collection: Environment.
c/El Arenal 36,	See page 412.
La Lechuza-Vega de San Mateo,	
35320 Las Palmas, Gran Canaria	
Tel +34 928 661436	
Email reserva@hotelrurallascalas.com	
Web www.hotelrurallascalas.com	

Hotel Fonda de la Tea

This charming small hotel sits amongst Gran Canaria's glorious peaks; the air sparkles and invigorates; the views of the mountains plunging to deep gorges are spectacular. The 19th-century inn had humble beginnings as a staging post, but these days Serafina welcomes you with pride. She is passionate about her hotel, her guests, and delightful Tejeda. The hotel has been lovingly restored, so modern and well-equipped rooms are designed for comfort and beds have stylish hand-carved headboards and great mattresses. Bathrooms are luxurious, all is immaculate. We loved the two rooms in the annexe across the lane. Dine in on hearty dishes, often organic, including eggs from Serafina's hens, or stroll to their sister restaurant. Sun yourself on the lovely terrace while children play in the park opposite or frolic in the open-air public pool. If you're an unfussy traditionalist, try the old-fashioned self-catering casita tucked away down a cobbled street; it too has breathtaking views. Hikers are in heaven, pretty villages abound and you can stargaze in the clear night air. Great value, too.

Price	€90–€99.75. Singles €52.50–€63. Half-board extra €18–€25 p.p. House €455–€630 per week.
Rooms	11 + 1: 5 doubles, 6 twins. House for 2-4.
Meals	Dinner by arrangement. Wine €30. Sister restaurant Cueva de la Tea 200m.
Closed	Mid to end June.
Directions	From Airport GC-1 for Las Palmas for 13km; GC-3 & GC-4 thro' Tafira to Santa Brigida. GC-15 thro' Vega de San Mateo. In Tejeda, pass church, thro' main square; on right.

Serafina Suarez Garcia
c/Ezequiel Sánchez 22, 35360 Tejeda,
Gran Canaria

Tel	+34 928 666422
Fax	+34 928 666443
Email	reservas@hotelfondadelatea.com
Web	www.hotelfondadelatea.com

Hotel Rural La Hacienda del Buen Suceso

Amid a sea of banana plantations in Gran Canaria's untouristy, windswept north, this jewel of a hotel will lure decadent souls. Owned and decorated by the Marchioness of Arucas, the perfectly proportioned colonial-style house is graceful and serene. Bedrooms share a taste of the building's opulence but each is individual: some flowery and swagged, others neutral and cool, a few with sloping ceilings or four-poster beds; each suite has a mezzanine level. Sink back and purr on alluring beds or dream in bubble-filled baths. It's a place to unwind, so sunbathe by the breezy solar-heated pool, luxuriate in the spa, stroll through the colonnaded verandas, recline on the sofas in the drawing room by the fire, order an aperitif from the patio bar. Dine by candlelight in the immaculate restaurant; or step out for some non-touristy options: charming manageress Maria Gabriela knows the best places. Historic Arucas is 15 minutes from Las Palmas but is the perfect launch pad for exploring the Gran Canaria that tourists don't know: the mountainous centre, the rugged north coast and the green, wooded west.

Price	€115.50–€157.50. Suites €135.50– €183.75. Half-board extra €19 p.p.	
Rooms	18: 13 doubles, 5 suites.	
Meals	Dinner €19. Wine from €8. Restaurants 1km.	
Closed	Never.	
Directions	From airport, GC-1 to Las Palmas; GC-2 for Galdar & Guía, to Bañaderos. GC-330 for Arucas; 1km before Arucas, right at r'bout (signed).	

Maria Gabriela Viani Colombo
Ctra. de Arucas a Bañaderos km1,
35400 Arucas, Gran Canaria
Tel   +34 928 622945
Fax   +34 928 622942
Email   hacienda@haciendabuensuceso.com
Web   www.haciendabuensuceso.com

Hotel San Roque

One of our favourites: an 18th-century mansion that has become a luxurious yet wonderfully unstuffy and family-run hotel. Local hardwoods and earthy colours have been introduced with a flourish. It is lavish, bold yet subtle. An immaculately dressed bed floating on a sea of gleaming parquet, a new Deco rug, contemporary art. Each room is different, with deliciously coloured stuccoed walls, big old rafters and Bauhaus or Glasgow School furniture. At every turn the eye is drawn to something striking, such as the soaring steel sculpture in the courtyard – a chic outdoor space with original wraparound wooden balcony transformed by terracotta walls, white armchairs and potted plants. And so many opportunities for decadence: sauna, pool, music, tennis, Canarian cuisine… and breakfast as late as you want. The natural sea pools along the front are a delight, as is the rugged coastline with its dramatic backdrop of mountains rising steeply behind the lovely old town. Garachico embodies the Isla Baja: 'secret Tenerife'. This is the serene jewel in its crown. *A Rusticae hotel. Golfing discounts available.*

Price	€175–€250. Suites €280–€350.
Rooms	20: 16 doubles, 4 suites.
Meals	Light lunch €10. Dinner €27. Wine €10–€105.
Closed	Rarely.
Directions	From southern airport m'way past Santa Cruz, La Laguna & Puerto de la Cruz. On past San Juan de la Rambla & Icod de los Viños to Garachico. Here, 4th left into cobbled street; 1st left. On right.

Dominique Carayón Sabater
Esteban de Ponte 32,
38450 Garachico, Tenerife

Tel	+34 922 133435
Fax	+34 922 133406
Email	info@hotelsanroque.com
Web	www.hotelsanroque.com

Hotel Rural El Patio

Much comfort, a fabulous setting and not a whisper – other than the dawn chorus and the swish of waves breaking on the distant shore. El Patio sits in one of the oldest and lushest banana plantations in Tenerife. Rustically elegant bedrooms, each opening out onto a balcony, are housed in three separate buildings, each with a fascinating history. The listed 16th-century mansion and its 25-acre estate have been in the Ponte family for 500 years, and signs of the past are delightfully present: a 1565 chapel at the entrance to the estate, a 400-year-old dragon tree on the exuberant patio. But time has not stood still, and now you have a heated swimming pool, a solarium, a fitness room, a tennis court and even a golf-practice area for your pleasure. Charming, courteous Canarian aristocrat Baltasar Ponte Machado is a plain-speaking man who has strict rules – rules designed to make you feel delightfully at home. He gives you keys to the bar – just help yourself and settle up when you leave – and to the front door, so you may come and go as you please. It's good value, too.

Price	€71–€124.
Rooms	26 twins/doubles.
Meals	Dinner from €17.
Closed	11 May-10 July.
Directions	From airport for Puerto de la Cruz & Icod de los Viños. Hotel 4km after Icod, on Garachico road, sharp steep right turn on bend onto signed track: negotiate with care!

Baltasar Ponte Machado
Finca Malpaís 11, El Guincho,
38450 Garachico, Tenerife

Tel	+34 922 133280
Fax	+34 922 830089
Email	reservas@hotelpatio.com
Web	www.hotelpatio.com

Casa Cantarilla

Between blue seas and the lava fields of Timanfaya National Park, the perfect hideaway for all who seek peace, nature and civilised company. Enter a flower-filled patio from which stairs lead up to a huge balconied master bedroom; dramatic views and a four-poster bed await. It's a serene, light-filled haven, with gleaming pale furniture and floors. Gaze out to sea while you laze in the bath; the bathroom is equally generous. Downstairs is the welcoming rose-washed courtyard sitting room – books and art at every turn – and there are a cosy double and an airy studio with practical kitchenette, too. Well-travelled, eloquent and engaging, ex-Oxford don David and writer Penelope entertain you over a 'slow food' dinner – much of it home-grown or organic; for breakfast, there may be Spanish omelette courtesy of the bantams (they keep goats, too, though not for breakfast!). Three patios give you the choice of sun, shelter or shade or a dip in the open-air jacuzzi; beaches and rock pools are within easy reach. If you prefer self-catering, ask for their casita in the charming fishing village of El Golfo. *Internet access.*

Price	€50–€80. Casita €500 per week.
Rooms	3 + 1: 1 double; 2 twins/doubles each with separate shower (1 with kitchenette). Casita for 5.
Meals	Dinner €20. Wine €5–€20. Restaurants 1–2km.
Closed	July & August.
Directions	From Arrecife LZ-20 thro' San Bartolomé to Tinajo. Left at r'bout onto c/Volcanes. Continue 1km; right opp. phone box onto c/Tablero. Continue 1km; right at x-roads onto Camino Cantarilla; on right.

David McFarland & Penelope Farmer
Camino Cantarilla 2, Tajaste,
35560 Tinajo, Lanzarote

Tel	+34 928 840319
Email	casacantarilla@yahoo.co.uk
Web	www.casacantarilla.org.uk

Casa Amatista

Rest mind and body in this delightful retreat of apartments and a Mongolian yurt. Warm, hospitable Daniel and Zanna are passionate about sustainable living: all is recycled or composted. In the compact bathrooms, showers are solar-heated and waste water filtered for the garden. And what a garden! An oasis of exuberant greenery in Lanzarote's arid landscape, it bursts with flowering shrubs, organic fruit trees and aloe vera amidst volcanic nooks and crannies. Laze around the pretty solar-heated pool (there's a sofa in the shade) or climb to the solarium for views of the Timanfaya volcano. Each light and airy open-plan apartment is different, with a simple kitchen and private terrace. Zanna's creative touch is evident in the natural design and flowing shapes of the houses, paths and cosy corners; prints, wall hangings and splashes of fuchsia and lime green. In the wood-floored Group Room, join in yoga or weekly meditation sessions; there are alternative therapies too. Amiable Bonnie the dog loves to be walked, and nearby beaches cry out to surfers and sunbathers; nature lovers will find plenty to explore, too.

Price	House €110–€120. Studio & casitas €60–€80. Yurt €60. All prices per night.
Rooms	House for 6. Studio for 2. 3 casitas for 2. Yurt for 2.
Meals	Restaurants 2km.
Closed	Never.
Directions	From airport LZ-2 to Arrecife. LZ-20 thro' San Bartolomé; at r'bout 2nd exit to Mozaga. At r'bout 3rd exit to La Vegueta. At x-roads left to Mancha Blanca; left by pink house onto Camino de las Huertitas. Right after 400m (signed); on left.

Ethical Collection: Environment.
See page 412.

Daniel Jacobi & Zanna Barge
Camino las Huertitas 11,
35560 La Vegueta-Tinajo, Lanzarote
Tel   +34 928 840867
Email   info@villa-amatista.com
Web   www.villa-amatista.com

Entry 346   Map 19

Caserío de Mozaga

Artists and photographers flock to Lanzarote for its special light; this intimate hotel in the little whitewashed village of Mozaga is a favourite. Gonzalo and his sister have lovingly restored their 18th-century family farmhouse, built on ancient volcanic rock in the very centre of the island. Old family photos and furniture remind you it's a genuine Canarian home, cherished and authentic – staff welcome you in the same hospitable style. Nearby, you can visit the well-known family vineyard with its small museum. Inviting farmhouse style rooms are cool and simply dressed in plain fabrics, and bathrooms are generous. Enjoy sophisticated Mediterranean and local dishes in the popular and softly lit restaurant, housed in former stables – once the home of a camel! Breakfast is varied, plentiful and delicious. There's a charming terrace and volcanic garden in which to relax, with a hammock for dreaming in (and a small library with board games if the weather turns). Beaches and markets are close by; couples in search of quiet relaxation and the authentic Lanzarote will be in heaven. *A Rusticae hotel.*

Price	€63–€110. Singles €51–€83. Suites €80–€167. Half-board extra €37 p.p.
Rooms	6: 2 doubles, 1 twin, 1 single, 2 suites.
Meals	Breakfast €10.
Closed	Never.
Directions	From airport LZ-2 to Arrecife. LZ-20 thro' San Bartolomé; 1st exit at Monumento Al Campesino; 1st left to Mozaga. Caserio de Mozaga 100m on right.

Gonzalo Bethencourt
Mozaga 8, 35562 San Bartolomé,
Lanzarote

Tel	+34 928 520060
Email	info@caseriodemozaga.com
Web	www.caseriodemozaga.com

Finca Malvasia

Follow a track through lush vineyards to these apartments; they glow among the starkly beautiful volcanic landscape of La Geria. The low white buildings welcome you with their stylish and uplifting lines. Inside, exposed stone and inner gardens add drama to coral sofas, tiled floors and sleek white walls. Whitewashed bedrooms and neutral furnishings are lightened with gorgeous splashes of colour, while modern-rustic bathrooms offer waffle robes. A turquoise lagoon pool (toddlers have one too) sparkles amid palms and yuccas, an idyllic spot for a sunset glass of wine. Help yourself to the honesty bar, barbecue by the pool, dine on your terrace. Kitchens are well-equipped, but do ask Tarnya about restaurants, markets and the best wines; a Spanish platter can be arranged on arrival. Richard and Tarnya are passionate about the island and are the kindest hosts; little Joss and a wagging dog complete the family feel. It's hard to tear yourself away from the pool, but the beaches are an easy drive. There's hiking in winter and spring, and surfing and cultural delights all year round. *Breakfast & private chef on request.*

Price	Apartment for 2, €120. Apartments for 4, €140–€160. All prices per night.
Rooms	4 apartments: 1 for 2, 3 for 4.
Meals	Breakfast €10. Dinner €25–€50, by arrangement. Wine from €10.
Closed	Never.
Directions	From LZ30 for La Geria/Uga. In Masdache, left at Teleclub snack bar. Continue on winding road 3km, right onto Camino El Oratorio, signed Finca Malvasia. Continue 1km thro' vineyards; at end of lane.

Tarnya Norse-Evans
Camino el Oratorio 12-14, Masdache,
35572 Tias, Lanzarote

Tel	+34 928 173460
Email	info@fincamalvasia.com
Web	www.fincamalvasia.com

with undiscovered beaches and vibrant fishing villages; the celebrated St James pilgrimage route runs westwards to Santiago de Compostela.

Basque and Galician are spoken in their respective regions and great pride is taken in their cultural identities. The cuisine is among the best in Spain, with Atlantic seafood playing a major part, from fabulous tapas to the stunning world-class gastronomy of San Sebastián.

Eastern Spain

An area of wild and wonderful extremes. To the north of **Catalonia** are the Pyrenees – hiking trails, rushing rivers, ski resorts, rich fauna and flora – and tiny independent **Andorra**. To the east: the rugged coves of the Costa Brava and the golden sands of the Costa Dorada; below, the Costa del Azahar and the Costa Blanca in **Valencia**. Inland: the drier, vine-covered Penedès in Catalonia, famous for its sparkling *cava* and white wines. In Valencia, citrus groves flourish and rice paddies shimmer.

Catalán is spoken throughout, and Cataláns are known for their proud independence, dynamism and strong work ethic. The region is home to some great modern artists: Miró, Dalí, Gaudí, Picasso; Barcelona has fine collections of Picasso and Miró's work, Dalí's can be seen in nearby Figueres. Vibrant Barcelona is famed for its art and culture – including Gaudí's unique and surreal

Northern Spain

Mountains and sea characterise the area that stretches from the **Basque Country** through **Asturias** and **Cantabria** all the way to Spain's wild western coast in **Galicia**. Expect rain at any time of year: the moist climate explains this lush paradise. Bordered by the Pyrenees, the Basque Country flattens out to the seaside cities of San Sebastián and Bilbao (famous for the Guggenheim); beaches reach all along the gentle Cantabrian and Asturian coasts. Just inland lie the magnificent mountains of the Cordillera Cantábrica, hugging the Picos de Europa National Park. Galicia's western coast is fringed by estuaries (*rias*)

buildings – and its nightlife. Lovely Valencia is best known as the home of Spain's most famous dish, paella, and for the exuberant festival of *Les Falles*.

Central and North-Eastern Spain

The whole of this area, from mountainous **Navarre** in the north, through **La Rioja** and **Aragon** to the vast rolling spaces of the plains of **Castile and Léon**, are redolent with history. Many of the battles that sowed the seeds of modern Spain were fought here, and ancient sites of learning (Zaragoza, Salamanca, Valladolid), where Spanish is spoken in its purest form, rise in the midst of a farming landscape. Don't miss the wineries of La Rioja and the beautiful cities of Zaragoza and Pamplona (most famous for its bull run). UNESCO-listed sites abound, from the exquisite La Alberca to the monumental cathedral of León. **Castile-La Mancha**, historic crossroads of itinerant herders and home of Don Quixote, has Toledo and its hilltop old quarter as its cultural highlight; for ramblers there are the alpine meadows and azure lakes of the Sierra de Gredos.

Stylish **Madrid** presides from its high *meseta* – and when you're sated with culture (and tapas) seek respite in the lush pine forests of Sierra de Guadarrama, or the Royal Palaces of La Granja and Aranjuez. Be prepared for the continental climate in central Spain: baking in summer and freezing in winter!

Southern Spain

Extremadura sits to the west: tough, sparsely populated, strewn with vast estates and cork and holm oak pastureland. It's also full of gems: Roman ruins and conquistadors' palaces. Below and to the west are the eight provinces of **Andalusia**, with the Alpujarras and the Sierra Nevada to the north (noted for the highest mountain pass in Europe, and winter skiing). To the south is the Mediterranean Costa del Sol, famous since the 60s for 'sangria and sun', and the Atlantic Costa de La Luz, beloved of surfers. To the east are the important fruit- and veg-producing provinces of Almeria and **Murcia**, and the Mar Menor, the largest saltwater lake in Europe, separated from the sea by a long sand spit.

The climate ranges from semi-desert at the Cabo de Gato to subtropical on the Costa del Sol; inland areas can be baking hot in summer and cold in winter. Away from the costas are the *Parques Naturales* (literally "nature parks") with landscapes and flora and fauna of great beauty and variety. Andalusia, land of fighting bulls, flamenco and fiesta, was deeply influenced by half a millennium of Muslim rule during the Middle Ages. Stunning Moorish architecture abounds in its cities: Granada and the Alhambra; Sevilla and the Giralda; Cordoba with its Mezquita. Jerez is renowned for its sherry bodegas.

Balearic Islands

Of the three major islands, Mallorca is the largest and most developed, but there are many lovely places to discover away from stylish Palma, like the villages tucked into the northern mountain range, popular with walkers. The Port of Pollensa is yachtie heaven – as is Maó in Menorca, with its spectacularly long and deep harbour. Menorca, the least developed of the islands, is dotted with white villages and megalithic monuments. Ibiza, the party island, has many delightful corners away from the major towns. But the islands are best known for their rugged coves and spectacular bays, their pine trees, golden sands and crystalline waters. There's interesting architecture to explore too, reflecting the influences of occupying forces over the centuries.

Canary Islands

Volcanic in origin, the topography of the islands is hugely varied; it's not unusual to find two or three climatic areas within one island. The largest, Tenerife, has golden beaches to the south, the volcanic Teide National Park in the centre – the highest peak in Spain – and lush greenery to the north. The dramatically mountainous and wooded heart of Gran Canaria rises steeply from beaches and dunes then drops again to banana plantations and bustling Las Palmas in the north. In the centre of Lanzarote is the Timanfaya National Park – dramatic, arid, volcanic. Enjoy this island's wines; with the lowest rainfall in Spain, vines are grown in volcanic soil that absorbs evaporation and dew provides the sole source of irrigation.

The Canaries are a paradise for birdwatchers, botanists and nature lovers: the rich flora and fauna include many unique species. Beaches and surfing aside, the year-round benign climate and varied landscape is also a lure for walkers and hikers; each island has a wonderful variety of routes to explore.

Photos: www.istockphotos.com

You can expect this book to lead you to places that are original, individual and welcoming. We hope that it will bring you closer to the Spain we love, a country whose people are convivial and spontaneous, love to chat and are usually beautifully mannered. But please don't judge Spain by your own cultural yardstick: the Spanish language can be as rich and convoluted as it can be economical and austere, and any apparent abruptness is unlikely to be intended. And don't be surprised by the amount of gesticulating, hugging and kissing you'll encounter – Spaniards are very tactile and express themselves physically as much as verbally.

Relax The Spanish concept of time can be fairly loose; Spaniards firmly believe they determine the course of time and not the other way round. You will have to take this on board and relax about time when in Spain. Enjoy all those little things that can make life so enjoyable, with which Spaniards regularly indulge themselves. The *sobremesa*, the ubiquitous chat over coffee after lunch; a siesta to cope with the rigours of the hot summers; or the *paseo*, the stroll down the main street at dusk with no specific purpose in mind other than that of encountering friends and neighbours.

Noise One of the first things you'll certainly notice is the Spanish in-built tolerance to noise: from two-stroke mopeds roaring up and down late at night to pre-dawn church bells, from distant barking dogs to vociferous – almost certainly friendly – bar conversations. The best attitude to take is to consider it one of the country's idiosyncrasies and part of your travel experience. Or pack some ear plugs!

Opening hours As a general rule:
* Shops open 9am–1.30pm, 4.30/5pm–8/8.30pm Monday–Friday; 9am–1.30pm on Saturdays.
* Banks are usually open 8am–3pm Monday–Friday.
* Post Offices generally open 8.30am–2.30pm Monday–Friday; 9.30am–1pm on Saturdays.

Photo above: Chris Lucas
Photo right: www.istockphotos.com

Regional spelling of place names

In areas where there are two languages (Galicia, the Basque Country, Catalonia, Valencia and the Balearic Islands), place names will often have two spellings. Orense will be Ourense in Galicia; Lerida will be spelt Lleida on road signs in Catalonia (Cataluña in Spanish, Catalunya in Catalán). In the Basque Country regional spellings usually accompany the Spanish one, eg Vitoria will be signposted Vitoria-Gasteiz. We try to use the ones that you are most likely to see: this may mean one version in the address, another on the directions on how to get there. We have no political agenda!

Public transport

Trains, buses and taxis are cheap in Spain. You can meet people, start a good conversation, and get much more of a feel for the country by travelling this way.

Spain has a number of high-speed rail links; visit www.renfe.es/ingles for details of these and other national rail services. Some regional lines would bring a tear to a rail-buff's eye, such as the one between Ronda and Algeciras. In the north, FEVE (www.feve.es) runs several narrow-gauge trains, which usually travel through extraordinary landscapes and have retained the magic and romance of the old railway journeys. Look out for the national coach company if you want to travel by public transport; Alsa Enatcar (www.alsa.es) is the equivalent of National Express, with concessions in every major town and some of the most comfortable coaches you will find in Europe. And they are relatively cheap and tend to be swift too.

Road nomenclatures

A = motorways (usually with a toll); E = new European nomenclature for motorways or free dual carriageways; N = national roads (equivalent of British A roads) some of which have been converted into dual carriageways.

For minor roads, each region has its own numbering system, the letter(s) usually standing for the particular region, eg CV = Comunidad Valenciana; A = Aragón. Characteristic of most roads in Spain are the km markers – invaluable in the more remote areas.

Driving

It is compulsory to have in your car: a spare set of bulbs, a car jack, a spare/emergency wheel, two warning triangles, a visibility jacket (which you must carry in the front of the car, not in the boot), and a basic first aid kit. It is also compulsory to carry on you your driving licence and the car documents, whether you have a rental car or your own. Impromptu road checkpoints are not an unusual occurrence. These are usually carried out by the Guardia Civil – in green fatigues – who, however intimidating they may look, are courteous and extremely helpful should you have an emergency.

Walking and cycling

Do take advantage of the nationwide network of *Vias Verdes* or 'green ways' to walk, cycle or ride along disused narrow-gauge railway lines (www.viasverdes.com/GreenWays). In spite of Spain's rugged terrain, the tracks are mostly flat and smooth which makes them highly accessible to all. The routes span many of the mainland provinces; enjoy stunning views and fascinating glimpses of history as your route passes through everything from nature reserves to cities, via railway viaducts, bridges from the ancient to the new, and tunnels lit by solar-power. In La Mancha, take the long-distance, windmill-peppered *Ruta del Quijote* and follow in the footsteps of Quixote (www.donquijotedelamancha2005.com).

Many of you may want to stay in environmentally friendly places. You may be passionate about local, organic or home-grown food. Or perhaps you want to know that the place you are staying in contributes to the community? To help you we have launched our Ethical Collection, so you can find the right place to stay and also discover how each owner is addressing these issues.

The Collection is made up of places going the extra mile, and taking the steps that most people have not yet taken, in one or more of the following areas:

• Environment Those making great efforts to reduce the environmental impact of their Special Place. We expect more than energy-saving light bulbs and recycling – in this part of the Collection you will find owners who make their own natural cleaning products, properties with solar hot water and biomass boilers, the odd green roof and a good measure of green elbow grease.

• Community Given to owners who use their property to play a positive role in their local and wider community. For example, by making a contribution from every guest's bill to a local fund, or running pond-dipping courses for local school children on their farm.

• Food Awarded to owners who make a real effort to source local or organic food, or to grow their own. We look for those who have gone out of their way to strike up relationships with local producers or to seek out organic suppliers. It is easier for an owner on a farm to produce their own eggs than for someone in the middle of a city, so we take this into account.

How it works

To become part of our Ethical Collection owners choose whether to apply in one, two or all three categories, and fill in a detailed questionnaire asking demanding questions about their activities in the chosen areas. You can download a full list of the questions at www.sawdays.co.uk/about_us/ethical_collection/faq

We then review each questionnaire carefully before deciding whether or not to give the award(s). The final decision is subjective; it is based not only on whether an owner ticks 'yes' to a question but also on the detailed explanation that accompanies each 'yes' or 'no' answer. For example, an owner who has tried as hard as possible to install solar water-heating panels, but has failed because of strict conservation planning laws, will be given some credit for their effort (as long as they are doing other things in this area).

We have tried to be as rigorous as possible and have made sure the questions are demanding. We have not checked out the claims of owners before making our decisions, but we do trust them to be honest. We are only human, as are they, so please let us know if you think we have made any mistakes.

The Ethical Collection is a new initiative for us, and we'd love to know what you think about it – email us at ethicalcollection@sawdays.co.uk or write to us. And remember that because this is a new scheme some owners have not yet completed their questionnaires – we're sure other places in the guide are working just as hard in these areas, but we don't yet know the full details.

Ethical Collection in this book
On the entry page of all places in the Collection we show which awards have been given.

A list of the places in our Ethical Collection is shown below, by entry number.

Environment
11 • 33 • 38 • 44 • 70 • 103 • 133 •
135 • 141 • 177 • 217 • 235 • 236 •
239 • 243 • 245 • 256 • 271 • 275 •
285 • 286 • 287 • 288 • 291 • 311 •
316 • 323 • 340 • 346

Community
11 • 33 • 103 • 306 • 311 • 323

Food
33 • 44 • 70 • 114 • 133 • 141 • 243 •
271 • 275 • 286 • 288 • 291 • 306 • 311

Ethical Collection online
There is stacks more information on our website, www.sawdays.co.uk. You can read the answers each owner has given to our Ethical Collection questionnaire and get a more detailed idea of what they are doing in each area. You can also search for properties that have awards.

Photo above: The Hoopoe Yurt Hotel, entry 243
Photo right: Mas Vinyoles, entry 103

Fragile Earth

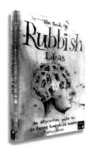

The Book of Rubbish Ideas
An interactive, room by room, guide to reducing household waste
£6.99

This guide to reducing household waste and stopping wasteful behaviour is essential reading for all those trying to lessen their environmental impact.

Ban the Plastic Bag
A Community Action Plan
£4.99

In May 2007 Modbury in South Devon became Britain's first plastic bag free town.
This book tells the Modbury story, but uses it as a call to action, entreating every village, town and city in the country to follow Modbury's example and... BAN THE PLASTIC BAG.

One Planet Living
£4.99

"Small but meaningful principles that will improve the quality of your life."
Country Living

Also available in the Fragile Earth series:

The Little Food Book   £6.99
"This is a really big little book. It will make your hair stand on end" *Jonathan Dimbleby*

The Little Money Book   £6.99
"Anecdotal, humorous and enlightening, this book will have you sharing its gems with all your friends" *Permaculture Magazine*

To order any of the books in the Fragile Earth series call 01275 395431 or visit www.fragile-earth.com

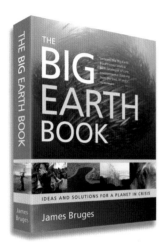

The Big Earth Book
Updated paperback edition
£12.99

We all know the Earth is in crisis. We should know that it is big enough to sustain us if we can only mobilise politicians and economists to change course now. Expanding on the ideas developed in *The Little Earth Book*, this book explores environmental, economic and social ideas to save our planet. It helps us understand what is happening to the planet today, exposes the actions of corporations and the lack of action of governments, weighs up new technologies, and champions innovative and viable solutions. Tackling a huge range of subjects – it has the potential to become the seminal reference book on the state of the planet – it's the one and only environmental book you really need.

What About China? £6.99
Answers to this and other awkward questions about climate change

"What is the point of doing anything when China opens a new power station every week?"

All of us are guilty of making excuses not to change our lifestyles especially when it comes to global warming and climate change. *What About China?* explains that all the excuses we give to avoid making changes that will reduce our carbon footprint and our personal impact on the environment, are exactly that, excuses! Through clear answers, examples, facts and figures the book illustrates how any changes we make now will have an effect, both directly and indirectly, on climate change.

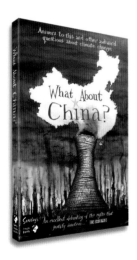

"An excellent debunking of the myths that justify inaction" *The Ecologist*

Slow down with Sawdays

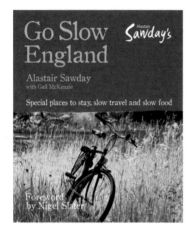 

Special places to stay, slow travel and slow food

The Slow Food revolution is upon us and these guides celebrate the Slow philosophy of life with a terrific selection of the places, recipes and people who take their time to enjoy life at its most enriching. In these beautiful books that go beyond the mere 'glossy', you will discover an unusual emphasis on the people who live in Special Slow Places and what they do. You will meet farmers, literary people, wine-makers and craftsmen – all with rich stories to tell. *Go Slow England* and our new title *Go Slow Italy* celebrate fascinating people, fine architecture, history, landscape and real food.

RRP £19.99. To order either of these titles at the Reader's Discount price of £13.00 (plus p&tp) call 01275 395431 and quote 'Reader Discount SP'.

"*Go Slow England* is a magnificent guidebook" *BBC Good Food Magazine*

Have you enjoyed this book? Why not try one of the others in the Special Places to Stay series and get 35% discount on the RRP *

British Bed & Breakfast (Ed 13)	RRP £14.99	Offer price £9.75
British Bed & Breakfast for Garden Lovers (Ed 5)	RRP £14.99	Offer price £9.75
British Hotels & Inns (Ed 10)	RRP £14.99	Offer price £9.75
Devon & Cornwall (Ed 1)	RRP £9.99	Offer price £6.50
Scotland (Ed 1)	RRP £9.99	Offer price £6.50
Pubs & Inns of England & Wales (Ed 5)	RRP £14.99	Offer price £9.75
Ireland (Ed 7)	RRP £12.99	Offer price £8.45
French Bed & Breakfast (Ed 11)	RRP £15.99	Offer price £10.40
French Holiday Homes (Ed 4)	RRP £14.99	Offer price £9.75
French Hotels & Châteaux (Ed 5)	RRP £14.99	Offer price £9.75
Paris Hotels (Ed 6)	RRP £10.99	Offer price £7.15
Italy (Ed 5)	RRP £14.99	Offer price £9.75
Spain (Ed 8)	RRP £14.99	Offer price £9.75
Portugal (Ed 4)	RRP £11.99	Offer price £7.80
Croatia (Ed 1)	RRP £11.99	Offer price £7.80
Greece (Ed 1)	RRP £11.99	Offer price £7.80
India (Ed 2)	RRP £11.99	Offer price £7.80
Green Places to Stay (Ed 1)	RRP £13.99	Offer price £9.10
Go Slow England	RRP £19.99	Offer price £13.00
Go Slow Italy	RRP £19.99	Offer price £13.00

*postage and packing is added to each order

To order at the Reader's Discount price simply phone 01275 395431 and quote 'Reader Discount SP'.

If you have any comments on entries in this guide, please tell us. If you have a favourite place or a new discovery, please let us know about it. You can return this form or visit www.sawdays.co.uk.

Existing entry

Property name: _____

Entry number: _____ Date of visit: _____

New recommendation

Property name: _____

Address: _____

_____

Tel/Email/Web: _____

Your comments

What did you like (or dislike) about this place? Were the people friendly? What was the location like? What sort of food did they serve?

_____

_____

_____

_____

_____

Your details

Name: _____

Address: _____

_____

_____ Postcode: _____

Tel: _____ Email: _____

Please send completed form to:
SP, Sawday's, The Old Farmyard, Yanley Lane, Long Ashton, Bristol BS41 9LR, UK

Singles

Single room OR rooms let to single guests at half the double room rate or under.

Wheelchair-accessible

At least one bedroom and bathroom accessible for wheelchair users. Phone for details.

Travel without a car

Within 10 miles of a bus/coach/train station and owner can arrange collection.

Quick reference indices

Close to town

These places are in town or within easy walking distance of a town.

On a budget?

These places have a double room for €100 or under.

Quick reference indices

Riding

Riding can be arranged nearby.

Quick reference indices

Alastair

Sawday's

British self-catering

A whole week self-catering in Britain with your friends or family is precious, and you dare not get it wrong. To whom do you turn for advice and who on earth do you trust when the web is awash with advice from strangers? We launched Special Escapes to satisfy an obvious need for impartial and trustworthy help – and that is what it provides. The criteria for inclusion are the same as for our books: we have to like the place and the owners. It has, quite simply, to be 'special'. The site, our first online-only publication, is featured on www.thegoodwebguide.com and is growing fast.

Cosy cottages • Manor houses
Tipis • Hilltop bothies
City apartments and more

① Andalusia   **② B&B**

③ Cortijada Los Gazquez

④ The Beckmanns have joyfully restored five houses that make up this cortijada. The ceilings are lofty, the finish is perfect, the thinking is environmental, the family is delightful. There's Simon, artist and designer, Donna, illustrator, Solomon and Sesame, twins; they are completely dedicated to their restored family house and cannot wait to cook for and entertain their guests. Rooms weren't quite finished at the time of our visit but promise to be warm, simple and light, with a fun/funky twist. Olive oil soaps sit by cool concrete basins, pine logs furnish roaring fires, rainwater is harvested, and wind and solar power keep floors toasty and water piping hot. Reed beds eliminate impurities and the water irrigates the land; soon there will be a natural pool and a wood-fired sauna. And the landscape? The farmhouse sits magnificently and remotely in the *parque natural* surrounded by fruit, almond and olive trees… the view of La Sagra mountain is beautiful in every weather. Ramblers, artists, nature lovers will be very happy here. All you hear is the call of the eagle and the owl at dusk. *Minimum stay two nights.*

Price	€85.
Rooms	6: 3 twins/doubles, 3 doubles.
Meals	Dinner with wine, €18.
Closed	Christmas.
Directions	At Velez Blanco Visitors Centre (signed) 1st right, signed Las Almahollas. Left at fork, follow road for 8km. At junc. follow signs to Los Gazquez.

⑤ ⑥ ⑦ ⑧ ⑨

⑩ Ethical Collection: Environment; Community; Food. See page 412.

Simon & Donna Beckmann
Hoya de Carrascal,
04830 Velez Blanco, Almería
Tel   +44 (0)20 7193 6056
Email   info@losgazquez.com
Web   www.losgazquez.com

⑪ Entry 311   Map 17    **⑫**